Old Provence

D0112341

Lost and Found Series

New editions of the best in travel writing—old and modern—from around the world

The Pilgrimage to Santiago by Edwin Mullins
Two Years in the French West Indies by Lafcadio Hearn

Classic Travel Writing

Old Provence

Theodore Andrea Cook

Interlink Books

An imprint of Interlink Publishing Group, Inc.
New York • Northampton

This edition first published in 2001 by

INTERLINK BOOKS
An imprint of Interlink Publishing Group, Inc.
46 Crosby Street, Northampton, Massachusetts 01060 and
99 Seventh Avenue, Brooklyn, New York 11215
www.interlinkbooks.com

First published 1905
Foreword © James Ferguson 2001

All rights reserved.

Library of Congress Cataloging-in-Publication Data

Cook, Theodore Andrea, Sir, 1867–1928.
  Old Provence / Theodore Andrea Cook ; foreword by James Ferguson.
  p. cm. -- (Lost and found series)
Originally published: New York : C. Scribner's Sons, 1905. With new foreword.
Includes bibliographical references and index.
  ISBN 1-56656-372-0
  1. Provence (France) --History. I. Title II. Series.
  DC611.P964 C7 2001
    944'.9--dc21   00-011339

Line drawings: Nicki Averill
Cover image: Courtesy Éditions Clouet

Printed and bound in Canada

To request a free copy of our 48-page full-color catalog,
please call us at **1-800-238-LINK**, write to us at
Interlink Publishing, 46 Crosby Street, Northampton, MA 01060
or visit our website: **www.interlinkbooks.com**

CENTRAL ARKANSAS LIBRARY SYSTEM
JACKSONVILLE BRANCH
JACKSONVILLE, ARKANSAS

Contents

Volume Two

Queen Jeanne—Her Sale of Avignon—Fêtes at Barthelasse—
Innocent VI—Rienzi's Last Triumph and Death—Cardinal
d'Albornoz—The Chartreuse in Villeneuve—The "Virgin of
Pity"—"Coronation of the Virgin"—Urban VI—His Buildings
at Avignon—Visit to Rome—Henry of Trastamare—Du
Guesclin's Grand Companies—Philippe de Cabassole—Death
of Albornoz—Rival Claimants for Provence—Gregory XI—
Queen Jeanne's Fourth Husband—Cardinal Pierre de Luna—
Catharine of Siena in Avignon—Death of the Pope after visiting
Rome—Two Popes—Urban VI in Rome; Clement VII in
Avignon—The Great Schism—Coronation of Louis d'Anjou—
Assassination of Queen Jeanne—Boniface IX in Rome, and
Benedict XIII in Avignon—Marshal Boucicaut and His
Army—Rodrigo de Luna—The Escape to Châteaurenard—
Innocent VII in Rome—Gregory XII in Rome—Attempts to
End the Schism—Three Popes Instead of Two—Alexander V—
John XXIII—Benedict XIII Holds Out Until His Death—
Martin V—End of the Schism.

Foreword

THE Pont du Gard amazes. Nothing prepares you for your first sight of this living testament to Roman engineering genius, with its massive stones rising three tiers high in a symmetry both functional and designed to impress. Even after repeated visits you forget how the edifice, made of great hewn blocks from the nearby quarry, some weighing six tons and assembled without mortar, catches the late afternoon light, stretching from one wooded hillside to another over a river that is either raging winter torrent or summer-baked trickle. The most reluctant of child tourists, fearful of yet another dull outing to some renowned ruin, are awe-struck by the Pont du Gard and its sheer majesty. Roman relics are rarely so spectacular.

The authorities are beginning to treat the aqueduct with more veneration these days. Until quite recently, you could drive your car over the wide first level for no reason other than an interesting and gratuitous diversion on the road between Uzès and Avignon. It was also possible to walk across the very top of the structure, warily peering down into the abyss below and hoping that no unexpected gust of *mistral* would put a sudden and tragic end to a day out. The true exponents of *sang froid* were known to sit with legs dangling over the edge, some enjoying a picnic. Today, such recklessness is frowned upon, but nobody seems to mind if you scramble round the massive foundation stones at the water's edge. Some two thousand years old, some 150 feet high, the structure is imposing but invites the onlooker to approach, to touch its ancient masonry.

The Pont du Gard was built to carry fresh spring water from around Uzès to the city of Nemausus, now known as Nîmes. In this hot and busy place, surrounded by all the least attractive features of modern French consumerism, stand two further reminders of southern France's Roman past. Like the aqueduct, the amphitheatre impresses by its sheer scale and the state of its preservation. True, there are larger Roman amphitheatres in existence, but none so intact. The tiers rise in uniform gradient within the unbroken oval exterior of arched arcades, reached by a network of steps and inner, barrel-vaulted, galleries. The holes gouged out of the top stones to hold awning poles can still be seen. Today, *les Arènes* host rock concerts, opera and, most picturesque, the bullfights—both Spanish and Provençal—that punctuate the spring and summer calendar.

A ten-minute walk along Nîme's plane tree-shaded boulevard takes you to the Maison Carrée, a building that despite its name is neither house nor square-shaped. Dating from the first century AD and a little younger than the amphitheatre, this rectangular temple was erected to overlook the city's forum and to display its builders' mastery of Greek-inspired classical symmetry. Its flight of wide steps lead the visitor to a triangularly pedimented portico held up by six columns, each decorated by an elaborate Corinthian capital. But here the effect is not one of scale; rather, the Maison Carrée is reduced in size both by the surrounding older buildings and the daring location of the towering modern art museum directly opposite the square. Again, it encourages the visitor to come closer, to climb the steps into the cool interior, from where the statue of an uncertain divinity has long since disappeared. Now a museum is fittingly installed inside, featuring Venus, Apollo and the water spirit herself, Nemausus.

Throughout Provence towns and villages are littered with the remains of five centuries of Gallo-Roman civilization. Different locales reflect different phases within this long period of occupation. The defensive walls, towers and gateways that once encircled towns such as Arles testify to the perils of early settlement and the threat of Barbarian or Teuton aggression at the end of the *Pax Romana*. The settled phase of the last decades BC and first and second centuries AD finds its proud expression in the great public buildings: the theatre and triumphal arch at Orange, the amphitheatre at Arles, the mausoleum at St.-Rémy-de-Provence. Like the Pont du Gard, these buildings speak of permanence, of the unshakable Roman belief in their own staying power.

This confidence was illusory. By the end of the fifth century, after an earlier but unsuccessful Visigoth invasion, Roman Provence had fallen. And so began that long period that we know as the Dark Ages.

The Romans' monumental buildings fell into disrepair; some were used as convenient quarries by those in search of ready-made building materials. Others suffered the indignity of being used in ways that their architects would never have imagined. The Maison Carrée, we are told, was at one point turned into a stable. The amphitheatre at Arles became a sort of self-contained medieval village, in reality more like a slum, which was stricken by repeated epidemics of plague.

And yet, as Theodore Andrea Cook makes abundantly clear in the pages that follow, Roman Provence never disappeared, but merely hibernated across the centuries of neglect and vandalism. His book thus evokes "a classic past which is not dead, but sleepeth: which embraces you as you step into it." It was not until the nineteenth century that excavations and restorations began fully to reconstruct the glories of the Pax Romana, but in the intervening centuries the theatres, arches and arenas had proved their durability simply by surviving.

The Roman and pre-Roman past that Cook traces is but part of the Provençal landscape that he found in the first years of the twentieth century. Fascinated by the military and political struggles of such figures as Marius, Augustus and Marcellus, conscious of the complex relationship between the province and the Roman political centre, the author is also drawn to that other great period in the region's history—the five centuries dominated by the Counts of Provence.

In what was originally the second volume of *Old Provence*, Cook recreates a medieval world of Christianity and warfare, of chivalry and treachery. Exploring fortresses and churches, he traces the development of the Provençal Romanesque in exquisite architecture such as St. Trophime's doorway and cloisters in Arles or the west doorway of the abbey at St. Gilles. His irrepressibly romantic sense of history leads him also to the great citadels and castles, ranging from Carcassonne, the hilltop stronghold of the Albigensian resistance to the Crusaders' fortress of Aigues-Mortes, set in the desolate flatlands of the Camargue. But the site that most inspires Cook's imagination is the ghostly "Ville Morte"of Les Baux, once the impregnable fortress of the strongest seigneurs in southern France, but destroyed by Louis XIII in the 1630s. Here, he is moved and chilled by the "insistent mortality of its irretrievable decay." And, of course, he visits and re-visits the Palace of the Popes in Avignon, the vast stone headquarters of the papacy between 1309 and 1403 that made the city the centre of Christendom.

Sportsman, Francophile and Classics scholar, Theodore Andrea Cook was a man of many enthusiasms. But what is perhaps most compelling about his observations of Provence is his insatiable human curiosity. He was not just another Edwardian traveller, scrambling over the ruins of some distant civilization. For what appealed to him was precisely the links, the historical continuity that bound together Roman Provence, medieval Provence and the Provence of 1900. Architecture and archaeology provided him with the outward, tangible evidence of those links, but it is the human experience, the myriad life stories that the buildings suggest that is his real passion. Whether Roman gladiators or medieval crusaders, poets or troubadours, the past inhabitants of Provence emerge as flesh-and-blood individuals from his readings of Latin inscriptions or Romanesque motifs.

Cook was perhaps gloomier than he might have been about the future of Provence. He leaves the region's history with its annexation in 1484 by Louis XI into the Kingdom of France, but five hundred years later still frets about the desecration of the Palace of the Popes and the dilapidation of other monuments. His elegiac vision of the land of Petrarch and good King René is coloured by a gentle sense of melancholy and decline, by a feeling that the past, for all its modern-day reminders, is to be mourned as well as celebrated.

But significantly, 1905, the year in which *Old Provence* appeared was also the year in which Frédéric Mistral, architect of the Félibrige and promoter of the Provençal cultural renaisssance, received the Nobel Prize for Literature. Despite his romantic pessimism, Cook was aware that Provence's individuality—cultural, linguistic, historical—was perhaps again to find expression:

After her years of fighting and of love, tired out too soon by passions that had left her wellnigh strengthless, Provence fell upon a long sleep in the encircling arms of France. With Aubanel, with Mistral, and the Félibres, she is awaking to the new dawn of a distinctive personality that has never been completely overshadowed by the insistent claim of more extended patriotisms.

Today's Provence, with its developed tourist industry, its expatriate retirees and declining agricultural traditions, would probably be quite alien to Cook. Mostly gone are the small hostelries, the unhurried carriage rides, the sometimes wild landscapes, replaced by motels, motorways and industrial complexes. But tourism has helped to conserve rather than destroy Provence's ancient and medieval treasures; the Palace of the Popes is now restored to some semblance of its former glory by the entrance tickets bought by millions of visitors. And almost all of what Cook describes and interprets is still there, more protected, perhaps slightly more bureaucratically arranged, but there none the less. It still amazes, it still invites you to touch centuries-old limestone, warmed by the sun, or cool marble. Above all, it still invites you, as it did Cook, to go to Provence: to see and touch for yourself:

But it has become quite clear to me that to understand the history or the life of old Provence you must see the country. The tale of the Rhone valley is incredible until you know the Rhone. The classical authorities present a merely unintelligible maze till you have walked over the battlefields they describe.

James Ferguson
Uzès, August 2000

Preface

Veson li vièi mounumen de l'istòri de Prouvènço
Veson li vièi mounumen
Emé soun ensignamen...
—L'AMIRADOV

Tarascoun, e Bèu-Caire, e Toulouso, e Beziés,
Fasènt bàrri de car, Prouvènço, li vesiés...
I TROUBAIRE. CATALAN.[1]

THOSE who have done me the honour of reading *Old Touraine* will need little by way of preface to these pages. The history of Old Provence has a somewhat different treatment only because I have had towns to deal with instead of castles, and because I have had far more space to cover, both in territory and in time, than was involved in describing the châteaux in the districts of Tours and of Blois. The Seine seems full of commerce and of government; the Loire still mirrors the pleasure-palaces of the Valois court upon its golden stream; but the valley of the Rhone has been the highway of the nations, the path of conquerors, the battlefield of the invader; and its boatmen still call one bank "Empire", and the other "Kingdom", though the names have long ago lost all significance in relation either to the east or to the western shore. But Provence, united, as she has been, to the crown of France for more than four hundred years, has preserved a more distinct individuality than almost any other region within French frontiers. It was indeed, at one time of her history, quite as likely that Provence should absorb the territories of Capets and of Valois as that the reverse process should eventually occur; and the extraordinary influence exerted in European politics of the thirteenth century, by the four daughters of Raymond-Bérenger of Provence and Béatrix of Savoy, was only equalled by the profound significance of the presence of the Popes at Avignon in the fourteenth, a fact which concentrated the thoughts of Christendom upon the Valley of the Rhone for more than a hundred years.

These salient characteristics in the history of Provence have guided me in my treatment of so large a theme. The whole of my first volume has been devoted to the Phoenicians, Greeks, and Romans, who have here left traces upon the soil of France that are as remarkable as any to be found in Italy, and that have often been preserved among far less discordant surroundings. In Arles, in Nîmes, near St. Remy, at Fréjus, at the Pont du Gard, has stayed the completed vision of a classic past which is not dead, but sleepeth; which embraces you as you step into it, without a trace of crude survival or barbarous anachronism. This first volume, then, may be used alone, if necessary, as a description of the Roman Empire on the Rhone, illustrated by Greek and Roman monuments.

I have made full and frequent use of the inscriptions and epitaphs in all parts of Provence, in order to give as many details as possible of the life of the Romans on the Rhone among the buildings they have left; and I must here express my deep gratitude to Professor Pelham, President of Trinity College, Oxford, for his kindness in saving me from many a mistake, in evidence which must inevitably be submitted to an expert constantly conversant with such matters. It is, however, in the correction of errors only that Professor Pelham's invaluable aid is here acknowledged. The use made of this material, and the deductions based on it, are mine alone. Those who are familiar with classical versions of the campaigns of Hannibal or Marius may perhaps detect a certain curtly decisive pose about some of my statements which they will not consider justified by the authority conveyed upon my title-page. But I have no space either for redundant explanation or for insincere apologies.

My conclusions are the result of working on the spot; and when they differ from those of previous writers who, in their studies, know far more of the classics, I would ask the critic to suspend judgment until he has realised the differences involved in the two methods employed. The systems of such men as M. Gilles, M. Lenthéric, or M. Bérard, who have gone to sunny Mother Earth, to the fair flowing of her streams, and to the barriers of her mountain-ranges, may at last seem productive of results which no student nurtured in the cold, clear lamplight of textual criticism could accept. If I have sometimes taken a middle course, it is not from considerations of safety that I have made my choice. But it has become quite clear to me that to understand the history or the life of old Provence you must see the country. The tale of the Rhone valley is incredible until you know the Rhone. The classical authorities present a merely unintelligible maze till you have walked over the battlefields they describe.

Many who know Provence already will wonder at my omissions. But I have preferred to say nothing of places which tell their own tale, Martigues, for instance, and many more, which will be constant discoveries of fresh delight to every traveller. I have determined to write a book, and not a library; and in the selection that became inevitable I have been guided as much by considerations of what was typical, within the most generous of geographical boundaries, as by the determination to be able to refer the reader to the actually existing framework of my story. Little of Marseilles that was built before the fifteenth century remains, except its churches; the Roman buildings of Narbonne were broken up by that enlightened friend of the Arts, François I, to make fortifications; so I have said more of St. Remy, or of Fréjus, than of either.

My second volume begins in the vague mists of a "transition-period", which scientific research will no doubt wholly clear away as soon as it has settled such comparatively simple problems as the explanation of Etruscan nationality and language. But with the passing of the year 1000, and the building of St. Trophime and St. Gilles, we emerge into modern times. With Les Baux and Aigues-Mortes we pass on to the period of wars, Crusades, and fortresses, when the races were in the melting pot and the sword solved every problem. At Avignon we meet the Popes; and hard by are the shades of Laura and of Petrarch. The good King René, a bunch of grapes in one hand and a scroll of verses in the other, smiles at us from Aix and Tarascon. Across the river lies Beaucaire, where Aucassin loved Nicolete. When Charles of Anjou left Provence to Louis XI of France, in 1484, my labours end.

> *"La Prouvènço cantavo, e lou tèms courreguè;*
> *E coume au Rose la Durènço*
> *Perd à la fin soun escourrènço,*
> *Lou gai reiaume de Prouvènço*
> *Dins lou sen de la Franço à la fin s amaguè."* [2]

I have not wearied the reader with large lists of authorities for various interesting points which occur before 1484. He must, for instance, take it for granted that Dante passed through Provence on his way to Paris, and certainly knew more of the country than the author of *Aucassin and Nicolete* did of Beaucaire. The best short account of early painters in Provence, especially of the famous "Buisson Ardent" at Aix, is in M. Paul Vitry's annotated catalogue of the "Exposition des Primitifs

Français", held in the Louvre in 1904. It will also be noticed that I reject the Provençal version of "Laura", as it is given in De Sade's *Vie de Pétrarque,* which seems to me as erroneous as it is bulky. Though the volume published in 1904 by Mr. E. J. Mills will not wholly recommend itself to the critical historian, it is valuable as drawing attention to the evidence in Petrarch's own writings; and all who care to investigate the subject for themselves should read the edition of the Letters published by Fracassetti in 1859, and numerous tractates by Pierre de Nolhac (of Versailles), whose great contribution to literature was the discovery of Petrarch's own finally revised manuscript of the *Rime.* Until the publication of the works of M. Segré at Rome, and M. Cochin in Paris, the Essay by Mézières held the field, but it has lost its value since the most recent discoveries.

As a last word, let me advise the traveller to visit Provence in spring. He should go from Paris to Toulouse, working along south and east by way of Carcassonne to Béziers or Narbonne (with possible excursions to Foix or Perpignan) and so through Montpellier to Nîmes. Visitors who have begun their tour in autumn would do well to spend their winter on the Côte d'Azur. But in any case it is a pleasant journey, after the Camargue and the Crau are passed, to travel round the coastline from Marseilles to Monte Carlo. Of the Riviera I have little here to say. All character has been stamped out of it by the levelling cosmopolitanism of alien luxury. The pleasure-ground of Europe, lovely as it may be for the foreign visitor, has had to pay the price; and on your return to the Rhone valley from Monte Carlo you will do well to go inland by Vence, and Grasse, Draguignan, and St. Maximin, and so to Aix en Provence, a pleasant town of fountains and front-doors and shady boulevards, with memories of the good King René and an excellent library. St. Gilles and Les Saintes Maries, on the west side of the Rhone, you will have visited from Nîmes. On the east are Vaucluse and St. Remy. The stream itself is bridged, as you move up it, by Arles and Trinquetaille, by Beaucaire and Tarascon, by Avignon and Villeneuve; from these last, by way of Orange, lies your road home.

The lovely voyage down the Rhone from Lyons is better done in summer than either in spring or autumn, the two best seasons for Provence. But when summer travelling is necessary, go down the river as far as Beaucaire, and make straight from Tarascon to St. Remy.

If one result of these pages be to send more Englishmen to what was once a fief of Richard Coeur de Lion, I shall be well content; they will at least help to repay a little of that obligation under which we were first laid by St. Augustine at Arles.

Theodore Andrea Cook
Chelsea, 1905.

NOTES

1. "They see the ancient monuments of old Provence, with all they have to teach…Tarascon, Beaucaire, Toulouse, and Béziers. Provence! thou hast seen all of them at bay behind the ramparts of their flesh and blood …"—MISTRAL, *Lis Isco d'Or.*

2. "Time slipped by as Provence sang her songs; until, as the Durance at last loses her stream within the Rhone, so the gay kingdom of Provence laid herself to rest upon the bosom of France."

VOLUME ONE
CHAPTER I

Introductory

> *"Pesto, lioun, sablas, famino, dardai fòu,*
> *Avié tout afrounta ! Li loop, Li tartarasso*
> *Seguissièn trefouli sa cavalo negrasso*
> *Car sabien que l'aurié de mort on terro-sòu"...*[1]

THE quotation from Aubanel which I have set at the head of this chapter resumes, in the best phrases I have ever read, one of the great characteristics of Provençal history—the blood that has been poured out so often and so terribly upon her soil. They will remind the reader that the country through which Hannibal's Numidians marched towards the sack of Italy was also the scene of the slaughter of the Barbarians by Caius Marius; that the citizens who once filled the amphitheatres of a Roman Empire were afterwards the victims of many a Christian Crusade; and that beside the Palace of the Popes at Avignon the Rhone has run red from the battlefields of Romans, Saracens, Spaniards, Englishmen, Italians, and French. After her years of fighting and of love, tired out too soon by passions that had left her wellnigh strengthless, Provence fell upon a long sleep in the encircling arms of France. With Aubanel, with Mistral, and the Félibres, she is awaking to the new dawn of a distinctive personality that has never been completely overshadowed by the insistent claim of more extended patriotisms. In France, yet not of it, Provence has forged her dialect into a language as different from the French as are her olives and her Arlésiennes from the apple-orchards and the milkmaids of the North. How magnificently concentrated in expression, how resonant in harmony, how characteristic in its phrasing that language can be, the lines which I shall quote here and there among these pages will be more than sufficient proof.

Many different nationalities have passed through Provence, and danced upon the bridge of Avignon, or bought at the market of Beaucaire; Greek, Spaniard, and Italian have joined the farandole of Arles; the very soil seems eagerly to thrust forth its thirsty sands towards the sea, with something of that impulse towards maritime adventure which inspired the Crusades and the campaigns of Sicily. The torrent of the Rhone is symbolic of the country: dazzling in the sunshine, strong and barbarous in the shade, with no respect of persons or of places, yet with a beauty that is irresistible. Its oratory was typified in Mirabeau. Its poetry lives in Frédéric Mistral.

That strange centrifugal force which has so often animated Provence seems soon to have driven all her great towns to her frontiers. In her heart were the dying colonies of a different race. When all her towns were gathered under one standard, it was to the fatal conquest of Naples that they were led; and Provence herself was never reunited. It was the same with her religious life, which had scarcely recovered from the horrors of the Albigensian Crusade, when the deathblow was dealt by the Papal court at Avignon. Like the Rhone, which moves more and more slowly as it nears the sea, until its waters lose themselves in plains and marshes, so Provence has never reached the zenith of her destiny. The sands of time have choked her fortunes, and she lives but in the mighty ruins of her past.

To the student of history there can be no more beautiful, no more pathetic region in Europe than the valley of the Rhone.

What we call civilisation, as Anatole France has said, is merely a conveniently summary description of contemporary life. Everything that is past we label barbarous. In time we, too, shall become the barbarians of a more civilised and enlightened future; just as Rome, with all the Roman Empire meant, is merged in that dark night of uncouth disorder before we had ourselves arisen. If we consider the ideals of various ages in the perspective thus suggested, we shall find that they present a curious kaleidoscope of differing results.

Here by the Rhone, for instance, we see the reasonable Roman gods, their utilitarian goddesses, full of good sense and kindliness, taking a due share in the divinely organised society. Here, too, we can realise a little of that difficulty which beset the cultured Roman when he was asked to believe in a Divinity which was as much offended by the existence of other creeds as by the worship of the deity in other forms. To the tolerant Roman all religions were but as shafts, loosed, it is true, from different quarters, which were no concern of his, but aimed at the same centre he recognised himself, a central sphere of perfect light, which could be caught in various prisms, and might be reflected in as many varying hues, but which remained essentially the same. For him religion duly recognised the proper bases of mundane society; and if the better-born enjoyed the favour of the greater gods that was but a natural consequence of a divinely sympathetic aristocracy. Yet, as the Roman Empire grew, and as by far the greater number of its inhabitants were either slaves or freedmen, a religion that directly appealed to them was supported by an infinitely vaster audience than that which appreciated the ritual of their masters. So Christianity, as soon as the truth which underlay its tenets had been realised, went on, by sheer weight of numbers, until it conquered Rome herself. But mark the first results. By the Popes were introduced these Christian persecutions which devastated Provence far more than any pagan rites had ever done, or ever wished to do. Religion at first seemed to mean the increase of persecutions, and to imply, not Rome, not Protestantism, not even Christianity, but a balance of differing phraseologies chiefly depending upon abstruse and legal considerations.

By the Rhone, too, we can realise that it was a mere matter of exact knowledge which led to Rome's greatest political mistake. She imagined that the conquered Parthians and Germans were on the true limits of the world; so the Universal Peace, of which Augustus sincerely believed himself the forerunner, was shattered by the inroad of those outer Barbarians, unrecognised by Rome, who for fourteen centuries after their arrival in the South fought over the making of modern Europe. Ever since their coming the growth of civilisation has meant the growth of war, and that, too, in exact proportion to the increase of knowledge and the extension of colonial possessions: for the discovery of the New World only convulsed the Old with even greater pangs of rivalry and contest. It remained for the twentieth century, and for another imperial advocate of Universal Peace, to conduct the bloodiest campaign seen since the Roman Empire, and to lose as many men as Varus or as Crassus on battlefields even further from his base. So peace now seems to rest, not on the philosophy of an Augustus, not even on the balance of power as between the nations which have inherited his Empire, but on the available cash-balances of various Chancellors of the Exchequer.

Though the eternity of the Roman Empire soon became as obviously untrue as its pretensions to universal dominion had always been, it is curious that Roman laws and civilisation have been inherited and enjoyed by every great nation of the modern world save one, the Chinese Empire. China has maintained an attitude of unruffled reserve for more than two thousand years. On one side of the world she ruled vaster masses of population than Rome on the other ever knew. Like Rome she claimed the possession of the whole habitable globe.

The attitude of the two Emperors, during the age of the Antonines for instance, recalls the old French story of the atheist who bowed before a crucifix: "Ils se saluaient, mais ils ne se connaissaient pas." The Chinese Emperor must have vaguely heard of the existence of the Roman Emperor, and no doubt smiled, with some indulgence, at the news of his extraordinary claims. Their representatives saluted distantly, but the principals were careful not to meet. In fact China maintained a more or less respectable and a fairly unmolested seclusion until five Great Powers had guaranteed her integrity, and two had come to bitter blows about it.

The builders of the Pont du Gard, the men who raised the theatre of Orange, or the aqueduct of Fréjus, seem even today to have been the agents of some greater power than the world had seen before, or has seen since. But the Empire for which they built has been outlasted by their arches; the Provence they knew has vanished; it is their Chinese contemporaries who have survived. It is thought significant, sometimes, that China appears as little in the military calculations of Western Europe now as did the Goths and Huns in those of the later Roman Empire they destroyed.

Beneath the broken shadows of St. Remy's triumphal monuments, or among the mighty tiers of seats within the ruined amphitheatre of Arles, we begin to understand, in a new way, the ancient truth that continuity of fame and strength depend neither on material forces nor on enlarged dominion. Provence will live, not because of her Roman ruins, her mediaeval fortresses, her modern industries, but because some unknown singer saw the daisy-flowers that seemed black beneath the feet of Nicolete, so white was the maiden, as she went tip-toe through the moonlit garden of Beaucaire; or because such poetry as Petrarch's was inspired by her women and fostered by her skies.

> "Bluio Sorgo, dins sa barco,
> Amourous coume n'i'a plus,
> L'as pourta dins soun trelus
> Toun Petrarco.
> E la Sorgo dis:
> Ero un paradis !
> Parlo-nous toujour de Lauro
> O douço auro !
> Tu que, sèmpre à soun cousta,
> Caressaves sa bèuta.
> Jovino e puro coume l'aubo,

> *Quand venié dins lou valoun,*
> *Boulegaves soun péu blound*
> *E sa raubo.*
> E l'aureto dis:
> Ero un paradis!" [2]

It leaves me comparatively unmoved to hear the decorous observations of John Evelyn on the valley of the Rhone, or to follow the conscientiously agricultural footsteps of the worthy Arthur Young in Montpellier or Narbonne. But I must confess to a joyful thrill of expectation as I draw near the Ringing Isle with Pantagruel, and learn that, by the primal institution and fatal destiny of the stars, there was but one single Papegaut alive at one time among its venerable winged inhabitants; or as I join in Epistemon's warnings, and urge his amorous giant to leave the pretty girls of Avignon and Arles alone. Their immemorial charms are fresh with each returning spring, because in their beauty, born on historic soil, is concentrated the best of all their hot-blooded, warring, loving ancestors.

> *"Mar que reboumbello,*
> *Bos plen de rumour,*
> *Digas à la bello*
> *Moun làngui d'amour!"* [3]

The life that will last in Old Provence is the life of the imagination; and that is why the significance of the Félibres is so much deeper than has sometimes been acknowledged. "Born to a gardener and a gardener's wife among the gardens of St. Remy," Roumanille was the first modern poet to write in Provençal, and he gave an unanswerable reason: "Since our mothers do not know French enough to understand the songs inspired by the tenderness of their children, let us sing in the language of our mothers..." He was elected head of the Félibres at Fontségugne, near Avignon, in 1854; and with him were Matthieu, Aubanel, Tavan, Gièra, Brunet, and Mistral. The movement was neither separatist nor, in the larger sense, antipatriotic; for as Felix Gras wrote, so might they all: —"J'aime mon village plus que ton village; j'aime ma Provence plus que ta province; j'aime la France plus que tout." They have but preserved those differences that were worth preserving: those differences in dress, in speech, in beauty, that are the savour of life and the condition of improved survival. So here I give you the toast to which these pages have served as the preliminary speech. I give it in the words of Aubanel, and I couple with it the name of Frédéric Mistral:

> *"Dins la coupo d'argènt*
> *A plen de bouco*
> *Beven lou vin tant gènt*
> *De nòsti suco.*
> *Catalan, Prouvençau*
> *Tout bon felibre saup*
> *La lèi d'escréure*
> *E la de béure!"* [4]

Drink it before you begin my second chapter, and remember it as you read the story of Provence.

NOTES

1. "Pestilence, lions, and the burning sands
   Sunstroke and famine, he had faced them all.
   Gladly the wolf and vulture followed him
   And his black mare, because they knew his track
   Was marked by heaps of dead..."

2. "O azure stream of Sorgue ! Thou didst bear the boat of thy Petrarch, in all the splendour of his fame, that never-equalled lover. And the Sorgue replied, '*Ah! that was Paradise indeed!*'" O gentle breeze! Speak to us always of Laura, thou who didst ever play around her and caressed her beauty, and when she came, in all her youth and purity, into the valley, didst stir the tresses of her fair hair and the folds of her dress. And the soft breeze answered, '*Ah! that was Paradise indeed!*'"

3. "Waves of the sounding ocean,
   Trees that whisper above,
   Tell my heart's emotion
   To the lady of my love!"

4. "Full-mouthed from the silver cup,
   Let us quaff a measure;
   With the good wine fill it up
   That was grown for pleasure.
   Catalan and Provençal,
   We know, good Félibres all,
   Both the duty of high thinking
   And the beauty of deep drinking!"

CHAPTER II

The Dawn of History

"Vesti de pèu, rufé, barbare,
Nòstis aujou, Ligour, Cavare,
Se disputant lou sòu avare,
Di mount trevant li cauno o de la mar li bord.
Ensèn, li Fado bouscassiero
D'aquelo raço baumassiero
Meravihant la vido, ispirant li counsèu;
Pièi li galèro de la Grèço
Sus l'aigo lindo que le bresso."
—CALENDAL.[1]

WHAT may be imagined to be the vestiges of prehistoric man are too often but the materials for antiquarian dispute. Limiting myself not only to visible relics, but to those concerning which a definite opinion is at any rate possible, whether it be right or wrong, I need only say that the earliest trace of humanity in Provence has been found in the stone instruments at the foot of Mont Ventoux in the Vaucluse country, wrought out of the flint from its south-western slopes, and lying among the bones of the hyena, the rhinoceros, the giant stag, and the auroch.

The Ligurians and the Iberians are the earliest inhabitants of Provence to whom history has given a name. The first came from Italy; the last from Spain. "To them enter" the Gauls or Celts from the north. The earliest recognisable Provençal population was something of a mixture of them all. Ligurian strongholds have been traced upon the hill of Barri in the north of Vaucluse; upon the precipitous fastness of the Mourre de Sève; upon the slopes above Beaumes-de-Venise; upon the bastions of the Alpilles, east of St. Remy, near the Château de Romany, and elsewhere. But in the dolmens, cromlechs, and menhirs, those vast, legendary stones that in England, in Brittany, and in Provence as well, have troubled the imaginations of so many centuries, we can find more satisfactory evidence of prehistoric life. In the list of "Monuments Historiques," which are under the especial guardianship of the state, occur the dolmens of Aiguèze, Barjac, and Campestre in the Department of the Gard; of Fontvieille in the Bouches-du-Rhône; of Minerve and Soumont in the Hérault; of Villeneuve-Minervois in the Aude; of Cabasse and Draguignan in the Var; and of St. Césaire in the Alpes Maritimes.

There are many others; but they are not the finest of their kind, and they are more valuable to the student of folklore or to the poet in search of a romantic background for the shadowy past in which he frames his fantasies than to the traveller who desires to reconstruct a little of the history of the land he visits. So we must leave them as the mere suggestion of those far-off primitive religions which have been common to many other countries, and we must search a little more closely for the particular characteristics of Provence. As in so many other cases those characteristics may be sought now, as they were formed long ago, first of all in the conformation of the soil and the movement of the waters over it.

The brilliant researches of M. Victor Bérard along the coastline of the Mediterranean have just done for the geography of Homeric society what Lenthéric and others did for the Rhone valley and its shifting seaboard. How small is the value of unaided archaeology, how narrow the horizon of the specialist who confines himself to philological or even anthropological speculations, such studies as these reveal but too clearly. In earth and sea and sky, in river and hill and pasture we may still examine the conditions under which our predecessors lived in towns and harbours that we know today; we may discover the laws of climate, of tide, of watershed, of geological formation which bound them, as we too are bound; from the results which are now visible in certain well-known natural surroundings we can argue not merely the habits, the trade, the social civilisation of modern populations, but we can also infer the life of far more ancient peoples on the same spot long ago; we can even go further, and demonstrate the changed social conditions that have been produced by such changing natural features as the coastline, the deltas, and the riverbeds of the valley of the Rhone.

Take, for instance, a list of the great seaport-towns on the Atlantic coast: all are on the estuary of a river—Lisbon, Bordeaux, Nantes, Antwerp, London, Hamburg. Now take a similar list on the shores of the Mediterranean—Barcelona, Leghorn, Salonica, Miletus, Alexandria,

Marseilles: all are near the mouth of a river, but none of them are on the estuary itself for there are no tides to sweep their harbours clean, to break the bars of silting sand, to check the constant alterations, in depth and contour, of the mud-banks that impede free navigation. The geographical description that suits a place today will not only predict its future, it will explain its past. We can thus understand, on examining any given historical site, why it was selected as a habitation, how long it remained advantageous, when and why it became deserted, what conditions of contemporary life and politics it suited, and to what other conditions its situation and possibilities were unfavourable.

A consideration of the towns of Brittany will furnish a good example of this. The ancient and famous cities of the duchy were—Dinan, Tréguier, Lannion, Morlaix, Landerneau, Quimper, Hennebont, Auray, Vannes, and Nantes. Their ancient livelihood came from the sea; but they had to be in some measure protected from English or Spanish ships and from other corsairs of the deep, so they were built at the highest point the tide touched up the streams to which they serve not only as harbours but as bridges. With the policing of the seas their ancient wealth and power have been transferred to towns like Brest, Saint-Malo, Lorient, Quiberon, or Saint-Nazaire, which have absorbed all their old commerce and are living the new life that has ebbed away for ever from the older havens. If we knew nothing of Cherbourg whatever, we might infer that its modern importance was solely military or strategic; for there is no other explanation of the existence of a town in an isolated bay that is not connected by a river with the inland.

Throughout all of its history which we can trace, the towns of the Mediterranean have been dominated by the existence of a succession of sea-powers, whose sea-laws and sea-police are responsible for the life of the inhabitants for the time being; but powers, and police, and laws alike were all subject to the working of the same natural forces which we still watch at work, which we can still see moulding and modifying the character and the commerce of the modern Provençal. The archaeologist may tell you, judging from the only things he admits as evidence, that France owed little to the Greek colonies in the Mediterranean beyond some coinage and some letters of the alphabet; and with that he will dismiss the subject. But, even if this were all the debt, an interchange of coinage implies commercial traffic, and the interchange of alphabet implies commercial correspondence; and when the inevitable laws of the Mediterranean world are considered, it is seen that both the traffic and the correspondence are the most natural results possible.[2] Broad, vital principles still regulate the course of empire and the choice of harbours. The modern battleship cannot stay where the old flat-bottomed trading-sloop was moored beside the shelving shores of some small estuary. The Power that insists on coaling-stations does not choose her ports as nations choose them which have stores of drapery, or bales of spice, or crates of pottery to sell. As the supremacy of the seas has passed from the Power which affects one form of commerce to that which chooses another, so the disposal of harbours, the making of roads, the rise and fall of urban centres have changed with them; and sometimes it is only in a half-forgotten name that the passing of some foreign domination is remembered upon a shore far distant from the motherland of a speech already dead. Even if the witness of contemporary writers, or of contemporary monuments were non-existent, this series of changes could be traced upon the soil and upon the water of the sites that still reveal their history. From the Mediterranean of today we can evoke the phantom of that Homeric sea of thirty centuries ago, and of that mild coast of old Provence "whither came the Phoenicians, mariners renowned, greedy merchantmen, with countless gauds in a black ship," the sailors who beguiled the daughter of Arybas of Tyre so that she stole the nurseling of her foreign master and bore the boy away with the pirates of her own blood who fared along the coast. It is the custom now to choose an English governess or an Alsatian nurse, just as it was fashionable to take a Phoenician woman for a foster-mother long ago; just as Paris of Troy sent to Sidon for women to embroider the tissues of his palace, just as Roger Guiscard took the silk-weavers of Byzantine Greece to decorate his Italian pleasure-chambers.

These first Phoenician sailors—dark-haired and dark-eyed pirates, shifty bargainers, resolute mariners, cunning fighters—are the first of the ruling powers of the Mediterranean with whom we need concern ourselves. Their ships sailed to and fro with cargoes of manufactured produce; they searched first for provisions and wine; and secondly, for forests and good wood for building. When the Athenians first saw the virgin forests of Sicily they realised the material of naval empire. The fatal Sicilian campaign itself is a proof of the brief lives of the classical fleets. The earlier trading boats lasted even a shorter period. Constantly being dragged up the stony beach for safety, the corsair's barque needed constant repair. Egypt and Alexandria were a perpetual market for ship-building wood, and wherever the Phoenicians sailed for wood or for provisions they established little trading-ports in hundreds, and they stayed in them for years at a time. A commerce in slaves, especially in women, went on merrily and continually. Voyages implied neither a hurried transit nor a short stay in port. Every night on the way the boat was hauled up on shore, and the men slept beneath a tent. At every bay and river mouth and cape they stopped and made investigations. When it was possible to save a sea-voyage by dragging the ship on dry land across an isthmus, they always went by dry land. They knew only the dangers of the sea; they trusted it and loved it less.

When Hiram was King of Tyre, the Phoenicians were exploiting the Pyrenees for gold and silver. Their way lay along the coastline, and without doubt they washed the sands of the Rhone valley for the gold which is still found in the powdered rocks that are crushed in the waters of its streams. Personified as the spirit of Phoenician adventure, Herakles is warned by Prometheus of the dangers of his journey from Caucasus to the Hesperides. Foremost among them are named (in the verses of Aeschylus which have been preserved by Strabo) "the brave army of the Ligyes." There, "upon a soft and swampy soil, thy arrows will fail, and not a stone will be there. But Zeus will pity thee and will rain down pebbles and round stones upon the earth, and with them thou shalt disperse the Ligyans." Such is the legend of the Phoenicians in the plain of the Crau, between Arles and the sea, and the "round stones" are there unto this day.

It was chiefly pottery, and arms of bronze, dyed stuffs, and glasswork, that the first Phoenician traders brought to the coast of Provence on their way to the mines of Spain. They took gladly in exchange the wood and hides, the coral, the carbuncles, the fish, of the Provençal villagers. When tin grew difficult to find in Spain they went as far afield as Cornwall and the Isle of Wight for it, and they came back along the valley of the Seine and down the Rhone, one of the most ancient commercial routes of France, of which one of the oldest southern stations was Heraklea, or Saint-Gilles. That Herakles, in all these suggestions, is the Phoenician Melkarth seems quite clear. The legend of the hapless Pyrene points in the same direction. The town founded in honour of the son of Herakles, Nemausus (Nîmes), is another indication of the same traditions. In "Portus Herculis," the ancient name of Villefranche, we can still trace the Phoenician name for the harbour they built near Monaco. It will be observed that Marseilles has not yet been mentioned. That famous city was created by the Greeks. In the name of "Phoenicae Insulae," "les isles Phoenices," we can trace the passage of the Phoenicians along the coast; but they stopped on the island of Château d'If, on Pomègues, or on Ratonneau, not on the mainland.

Already the origins of civilisations in this land of Ligurians, Iberians, and Celts have been clearly revealed; the interchange of ideas, of language, of commerce involved in the Phoenician period of Mediterranean sea-power has become more visible; the road that led from Italy and the east all round the coast to Spain, the Via Herculea of the Phoenicians, has been almost trodden into the visible track which Hannibal followed, and which Marius guarded, later on; which was to become the Via Domitia from Beaucaire to Spain, and the Via Aurelia from Tarascon to Rome.[3]

Throughout most of the historic transformations which these names involve, it must be remembered that the country round Arles and south of it was very different from what it is now. A vast triangular lake communicating with the Rhone and with the sea was bounded on the north by Beaucaire, on the east by Fos, and on the west by Cette; its waves overpassed what now is the mouth of the Rhone, and dashed against the cliffs of Lunel or of Nîmes, or foamed upon the precipitous rocks of the Alpilles, north and east of Tarascon; above its waters the site of Arles showed slightly, the island of Montmajour rose higher, the hamlet of Castelet was visible. The Rhone itself was lost in these long lagoons not far south of Avignon. The Durance passed close to where Saint-Remy still preserves the memory of the Roman legions. The work of filling up these lagoons was going on then, and has been going on almost ever since, in the constant deposition of solid matter by these two rivers. The Camargue and the plains of Arles are but one result of these alluvial deposits.

Like Holland, Arles and her plain owe their present position to the dikes alone: sixty-eight kilometres of them on the right bank of the "Rhône d'Arles," seventy-two on the right bank of the "Rhône de Saint-Gilles," and a hundred and ten kilometres on both sides of the Camargue. No one seems to have asked whether, like Egypt, Provence might not owe far greater prosperity to well-regulated floods than to the unproductive aridity of her protected plains. The current now carries seventeen million cubic metres of alluvial soil out to sea every year, where it forms bars, quicksands, and shoals, which destroy the possibility of navigation, and which might have covered one hundred and twenty acres of the Camargue with a couch of soil twenty-five centimetres thick. These deposits have been more or less prevented from benefiting the country since the fourteenth century, and even earlier. One result is "the dead towns of the Gulf of Lyons." The sea has left them, and there are no cornfields to take their places. If the Nile were similarly treated, Egypt would perish in less than two hundred years. Arles was once known not only as "Gallula Roma," but as "Theline"⁴ or "Mamillaria Arelas"; and the riches from which it nourished Gaul were the products of its fertile soil. Now, out of 160,000 acres of its plains only 18,000 are cultivated profitably, and these 18,000 are all alluvial soil deposited by the Rhone wherever the flood-water of the river has free course; the rest is arid desolation.

Of all the cornfields and pastures which led the imaginative Greek to see the bounteous bosom of nature herself in the city which possessed them, perhaps the most typical relics are to be found in the long islands, regularly submerged from time to time, which the Provençal still calls "*segonnaux*,"⁵ with the echo of a tongue yet older in his ancient land than was the Greeks'. Their value and their productiveness may give some faint notion of the loss entailed to the Camargue by the diversion of these fertilising streams, which might have been allowed gently to pour over the soil by degrees each rainy season. The dikes have not only stopped this process; they have created a separate danger, the danger of the sudden and tempestuous floods which have desolated Provence from time to time ever since the dikes were built, and of which the more modern examples of 1840, 1841, and 1856 were each terrible enough, it might be thought, to have provided final lessons to the blindest of bureaucracies. When, in the last of these, the Chaussée de la Montagnette was burst by the pressure of the water it held back, the houses in Tarascon were flooded up to the first floor, almost without any warning. If the prefect of the district had not promptly cut the railway embankment and allowed the flood to disperse itself over the plain, the town and its inhabitants must have perished. The element that was meant to provide harvests on a thirsty soil, and to give easy passage to the village populations and their produce in light boats and barges, had now become a devastating terror which cut off one community after another from its markets, its business centres, even its food.

Yet the dikes remain, and no doubt will continue. But it is essential to remember the difference between our own enlightened times and those more barbarous ages when Arles was not only beautiful, but prosperous as well.

Every great river obeys much the same laws. In the early part of its course from the parent spring it usually flows swiftly, on a fairly rapid incline of descent, and always eats away large quantities of rocks, earth, and soil, which are gradually ground up by the violence of the stream, and are borne downwards by its turbid waves until the river flows more gently. In the second stage, the river's bed would be perpetually growing deeper and wider but for the compensating process carried on by the deposit of solid matter contained in the water. In the third stage, the angle of descent has become so nearly flat that the water of the stream tends to sideways, and the solid matter, now reduced to mud and sand, tends to form banks and bars. The Rhone is the most important river, after the Nile, which flows into the Mediterranean, and its current is the fastest in Europe over an extent of about 840 kilometres from its the Furca glacier of the St. Gothard range. The enormous quantity of detritus it brings down from the Valais is considerably purified on passing through the Lake of Geneva, into which it has fallen from a point 1388 metres higher up, on a slope of over seven in every thousand. By the time the stream reaches Bellegarde its triturated rocks have become gravel, and the slope is just over one in every thousand metres. From Lyons to the sea it becomes navigable, with a slope of a half metre (or less) in every thousand metres. The rapidity of its current varies from one and a half metres a second at ordinary times to more than four metres in flood. Between Beaucaire and Arles the solid contents of the water have become sand and mud, and the slope is reduced to less than one-tenth of a metre in every thousand metres. At Arles the river divides into the Great Rhone on the left, and the Little Rhone in the right, while the Camargue, between them, is furrowed here and there with traces of various other courses by which the Rhone's waters have at different ages made their way towards the sea. The fifty kilometres from Arles to the bar are on so slight a slope as to be almost level, and the deposits are therefore seen at the maximum of their activity.

I have gone into all this detail because the history of Provence is unintelligible unless you realise the influence of natural forces on the country and on its inhabitants; and because the tideless Mediterranean, and those rivers of which the Rhone is far the greatest, provide the sole explanation of what you can see today and of what you will soon learn of yesterday. The laws I have explained are of universal application. Alexandria and Marseilles are placed in their actual relation to the Nile and to the Rhone for precisely the same reasons as Venice or Trieste and Odessa are situated in their existing relations to the Po, and to the Danube. All four rivers exhibit the similar phenomena of the delta.

Provence is the delta of the Rhone; and every river of the district I shall deal with that flows into the sea exhibits the same characteristics. The depth of water on its coastline corresponds exactly to the character of the soil upon the seaboard. Where the Esterels and the maritime Alps rise above the sunlit waters of the Côte d'Azur, the sea is deep. Where the Gulf of Gascony bathes the plains of Arcachon, where the North Sea rages round the dikes of Holland, and where the Mediterranean receives the waters of the Rhone, the sea is shallow, so shallow that at Aigues-Mortes, on the coast of the Camargue, or at Cette, a man may walk out several hundred yards upon the sand. These shoals, when combined with the prevalent south and south-east winds, make navigation in this part of the Mediterranean very difficult; but another result, which is more visible to the traveller on dry land, is that the sea has slowly but surely withdrawn from its ancient shores; the mass of débris brought down by the rivers has slowly but surely encroached upon it; and towns that once were flourishing seaports are now but the dried-up mummies of a life which has left them with the waves that once broke upon the quays so long deserted.[6]

The delta of the Nile was once far larger than it is now, as was that of the Rhone; but in the Egyptian river it was always Heliopolis which marked the bifurcation of the stream, as it was always Arles as long as we can trace the Rhone. The name of Fourques ("Furca") preserves the ancient memory of this bifurcation of the Rhone at the extreme north of the Camargue, near Trinquetaille, the suburb of Arles. In each delta there are well-marked depressions between the branches of the stream, depressions which continue in a chain of lagoons until the "cordon littoral" is reached. The swamps of Mareotis, the lakes of El Madieh, Ed-Kou, of Bourlos, or of Menzalch, are similar formations to the lagoons of Venice, or to the Lake of Valcarès, the swamps of Arles, or of Aigues-Mortes. Some of the Provençal lagoons are filled up already, others will soon disappear; and throughout the process, the actual seaboard retires further and further from the Provençal towns. Narbonne, for instance, which once stood above a navigable lagoon, is now several miles from any open communication with the sea; and I can think of no better example of this process than the town which was once a Celtic seaport, then gave its name to the whole Roman Province, and is now—Narbonne.

There existed a fishing village, and perhaps more than that, on the spot where Saint Louis built the Tour de Constance and dredged the lagoons of Aigues-Mortes for the embarcation of his crusading fleet and army. Indeed, a deed of Charlemagne, signed in 701, speaks of a "Tour

Matafère" in this place, and of the famous monastery of Psalmodi, a little to the north. The very names used in the district at those remote periods—"Pinèdes," "Sylve-Godesque," "Sylve-Real"—suggest the fertility of pine-forests among the mouths of the Rhone, which have long since disappeared. At a very early date, the industry of collecting salt from the shallow beds of the lagoons took the place of every other industry, and seems to have been known here far earlier than in any other part of France. The possession of rights in the collection of this salt was the subject of a legal arrangement between the Seigneur of Uzès and of the Abbot of Psalmodi in 1284; and these rights eventually passed to the Crown itself, whose restrictions and taxes in favour of the royal monopoly lasted in their full unpopularity up to the days of the Revolution.

Even in 1881 the state drew a revenue of some ten million francs from that source; and one of the most interesting signs of the geographical changes which I have here tried to emphasise is the canal from Aigues-Mortes to the Rhone at Beaucaire, which was one of the first necessities of that difficult navigation of the Rhone delta already described, and which has resulted in Aigues-Mortes, dead as it may look, having more life left in it, and more promise of future commerce, than Narbonne. The smoke from the railway trains is already blackening the ramparts of the Crusaders, in whose days some fifteen thousand souls dwelt in a town built to hold forty thousand, and, until quite recently, peopled only by the spectres of the past. But as the Harbour of the King, as the great royal customhouse of Languedoc, Aigues-Mortes exists no longer. Its only prospects, apart from the salt industry, are to be found in the gradual reclamation for agriculture of its surrounding plains; for the various schemes suggested for its resuscitation as a seaport are more philanthropic than practical.

In almost exactly the same way, it is the loss of the navigation of the lower Rhone that has brought down the imperial city of Arles from its old splendour to the pathetic ruin of her ancient greatness, which we know and love today. Yet another instance of vanished commerce is the once famous, and now almost unknown, Fair of Beaucaire, where the merchants of the East, the traders of Venice, and the sailors of the Mediterranean met the Provençal farmers at a great exchange which spread broadcast the traffic of the west of Europe. Beaucaire, in her turn, has been ruined, not only by the railway which has destroyed the river trade, but also by the increasing dangers of the Rhone itself and of the bars that close its mouth. It is possible, even now, to imagine the watery plains which I have described between Arles and the sea covered with those earliest vessels of remote antiquity, the rafts that rested on inflated skins. Feverish antiquarians have struggled now and again to revive these ancient processes. A professor of Avignon University was watched by large crowds guiding his raft on skins from one side of the Rhone to another, and even for some distance down the stream. The Chevalier de Folard, fired by the study of Caesar, and by stories of Hannibal, desired at the same time to reintroduce their ancient method of crossing rivers as the established discipline of French armies. But neither of them succeeded. The days of the " Utriculaires" passed away when the great lake from Arles to the sea disappeared, and these prehistoric vessels will never be seen again in Provence. Venice has preserved her gondolas, for her canals are with her still. Where the light rafts of early populations carried commerce and civilisation in all directions across the Camargue and the long lagoons of the Rhone delta, there is now only silence, abandonment, and fever—the price of some two thousand years of progress.

Where Celts, Ligurians, and Iberians had lived so many years ago, the Phoenicians, as I have said, were the first visitors who brought a real breath of foreign, exotic, fascinating travel. But their establishments were generally temporary markets, with foreign interests, rather than abiding resting places of a people who meant to make the new land their home. The Greeks were the first foreigners to live in Gaul, and radically to change the essential elements of Gallic life; and of the Greeks the Phocaeans were the earliest colonising race.

The last to settle on the Ionic coasts of Asia Minor, these Phocaeans found themselves upon a sterile and narrow peninsula, and were naturally driven to make explorations westward, and to go further in search of a new home than any mariners of their race had gone before. The tales of monsters and of pirates with which the wily Phoenician pilot terrified the childhood of antiquity, and kept his own routes clear of enterprising strangers, had no effect on the audacious Phocaeans. They built their long, swift penteconters, the greyhounds of the ancient sea, on purpose to face the unknown perils of a longer voyage and a more dangerous adventure than any Greek had yet faced; for their explorations began where former voyages had left off.

From Corfu, the legendary home of Nausicaa and the Phaeacians, they crossed to Italy and sailed along the coasts even to Spain, even beyond the Pillars of Hercules and Calypso's fairy isle, to that Tartessus which Coleos the Samian had only reached before them because he had been driven out of his true course by a tempest along the coast of Africa. It was after their first long voyage of exploration that the Phocaean mariners, on their return home, decided to found a colony with the regular rites, and to found it at Marseilles. The oracles of Delphi or of Dodona were consulted. The names of the colonists were inscribed in the temple registers at home, together with the agreement entered into between the travellers and their mother state. The gods of the old shrine, the fire from its Prytaneum, were carried overseas to the new site. Aristarche, a lady of Ephesus, warned of her duty in a dream, went with them. Simos and Protis were the leaders of the expedition of young men who trusted to find their wives in their new home, and thus ally themselves at once with the inhabitants by the strongest and most enduring ties. This is the process that is suggested in the charming tale of the old chroniclers, a tale that contains far more truth than legend.

Simos and Protis, anxious to secure the friendship of the Segobrigians before the whole Phocaean expedition landed, went up to the stronghold of their king, Nannos. They had discovered that from the Rhone westwards towards Spain was the country of the Iberians. They evidently preferred the territory eastward of the Rhone, towards Italy, in which dwelt the Ligurians or Ligyans, of whose tribes the Salyes, the Comani, and the Segobrigii were the most important. These last must have lived somewhere along what is now the chain of the Esterels, and the foreign travellers arrived just as King Nannos was about to celebrate the betrothal of his daughter Glyptis, who was to choose her husband, as the custom was, by offering a full cup of wine at the banquet to the man who pleased her most. It was to Protis—for the other name, Euxenos, only signifies the same, honoured guest—that she gave it. The Mas-Salia, which was her dowry, was the small Salyan village above what is now the Old Harbour of Marseilles; and in the last paragraph of this chapter I have mentioned some rude carvings that recall the Salyan tribes who once lived at Entremont near Aix. The Greek explorers landed under the happiest auspices, and began to look about them.

The choice of their leader was soon justified. Here was a bay ringed round with hills, from which there jutted a peninsula on which to found their city, with her harbours upon either side. Here was their "Lamptera"; here their " Naustathmos"; here, too, even the three islands that protected these Phocaean originals; for Château d'If, Pomègues, and Ratonneau were the Bancheion, the Elaiousa, the Alopeke, of their Ionic shores. It was Phocaea once more beneath another sky. The images of their Phocaean divinities were placed round that of the Artemis they had brought from Asia Minor, in the first temple built to her worship on the coasts of Gaul; and some of these carved gods and goddesses remain unto this day. Following the example of Protis, his young men took to themselves wives of the daughters of the country, and the new colony grew and flourished, gradually imposing its arts, its religion, its civilisation, upon the receptive populations all around.

But the Phocaeans of Marseilles did more than this. Restless and bold mariners, they were not content with the one harbour that had held one expedition. This was but the nucleus, the fruitful centre of more exploring voyages both from itself and from the mother-country. To the east, in the country of the Ligyans (descendants of those Italian tribes of Siculi, whom the Greek mariners had passed on their adventurous westward voyages), the Massaliots founded outposts, ports with a sheltering island wherever possible, like the Stoechades at Hyères. Here, too, they founded Olbia, Antipolis (Antibes), and Nicaea (Nice); and hence they did a rich trade in timber, cattle, honey, skins, and fish. Along the westward coast they advanced steadily towards the Pyrenees, by way of Agathe (Agde), and Emporiae; taking possession, as they went on, of the Rhodian settlement (Rodez) between Emporiae and the mountains.

Still further they sailed, along the coast of Spain itself, where they found salt, metals, and dye stuffs; and opposite the Balearic isles they built Hemeroscopeum, a kind of fortified ironworks and fisheries combined, with a sanctuary of Artemis. Beyond the Straits of Gibraltar they sailed on, even to the mouth of the Baetis (the Guadalquiver), and so at last to the legendary riches of Tartessus, the Tarsis of the dawn of history, "where was good copper." Nearly all these foundations still exist; but Rhodanusia and Heraclea, at the Rhone's mouth, have vanished from our ken. Inland towns like St. Remy, Tarascon, Vaison, and Avignon (as they are called now) were connected with Marseilles by links of commerce and communications that grew stronger every year.

Realising that agriculture is one of the deepest foundations, after intermarriage, for the prosperity of aliens who propose to stay, the Phocaeans brought with them their own olive-trees; and in the greatest beauty of today's Provence, as in her best harvest, we can still trace the wisdom of her first Greek colonists. It is practically certain, too, that they brought over more highly developed varieties of the fig, the cherry-tree, and the chestnut; and there is little doubt that they began the culture of the vine on systematic methods. Their coins were probably the first that ever circulated from hand to hand in these early days of commerce. For if Pheidon, King of Argos, was the first Greek to circulate gold coins in Aegina, stamped with the tortoise of Aphrodite, he was only enabled to do so because the Mediterranean coasts already knew and accepted the money and weights instituted by Lydians and Phoenicians on the coasts of Asia Minor, the rounded pieces of pale yellow Ionic gold, formed out of electrum from the Pactolus, and coined as staters in 720 B.C. Massalia was founded a hundred and twenty years later than this, and no doubt its founders brought with them the coins to which they were accustomed, and the usages of local minting which they had known in Asia Minor. Coins have been found in the districts in and near Marseilles which were struck in nearly every Greek town in Asia Minor; and among the types upon them are the lion of Cyzicus, combined with the "griffon" of Phocaea, which is the trace of a commercial union so valuable that the greater number of Massalian coins retained this stamp of the lion's head, almost as frequently as that of the Artemis who was the special goddess of their sacred rites. To her presentment they added, later, the figure of a crab, on the reverse, with the letter M beneath it. But the emblem of the lion lasted longest as the symbol of Massaliot marine supremacy, even as it was to be that of Venice and of England later. Some antiquarians have even seen in this coin the derivation of that much-contested name, the Gulf of Lions. But I do not propose to discuss so difficult a problem. The older names of Gulf of Narbonne and Gulf of Marseilles are far more appropriate, and need never have been altered.

It will be remembered that a lion typified too the sea trade and the sea power of ancient Arles. "Ab ira leonis" is the town's motto even now; and it may well indicate an early tie with the Greek colony which had a lion upon its coinage alike by right of heritage and of its own supremacy. The Phocaeans of Marseilles cannot have forgotten that when they were originally sent out from Athens, it was their swift appreciation of the women of Cyme which gave the most Hellenic colony in Asia Minor its deepest hold upon the country by the most pacific methods possible. The equally harmonious traditions of the marriage between Protis and Glyptis reveal that this successful policy had not been forgotten when the Phocaeans founded colonies in their turn and came to Gaul. If the principle had needed further confirmation, it would have derived it from the incident which saved the young city from the treachery of "Comanus," the king of the Segobrigians, who followed Glyptis's father.

It was the love of another Segobrigian damsel which revealed the plot to a young Greek, and enabled him to warn the authorities in time. The treacherous Segobrigians were massacred to a man, and once more the colony profited by the women of the country. At Arles no doubt the same process went on. Arles was already founded when Massalia was born. But this only meant that the young and daring Ionians were received with a more certain welcome when they came; and there is no town in the world where the mingling of Greek blood with that of Eastern races, and with ancient Gallic stock, can be more clearly traced than in the streets of modern Arles.

The beauty of the Arlésienne is the one traveller's tale that never disappoints either the most sceptical of modern visitors, or, hardest test of all, their even more unbelieving wives and daughters. I saw her first ten years ago, as she is drawn in one of my mother's illustrations for this book (in vol. ii.). Only last spring I had the happiness of verifying my first impressions. At the gate of the old Roman Theatre, which is guarded by a concierge with military memories and a better conscience than his predecessor, sat a beautiful woman with dark hair that shaded a warm olive cheek, beneath which the blood flushed visibly. Her quiet eyes, her beautifully proportioned face, her gentle dignity were all that I remembered of her race. They were the gifts that race alone can give. Not until she opened her lovely mouth could you realise she was a daughter of the people.

A few days before, Mistral, the poet of Provence had called a gathering of the girls of Arles in that same Roman Theatre which is so fitting a framework to their classic charms. Like the columns which were set there by Greek workmen so many centuries ago, these women seem the immortal relics of a golden age that has, elsewhere, vanished from the earth. Greek, Roman, Saracen, and Frank have had their say in the moulding of those perfect features. But it is the Greek that has prevailed. Upon the coins of Evaenetus of Syracuse, in the head of the Persephone he modelled for the Greeks of the fourth century before Christ, you may trace the type that has survived. In no other country but the land that has preserved the Aphrodite of Arles, the Maison Carrée, the Triumphal Monument of Marius, could such a type have lasted for so long. The soil itself of modern Hellas has not proved so favourable to the preservation of these noble racial distinctions; and even in Arles those exquisite refinements of line which give character and beauty are denied to the male. The woman only has preserved the delicate chiselling of the antique gems and cameos in which her far-off ancestors delighted to portray the faces of their gods and goddesses. The town of handsome men is Tarascon; but their type is again entirely different. It would seem that, by some process which wiser heads than mine may possibly explain, the mothers that were to mould the future generations of Provence had received, at the very beginning of Provençal civilisation, that eternal stamp of Greek beauty, of Hellenic dignity and proportion, which was to remain pure and unsullied however often a fresh issue of human currency was called for. The pattern of the mint was fixed, once and for ever, by the Attic blood that the Phocaeans brought to the valley. Neither in Narbonne nor in Nîmes; not in Avignon, not at Carpentras, not at Orange, has the same type survived; not even at Marseilles, the first cradle of that fertilising race. Wherever, in other towns than Arles, a distinctive type stands out it may be either the bronzed face, the slightly angular features, the blazing, feverishly active black eyes of the Saracen; or the massive form and riper beauty of the Roman matron; but it is never the perfection of the Greek. The very rarity of the type, the precise restriction of its area, give it a greater value, suggesting one of those strange, inexplicable results of Nature; working at her will, in her own way, and in no other. At Marseilles the Phocaeans may have planted their arsenals, founded their markets, trained their sailors. But at Arles they loved, and bred. "Theline Vocata Graio incolente." Here was the bosom upon which the weary seafarer reposed, and here he paid back to posterity the debt he owed the woman of his choice. By such almost intangible, yet infinitely precious and permanent results in human framework and in certain architectural types which I shall mention later, must we be content to trace the presence of the Greeks in old Provence.[7] By the time the Romans had come over we shall find more visible evidences of life; and in many of the monuments and statues that the Roman domination left behind it in the valley of the Rhone we shall see very distinct proof that the Greek art and the Greek love of beauty had been carefully preserved. "Graecia capta ferum victorem cepit." It is not only in the mighty amphitheatres, the rugged aqueducts, the vast remains of structures which seem built to defy the elements, and Time itself, that Rome has left her indelible mark upon Provence. It is in the Greek workmanship and design which Rome preserved as well; and of this I have given several examples in my illustrations. It is, indeed, astonishing that more is not known of a district which preserves monuments of Roman life as interesting as can be found in Rome herself, and which probably gave the lead—in at least one important instance—in an architectural development which spread from Provence over the whole Roman Empire, I mean the Triumphal Arch at St. Remy.

After suffering a temporary eclipse from the jealousy of Carthage the Massaliots returned from this enforced exile in Italy, and their city rose, from 470 B.C. onwards, to her true position, as the Greek capital of Gaul, taking, one by one, under her dominion, the various other colonies that either Phoenician or Greek enterprise had founded on or near the coast. Among these were Monaco and Saint-Gilles. Even in the Balearic islands they established their sway more firmly by the foundation of Artemisia. The Iberians in the west seem to have accepted this change of power more contentedly than did the Ligurians to the east, with whom the Massaliots had many a sanguinary struggle. It was against these persistent enemies that Massalia was finally obliged to call in the help of Rome. C. Sextius Calvinus was sent, and at Aquae Sextiae (Aix) he left the military station which recalled his victory over the Salyans. When the vanquished barbarians' king, Teutomalius, took refuge with the Allobroges, C. Domitius Enobarbus was sent out, with the usual Roman thoroughness, to conquer them in their turn, which he did with complete success in the battle between the Ouvèze and the Sorgue. He was succeeded by Quintus Fabius Maximus, who finally crushed the Allobroges near the Isère. Victorious Roman legions had set foot upon Provence. Their mark has never left it; and it is in commemoration of the victories just mentioned that the first Roman monuments in Provence were built.[8]

Of the Celtic tribes that had moved out of Germany about 300 B.C., a certain proportion passed down the Rhone Valley. The disturbance created among the Iberians and Ligurians of Provence may easily be imagined; and it is significant that when the legions of Sextius, Domitius, and Fabius were called to help Massalia in the turmoil of contending nations there were not only Ligurians to conquer but also Volcae, Allobroges, Vocontii, Helvii, and Cavares. Their defeat was not finally effected until the reign of Augustus; and the trouble given by their presence first becomes notorious in history when Hannibal was on his march to Rome, and crossed the Rhone between Beaucaire and Tarascon to gain the highway to the Alps.

Discussions have raged long and hotly over the route of Hannibal. I do not pretend to greater authority than that of any previous writer on this difficult problem. But I have examined the locality and I have made up my mind, after considerable labour, that a certain route is right, and without further complication or argument I shall give the one which was first suggested by Gilles in 1872, and which no subsequent theories have ever shown to be impossible. Certain facts in the problem are undisputed; such as the point of disembarkation of Scipio's attacking forces, and the direction of existing roads. The great highway from Spain to Italy, for instance, crossed the Rhone at Tarascon, and there split into two, one part going by way of St. Remy towards what became later the Via Julia Augusta southwards, the other going further up the Rhone by Avignon, and towards the Alpine Passes eastward. The only existing road Hannibal had to use was the one that led him to Beaucaire, and when once he had crossed to Tarascon, the third undisputed fact is that he then crossed the Durance near its mouth. This river joins the Rhone close to Avignon, and Hannibal crossed it from south to north, proceeding up to Orange, and further north still, before he turned eastwards on the road to Gap, to Embrun, to Briançon, and so to Mont Genèvre.

The destruction of Saguntum was the determining cause of a war for which Hannibal had made long and careful preparations. The friendly spies from Marseilles had scarcely informed Rome that he had passed the Ebro when he was across the Pyrenees, and marching by way of Perpignan, Narbonne, Béziers, Montpellier, and Nîmes, upon Beaucaire. He reached the Rhone in fact before Scipio's army had had time to interfere with him at all, and he therefore had full leisure to choose between the two routes that offered themselves, either to north or south. Scipio meanwhile had disembarked at Fos, near the south-eastern corner of the Camargue, and just north of the eastern mouth of the Rhone, at the foot of the Salyan hills, four days' march from Beaucaire. At that time, as we have seen, the plain from Arles to the sea, that is between Arles and Fos, was so covered with immense though shallow lakes that the only route from Fos to Tarascon, on dry land, lay through Istres, Le Merle, Aureille, Mouriès, St. Remy, and Maillane. It was by this route that Scipio's three hundred cavalry scouts marched to their first skirmish with Hannibal's Numidians, doing about fourteen miles a day. The barbarian inhabitants who opposed the Carthaginian's passage of the river were the Cavares, and if Scipio had been a little quicker there is no doubt that the Roman legions, backed by these clouds of irregular militia who knew the country, might have stopped Hannibal for ever. Even alone these hordes of enemies were difficult enough to deal with. So Hanno was sent from Beaucaire northwards to where the isle of Barthelasse gives a ford over the river between Avignon and Villeneuve. His Spanish mercenaries swam over on their shields, and came back to Tarascon in much less time than they had taken to go north, owing to the conformation of the rivers course. Their beacon fires were sufficient to terrify the Cavares into a hurried retreat, and Hannibal passed over safely to Tarascon, after gaining time for the transportation of his elephants by occupying the Roman cavalry with his Numidians. The arrival of an embassy from the Boii then decided him to take the northward route by Gap and Embrun.

Between Tarascon and Maillane took place that fierce little conflict between Scipio's advance-guard and the Africans, which was so sharply contested that one hundred and forty of the Romans perished before the Numidians were put to flight with the loss of two hundred of their numbers in rather less than an hour's hand-to-hand combat. The reconnoitring party, having made out the main body of Hannibal's army, returned at once through St. Remy to their general's headquarters at Fos. Scipio then advanced in order of battle, leaving his baggage on his fleet at anchor, but marching without undue haste, believing at every moment that he would meet the Carthaginian army advancing along the southern road after its passage of the Rhone. But Hannibal had had a fatal advantage in his start, and with his infantry ahead, and his cavalry and elephants behind, was already marching to the north and east by way of Frigolet and Avignon where he crossed the Durance, the only hindrance in his march from the Rhone to the Alps,[9] for the Allobroges had been won over to a friendly neutrality. Once more Scipio had his chance, for the crossing of the Durance in its autumn flood, at Barbentane by Avignon, was a dangerous operation which cost the Carthaginians a heavy loss in men and animals by drowning. But Scipio was again too late. If he had pitched his headquarters at St. Remy, as Marius did long afterwards, he might have had time to strike, first at the Rhone passage and then at the Durance, if another blow had been necessary. But with a base so far away as Fos he could do nothing. With totally wrong conceptions as to Hannibal's daring plan of campaign after Tarascon and Avignon, Scipio was equally powerless after he had started from Fos; for he was continually making slow preparations to fight an enemy who was continually marching as fast as possible away from him. The slaughter of Lake Trasimene and the disaster of Cannae were the price Rome paid for the indecisions and delays of Scipio in Provence.[10]

The sad silence in which the mistakes of Scipio have been wrapped by Roman chroniclers is reflected in the utter absence of all legends, and of almost every trace of his campaign in Provence itself. The difference observable when we reach the days of Marius is extraordinary but not unreasonable. Hannibal passed like a thundercloud. His goal was Rome, and he paused not on his way. The invading hordes whom Marius annihilated were a menace to every population on their route. The massacre of their whole strength upon the plains near Aix was a catastrophe which no nation could observe unmoved. The Provençal has never forgotten it, and from his memories of that bloodstained cataclysm have arisen some of the most enduring and the most beautiful of his beliefs. But the campaign of Marius came after those of Domitius and Fabius already mentioned, and it is with the triumphal monuments of these two last-named generals, at Vienne and at Cavaillon, that I must first briefly deal.

Both of these monuments, the earliest of their kind in Provence, are the primeval types of a building peculiar to the Roman genius. They assumed the form of a tall pyramid or obelisk, a form which was successively modified until it reached perfection at St. Remy, where in the same enclosure is the first triumphal arch built outside Italy, which was the type that eventually replaced the pyramidal form.

After C. Sextius Calvinus had established his military headquarters at Aix, his work was handed on to the proconsul Domitius, who fought the combined forces of the Allobroges and the Arverni in 121 B.C. at Vindalium, the meeting-place of the Sorgue and the Ouvèze, in the country of the Cavares. The same enemies rose again the next year against Fabius, the next proconsul. He beat them even worse than his predecessor had done, and took their king, Bituitus, prisoner on the field of battle at the confluence of the Rhone and the Isère; and it was to celebrate the second battle that the first triumphal monument in Provence was erected by Fabius at Vienne.[11] This is the "needle" or "pyramid" which stands on the level ground near the river, a little to the south of the town. It has been called the "Tomb of Pilate"; it has been described as the tomb of Alexander Severus, or of one Venerreus who is the mythical founder of Vienne; even as the mausoleum of Augustus himself, and many other guesses have been made about it. In the archives of the town it is spoken of as the Tower of Mauconseil, and its evil reputation is reflected in the legend reported by Gervase of Tilbury that the devil himself had set it up. A less daring archaeological interpretation held that it was the "spina" of some vast and vanished Roman circus, round which the racing chariots made their turn. It is, as a matter of fact, the "monument in white stone" of which Strabo speaks, the monument set up by Fabius in the capital of the Allobroges after he had beaten them in the plains between that town and the Isère. The ruins of the two temples which set up at the same time are among the many Roman remains at Vienne, of which the temple of Augustus and Livia is by far the most important [12]

The pyramid at Vienne is built of huge, hewn stones, beautifully jointed without cement, though originally cramped with iron. It rests upon the square roof of a portico which is pierced with an arch on each of its four sides, and ornamented at each angle with engaged columns. Though the pyramid itself is hollow, the enormous weight resting on the portico is the most astonishing feature of a construction which is otherwise quite plain, and even unfinished in the carving of its details.

As became the reputation of Domitius Enobarbus, the monument he set up (later than the one at Vienne), for the victory won before Fabius arrived, was far more finished in style and much more elaborately decorated. In plan the same as that at Vienne, the monument of Cavaillon originally showed a similar portico with four arches and carved Corinthian columns with a cornice above it, and other decorations in detailed work, among which are winged Victories at each angle. Above was placed by its founder a pyramid which has now disappeared. This loss of its chief feature, and the concealment of the plan by subsequent débris, at first led many observers to consider the ruin as the remains of a triumphal arch. But this is not the case. Such arches did not appear in this connection till much later, and this monument was of the original type from which other buildings of the kind were, as we shall see, descended. The victory of Domitius over the combined tribes took place at Vindalium in the territory of the Cavares, which is now Bédarrides, the strategic position commanding the plain from the Rhone to the Alps, which was the natural battlefield of the tribes against the advancing legions. His monument was placed at Cavaillon ("Cabellio Cavarum") because that was the chief town of these conquered populations before Orange attained importance as an Augustan colony. The position of the monument has no doubt been changed since its first building, for the present arches have no real foundations such as would have been necessary for a structure originally at least seventy-five feet in height to the top of the pyramid which surmounted it. The wrongly placed pilasters of the western arch are also evidence of an ignorant reconstruction, in which, no doubt, the whole building suffered sufficiently to begin the state of ruin in which it now exists.

Besides these monuments of Roman victory, it will be interesting here to point out that in the Museum of Aix are preserved some ancient bas-reliefs which recall Gallic battles and were carved by the Gaulish warriors, themselves inspired, no doubt, in these their first rude efforts by the artistic work they must have seen in or near the Greek colony of Marseilles. The three stone blocks at Aix are certainly pre-Roman; and they are equally certainly neither Greek nor Phoenician. Together they form a four-sided pillar, one side of which is left plain. On the front are spirited sketches of men and horses, and on the two sides are carved human heads, almost life-size, and apparently the remains of decapitated foes, who were clean-shaved. The cavalry on the front are naturally very much reduced in size, and sadly out of proportion, but the carvings clearly represent the fighting of barbarian horsemen. These most valuable relics of the aboriginal Gauls of Provence were found in 1817, in the old Salyan stronghold of Entremont on the plateau which dominates Aix to the north, and were presented, in 1862, by M. Sallebant, owner of the land, to the Aix Museum, where they are now numbered 305, 306, and 307.

NOTES

1. "First, dressed in skins, rude, barbarian, the Ligures and Cavares our ancestors fought for the niggard soil, dwelling in caves of the mountain or the seashore; and with them were the fairy folk of the forest, the troglodytes of eld, who cast their spells on life and swayed its counsels. Then came the galleys of the Greeks upon the cradling waters of the sparkling sea."

2. It is far from being my desire to depreciate unduly such results as those of Schliemann or Arthur Evans. My point is that, unaided by other studies, the most brilliant archaeological researches are at best indefinite. To take only the two instances I have quoted: instead of believing Mycenae to be the birthplace of primitive Greek civilisation, we find from Cretan excavations that it was more probably the decadence of a far older state of life, for Mr. Evans has revealed undoubted vestiges of human progress, which not only provide a middle term between the Egyptian and the Greek, but which show three periods of what he calls Minoan civilisation stretching as far back as 3500 B.C. and reaching forward to 1100 B.C. The myths of legendary Hellas are being restored to their right place in history; and the Phoenicians, from whom the Greeks inherited their maritime knowledge, are shown to have inherited it in turn from the Minoan mariners of an

infinitely older sea-supremacy. The earth alone, on which these various Powers arose and passed away, can give a constant key to the multifarious problems of their presence on her surface.

3. Hirschfeld considers that the name *Via Aurelia* properly belongs to the first section of the road, from Rome to the northern confines of Etruria. In these pages, however, I have followed the Provençal convention, which continues the name as far as Tarascon.

4. *"Theline vocata sub priore saeculo*
   Graio incolente."
   (Called Theline in an earlier age when the inhabitants were Greek)

5. "Veson dins li Segounau la meissoun que s'amaduro" ... *Lis Isclo d'Or.*

6. Exactly the reverse process in physical geography may be noted on the coasts of England, which, as Mr. Beckles Willson showed, are deprived by the sea every year of a tract of land the size of Gibraltar, and on the east coast alone as much territory is engulfed by the waves as would more than equal the island of Heligoland. The worst havoc wrought by this constant marine erosion is in Norfolk. Off Selsey, in Sussex, the line of anchorage is still called "The Park," and in Henry VIII's time it was a forest full of stags. Off the coast, in the Wirral district of Cheshire, a forest now submerged can plainly be seen at low tide. The legendary land of Lyonesse represents a whole lost tract of England between Land's End and the Scilly Isles. When the Phoenicians first came here, and landed on these islands, there is no doubt that the lie of the land was as different from that of modern Cornwall as is today's Provence from the Rhone-country of its oldest history. But of the two processes which have changed these countries, it must he confessed that erosion seems in the end less fatal to prosperity than undue extension.

7. Prosper Castanier in *Histoire de la Provence dans l'Antiquité* (Paris, 1896. E. Flammarion) gives a drawing in vol. ii. plate i. of the statue of Artemis which the Phocaeans brought to Marseilles. The original may be seen in the Musée Calvet in Avignon, and is a careful Roman copy of the Ionic carving. In the Museum of the Château Borély in Marseilles may be examined the remains of the forty-one shattered statuettes which were placed in the Pronaos of her temple, where Aristarche was high-priestess. In the Museum in Lyons is the Aphrodite of Marseilles, an archaic statue of no great merit, but of the highest interest, showing the long braided hair of the goddess and the dove upon her wrist. It is no doubt Phocaean work, as was the Artemis, and of about the sixth century B.C. M. Castanier also gives excellent reproductions of many types of early Greek coins found in Provence. But for more beautiful specimens of workmanship inspired by Greek art we must wait until the Romans reached the Rhone. The Phocaean statues just mentioned were buried (and thus preserved to us) when the Massaliots, on learning of the flight of their former countrymen to Rhegium after a naval battle in which Massalia had of course assisted, abandoned their city for a time in fear of the

Carthaginian vengeance, about 536 B.C. The monuments they put up after their return, in about 480 B.C., have totally disappeared. The period between this date and the siege of the Greek town by Julius Caesar has left no traces.

8. The immediate answer of Rome to the appeal of the Greek colony of Marseilles is only intelligible when the ancient history of the Phocaean mariners is remembered. In the distant centuries when Tarquin was king a Phocaean expedition had landed at the mouth of the Tiber and made alliance with the Romans before sailing further west. South of the Tiber, too, was that "Magna Graecia" which every Hellene loved. An even stronger tie was the common hatred felt by both Romans and Greeks for the Etruscans, those descendants of the Pelasgi whom the Hellenes had chased out of Greece, whose fleets, allied with Carthage, had at one time crushed the Phocaeans and Massalia, and whose yoke the Romans only finally threw off about 400 B.C. This independence was probably not achieved without the sympathy and even the assistance of the same old friends in Massalia, whose swift pentaconters had so impressed the Romans two hundred years before. When Phocaea, the mother-city of Massalia, was sacked by the Persians, and after both colonists and original citizens had had to fly from their own cities, in fear of further outrage, it was at Rhegium that they first sought safety, and at Velia in Lucania that they founded a new home. Here was yet another bond between the Italians and these Greeks.

Such traditions are not easily forgotten. As the centuries passed by, and it came to be Massalia's turn to struggle for her independence, her call for help was not made in vain to the growing republic on the Tiber which had suffered from Hannibal's army the same Carthaginian insolence that had well-nigh destroyed Massalia. Rome must have watched for long the rise of the Greek cities on the Mediterranean coast, and must have sympathised instinctively with those colonising and civilising influences of which she was herself to be the great exemplar of all time.

9. I read here (with I. Gilles) "*Inde per extremam oram Vocontiorum agri tetendit in Tricorios. Haud usquam impedita via priusquam ad Druentiam flumen pervenit; is et ipse Alpinus amnis,*" etc. (From there he proceeded past the borders of the Vocontii to the territory of the Tricorii. He found nothing to stop him anywhere until he reached the River Durance. This Alpine stream…) A slight change in the accepted punctuation of Livy gives sense instead of nonsense.

10. I claim no credit whatever for an explanation of the text of Livy and other classical authors, which is entirely due to the geographical labours on the spot of a Provençal historian, who has once more shown the supreme value of geographically scientific researches in the field of history. It may be added that Scipio only sailed from Italy on the 25th of September 218 B.C., when Hannibal had already reached the banks of the Rhone. The time taken by Scipio's voyage was employed by Hannibal in making those careful preparations for his passage of the Rhone which Livy has described in detail. When Scipio had reached Fos on the 28th, Hanno had been sent northwards on his forced match round by Avignon to take the barbarians in flank, which was effected on the 29th. The way being then clear, Hannibal's

infantry passed the Rhone on the 30th. On October 1st he sent his five hundred Numidians against the Roman scouts, and during the progress of the cavalry skirmish that ensued near Maillane he communicated to his army the result of his negotiations with the Boii and definitely decided on the northern route. On the *fourth day* after Scipio's fleet had reached Fos, Hannibal's advance-guard was crossing the Durance and his elephants were passing over the Rhone. On the next day (the 3rd of October) Scipio at length started, only to reach Tarascon on the 6th October and to find that he had made an error which was to cause Rome untold horrors in the years to come. His countrymen have said little about Scipio's mistake. But that they had read the lesson right is shown by the fact that when Marius, one hundred and eighteen years later, had to cut off the advancing army of the Teutones and the Ambrons, it was at St. Remy he waited for them, and chose his own battleground for their defeat. Scipio's camp, after his fleet had landed the army, was on the plateau of Saint-Blaise, or Castel Veïré, an old Celtic stronghold where the remains of Scipio's cautious fortifications can still be traced, in a straight line from east to west. The only other trace of the campaign ever found was the skeleton of an African elephant, dug up near Maillane in 1788, the memory of which is only preserved in Achard's *Geographical Dictionary*; and now even the authenticity of this blameless relic has been severely questioned.

11. Soon after 1540, ruins were dug up near the temple of Faustina at the eastern limit of the Forum in Rome, and one of the fragments bore the inscription: "Q. Fabius Q. F. Maxsumus Aed. Cur. Rest." Some twenty-five other fragments were found in 1882 (*Ann. Inst.*, 1859, p.307, and *Not. degli Scavi*, 1882, p.225) on the same site, which were supposed to belong to an arch erected by Q. Fabius Maximus, consul in 121 B.C., called Allobrogicus after his victory over the Allobroges. But whether these fragments really belonged to the arch of Augustus, erected near this point in 29 B.C., or whether they were fragments of an arch at all, I am inclined to think that the development of the arch as a triumphal monument cannot be dated before Julius Caesar.

12. Vienne is too far north even for my generous interpretation of the geographical limits of Provence. But it may be added that the inscription on this temple was finally deciphered, after a skilful use of holes left by the old bronze letters, by Édouard Bondurand of Nîmes, Archiviste of the Gard. It runs as follows—DIVO •AUGUSTO • CAESARI • OPTIMO • MAXIMO • ET • DIVAE • AUGUSTAE. (To the divine Emperor Augustus Caesar, best and greatest, and to the divine Empress) To this interpretation it has been suggested that the use of both DIVUS and IMPERATOR of the same man is unprecedented in inscriptions hitherto examined. Precedent, however, has little to do with proved facts. This building is now carefully restored, and as a complete specimen of its type is only second to the Maison Carrée at Nîmes. The fine group of two children struggling for a bird is the best bit of old sculpture in the town.

CHAPTER III

Marius in Provence

"…Pièi racountavo quouro e coumo
Eron vengu li fièu de Roumo
Bastissèire de vilo e ditaire de lèi
Caius Cauvin—e Caius Màri
Lou grand vincèire poupulàri
Qu'engruno a-z-Ais sorto soun càrri
Lou front d'un mounde fèr e i'e staco si rèi."
—CALENDAL.[1]

FAR more terrible than the dangers surmounted by Fabius and Domitius was the peril that threatened both Provence and Italy when the Cimbrians and the Teutons advanced by slow and devious but unrelenting marches from the Baltic Sea, through Germany, towards the promised land of southern Europe. Joined by the Ambrons of the Bernese Oberland, this torrent of warlike humanity numbered no less than twelve hundred thousand souls, of whom three hundred and sixty thousand were fighting men. Fresh from his triumphs in Africa, Marius was called upon by Rome to stem the invasion, and the unexpected march of the Teutons into Spain gave him time to make preparations to meet them after they had recrossed the Pyrenees and as they passed along the Rhone valley on their way towards the Alps. The Cimbrians he was to deal with later. We have now to reconstruct the salient details of a campaign which has never been forgotten in Provence, and in doing so I shall be obliged to make as many references to the modern map, and to those earlier geographical conditions already mentioned, as were necessary in explaining the advance of Hannibal.

The naval base of Marius's army, which kept up a considerable amount of his supplies, was near that same Fos where Scipio had landed long before him. But the famous "Fosses Mariennes" were not here, nor did they join the Rhone at any point, for Marius did not camp close to either bank of the Rhone. The Barbarian army, advancing from the Pyrenees as Hannibal had done, would be obliged to leave the line of the coast soon after Béziers because of the immense lagoons which stretched from Aigues-Mortes, from St. Gilles, and from Beaucaire, towards the sea. They had to reach Beaucaire by way of Nîmes, and they, too, crossed the river to Tarascon. From there they marched eastward across the Tarascon plain, turning a little southerly past Maillane, and working up the foot of the Alpilles at St. Remy. It was on the foothills near St. Remy that Marius pitched his fighting camp to wait for them; and that camp was chiefly provisioned by the port of the "Fosses Mariennes" at St. Gabriel, or Ernaginum.[2]

Marius only began the "trench or canal," which Plutarch describes, after he had learnt that his enemy was approaching, and as part of the final preparations he had so carefully elaborated for a campaign which, I have often thought, shows many points of resemblance with that which ended in Kitchener's victory at Omdurman. Plutarch's phrase is that through this canal Marius "drew off water from the river towards a convenient spot where the water flowed towards the sea, smoothly and tranquilly, without being harassed by the wind or waves of the sea. This canal still bears his name." His complete system of "waterworks" therefore consisted in (1) the natural lagoons between Ernaginum and the sea; (2) the "Fossa Mariana," which he dug out from the Durance towards Ernaginum. The natural lagoons, decreased in size by the Abbé of Montmajour in the thirteenth century, and again by Van Ens in 1642, were almost completely dried up by the opening of the Canal de Bouc in 1835; and the water which formerly found its way to the sea between Fos and the mouth of the Rhone is now entirely diverted. It remains only to fix the exact situation of the "Fossa Mariana," which was artificially constructed. This was what is now called the Canal des Lonnes (or sometimes Duransole), which leaves the Durance opposite Château-Renard in a south-western direction towards Laurade. Of this canal, and of the lagoons which it made practicable, one of the chief officers responsible was that Flavius Mamorius whose title of "Comes Ripae" is mentioned on the tomb preserved at Arles, and whose duties extended from Château-Renard to the south of that Lake Galégeon by which the waters eventually reached the Mediterranean. The distance from Château-Renard to Laurade is about fifteen kilometres, with a slope of rather more than a half in every hundred metres; and it was far from necessary to canalise the whole distance in order to ensure the waters of the Durance flooding the whole plain towards the south and west. This therefore is the reason why, during the three years Marius waited in Provence, he put off the final construction of his water-system until the last year, when tidings had reached him of the slow advance of the Barbarian hordes across the Pyrenees.

As was only natural, there are certain traces still visible of this long sojourn of Marius and his army along the slopes of the Alpilles, and the stone-carving at Les Baux, now known as the "Three Manes," is in reality the monument of Marius, of Julia his wife, and of Martha his prophetess. A drive from St. Remy to Les Baux, one of the most interesting and beautiful excursions in Provence, will at once show the importance of both places in the campaign, for they mark the eastern extension of the position held by Marius on the north and south slopes of this magnificently picturesque chain of hills. It is a district filled with legend and with fairy lore, and in the chapter on the ruined citadel of Les Baux we shall hear more of it.

The slopes of the Alpilles, on each side, have yielded a rich harvest of Roman remains of every kind. During his long wait, Marius no doubt had several camps in the immediate vicinity of Les Baux, with important outposts to the north. But when at last news reached him of the Barbarians' advance, when he had completed his system of waterworks, and when it became necessary, not only to watch the ford of the Rhone between Beaucaire and Tarascon, but also to keep in touch with St. Gabriel, the vital point of his supplies, he chose a camp on level ground at St. Remy, rather to the south of the present town, with his right flank protecting and resting on the defiles that led to his old stronghold of Les Baux, and so to safe retreat southward; and with his left flank guarded by the waters he had just led southwards from the Durance towards Maillane. The old Celtic citadel which became the Roman Glanum protected his rear, and in front a simple palisade upon an earthwork was enough additional fortification to the torrent of Jonquerolles.

Two objections to this choice occur at once. Why did he not attack the Barbarians while they crossed the Rhone, and why did he leave the route towards Orgon, Aix, and Italy wide open? He had two reasons; and his success proved that they were right. He desired, first, to accustom his soldiers to the sight of the Barbarian army, whose exploits and ferocity had been unwarrantably exaggerated; and he desired to do that at a spot where the narrowness of the route would compel the

Barbarians to pass by slowly in a narrowed formation, while his own men would easily be able to repel any attacks that might be made during that passage. His second wish was to destroy the invaders utterly and irremediably upon a battlefield that he had chosen previously, and which they must necessarily accept. All turned out as he had planned it.

Conditioned as it was by the waters on the plain, the march of the enemy from Tarascon led them to the attack of Glanum (St. Remy), rather from the east than from the west, and they passed close enough to Marius's camp to shout insults to the Roman soldiers on their way. Finding that hard words broke no bones, and that Marius remained immovable, they attacked his camp, but were repulsed so decisively that they proceeded on their march along the northern slope of the Alpilles by the Via Aurelia, which led from St. Gabriel to Orgon. From here they proceeded by way of Lambesc and St. Cannat; through Eguilles, to the plain of Les Milles, by which flows the river Lar, a short distance west of Aix. Here they camped south of the Lar (or Arc), and the army of Marius, which had followed hard upon their rear-guard, step by step, encamped upon the northern bank, where his water-supply was very limited. This was again part of a prearranged plan. By the time he had arrived here the advance-guard of the Barbarians, comprising the whole forces of the Teutons, had already reached those fateful plains on which their death was to bestow so terrible a name.[3] He therefore had only the Ambrons to deal with, and when his thirsty soldiers, tired of pursuing an enemy whom they now longed to conquer, shouted for water, he pointed to the river that flowed along the Ambrons' camp, and bade his men go down and take it. A number of the Roman camp-followers and servants did, in fact, "go down" to get water, and the enemy at once advanced upon them, though many of the Barbarian chiefs were still engaged on their midday repast.

At first both sides shouted the same war cry; for against the invading Ambrons rushed a fierce remnant of the same populations which had been left in Liguria, and now fought for Rome. Behind these hot-blooded skirmishers tramped the living wall of steadfast Roman legions, and the Barbarians who had crossed the Lar to the attack soon found themselves repulsed again among the boulders of its stream. And now the irresistible advance swept over it, and on; driving back the routed Ambrons with terrible slaughter up to the very lines of the wagons that guarded their central camp. Then the Roman trumpets sounded a retreat, and the Roman soldiers moved back steadfastly to camp, where, through the whole of that portentous night, they heard the lamentations of the Barbarian host and their hoarse cries for vengeance. By degrees these sounds grew fainter. Panic, in that unknown darkness, terror of that conquering foe across the stream, had done their work at last. In tumult and in shouting the night wore slowly on, and the Barbarians fled, fled beyond Aix, until in that great plain which already held the Teutons, the Ambrons joined them and prepared to fight again. The whole army of the invaders was now gathered on the battlefield which Marius had chosen.

In the dawn after the combat of the Lar the Roman troops pressed forward relentlessly upon the tracks of their predestined prey. Both forces thus passed along the Via Aurelia by way of Le Tholonet, Beaurecueil, and Châteauneuf, going through the hills north of Trets by La Grande Pégière, which is on the actual modern road from Paris to Antibes. The Barbarians fixed their camp at Tegulata (so called from its tile factory) which is known as La Petite Pégière. Round this centre were grouped their chariots and wagons, and their mighty army stretched across the Lar (or Arc) southwards (to the north-east of Trets), and as far as Pourrières to the north. When the Romans were within touch of their outposts, they halted, about a mile and a half west of La Grande Pégière, and occupied the hills which stretch from Trets to Puyloubier, from the stream of the Lar to the eastern foothills of Mont Ste. Victoire. Knowing the country well, Marius then sent three thousand infantry under Claudius Marcellus from Puyloubier towards the north and east, as far as Puit-de-Rians. This was the highest point of the turning movement, and Marcellus's infantry then marched south, past Pain de Munition, towards the wooded valleys near Pourrières, where they were well under cover. On the hill at Pain de Munition (Annonae Munitio) was an old Celtic fortification, which was rapidly strengthened; and it formed even a better retreat in case of disaster than the other camp, also fixed upon before, upon the hills just north of Trets. Its importance as a centre for baggage and for reinforcements[4] would have alone justified the turning movement of Marcellus, even if that movement had not been planned with a very different, and a very forcible, immediate object.

It was now the second day after the preliminary skirmish some miles back. The Roman army had rested. Its reserves and provisionhad had been secured. Marius at length advanced straight on the Barbarian camp, throwing forward a cloud of light cavalry as he came. Without waiting for the attack to develop, Teutons and Ambrons both rushed into the fray and engaged the main body of the Roman army while yet it was among the foothills of the descent. Once they were rolled back, and once they rallied; but then Marcellus, marching by a route which completely screened his troops, reached the rear (or eastern side) of the Barbarian camp, and fell upon the centre of their headquarters. The cries of their women gave the first news that this great turning movement had proved successful in its aim. The Teutons drew back at once to grapple with Marcellus, and like a thunderbolt the Roman legions fell upon them as they turned. A hundred thousand fighting men were slain in that awful carnage on the right bank of the Lar. Three hundred thousand of the camp-followers and women were exterminated or sold in every slave-market along the coast. The stream of the Arc was choked with blood. The plains were thick with corpses. So complete was their defeat that the principal fact which history records of these Barbarian wanderers is their entire extermination.

Upon an enormous pyre in the very centre of the blood-stained encampment of his enemies at Tegulata, Marius celebrated his victory by a holocaust of all the booty which was not divided among his soldiers or reserved for his own formal triumph. Traces of a deep layer of ashes, of melted lead and other metals, of burnt earth and calcined pottery, have been lately found where this great pyre once flamed to heaven so long ago, and proclaimed the victory of Marius to all the countryside. Plutarch adds the picturesque touch that the messengers from Rome bringing news of his fifth consulate arrived just when Marius was lighting the pyre. The episode is only important as suggesting the date of the battle in the spring, and the 24th of April is the date tradition gives it. Within fifty metres of the same spot, which is east of the bridge that bears the modern road, are some few vestiges of a stone triumphal monument, which was erected by the soldiers of Marius just south of the river. A fifteenth-century tapestry existed in 1804, and was then described by M. Fauris de Saint Vincent as showing a high pyramid supporting a strong square base which bore, he says, a sculptured bas-relief of three Roman soldiers carrying a general upon the shield lifted upon their shoulders. But the historian Bouche, describing "Le Triomphe de Pourrières, which is near the bridge of La Petite Pégière on the river Lar," suggests that the three soldiers each carried a buckler; and evidently from some confusion with the old name of Tegulata, it was at one time thought that these men were each carrying a tile. The arms of Pourrières, taken in 1697, preserved the same monument,[5] which those readers who have followed my descriptions of the monuments to Fabius at Vienne and to Domitius at Cavaillon, will have no difficulty in recognising as another erection of the same type, a pyramid upon a quadrangular base, which here preserved upon the spot the memory of Marius's greatest victory in 102 B.C. His triumphal monuments in Rome itself were destroyed by Sulla long before this one near the Arc had crumbled into oblivion. But the great Roman general was not to be without his own commemoration on the soil of Provence; for, as we shall find at St. Remy, Julius Caesar, who cared for his relative's memory in Rome, erected also, upon the site of the camp where Marius first saw the Barbarian host, one of the most beautiful examples of triumphal architecture which remains in the world.

There is still, above that mighty battlefield, a memory of Marius which will remain while the everlasting hills endure, for Mont Ste. Victoire is called after his victory upon the plains of Pourrières, and on its summit is a church dedicated to the victorious saint, which replaced the Cassianite convent built on the ruins of a far more ancient shrine. To this old convent, it will be remembered, that Scott describes the visit of the Earl of Oxford's son to Queen Margaret, in *Anne of Geierstein;* and on the narrow platform near the modern church, above the giddy precipice that falls sheer down into the plain, the villagers used to go every year upon the 24th of April, until the Revolution of 1793 swept away this picturesque custom with so many others. A former curé of Pertuis, the town from which Marius drew his chief corn-supplies, has fortunately preserved the memory of a vanished rite, together with the music to which the procession marched from Vauvenargues towards the mountainside. As soon as all had arrived upon the summit a vast bonfire was lit, and round it, with garlands on their heads, the peasants danced the farandole with shouts of "Victoire! Victoire!" As the start was only made in the late afternoon, it was long after midnight before the men and women returned to Pertuis, all carrying boughs and branches, and shouting as before. At dawn the curé of Vauvenargues, the village near Mont Ste. Victoire, on the route taken by Marcellus and his three thousand, celebrated Mass. Immediately afterwards all moved on towards the Garagaï (the abyss of Caius Marius), to see the rocky cleft down which he hurled a hundred prisoners the day after the battle, by the advice of Martha, his prophetess.[6]

The journey from Aix to Vauvenargues is still an easy one for any visitor who cares to see these haunted precipices for himself, and takes less than two hours to drive, on the left-hand side of the valley called "Infernet," beyond which rises the height of Mont Ste. Victoire. There are the remains of a huge château, part of which is still inhabited and finely furnished. In a ravine to the south-west is a farm called "Le Delubre," but there are no vestiges of the ancient temple from which its name may have been originally derived. From here guides and mules can be procured for the famous ascent of the mountain, which is easy enough, and may also be made from Cabassols, which is slightly nearer Aix. In two hours you reach what is now called the Hermitage and Chapel of Notre Dame de la Victoire, with the ruins of a cistern and an older convent near it. Though the view is fine here, it is still grander from the western point of the mountain, on which has been erected the great iron "Cross of Provence." From this spot the whole battlefield of Marius is stretched out below you, and within about two hundred and fifty yards is the famous "Garagaï," the dangerous and legendary chasm whose mystery no man has yet solved. On the southern slopes it is a stiff climb down, but there are the ruins of a Roman aqueduct, and the traces of a Celtic hill-fort to be seen, which may reward the more adventurous traveller. The whole place is filled with memories of a dead civilisation, and must be crowded with the ghosts of that great army which was slaughtered in the plains beneath. But the peasants will not seem to know much more of the details of what happened there so long ago than Thiebault could tell Arthur Philipson, when he explained to the English visitor that the great victory had been "gained by a Roman General named Caio Mario, against two large armies of Saracens, in gratitude to Heaven for which victory Caio Mario vowed to build a monastery on the mountain for the service of the Virgin Mary, in honour of whom he had been baptized." But if many of the historical details have been forgotten by the people whom they chiefly affected, the folklore and the religion of Provence have preserved many traces of the campaign of Marius which even the French Revolution could not utterly destroy, and Ste. Victoire herself, now added to the calendar of the Church, is but the Christian personification of the greatest Roman victory on Provençal soil, a touching instance of that infant piety which, as Gregory of Tours observed, made use of local traditions as the basis of early Christian faiths, and gave to ancient superstitions a new meaning for the worshippers of Christ.

A very extraordinary example of this metamorphosis is closely attached to the story of Marius; and the process of development will appear perfectly natural to those who remember that when the first preachers of Christianity reached Provence, the remembrance of the salvation of that country, and of Italy herself, from the Barbarian hordes was still distinct, and still as great a fact in the contemporary life of both Provence and Rome as the Napoleonic wars are to ourselves. For if it was near Aix that the Ambrons and Teutons had been annihilated by Marius, it was at Vercellae that the other half of the invading army, the Cimbrian tribes, were crushed in the valley of the Po by Marius and Catulus. This is why the statues of the two generals are seen together on the triumphal monument erected to them by Caesar at St. Remy, and this is the reason that a Christian legend attached to the local memories of their campaigns would be acceptable both to Provençal hearers and to Roman colonists. The origin of that legend is to be found, strangely enough, in the prophetess Martha who commanded the human sacrifice in the Garagaï, and whose effigy was carved beforehand with that of Marius and of his wife Julia on the "stele" at Les Baux.

At the present time I know no place in the world which gives so deep and melancholy an impression of remote antiquity as does Les Baux, which should be first seen from the St. Remy side, not from the road that reaches it from Arles. It is here that Ezekiel might have seen the valley of dry bones; here may the belated traveller at night behold them shaking, bone coming together to his bone, "until the breath came into them and they lived and stood upon their feet, an exceeding great army." Here in the "Valoun d' Infèr," which hides the "Trau di Fado," might Dante have conceived his amphitheatre of hell: —

> *"In su l'estremità d'un alta ripa*
> *Che facevan gran pietre rotte n cerchio."*

And as we found traces of the Syrian prophetess in the cleft of the rocks above the battlefield of Pourrières, so near Les Baux, at the end of a small valley, called the Gorge of Hell, is a sombre cavern of the spirits, where Mireio and her Valebregan went to consult the sorceress Tavèn, as Saul long before them went to consult the witch of Endor, who "saw gods ascending out of the earth," or as Odysseus went down to Hades through the caverns of Avernus.

The sterile rocks around Les Baux gleam white like skeletons. The air of death is all the deeper for those dusty ruins of royal habitations whose princes have been dust for centuries, and for those few hovels, still inhabited, that cluster among the empty palaces like the evil excrescences of a foul decay. Among them, on the slope of the hillside, some forty yards below the little plateau of the modern village, are two carvings upon the white stone from which Les Baux itself was quarried. About three hundred yards apart, one of them is called Gaïe with two figures upon it; the other is called Trémaïé with three figures.[7] This latter was no doubt called Trémaïé because it was first supposed to be "tres Marii imagines" (three figures of Marius) which afterwards became "les trois Maries." The change to "les Saintes Maries," assisted by the pious exegesis of the local curé, was not long in coming; and the chapel that is built beneath the great triangular carved block soon consecrated the new name.[8] The sculpture faces south, and looks out above the valley of Entreconque, over the lakes, the river Rhone, the Crau, and on to the distant horizon of the sea itself. Originally the bas relief, which is five and a half feet high, by four and a half broad, stood twelve feet above the rocky soil immediately beneath it. The central figure preserves the mantle closed by buckles on the left shoulder, the lance decorated with wreaths and flowers, which Plutarch describes in his sketch of Martha the prophetess; it preserves also the Eastern head-dress, or tiara of camel's hair, which Raban Maurus describes in his *Life of St. Martha,* written in the middle of the ninth century, "Alba tyara de pilis cameli velata caput."[9] This is the Syrian "woman that had a familiar spirit," like the witch of Endor, whom Marius brought "in a litter with great reverence; by whose commands he made sacrifices at the time and in the manner which she ordered." The importance attached to her by Plutarch is evident from the space he gives to the story of her first meeting with Julia, the wife of Marius.

On her right is the only contemporary portrait-statue that still exists of Marius himself. Plutarch has described a carving of the great general which he saw at Ravenna, and which has now disappeared. It represented, says the historian, "a man of vigorous and austere nature, brought up to the military discipline of war, hardened by early poverty to privations and fatigues." He is represented at Les Baux as a small man, with a muscular neck, in the simple toga of a consul, with uncovered head, and quite short hair and beard. On the other side of the prophetess is Julia, his wife, a matron of ampler proportions, wearing a tunic beneath the usual stola of the Roman lady, one end of which covers her head and folds back beneath her left arm.

A most interesting fragment of inscription, copied by M. le Marquis de Lagoy when more remained of it, may still be traced. It is at any rate contemporary and authentic, and the only word that can he deciphered without any doubt gives us the name of the man who erected the stele. This was Caldus, perhaps that plebeian partisan of Marius, who forged his own way to the front, was made tribune in 107 B.C., and won his honours by hard work like his master. He it was who later on accused the patrician Pompilius of treasonable cowardice in the Cimbrian campaign; and he was lieutenant at Les Baux with Marius before he went to Spain; and in memory of his Spanish campaigns he struck the gold medals which record his rise to the Consulate in 97 B.C. The inscription on the carved stone known as "Li Gaïe," containing two figures, is neither contemporary nor properly connected with the sculpture. The fragments of writing that have been deciphered show the sixth century cursive characters of a Christian epitaph, and the digging of a grave beneath it has no doubt been responsible for the slope of the whole stone. A far more flagrant instance of the use of an ancient Roman monument by later inhabitants as a tomb will be found when we consider the wonderful buildings of St. Remy. The stone called "Li Gaïe" was probably a votive altar; and if the sacrifices at Lou Garagaï on Mont Ste. Victoire are authentic, it is easy to believe that human blood was shed at the same instigation upon this altar at Les Baux. The figures carved upon the stone are again those of Marius, whose head has been entirely mutilated by time and accident, though his consular toga remains; and of Martha the prophetess, on the spectator's right, in her camel's hair tiara, her buckled mantle, and the thyrsus in her right hand as on the other stone. But the top of the tiara shows traces of richer decoration, and its bands on each side fall over the ears as far as the middle of the breast. The neck, however, in the Gaïe seems unfinished and only roughly blocked out. The niche containing these carvings, which are only busts, instead of the full-length figures of the Tremaïé, measures seventy-one centimetres across by sixty-eight high, and as it faces south-west, it is best seen in the morning, while the setting sun gives the best view of the Tremaïé.

The traditions of the countryside have for long regarded the Tremaïé as the representation of the holy women whose shrine is in the fortress-church of Les Saintes Maries by the sea, and M. l'Abbé Paulet sees in their Roman carvings a pious Christian representation of Martha, of her sister Mary Magdalene, and of her brother Lazarus. At Les Baux, in very early centuries, it was believed that the three Marys after the death of Christ were sent out to sea in an open boat and miraculously reached

Les Baux, where their effigies were placed upon a rock to commemorate the event, at first roughly done upon a stone which only held two, and later on, full length upon a stone large enough for all three. As we have seen, the five figures on the two monuments really represented only three persons originally, but there is little else true in this harmlessly devotional legend. This story from Les Baux was no doubt the origin of all subsequent traditions about the miraculous voyage of the Saints. But we find it far more developed at Tarascon, at Arles, and elsewhere. There is good reason for this. It was at Ernaginum (St. Gabriel) that the inhabitants of Tarascon, bringing food to the port of the "Fosses Mariennes" for Marius's army, heard first of the victory prophesied by Martha, his Syrian prophetess. When news of the massacre of Pourrières arrived, it was Martha's prophecy which was remembered by the populations delivered from that terrible host which had devoured their country like a flame, and covered it with invaders of bestial countenance and animal ferocity. In the early days of Christianity, the change from Martha the prophetess to Martha the hostess of Christ, the sister of Lazarus, was but a slight one; and the legend that St. Martha on her arrival had freed the country from the devouring Tarasque was again a simple reflection of the annihilation of the Barbarian hosts.

But as the literature of the Church increased, and the audience to which her preachers appealed grew vaster, a new place of disembarkation for the saints had to be found on the Provençal coast, and this place was discovered where the village of Les Saintes Maries de la Mer now stands around its battlemented church, built at the end of the twelfth century. The entrance door at the side shows two lions carved in marble, which may well have been taken from some older Roman shrine; but the ship with two persons is contemporary, and is the "Navis in Pelago" of the miraculous voyage. A church was known here in the sixth century, when St. Césaire in his will mentions "Ecclesia Sanctae Mariae de Ratis"; and in the will of William, Count of Provence, in 992, it is called "Notre Dame de la Barque." Till 1061 there is then no question of anything but of a shrine to Our Lady Mary of the Sea; and by that title it is described in the wills of Calixtus II (1123) and Innocent III (1200), and a deed of Raymond Bérenger, Count of Provence, in 1241. The first appearance of the name "Les Saintes Maries" is in the procès-verbal of the search for the relics of the holy women, instituted by the good King René when he was at Aix in 1448. This consecrated the legend anew, and by 1744 the Arles tradition had absorbed the story of Les Baux, and an ecclesiastical writer speaks of the shrine of "Trimariarum," the Trémaïë of the monument we have just been examining.[10]

It is worth while emphasising just a little more closely the points of resemblance between the Christian legend and the monuments of Marius, though the "Tarasque" found at Les Baux need not necessarily be taken as the first link between the Syrian and the saint. On the right of the entry to the crypt of St. Martha at Tarascon is a panel-painting of King René kneeling to the saint, which shows an Eastern dress, and bands falling from it upon the breast, as shown on the altar at Les Baux. The famous carving of her with her Tarasque on the tomb of Aix I have mentioned in other pages, and of course we shall hear more of both at Tarascon, where the fête of the Tarasque on the 14th of April was celebrated every year since King René began it in 1474, until in 1904 I found to my great disappointment that M. Combes had commanded it to be given up at the same time as he tore down the crucifixes from the courts of justice. But St. Martha remains, and her Tarasque is without doubt the type of the invading terror crushed by Marius, and it is remarkable that this particular legend is not especially favoured in places so near at hand as Beaucaire or Nîmes, but is found at the place where the armies of Marius and his prophetess had the greatest influence. The church at Tarascon was finished in 1197 on the ruins of a much older shrine, and the crypt may well be of the fourth century, but the magnificent tomb of St. Martha was carved in white marble at Genoa in 1653. The fifth or sixth century bas-relief it contains shows how ancient was the worship of St. Martha on this spot, and indeed it may well have been at the very first introduction of Christianity, between 250 and 300, that the Syrian prophetess became the Saint from Palestine.

Julia, the wife of Marius, in the course of the transformation into Mary Magdalene, suffered strange chances. While St. Martha stayed at Tarascon, it would appear that Mary Magdalene went to bewail her frailties in the deserts of Sainte-Baume, but the recumbent statue now given her name behind the altar of the Grotto was unfortunately modelled by Houdon to represent Clairon, the actress, in 1803. Her tomb in the crypt of St. Maximin is of alabaster, with five scenes from the Bible carved on the front, and was probably a Christian tomb of the fourth or fifth century, like many of those preserved at Arles. No traces of Mary Magdalene exist in St. Sauveur at Aix. Nor is it easy to find at Marseilles any evidence of Lazarus, whom, as we have seen, the ancient carving of Marius was imagined by later hagiologists to represent. Still, it is perhaps significant that the saint is almost invariably carved with the short hair and beard of the Roman general, instead of the flowing hair and beard usual with the Jews. The oldest church in Marseilles, St. Victor, was not dedicated to him by the famous abbot of the Cassianite Abbey who founded it, and it was only in 1040 that Benedict IX connects the name of Lazarus with Marseilles.

If I took each of the other legendary occupants of the miraculous boat in turn, the result would be just the same. St. Trophime is one of them. The church now called after him at Arles was begun by St. Virgile in 625 in honour of St. Stephen, and only took the name of St. Trophime in the twelfth century when the cloister was carved and the saint's relics were transported from the Alyscamps, as those of the first Bishop of Arles. No greater proofs are obtainable of the arrival of St. Maximin, whose magnificent church in the town of the same name is one of the finest Gothic buildings begun at the end of the twelfth century in Provence. The tomb supposed to be his in the crypt is (like that attributed to Mary Magdalene) one of the same early Christian carvings of the fourth and fifth centuries which are preserved at Arles. There is no need to go further into the catalogue. All the supposed events of the legend are found to have taken place in the district covered by the campaign of Marius, from which in fact they took their birth. All the historical traces of the legend disappear when we search earlier than 1152, the translation of the relics of St. Trophime; and it is only completely accepted after 1448, the date of King René's search at Saintes Maries de la Mer. The result is then that the legend of the miraculous voyage of the saints to Provence arose in the twelfth century, attached itself to existing fables at Les Baux, and was incorporated in the theology of the faithful by King René. If these holy persons had in fact reached Provence so soon after the death of Christ, it would be difficult to explain the slow conversion of Provence, where, even under Constantine, the Christians were in the minority; where St. Martin (baptized in 354) was the first to preach against idolatry; where St. Hilary took the classic marbles of pagan temples and theatres to decorate the churches of 439; and where St. Césaire, in 542, found it necessary to destroy nearly every vestige of Roman art in his constant efforts to uproot the persistent paganism of the population.

The legend of the Saintes Maries, one of the most beautiful and most popular in all Provence, will lose nothing in the eyes of those who believe it, or the ears of visitors who hear it, because the historian can find no evidence of its material truth. It would scarcely perhaps be possible for any one to visit the strange old church of Saintes Maries de la Mer on the 25th of May without believing what that multitude of earnest pilgrims so ardently believe, as the shrine of the sacred relics is lowered into their midst, and all their sick are healed. Yet it is easy for one who has stood by the monuments carved upon the sterile hillside of Les Baux to understand how the legends of the countryside, and the stories of its childhood's faith, have gradually descended from the mighty memories of the plain of Pourrières and the victorious campaign of Caius Marius in Provence.

NOTES

1. "Then he told how the sons of Rome came down, the builders of cities and the makers of law: Caius Calvinus and Caius Marius, that great conqueror from the ranks of the people, who crushed the barbarian horde beneath his chariot wheels at Aix and bound their kings in chains."

2. In the choir of the church at St. Gabriel is preserved a Roman inscription, which runs as follows, with the abbreviations expanded: "*Marco Frontoni Eupori, Seviro Augustali Coloniae Juliae Augustae Aquis Sextis, naviculario marino Arelatensi curatori ejusdem corporis patrono nautarum Druenticorem et utriculariorum corporatorum Ernaginensium, Julia Nice uxor...*" This means that one Marcus Fronto was patron of the boatmen of St. Gabriel (Ernaginum), to which the "navy of Arles" brought sea-borne craft from Marseilles, while the "boatmen of the Durance" navigated boats from St. Gabriel to Fos across the swamps and lakes caused by numberless springs on a plain which easily held water (for there is only a slope of 13-17 metres in the 80 kilometres from Eyragues to the sea), and by the overflows both from the Durance and the Rhone. On these expanses, too, the rafts on skins and bladders were plied of the "utricularii," whose names are found in many Roman inscriptions. Near the amphitheatre at Nîmes was found the epitaph of the head of the Nîmes corporation, in the following terms: "*Lucius Valerius Secundus, magister bis Collegii utriculariorum Nemausensium, vivus sibi posuit.*" (Lucius Valerius Secundus, twice master of the College of raft-masters at Nîmes, placed this for himself in his lifetime) This man, however, might have merely been concerned in the making of skins, which were used in many different ways at that time, for wine or oil, as well as to float rafts. But when the name of a river is added, the connection with the raftsmen is clear. An inscription found inside the Nîmes Arena neatly indicates this. It runs as follows: "*Nautis Atricae et Ovidis loca numero xxv data decreto decurionum Nemausensium,*" which means that twenty-five places had been reserved in the Arena by the decurions of Nîmes for the boatmen of the Ardèche and the Ouvèze. The boatmen of the Rhone and Saône were naturally more liberally treated, as may be judged from another passage in the same inscription, which runs: "*Nautis Rhodanicis et Araricis (loca numero) XL,*

D.D.D.N." (40 places have been granted for the boatmen of the Rhone and the Saône) In the national collections in Paris, too, there is a tessera, showing a large swollen skin, such as was used for supporting the rafts, with an inscription recording the Utricularii of Cavaillon and Lucius Valerius, their chief officer. Suetonius speaks of Julius Caesar (cap. lvii.) using the same methods: "Were rivers in his way to hinder his passage? Crosse over them he would; either swimming, or els bearing himself upon blowed lether bottles" (Holland). Elius Aper and Cnaeus Cornclius are named as patrons of the Arles boatmen; Lucius Julius Secundus as one who left them money for annual sacrifices. Marcus Junius Messianus is recorded as four times their president. At Lyons is the tombstone of C. Liberius Decimanus, of Vienne, who established himself as "Utricularius" at Lyons; and of Arrius Attilius, procurator of the boatmen of Ernaginum; and of C. Catinus Driburon, a Lyons sailor—all apparently men of the highest domestic character. The epitaph of the head of the "Utriculaires" of Arles is still preserved there: "*M. Iunio Messiano Utricl. Corp. Arelat. Ejusd. corp. mag. IIII. F...*" (To M. Junius Messianus, boatman, head of the boatmen of Arles)

3. Pourrières, Campi Putridi.

4. Plutarch being almost the only classical authority for details here, I have chiefly followed him, but he does not seem to have enjoyed the advantage of studying the actual ground, and where his explanations do not accord with visible geography, I have usually chosen (from many authors) the solution of M. Gilles. The old fort on Pain-de-Munition is alone well worthy of a visit, for it is on higher ground than any other near the battlefield, and gives a splendid view of the amphitheatre where the tragedy was played out. It needs some courage to climb up to it, but if you persist for some two hours you will reach the vestiges of a kind of spiral path leading to the summit, a fortified platform six hundred metres above the plain. In the centre is a ruined tower, and round it no less than four lines of entrenchments are traceable. The inner circle, round the central ruin, is an irregular ellipse, whose largest diameter is about forty metres. At the foot of the third circle is a regular rampart of masonry with a fosse about two metres thick by three wide. The fourth circle, on the opposite side to the fosse, is incomplete, as the rocks at each end are in themselves sufficient defence. The blocks of hewn stone are laid together without cement, and in the course of time have almost fused in a solid mass. There is no doubt that Marius had foreseen the necessity for fortifying this ancient stronghold long beforehand, as a base for supplies which could be hidden there by the inhabitants, and as a strong refuge in case of utter need. In the end he made the brilliant, and probably sudden, choice of using it as the point from which Marcellus could safely make the turning movement that routed the Barbarians.

5. Heraldically as follows:—"D'azur, à une pyramide d'argent, maçonnerie de sable, sur la base de laquelle sont écrits ces deux mots Caius Marius, l'un sur l'autre en caractère de sable; la pyramide accostée en chef d'un P à dextre d'or, et d'un S à senestre du même."

6. The scene upon the balcony of the convent of Our Lady of Victory in *Anne of Geierstein* shows how long the traditions of this place were known and venerated, and perhaps indicates the reason why the good people of Vauvenargues only visited the Garagaï after they had been spiritually comforted and strengthened by the celebration of the early Mass. "Know," says Queen Margaret, in the pages of Sir Walter Scott, "that beneath these rocks, and under the foundations of this convent, there runs a cavern, entering by a secret and defended passage a little to the westward of the summit, and running through the mountain, having an opening to the south, from which, as from this bartizan, you can view the landscape so lately seen from this balcony, or the strife of winds and confusion of clouds which we now behold. In the middle of this cavernous thoroughfare is a natural pit, or perforation, of great but unknown depth. A stone dropped into it is heard to dash from side to side, until the noise of its descent, thundering from cliff to cliff, dies away in distant and faint tinkling, less loud than that of a sheep's bell at a mile's distance. The common people, in their jargon, call this fearful gulf Lou Garagoule; and the traditions of the monastery annex wild and fearful recollections to a place in itself sufficiently terrible. Oracles, it is said, spoke from thence in pagan days by subterranean voices arising from the abyss and from these the Roman general is said to have heard, in strange and uncouth rhymes, promises of the victory which gives name to this mountain. These oracles, it is averred, may be yet consulted after performance of strange rites in which heathen ceremonies are mixed with Christian acts of devotion. The abbots of Mont Ste. Victoire have denounced the consultation of Lou Garagoule, and the spirits who reside there, to be criminal. But as the sin may be expiated by presents to the church, by masses, and penances, the door is sometimes opened by the complaisant fathers to those whose daring curiosity leads them, at all risks, and by whatever means, to search into futurity."

7. It will be remembered that the hill near the camp of Caius Marius at Fos is known both as Gaïé and Maïé, from the two names of the general. Much the same is the case at Les Baux.

8. In 1902 the Abbé L. Paulet published *Les Baux et Castillon,* in which he bravely adheres to the saintly legend, "whatever may be the opinions which the antiquarian M. Gilles has published." The Abbé is of course right to be on the side of the angels.

9. The best way to reach these monuments is to take the path out of the Porte des Archers which goes to the north of the village out of the main road, keeping the "Croix de Machine" on your left. The first is "Li Gaïé" to the west, the second is "Trémaïé" to the east. These are also called "Li Santo." There was an excellent guide at Les Baux in the spring of 1904, but he does not take you to these carvings unless you ask for them.

10. The passengers in the miraculous ship of course increased as well, as time went on; and the beginning of their voyage is thus described in an old song of the Jews, quoted by Mistral: —

"Entrez, Sara, dans la nacelle,
Lazare, Marthe, et Maximin,
Cléon, Trophime, Saturnin,
Les trois Maries et Marcelle,
Eutrope et Martial, Sidoine avec Joseph.
Vous périrez dans cette nef.

Allez sans voile et sans cordage,
Sans mât, sans ancre, sans timon,
Sans aliments, sans aviron,
Allez faire un triste naufrage!
Retirez-vous d'ici, laissez nous en repos,
Allez crever parmi les flots."

CHAPTER IV

Rome at St. Remy and Orange

"Ansin, esfatant sa bassesso,
Aurenjo, futuro princesso,
Carpentras, Cavaioun, Saint-Roumié, Saint-Chamas,
S'arrengueirèron en carriero
D'arc-de-triounfle; li serriero
Vous durbiguèron si peiriero."
—CALENDAL.[1]

FOR the clear understanding of the next Roman monuments, all commemorating battles, which I shall describe in Provence, it will be necessary to give the briefest possible sketch of so much of the history of Rome as falls within my geographical limits, from the time when Marius returned to the capital up to the years when Augustus began the real pacification and consolidation of the district, and when nearly every monument that remains will be found to be of a civil or religious order, with the few exceptions that I shall note in their right place.

The natural consequence of Marius's victories over the Barbarian was the annexation of farms and estates for his veterans. Whether the native inhabitants expected to be freed from the Cimbri and Teutons without paying the price I know not; in any case it is certain that they objected to the payment. Their gratitude to Marius himself has continued to this day. But a very few years of Marius's soldiers was enough for them. There is no doubt that this discontent was increased by Roman misgovernment and Roman carelessness. The cauldron of Italy was still seething with those elements of discord that were to produce a different life and form of government. Just as, long afterwards, the last decades of the eighteenth century in France showed every symptom of the purging cataclysms that foreshadowed change and regeneration; just as a mighty master of men appeared to dominate the new Republic and to found an

Empire; so out of the horrors of the Servile War, out of the barbarities of the Marian and Sullan proscriptions, arose the dominating figure of Julius Caesar, and the foundation of the Roman Empire. Provence was neglected while greater stakes were being lost and won beyond her boundaries. The Salyes, the Celtiberians, and other tribes seized the opportunity to revolt. Naturally a stronghold of the Marian faction, Provence must have looked on with mingled feelings while the extremely dangerous rebellion of the Marian Sertorius gradually grew more and more menacing in Spain. Provence became a mere road for the armies of Rome's various faction-leaders, a mere source of supplies for one passing legion after another. The Senate had to send Pompey, their greatest general, against Sertorius, who held out until he was foully murdered by his own officers in B.C. 73. Fonteius was Pompey's lieutenant in Provence during those years; and Cicero's defence of him still forms the most damning indictment of his rule, still provides the most pathetic picture of the woes of this unhappy territory.

Fonteius was prosecuted in Rome for extortion and embezzlement by the inhabitants of Provence in B.C. 69. From the invectives which Cicero, then engaged on the other side, poured out against Verres only the year before, we may get some glimpses of the truth about Fonteius, whose chief claim to Roman sympathy was that he was represented as having saved the Roman capital of Narbo Martius from the rebels. That he extracted huge sums of money, vast supplies of forage, and numerous cavalry recruits, from the Provincials, is of course also set down to his credit by the patriotic advocate. But the people who had undergone these processes of extraction took another view. They were far from being, even at this time, the utter Barbarians depicted in Cicero's bitter phrases. Greek civilisation had done its work, and Roman colonisation had at any rate begun to spread its influences. The chief practical objectors to Fonteius had been those tribes of the Volcae and Helvii whose territory Pompey had handed over to the Republic of Marseilles, and who very naturally resented that process against the nearest Roman, being persons who knew nothing of Roman politics, and who were accustomed to direct dealing. It is significant that they had not at first been joined in open revolt by tribes which had given even more emphatic verbal expression to their sense of injury. The Allobroges, however, had not had their lands given to Marseilles; and their character and general proceedings are so different from those of all their more Barbarian neighbours that something must especially be said of them;

for, as will be seen, their action had the very greatest influence on most important events on both sides of the Alps. Let me, then, take their visit to Italy, to begin with, reminding you that their territory is at the extreme north of our boundaries, lying, roughly, between the Rhone and the Isère, from Lyons southwards through Vienne, and from Valence northwards towards Lake Geneva.

In the year of Cicero's consulship, a year of which he never ceased to boast, the Allobroges sent an embassy to Rome to complain of the unfair exactions which they, in common with the Provençal tribes, perpetually suffered. It happened that they arrived at the moment when the sinister and terrible shadow of Catiline was beginning to be cast over society in Rome. The leaders of the conspiracy, working for their own ends, urged them to revolt. Showing remarkable intelligence and loyalty, the Allobroges flattered Catiline's emissaries just sufficiently to secure damning proofs of guilt, and then explained the whole plot to the Consul. Cicero, in turn, used them for his private ends, and, having assured his own reputation, promptly turned them out of Rome without a shred of real redress for any of their grievances. So having had enough of Roman politics, they went home and revolted in good earnest, almost annihilating the legions of Manlius Lentinus. Pomptinus, who effectually crushed them not long afterwards, in 61 B.C., had to wait six years outside the walls of Rome before he was allowed to celebrate a well-earned triumph. But what are we to say when, in spite of this last insult, in spite of their defeat in battle, in spite of the contemptuous ingratitude of Cicero, we find the Allobroges the firmest friends of Rome in her next and greatest campaign in Gaul?

The only key to the enigma lies in the personality of Caesar. Here at last was a man they could trust. It is one of the many proofs of Caesar's greatness that he realised the Allobroges were indispensable. As a matter of fact, if they had not stayed staunchly faithful to him at the critical moment of the rebellion of Vercingetorix he would most probably have been overwhelmed, and the whole course of history would have been even more deeply altered than if the Catiline conspiracy had succeeded, as, but for the Allobroges, it might very conceivably have done.

To the Roman monuments in Vienne, I have already alluded as briefly as I may. They owed their beginning to the favour shown by Julius Caesar to the capital of the Allobroges. He saw that as the Roman dominions were spreading further north, they could not be held either by Aix on the east or by Narbonne to the south. The key to the larger position between the Isère, the Rhone, and the Alps, the vital link between his invading legions and his Italian base, must be Vienne. What Caesar recognised, his great opponent, Vercingetorix, perceived with no less keenness; and in B.C. 52 it was against Vienne and the Allobroges that Vercingetorix began the attempt, that proved eventually successful, to cut the line of Caesar's communications with his base. Had the Allobroges yielded either to the policy or to the arms of the Gallic leader, Caesar would have been fatally isolated. But they held firm to him; whether owing to his prescience in settling picked veterans at Vienne beforehand, or whether in deference to some personal charm in his own character, it would now be futile to conjecture. But the latter seems the more plausible hypothesis, for as soon as tidings of his assassination in Rome had reached them they rose in a body and expelled every Italian in their capital. The Roman military centre had in consequence to be shifted further north, to Lyons.

But throughout Caesar's masterly campaigns, Vienne was of the utmost strategic and military importance; and it was no doubt partly in memory of this that, even when higher honour was being paid in later years to her more northern rival, the fine temple to Augustus and to Livia was set up in Vienne. It was probably his confidence in the loyalty and the strength of this town that largely enabled Caesar to secure those unexpected reinforcements of German cavalry and light infantry from beyond the Rhine which finally enabled him to crush Vercingetorix at Alesia. After that, the victory of his lieutenant, Caninius, at Uxellodunum, completed the pacification of the north. With this and with a summary visit to Narbonne, the two years in Caesar's life between the defeat of Vercingetorix and the withdrawal to Arras are usually supposed to have been filled up. But the great commander left visible traces of his victory upon the soil of Provence before he quitted it, and it was in these two years that they were built. The first was the earliest Triumphal Arch[2] in existence outside Italy—the arch set up by Julius Caesar at St. Remy to commemorate the surrender of Vercingetorix; and the second is the exquisite triumphal monument he set up to the memory of Marius, which was placed at the focal point of Marius's campaign, and suggested the site that was to commemorate the honours and the conquests both of the uncle and the nephew. I will take them in the chronological order of the events to which they refer.

Owing to an utterly spurious inscription, the beautifully proportioned pyramidal monument on the "Plateau des Antiquités" at

St. Remy has often been called a mausoleum. On the architrave of the north side are engraved the words: —

SEX. L. M. JULIEI. C. F. PARENTIBUS SUEIS.[3]

The three Julii here mentioned may have been grandsons of a Gaulish chieftain, to whom, as was often the case, Augustus had given Roman citizenship, and who assumed, in consequence, the nomen *Julius*. Such persons were usually of wealth and distinction; but it is strange that there were apparently no official titles to add to the names given, and that the inscription is in a position which is so high up on the monument that I believe the letters were incised long after it had been completed; nor can I admit the possibility that three men of Gaulish descent, or three men who held no office, living in so small a town as St. Remy, would have had sufficient taste to erect so beautiful a work of art. They did something much simpler, something which is far from uncommon either in Provence or any other country full of classical remains. They calmly appropriated a fine "antiquity," wrote their own names on it, and buried the respected corpses of their parents within a building originally intended for entirely different uses. So old and so interesting an inscription need not be erased, in spite of the fraudulent attributions it has aroused in centuries of antiquarians; but it should be obliterated from the mind of any one who visits nowadays the monument that commemorates the victory of Caius Marius over the Teutons and Ambrons, and of Catulus, his colleague in the consulship, when their combined forces crushed the Cimbrians upon Raudine Plain.

Almost the first peculiarity that strikes an attentive observer of both these monuments is that they are not square with each other. The arch is set to the four cardinal points, but the higher monument is not, for it is squared so that the statues on its summit look out towards the north-east, towards the old belfry of St. Paul des Mausoles (now an asylum), in the direction from which the attack was first made on the Roman headquarters; and the form of Marius, carved beneath the cupola, still seems to watch over his encampment, and direct its stubborn defence against the Barbarian army. (See p. 34.) This is the reason why the whole building is set at a different angle to the arch, although so close to it, and although built at the same time, and of the same hewn stones. This, too, is the explanation of the horned helmet worn by an Ambron horseman in the cavalry combat depicted on the large carving of the north-eastern

Roman Triumphal Monument, wrongly called 'The Mausoleum'

side, beneath the spurious inscription, and of the same characteristic head-dresses found on the other relief representing an infantry skirmish. To the south-west is shown the triumph of the consuls. In front is a river (the Rhone, the Durance, or the Lar), by whose banks the Barbarians were beaten, holding an urn and a reed. On the left the bald-headed man is Q. Lutatius Catulus, and beside him is the short-haired Marius. Near them is a child carrying meal and salt for the sacrifice. After him stands the priest, his head bare, his hands crossed over the breast, and a winged Victory holds in her right hand the spoils of the conqueror, while behind her is a Barbarian wearing his hornéd helmet. Other figures of infantry and cavalry in combat fill out the design, and in one corner is a youth bearing the sacred shields of Numa for the general's triumph.

I quite admit that now and then it will require the eye of faith to pick out all these details. But I cannot agree either with M. Léon Palustre in his opinion of "la banalité des sujets représentés et la pauvreté de leur exécution"; or with M. Mérimée, who explained them as (1) a hunting-party, (2) a combat of Amazons, (3) the death of Patroclus, (4) a cavalry skirmish. If the inscription were genuine, I ask why these subjects should have been chosen for the tomb of two citizens of St. Remy. If the inscription is admitted to be false, I ask whether the monument decorated with such carvings could ever have been originally built as a tomb; however largely we interpret the well-known Roman feeling about the representations appropriate to the dead. Clearly, even if only a portion of the explanation here suggested for these carvings be correct, they recall a feat of arms; they commemorate a Roman triumph. The only great Roman victory over Barbarian warriors in this district was that which was planned within the camp of Marius upon this very spot. A pyramid, erected by his own soldiers, almost immediately after the massacre of the plains of Pourrières, commemorated the place of the final stand of the Barbarians. Fifty years afterwards an infinitely finer development of pyramidal architecture, in the style of such great Hellenic models as the Choragic monument of Lysicrates, was erected by the cultivated taste of his nephew, Julius Caesar, upon the spot where the Barbarians had first confronted the legions of Marius, and where Marius himself had dictated the whole strategy of his victorious campaign.

Those readers who have followed the architectural development of those pyramidal buildings which are a Provençal type of Roman triumphal monuments, will recognise here once more the same square basement we have seen before, the same four-arched opening above it, and a particularly graceful variation of the pyramidal structure that crowns all, a variation obviously due to Greek ideals, and never repeated in any of the other monuments of this same type, which I shall have to mention later on at Nîmes, for instance, and La Turbie. The square basement of the St. Remy monument, enriched by the reliefs just described, supports a story pierced with an archway in each face, with a three-quarter pillar of the Corinthian order at every angle, and a very beautifully carved frieze above them, of marine mythological monsters, referring to the "Fosses Mariennes." The highest part is a circular colonnade with a conical roof, which may now be incomplete. The openings in the archways and in the columns above them give an effect of lightness, even of aspiring beauty, very different from that at usually associated with either Greek or Roman architecture, and far finer, as I think, than the very singular and completely solid monument, of a somewhat similar form, at Igel, near Trèves, built in the last age of the Empire. The base of the St. Remy monument measures about twenty-two feet each way; the total height is over sixty feet; and it needs no great effort of the imagination to see in this exquisite piece of proportion the model of many early mediaeval church steeples in this part of Provence.

Few other leaders could have dared posterity to make comparison between their own campaigns and that which annihilated the invading Northerners beneath the crags of Mont Ste. Victoire. But Julius Caesar was able, without fear of comment, to erect the arch of his triumph over Vercingetorix beside the monument of the general which he set up at St. Remy, as he had restored the monuments of the great popular leader in the streets of Rome.

There is a political as well as a military significance in these buildings. Long before the Republic really fell, Roman society was already in structure, temper, and mind, thoroughly unrepublican. Marius had returned to Rome after his Provençal victories as the leader of the popular party. His military reforms had at once democratised the army, and attached it more closely to its leader for the time being, for he increased the efficiency of the legion, by admitting all ranks under voluntary enlistment, at the cost of a complete severance with all the ties which had formerly bound the army to the civil community and to civil authorities. In the ten years of civil strife during which constitutional government had been in abeyance, and the opposing political parties used legions who followed their generals even against their fellow-citizens, the turmoil had spread from the Roman forum to

Italy, from Italy to the provinces. The Sullan system was overthrown by Pompey, a typical example of that growing indifference to Republican traditions against which Cicero struggled until he lost his life; for Cicero was a man who represented more than Arpinum, the birthplace of Marius, more than his profession, more than merely senatorial ascendency; he was the champion of the Italian middle class, and by them he was made consul, especially to combat socialistic schemes on one side, and aristocratic exclusiveness and luxury on the other. Unfortunately he arrived too late. The future was with the nobly-born, the aristocratic Caesar, and Caesar saw at once that it was by posing as the people's champion, as the nephew of Marius and the son-in-law of Cinna, that he would finally succeed. The outbreak of Catiline for the moment gave Cicero the upper hand, and discredited the popular party; but Caesar had effectually cleared the memory of Marius, Cinna, and Saturninus, and publicly reminded the people of their services by setting up again upon the Capitol the trophies of the Cimbric War.[4] After he had conquered Gaul, he must have realised, in his own mind, what was the inevitable consequence. He must have at least coveted the position Pompey had already won. When the crisis came he was ready to cross the Rubicon at the head of his conquering legions and he was ready because, as there can be little doubt, his campaigns had riveted the convictions of his political experience, that the increase of Roman territory meant the downfall of Republican institutions Only as a portion of a Roman Empire could Provence be rightly held and fruitfully governed. There is something of these dreams of his in the two buildings at St. Remy: one to the great pacificator of Provence, the first conqueror of the invading Barbarians, who was also the leader of the political party with which Caesar had identified himself; the other to the conqueror of Gaul, the founder of the Roman Empire. You may see this in the very style of each. The exquisite Greek proportions of the monument of Marius not only do honour to the general, but commemorate the aristocrat who could achieve so perfect a conception. The Triumphal Arch, the first of its kind outside Italy, the type of all the chief triumphal monuments of the Empire that was coming, was the appropriate form to commemorate the conquests of that Empire's founder.

The St. Remy arch is about forty feet long by eighteen and a half wide, twenty-five feet to the under side of the vault, and is placed foursquare to the cardinal points. No earlier example of this form of

Triumphal Arch at St. Remy

building exists anywhere, though, as I have already noted, some authorities consider that earlier triumphal arches, now ruined entirely, were set up in Italy. This one is single, like that at Carpentras, set up by Julius Caesar's colonists; and, like it also, has engaged columns, with a considerable lateral thickness to receive bas-reliefs, which have vanished from St. Remy, but remain at Carpentras, though both have lost the capitals of the columns; and the attic, which was probably originally built on the later arch, was never designed for that of St. Remy.[5]

If the monument of Marius exhibited the happiest combination possible of Roman dignity with Greek proportion and elegance, the arch of Caesar is perhaps the most interesting, as it is one of the earliest developments of a building which Rome is said to have copied from Etruscan architecture. There is a reference in Pliny which suggests that the Greeks had developed this style, but I prefer to see in the St. Remy arch only the influence of Greek workmen, and the use of the Greek principle that monuments in the Corinthian style should never be too large. This is the smallest arch of its kind we know; and it was originally what is known as an equilateral arch, for I believe too much soil has now been dug away, and too great a height of its foundations thereby exposed. The carving on the northern side represents Julius Caesar, a small man, with his hand on his tall captive, Vercingetorix, whose head is still preserved, while that of his conqueror has disappeared. On the north-west the personification of triumphant Rome is seated on a pile of arms, beside which is a bound prisoner. On the south-east Vercingetorix is represented chained to a trophy formed of a tree-trunk, and beside him is the weeping figure of Gallia conquered, and a prisoner. The fourth carving, to the south-west, shows another male prisoner and a captured woman. Round the archivolt is an exquisitely carved garland of flowers and fruit, and on the narrow entablature just below the springing of the arch is a band of light relief carved with the "lituus," the sacrificial knife of the Pontifex Maximus, with flutes and other instruments of music. The vault itself is decorated with finely carved hexagonal caissons, deeply recessed, containing rosettes.

The whole construction, in large and finely fitted blocks, is as appropriate as the position and locality of the monument to the time when Julius Caesar built it. Glanum itself, the Roman town built near the modern St. Remy, had no special importance that such buildings should have been erected in it. It was only a "vicus" in the territory of Roman Arles; it was never the capital of a tribe; it therefore never developed into the see of a modern bishopric, with that continuity of history of which French towns give so many notable examples. But the site chosen for these monuments is one of the grandest in Provence when considered in the light of imperial history, when looked at as Julius Caesar, the maker of that history, would have looked at it.

To the south of St. Remy these marvellous buildings stand on the north side of the scarred and sun-scorched crags of the Alpilles, true Provençal hills: barren yet beautiful; grey, lilac, gold against the setting sun, but never green. Never had "antiquities"(as the country people call them) so finely picturesque a frame. From the lower part of the great camp where Marius awaited the Barbarians they look out over the plain that extends as far as Avignon, that is bounded by the horizon of Mont Ventoux, and of the hills that guard Vaucluse. Behind them, to the south, begin the crags crowned by the dusty solitudes of the fortress of Les Baux, by the misery and squalor of those mediaeval ruins that are in such terrible contrast to the sane and beautiful relics of classical antiquity.

When Madame James Darmesteter visited them, the peasants gave her their views of the matter.[6] "Some of them aver the figures [on the taller monument] to be the portraits of those twin emperors Julius and Caesar; but most of them, with some show of reason, consider that they

Triumphal Arch at Carpentras

commemorate the victories of Caius Marius, the hero of all this
countryside. The figures are twain, so the peasants have doubled the
general; Caius and Marius look out towards the Fosses Marienne... one
shepherd, however, offered me the best explanations. 'Those two

figures,' said he, 'represent the great Caius Marius and the prophetess Martha, the sister of Lazarus, and the patroness of our Provence. They were, as you may say, a pair of friends.' 'Dear me!' said I, 'I thought there was a hundred years or so between them.' 'Maybe,' said the good man, 'that may well be, madame; but none the less, they remained an excellent pair of friends.'"

This charming example of the legendary lore already explained in my description of the "Three Maries" was too good to be omitted, and it will show, better than anything, the hold upon the people's heart which these storied stones have held, and hallowed, for so long. In the north, traditions go back as far as, perhaps, the Great Revolution. Beyond that blood-stained trench the memory of the living past has almost vanished. But in Provence the horizon is far wider, far more mellow. Her citizens have peacefully inherited what the old kingdom of Arles handed on to them from Rome and Greece. In the contemplation of these vast and beautiful monuments of ancient Latin life, they have realised the inheritance of that ancient civilisation. They have acquired an unconscious dignity that, from the height of these departed glories, looks down with courteous superiority upon the new Barbarian hordes which modern travel brings within their gates. The sympathetic and intelligent visitor who travels in Provence will not so much feel that its Roman ruins have survived unto this day; he will be conscious of a strange translation from these modern moments of contemporary bustle to the elder centuries of a mild and bland antiquity.

"My countrymen," said Mistral, when I saw him in Maillane, "are not slaves like the men of Nice and Cannes who sell their soil to foreigners, or to syndicates from Paris and lose all individuality and freedom. We, on the contrary, have each our own land and home, our liberty and independence from our own toil, and therefore we have kept the local character of our old Provence. Fools prefer similitudes. They understand them better. When they see differences they try to smooth them down to the monotonous level of their own low instinct. The wiser man loves difference; difference in dress, in speech, in life, in looks; difference that has given Provence the loveliest women of all France in some of her towns, the handsomest men in others."

No one who looks at those two carved figures within their lofty colonnade can mistake the feeling of dignity they impress on the beholder. They look from beneath the cupola that stands out against the limestone hills, and their gaze seems to pass beyond the Triumphal Arch of their military victories to the peaceful conquest of their laws and civilisation that lies in the far expanse beyond.

I know few villages more beautiful for a week's sojourn in the month of April than is St. Remy. From the Hôtel de Provence you may be sure of happy adventure every morning, and of hospitable welcome every night. The village girls, in the beautiful costume of Arles, are like the maidens of Tanagra come back to earth again, maidens whom less favoured Londoners must look on as the terracotta statuettes upon museum shelves. The streets are avenues of plane-trees, garlanded, when I saw them last in April sunlight, with delicate little hanging balls of flower. The scent of roses and syringa is in all the air. Protected by the buttresses of the Alpilles, the gardens which are the chief business of that flowery town are full of blooms in odorous battalions of rich colour, divided by hay meadows and by orchards. Seeds are grown here for all the horticulturists of France; for many in distant England, too. There is a charming little irresponsible railway that jogs along from Tarascon across the fields to St. Remy. You pass one quiet farm after another, each screened against the Mistral by that line of tall, dark cypresses, which is one of the most beautiful characteristics of the country, until, amidst its orchards, and its oliveyards, its fig-trees, and its fields of flowers, you reach "La Ville Verte," the green and smiling town of St. Remy.

The earliest centre of habitation in this district was no doubt the Celtic station now known as Castellar, which is also called "Romany," which means "Roque Magne," and has in turn been spelt Romanif, Roumanille, Romanin, or Rogmanye. It means "the Great Rock." It is six miles east of St. Remy, on a northern buttress of the Alpilles to the west of Eygalières. Its earliest inhabitants were of the Desuviate family of the great Salyan tribe, and from their ancient walls they had heard of the elephants of Hannibal, the legions of delaying Scipio, and finally the Ambron army against which Marius came out from Rome. When the great Roman headquarter-camp was established in these regions they came down nearer, for purposes of barter, to the upper part of the Valley of St. Étienne, where there are still found remnants of their temples, of their mounded dwelling-places, around which countless fragments of Celtic pottery are discovered. By degrees they spread out towards the valley called "du Trésor," along the road towards Eygalières, a valley named from the little grotto in the southern slopes of rock which is popularly supposed to conceal the hidden hoard of some dead chieftain. After the army of Marius had passed on, some Romans and some

Greeks were left, and among them were absorbed the ancient Celtic populations in the new town of Glanum. Their old stronghold is now hidden under the ruins of a vast château, which was destroyed in 1793. Glanum (which may have been first called Clan) changed its name to Freta, when its site was altered; and that name in turn became St. Remy in the eleventh century. The site of Glanum has produced pottery of every kind: the black and fragile paste of Celtic ware; the delicate golden-coloured pottery of the Greeks, which is light enough to float on water; the thick, red, sturdy ware of solid Rome, and even the yellow, friable pottery of the Arabs, varnished to hold liquids safely, and ornamented with lines and geometrical patterns. By the second century, at latest, the Roman character, long predominant, was well assured by Roman government and institutions. Judging from the area covered by the ruined remnants that have been found, Glanum cannot have held more than two thousand inhabitants at most, who dwelt on each bank of the little mountain-stream that flowed through the town. There may have been villas outside. But the little town that began as a market-place for Marius's camp was never destined for a long or an extensive existence, and was never even walled in. An interesting relic of the very years of which I have just been speaking, the years between the campaign of Marius and the siege of Marseilles, has been found in the little silver medal, with a head of Persephone, and a bull, bearing the word Γλανικων (of the inhabitants of Glanum). This was discovered in 1824 by M. le Marquis Roger de Lagoy, and shows the influence of the Greek colony of Massalia over the regions from which Marius had driven the Barbarians, an influence which lasted till the independence of Marseilles was ended by the siege.

The Roman roads can still be traced which led through this district. The oldest line taken by the Via Aurelia left Tarascon at the Milestone of Hadrian opposite the temple, which is now the shrine of St. Martha, and went by way of Breuil and so across the Durance. At Maillane it passed in front of the Church of St. Peter. At St. André there was the Milestone of Tiberius. The chapels of Notre Dame des Pucelles at Eyragues, of St. Roch, St. Pierre, and Notre Dame, mark its stages towards the "Plateau des Antiquités" at Glanum, near St. Remy, and there it met the road from Nîmes to Cavaillon, and passed on to the south of St. Pierre by the old Gallic highway to the Farm of the Hugues. This road is only traceable by the temples, milestones, and buildings on its course. But the later Via Aurelia, still called the "Camin Aurélien," went from Tarascon to Laurade, and across to the temple which is now St. Étienne du Grès, arriving at Glanum along the northern foothills of the Alpilles. Several inscriptions mark its course, and a statue of Priapus, carved for it, is preserved in the Farm of Cloud as the centrepiece of a well-shaft. From the "Plateau des Antiquités," this second Via Aurelia joined the more primitive highway.

Glanum was destroyed by the invasions of 480, which did so much to ruin the monuments of Roman civilisation, and it is doubly fortunate that her two finest and most historic buildings survived the catastrophe which overwhelmed the rest. The population almost entirely deserted the site near them, and moved to Fretum, or Freta, which is almost exactly the site of St. Remy, and here were built their first ramparts. The name "Ager Fretensis" appears in charters of 982, and in that same year the Bishop of Avignon mentions in his will the name of various churches there. In the year 1000 it belonged to the princes of Les Baux, and at the beginning of the fourteenth century when the Counts of Provence were Kings of Sicily, a lady of the house of Les Baux is called "Princess of Fresta." The oldest part of the existing town is in the centre near the chapel of St. Peter; and there are remains of a temple, built of masonry like the Palace of Constantine at Arles, the north side of which, with a window, may be seen at the bottom of the Rue du Petit Puits, dating from the first half of the sixth century. The well which gave the street its name was the original fountain of the temple.

Freta herself was sacked by the Lombards in 571, and by the Moors in 737, after they had taken Avignon, and again after her name had been changed in about the tenth century. For some time longer, as we have seen, the ancient name survived as well; but that of St. Remy finally survived, and first appears in some letters patent of Alphonse II, Count of Provence, dated in 1198. The cathedral, which originally had a Romanesque belfry, was given a Gothic spire instead, in 1336, by the direct commands of Pope John XXII, and this is all that is left of the original building, most of which fell down in 1818, and was restored in a very different style from that of the little fourteenth-century work that remains.

The ruined tower, which rises near the ancient temple, already mentioned in the Rue du Petit Puits, is the remnant of the mint set up here by the Counts of Provence of the House of Anjou; and it is recorded in 1331 that the bankers of Marseilles made oath to the effect that they were ignorant of the value of the money coined at St. Remy. But it had a large local circulation, for Philippe-le-Bel had to give orders that all St. Remy coinage found in Nîmes and Beaucaire was to be destroyed, and none now exists; but a funeral inscription of 1305 gives the name of "Quintinus Anastasius de Luchio de Morantia" as that of the Master of the Mint.

Roumanille, the charming poet of Avignon, was born at St. Remy; but curiously enough its most famous child was Michael Nostradamus, who first saw the light here in 1503. His marvellous "powder" proved so successful against the plague in 1546 that he was given an annuity by the town of Aix; but professional jealousy seems to have driven him to literature, and in 1555 appeared the first edition of the rude quatrains that were to be his famous *Prophecies,* dedicated to his son César. Finding no honour in his own country, he went to Paris, where Catherine de Medicis was delighted to patronise him, with the result that his three hundred prophecies expanded in 1558 to a thousand, which were dedicated to King Henri II. His reputation was assured by the apparent prediction of that monarch's miserable death by a wound in the eye at a tournament, and Charles IX could do no less than grant him two hundred crowns with the post of physician-in-ordinary. He died in 1566, and by 1618 his prophecies were being used as reading primers for the school-children. The supposed prediction of the execution of Charles I by the Parliament gave his book great vogue again; and in the reign of Charles II we find Pepys recording (on Feb. 3, 1666) that "amongst other discourse we talked much of Nostradamus, his prophecy of these times, and Sir George Carteret did tell a story how at his death he did make the town [of Salon] swear that he should never be dug up or his tomb opened after he was buried; but that they did after sixty years do it, and upon his breast they found a plate of brasse saying what a wicked, unfaithful people the people of that place were, who after so many vows should disturb and open him such a day and year and hour, which, if true, is very strange." It is certainly true that he predicted 1792 as the beginning of a new era, and it was the Year One of the Republic. Perhaps it was this coincidence that led Napoleon to see predictions of his last campaign in 1814 in the lines that seem to foreshadow the famous landing at Fréjus from Elba. But when the son, César, tried to live up to his prophetic father's reputation, he was obliged to set fire to Le Pouzin in order to verify his own forecast, and was promptly trampled to death by the horse of the enraged General Montluc, who caught him in the act. The great Michael perpetrated a *History of Provence,* which, as far as I have ever traced its statements, is

about as useful as the *Prophecies,* and the one thoroughly deserves the
epigram which Etienne Jodelle wrote about the other: —

> *"Nostra damus quum falsa damus, nam fallere nostrum est*
> *quum falsa damus nil nisi nostra damus…"*

(I give what is my own when I give out falsehoods, for it is my
nature to deceive
And when I give out falsehoods I give nothing but what is my own…)

with which we may fairly leave a figure which is strangely out of place
in quiet, beautiful St. Remy.

Far better symbol, far more appropriately representative, of the
poetry and charm of all this district are the associations that cluster
round the name of Mistral, the true "genius loci"; not the poet only,
but the living shrine of every true Provençal from Avignon to Les
Saintes Maries. Along the quiet roads that are flooded with spring
sunshine, and verdant with the strange, green, palpitating shadows
thrown by those lofty pinnacles of cypress that rise, dark, sheer, yet
delicate, like cathedral walls, you may pass towards his simple country
house in the little village of Maillane. Its chief possession seems to be
the bust of that Lamartine who spoke of Mistral nearly fifty years ago
as "un poète né, comme les hommes de Deucalion, d'un caillou de la
Crau; un poète primitif dans notre âge de décadence; un poète grec à
Avignon; un poète qui crée une langue d'un idiome, comme Pétrarque
a créé l'Italien." No wonder the young writer, then only twenty-five,
answered with the dedication of *Mireille—*

> *"Te counsacre Mirèio: es moun cor e moun amo,*
> *Es la flour de mis an…"*

And near the bust of Lamartine is that of Gounod, who set those exquisite
verses to melodies no less delightful. Close by is one of those fascinating
carved coffers, which you may still find at Arles, in which the old
Provençal kept his loaves of bread. "Tout mon pays!" cried Daudet, "des
barreaux larges à passer le bras et une serrure de coffrefort!" The Mas du
Juge, the background to so much of *Mirèio,* and the birthplace of the poet,
is the big farm half-way from St. Remy, and before its door is still the long
stone table round which the farm hands sat at harvest home.

In his *Iles d'Or*, even more than in any other of his writings, Mistral has reflected and preserved that spirit of old Provence which is about us in St. Remy, which is not so touched with infinite sorrow as at Arles; not changed as at Nîmes; not imitated, as at Avignon; but sane, strong, deep-rooted, and deep-hearted.

> *"Environa de l'amplitudo*
> *E dou silenci di gara,*
> *Tout en fasent vosto batudo,*
> *Au terrado sempre amarra,*
> *Vesès, alin, coume un tempèri*
> *Passa lou trounfle dis empèri*
> *E l'uiau di revoulucion:*
> *Atetouni sus la patrio*
> *Veirés passa la barbario*
> *Emai li civilisacioun... "*

They have indeed beheld, these Provençals, "the pomp of empire passing far, like flying time—the lightning bolt of revolution, the decay of barbarian and of civilised communities." The monument of Marius and the arch of Julius Caesar are in their true setting still. It is but to hint at this truth that I have passed for a moment into those modern times that now surround them; and now I must return to them and to imperial Rome.

More marvellous remnants of antiquity than any monument of Provence may perhaps be found upon the soil of Italy and Greece, beneath the shadow of the Coliseum or in the sunlight of the Acropolis; the traces of an elder age may be discovered among the ruins of Baalbec or Ephesus, beside the pylons of Luxor, or beneath the cupolas of Samarcand; but for the completed vision of a classic past, for the full dream of an ancient life that is not dead but sleepeth, you must stand upon the "Plateau des Antiquités" at St. Remy, in the great amphitheatre of Nîmes or Arles, before the exquisitely proportioned colonnades of the Maison Carreé; or you must wonder at that cliff of masonry which is the Theatre of Orange, and the mighty arch which commemorates the triumphs of Tiberius.

Both the St. Remy buildings are types of other constructions found elsewhere. I shall have to speak of the towers at Nîmes and La Turbie in following out that form which began with the pyramid of Fabius and ends with the column of Trajan. I must now turn to the great arch which is suggested by its smaller and more perfect exemplar at St. Remy, the arch of Orange. Of Carpentras I have already spoken; here the arch is still single, but the taste of the architect is far from being at so high a level. At Orange the whole building, fine as is its general effect, shows an even greater decadence, which is by no means compensated by its far greater size. St. Remy, Carpentras, Orange: Caesar, Augustus, Tiberius—the list is short, but the tale of diminished skill and artistic feeling is clear enough.

The Triumphal Arch of Orange stands at the northern entrance to the town, and is about seventy feet long by seventy in height, and nearly thirty-two wide, set to the four cardinal points of the compass. Like most of these southern French arches, the lateral elevation is much broader than is usual in proportion to their length, and is also far more richly decorated than is the case in Italy, except perhaps in the Arch of Constantine. Another peculiarity is their engaged columns. And in their decoration the "motif" of chained captives is evidently a favourite one; "tristis summo captivus in arcu." The structure at Orange is pierced with a principal central arch and two smaller side arches, and is adorned with four attached Corinthian columns between the arches, supporting an entablature with a central pediment. Four similar columns, far closer together, are on the east side. Sculptures enrich the archivolts and frieze, and trophies of arms are placed over the side arches. The upper panel of the huge attic story, over the central arch, is filled with a large bas-relief of crowded, fighting figures. The rostra of the ships and other maritime emblems are remarkably well treated; and Ruskin observed particularly that the carvings of this arch afforded an excellent example of "sketching in sculpture," being surrounded with a deeply cut line, which emphasises their outline, just as an artist might do with his pencil upon paper. There are certain mathematical irregularities in the constructive measurements, to which I attach no importance as signs of decadence; in fact, they probably contribute very largely to the general effect of the mass, which is undeniably imposing; and neither beauty nor "proportion" depends on mathematics. But the design as a whole shows fatal signs of a loss of that delicate appreciation of appropriate balance and harmony which was the Greeks' best legacy to Rome. It seems to me to be the rough copy, made by uninstructed workmen, of the original at St. Remy; and its architect has only brought his ignorance into greater prominence by increasing the whole bulk of the great mass of stone he reared.

I shall try and say no single further word of depreciation. It is only my wish to emphasise the restrained beauty at St. Remy which has led me to criticise the magnificence of Orange; and it would be difficult, whatever phrase were written here, to lessen the delight of any one who sees that mighty monument of a great and warlike people, set at the head of the vast highway by which their legions marched towards the conquest of the north, and softened to the mellow tint of an exquisite gold against the brilliant blue of the Provençal sky. The town itself is full of a strange history, particularly significant to any Englishman; and in that history the arch has so great a part that no book which deals with the middle waters of the Rhone could possibly omit some mention of it.

The Triumphal Arch at Orange

As an example of the kind of work necessary to trace the varying opinions of these monuments, and to produce some final and logical conception of them, I am tempted to indicate a few "authorities" concerning the Arch of Orange. In February 1597 one Thomas Platter, of Basle, records his view that Marius built it, and that it was called the "Tour des Arcs," because its rectangular formation suggested the outline of a fortified tower. A few years later we find Peiresc using the most unimaginable adverb about its three arcades..." filletées le plus mignonnement qu'il se puisse faire en l'ordonnance corinthienne." A century later Millin can see no traces of any inscription, and gives a wide choice from Augustus to Hadrian for its date. It is strange that he did not notice the holes made by the rivets of the vanished letters on the northern architrave, just below the frieze, for it was by exactly similar traces that Séguier had just deciphered the lost inscription on the Maison Carrée. By 1815 M. Gasparin had observed these holes, and chronicled the discovery of an "L" in bronze among the soil and débris beneath them. This was a fragment of the word "IULI." Caristie recorded that in 1807 the arch was still encumbered to the height of some fifteen feet, with the ruins of the fortifications added by Raymond des Baux in the thirteenth century. As a matter of fact it was only by 1811 that the arch was cleared and the site put into something of its present state. On Caristie's report, and from the designs of Régnaux, the departmental architect, sufficient work was done to preserve what was left of the original Roman construction. Caristie reproduced the holes left by the bronze letters, but inaccurately, and showed that the northern frieze, never meant to contain an inscription, was originally designed for sculpture. Prosper Mérimée was artistically vague in 1834. Only in 1866 did a certain M. de Saulcy see the name "Tiberius" (and much more) in the shattered inscription; and the occurrence of the word "Sacrovir" on a Gaulish shield, carved on the northern front, showed he was on the right track; for it was the revolt of Sacrovir and Florus that the generals of Tiberius crushed in 21 A.D. M. de Saulcy's reading of the Emperor's name was further confirmed by Bertrand, who took a cast of the architrave, but could not successfully decipher the words it once had borne. It remained for Édouard Bondurand, Archiviste du Gard at Nîmes, to suggest the best solution of the problem in 1897.

This is no place for scholastic discussions; but I shall proceed to give the results of M. Bondurand's discovery, because Provence is a land of false attributions and spurious inscriptions, and one typical instance will be enough to show the process by which other statements in this book, more briefly given as they occur elsewhere, have slowly been arrived at. Between the 27th June of the year 24 A.D. and the 26th June of the year 25 this arch was dedicated to Tiberius; and at some period that was later than this, but not very far removed, the decurions of the colony restored it exactly to its primitive condition; but the record of this restoration, involving twenty-five fresh letters, necessitated a change in the inscription from its original two lines of equal length to a new upper line which exceeded the new lower line by thirteen letters at the beginning and by twelve at the end. It then read as follows : —

TI • CAESARI • DIVI • AUGUSTI • F • DIVI • IULI •
NEPOTI • AUGUSTO • PONTIFICI • MAXIMO •TRIBUNCIA

POTESTATE • XXVI • IMP • VIII • COS • IIII •
DDCCN • ARCUM • TRIUM • RESTITUERE [7]

which is, being interpreted, "In honour of Tiberius Caesar Augustus, son of the Divine Augustus, grandson of the Divine Julius, Pontifex Maximus, invested with the Tribunician power for the twenty-sixth time, Imperator for the eighth time, and Consul for the fourth time, the Decurions restored this Triumphal Arch."

It is worth while remembering in this connection that the Arch of Titus in Rome, containing only a single opening, shows the winged Victories in its spandrils which appear at St. Remy; but though small in size, and beautifully finished, it has no sculpture at the sides, which is a very obvious defect in a type of building that has no real reason for existence except as a magnificent frame for bas reliefs and carvings. The three openings of the structure at Orange may be compared with the arches of Septimius Severus and of Constantine, in Italy; and with them it very fairly holds its own. That at Rheims, once a hundred and ten feet wide, was larger than any of them, and was probably built in the last years of the Empire. This style of monuments must not be confounded with such a building as the Gate of St. André at Autun, or the far more elaborate Gate of Justice, known as the "Porta Nigra," at Trèves. The building known as the "Porte d'Auguste" at Nîmes is too obviously a town gate to be mistaken for anything else, and it probably had the light arcade above it which is preserved in the Porte St. André at Autun. Yet another form of Roman arch is to be found in Provence, and that is the beautiful entrance-gate placed at each end of a bridge, of which the fine arches on the bridge of St. Chamas are the best examples in the Rhone valley, and the most elegant in France.[8] The Triumphal Arch is, in itself, somewhat difficult to justify architecturally, though it is often quite successful as a picturesque commemorative monument; and I need only mention one more to complete all I shall have to say upon the subject.

This is the building long known to historians of Arles as the "Arc Admirable." Writing in 1687, Seguin (*Les Antiquités d'Arles*) could only trace this arch, which had then disappeared, by a deed of 1511, mentioning the "Arcus Mirabilis" in the Rue St. Claude. This monument, therefore, which for so many centuries had roused the admiration of those who saw it, had vanished more than sixty years before the Arch of Constantine was pulled down in 1743, so that one of the public streets might be widened. Fortunately, however, some fragments have been left which permit us to reconstruct it, as a smaller and more artistic example of the three-arch type at Orange. The largest of these fragments is the portico built into the wall of the hotel in the Place des Hommes, which was placed there in 1715, composed of pieces from various different monuments, for neither the columns nor their capitals were originally portions of the "Arc Admirable." Other remnants would no doubt be found in the old fortifications (made of such fragmentary stones from Roman buildings) near the Tour de Rolland. A portion of the bas reliefs of the attic story is preserved in the ancient theatre, together with the other vestiges which enabled M. Gilles to give a plan of the building as it was originally set up in honour of Augustus some years after his visit to Arles, in 43 B.C., a visit which is commemorated also by the busts of himself and of Marcellus, and by the splendid carving of his imperial wreath. This arch was called "Admirable," not only by reason of its beauty, but from the same motives which gave the name of "Tour Magne" to the triumphal monument in the pyramidal style set up to the same Emperor at Nîmes.

The vanished "Arc Admirable" was, as I have said, of much the same design as that of Orange, though in better proportion and finer workmanship; and the surviving monument further up the Rhone will give some measure of our loss at Arles. In the same way, that mighty cliff of masonry which is the Theatre of Orange, will suggest something of the smaller and more beautiful construction of which two lonely pillars and a large part of the auditorium still remain at Arles.

Orange played no important part as a Roman city; it was never as prominent as Arles, as Nîmes, or even as Vienne; yet the Roman buildings are all that remain of value in the town, and the size of them is a significant indication of that Roman character and civilisation which it is my business to describe in Provence. The hill of Orange was the original settlement, and the modern town is built on the site of the first attacking Roman camp, as Dorchester below the hill of Sinodun, without a winding Thames. The colony of Arausio began forthwith to take its amusements very seriously. They used the mass of the old hill as the material for their auditorium, and on its slope they built their stone seats in a semicircle. Opposite to them rises that stupendous wall of massive dark-brown stones, laid weightily one upon another, erect, eternal as the framework of the everlasting hills, and resonant still to every tone of modern tragedy. It overtops the town without a rival; and of all Roman theatres we know it is the most impressive, for there is no building of the kind that can compare with it as a whole. That part of the wall which faces the city is chiefly imposing from its sheer bulk. As we see it now, it rises in a single mass from the ground, but originally it must have looked like one side of the nave of some vast minster, with its aisle and clerestory; for there was an arcade in advance of it, and the plain second story was once covered by a sloping roof, with a long range of smaller round-headed arches, which forestall the clerestories of Pisa or of Lucca. It is about one hundred feet high, thirteen feet thick, and over nine hundred feet in length. On the side facing the hill it was once faced with marble, set about with carvings, and formed the permanent scenery at the back of the rather shallow stage which the spectators saw; a scenery so tremendous that it seems only appropriate to tragedies "presenting Thebes' or Pelops' line"; and so durable that only those tragedies themselves can claim an elder place among the few accomplishments of man which have so long outlasted the generations that produced them.

On great municipal occasions, the Roman theatre is still used. Once every year the Comédie Française produces a classic tragedy there, and the alexandrines of Corneille or Racine wake the echoes that are still stirring with the mighty lines of Æschylus or Sophocles. Sometimes the Provençal poets, called the Félibres, are gathered here; but for a true Provençal fête the smaller, lovelier theatre of Arles is a far better setting, with that soft charm of melancholy beauty which Arles alone retains. The sheer bulk of Orange is too overwhelming for our modern life. It was but the pleasure-place of the old Romans; yet how many of our most pretentious buildings will last even a quarter as long? Our Gothic churches, mere architectural babes in time compared with it, are fast tottering into decay already. Our modern buildings, our flimsy town halls and stucco palaces, will be dust when the Theatre of Orange is still serenely strong; and I prefer to see that theatre, not filled with modern actors, or with modern crowds, but as my friend saw it some few years ago: "...its sweep of steps graciously mantled in long grass growing for hay, and full of innumerable flowers; its stage tenanted by bushes of red roses and white guelder roses; the blue, empty circles of its wall-space rising serenely against the flame-blue sky. Never have I seen the huge strength of Roman antiquity appear more sweetly venerable, more assimilable to the unshaken granite structure of the globe itself, than thus, decked and garlanded with the transitory blossoms of its eighteen-hundredth spring."[9]

Those steps rouse many dreams; for few foreign cities are so often spoken of by Englishmen as is Orange, and few places have ever roused wilder confusions of thought; for Orange gave its name to a line of princes, one of whom was also a king of England, and from that king a political party in the British Islands and colonies thought proper to take its title. The fact that the town is on a tributary of the Rhone, and lies a little off the main line, has preserved it from too much attention on the part of the incurious English traveller, who hurries past it to the Riviera. Arausio, the Roman colony, is known only from geographers, and from its own remains; and the power and ubiquity of Rome have never been better exemplified than in the existence of such mighty works in a place historically so insignificant. Its mediaeval history begins with a certain William, of the house of Adhémar, called Duke of Aquitaine in the days of Charlemagne, who delivered Orange from the Saracens. There is a tale of this Guillaume d'Orange, who came home wounded after Roncesvalles,[10] the last survivor of that day of slaughter, suddenly aged and pinched and grey, upon a sorry varlet's nag. So the porter could not recognise him, and the lady of the castle would not let him in. "My husband," she cried, "would come a conqueror, with his captives behind him, covered with glory and honour." And when she heard that he had come from Roncesvalles: "Less than ever my husband," she cried again, "for he would not have lived when all those heroes died." At last he was let in; and there is nothing now of all his castle left upon the hill, save one weak buttress and a tottering wall. But they remind us of such a tale as the great stones of Rome could never tell; for "the monuments of the Middle Ages are other than of stone." By the end of the eleventh century and the beginning of the Crusades, we find a living and distinct Count of Orange, at the time when the Burgundian kingdom had arisen out of the ruins of Charlemagne's empire, and had been again united to the imperial crown with its fellow-kingdoms of Germany and Italy. Orange was no part of France then; it was a member of the kingdom of Arles, and its counts were vassals of the Emperor under the Counts of Toulouse, who claimed the imperial fief of the Provençal March. The greatest of the Crusading counts was Raimbauld II, whose modern statue now stands in the market-place; and in 1150 another of his name appears as a devoted troubadour, so loyal to a neighbouring countess that he left no heir for his inheritance, and Orange passed to his brother-in-law Bertrand, of the great house of Les Baux, the first to receive the title of prince, granted by Frederick Barbarossa, as he passed by Orange on his way to his Burgundian crowning at Arles. With that title, then so rare that from Orange to Snowdon there was but one other, the Prince of Aberffraw, Bertrand received the right of coining money, and marching with his banners displayed from the Isère to the sea and from the Rhone to the Alps. In 1215 Frederick II granted Bertrand's son, William, a charter (dated at Metz in 1215), which further granted him the whole kingdom of Arles and of Vienne, which was probably only the vicariate of the Empire within its bounds; at any rate, some such rights existed, for they were formally renounced by a later Prince Raymond of Orange to Charles of Anjou, and throughout the thirteenth century the Princes of Orange did homage to Provence for the greater part of their dominions.

The Princes of Les Baux turned the triumphal arch into a fortress, and held the castle on the hill above the town. By some strange hazard, this little scrap of the old kingdom of Arles lived on, side by side, with its neighbours of Avignon and the Venaissin, long after Pope and prince alike had been surrounded by the gradual annexations of France; even after Lyons, Vienne, Provence, Bresse, Besançon, and the Burgundian counts had been swallowed up. It is difficult to realise now that the character of France, as regards these places, was that of an encroaching enemy. The siege of Avignon, by Louis VIII in his Albigensian crusade, first showed his danger to imperial Burgundy. The acquisition of Provence by Charles of Anjou meant as much to Burgundy as did the later Sicilian crown to the Italian states. It was not a long step from doing homage to the king's brother to doing homage for Orange to the King of France himself. The Dauphin Charles (afterwards Charles V) had received the vicariate of the kingdom of Arles from his imperial namesake; but the only reality was the superiority of France. To this Dauphin had Raymond of Orange done homage in 1349, and by 1393 Orange had passed by female succession to the house of Challon, a French lordship in ducal Burgundy. Louis XI exacted homage in the fullest terms in spite of good King René's grumblings; but when, in the next reign, Orange had been completely surrounded by French territory, Louis XII good-naturedly declared Prince John II its independent sovereign. The full significance of this was not apparent until in 1531 René of Orange began the connection of the old Burgundian county with the house of Nassau. For thereafter the Princes of Orange, technically the peer of any sovereign with whom they had to deal, also became the first nobles in the outlying dominions of the Spanish crown, the first citizens and the first magistrates of a great commonwealth; though they took their title, being of the house of Nassau, from a precarious little principality in the Rhone valley, which they most probably never cared enough about to visit.[11] It was as a sovereign prince, owning the Emperor as his only superior on earth, that William the Silent could make lawful war upon the Duke of Alva. The independent sovereignty of tiny little Lichtenstein, which you may drive through in half an hour on the Ragatz road between St. Gallen and Graubünden, is the only modern parallel.

During the days of the Nassau princes France was perpetually seizing Orange and giving it back again by treaty. But Prince Maurice made the castle of Orange, upon the hill above the theatre, one of the strongest fortresses in Europe; and it was Louis XIV who swept away well-nigh every trace of those too presumptuous ramparts. The independence of the principality only came to an end when William, the Tenth of Orange, set forth for the deliverance of the Protestant religion and the liberties of England, and thereby became William the First of Ireland, Second of Scotland, Third of England, Fourth of Normandy, and Tenth of Orange. Though the formal incorporation of the town with the French province of Dauphiné was delayed till 1731, it had become a part of the French dominions by 1714, in virtue of the treaty of Utrecht. It is now a quiet, unimportant, yet charming little town, filling up its ancient girdle with ample spaces of green garden, and surrounded by lovely meadows of luxuriant flowers, that cover the sweet and fertile plains of Orange with a beauty that is appropriate to its best memories of idyllic Greece and Rome.

It was the arch that brought us from St. Remy to Orange, and to St. Remy's building I must now go back again, to pick up the thread of Julius Caesar's campaigns which we dropped beneath the shadow of the arch he built. It will need but a few pages before we can move on to Arles.

NOTES

1. "Thus rose from the darkness of their prime, Orange, the princess of the coming age, Carpentras, Cavaillon, St. Remy, St. Chamas; and thus their mighty thoroughfare was dressed with the Triumphal Arches, when the quarries of the granite hills were opened."

2. Good authorities assert that the earliest triumphal arches in Rome were those erected by L. Stertinius (196 B.C.) in the Forum Boarium and in the Circus Maximus, out of spoils gained in Spain (Liv. xiii. 27, and xxxvii. 3). All others, with the possible exception of the fragments ascribed to the arch of Q. Fabius Maximus Allobrogicus, are later than the arch of St. Remy.

3. M. Gilles is not so accurate as usual in his treatment of this inscription. The only possible reading, which is quite in accordance with good usage in the Augustan age, is that given in the "Corpus," which is:—SEXTUS LUCIUS MARCUS JULIEI, CAI FILII, PARENTIBUS SUEIS, meaning that "Sextus, Lucius, and Marcus, Julii, and sons of Caius, dedicated this monument to their parents." Both JULIEI and SUEIS are forms found in the first century A.D. at latest, and the same date is indicated by the absence of cognomina. Granting that such spelling lasted a little longer in the provinces than at Rome, I cannot put the inscription much before 100 A.D., whereas the whole style of the monument itself is at least a century earlier, if not more. It is also my opinion that the word "PARENTIBUS" can only refer to both father and mother; but unfortunately the statues beneath the cupola are both men, and the truth that their original heads were replaced some time ago by restoration, does not affect the fact that each body wears the simple toga of the consul on active service. It is only fair to add that other translations have been offered for the letters of this inscription, but they only increase the difficulty of imagining that the inscription is contemporaneous with the origin of the monument. Nine of these versions are before me, and it will be sufficient to select the two least appalling examples. They are (1) "Sexto Laelio Monumentum Juliei intra Circulum Fecit Parentibus Suis," and (2) "Sextus Lucius Maximus Julii consulis, filius Parentibus Suis."

4. This, no doubt, is one reason why Caesar placed the statue of Catulus, together with that of his uncle, within the St. Remy colonnade, a thing which we can scarcely imagine Marius doing, even if Catulus had actually assisted in the Provençal campaign. Fifty years afterwards, however, the unity of the St. Remy camp with the battle of the Raudine plain was seen in its true perspective by the heir of Marius's successes.

As Plutarch says, in North's translation, the proof of the love and goodwill which the people bore to Caesar was given "at the death of his aunt Julia, the wife of Marius the elder; for being her nephew he made a solemn oration in the market-place in commendation of her, and at her burial did boldly venture to show forth the images of Marius... the people rejoiced at it for that he had brought as it were out of hell the remembrance of Marius's honour again into Rome... and when Caesar was Ædilis he secretly caused images of Marius to be made... showing by the inscriptions that they were the victories which Marius had won upon the Cimbrians... the tears ran down many of their cheeks for very joy when they saw the images of Marius..."

5. The Carpentras arch, of which I give an illustration for purposes of comparison, is in the centre of the town, in the courtyard of the Palais de Justice. The town is twenty-seven kilometres by train from Avignon, along the line through Sorgues, Entraigues, and Monteux; and as I shall have no further opportunity of mentioning it, I may add here, that this ancient capital of the Meminian tribe of Gauls is well worth visiting, for the cathedral of St. Siffrein, its museum, and the Palais de Justice which guards its ancient arch. The greater size of this monument permits the possibility of the attic story that would crush the St. Remy building. It is placed foursquare to the cardinal points, and the bas-reliefs on each side show two captives bound and attached to a trophy. The two shown in my picture are different types of the mountain-tribes whose subjection was completed by Augustus after Caesar had conquered the peoples of the plain. The knife (perhaps a "scramasax"), carved below the rustic warrior, who is clothed in a sheepskin, seems very like the Ghoorka kukhrie, but I am unable to suggest any reason for the resemblance between weapons from places so far distant from each other. His comrade, much better dressed, and armed with the light double-headed battle-axe, may well represent Sacrovir himself. Many of these details are to be found in the larger monument, set up in the next reign at Orange. This arch was built in commemoration of the victories of Augustus, and an inscription to that effect was no doubt placed upon the attic story which has now disappeared, as a similar inscription to Tiberius can be traced upon the arch at Orange. The St. Remy arch needed no such inscription, even if its simple and beautiful proportions had admitted the addition of an attic, for its carvings reveal the leader in whose honour it was built as clearly as do those on the monument of Marius, which originally had no inscription either.

6. Recorded in the *Contemporary Review* for November 1892.

7. The last line is peculiar. "DC" is usual for Decurio. But the form "DDCCN" is unique for the plural number. The form D • N • for Dominus Noster, and DD •NN for the plural, may be compared. "ARCUM TRIUMPHALEM" is unknown to classical Latin, and would only be possible to decurions who set up this inscription at the restoration of the arch in about the fourth century. The abbreviation "TRIUM" for "TRIUMPHALEM" has usually been explained as due to fracture of the stone in other cases. On the whole M. Boundurand has failed to convince the best authorities that his reading of the last line is right.

8. The railway from Arles runs on the east (or left) bank of the Rhone across the Crau to St. Chamas, where there is a beautiful view of the Etang de Berre. The Pons Flavia crosses the Touloubre in a single span of solid masonry, the entrance arch at each end being decorated with Corinthian columns and entablature. The columns are surmounted with lions, and there is an inscription on the frieze. Some distance north, on the slope of the Vernégues hills, between the Rhone valley and that of the Durance, is a single Corinthian column, in the pure Greek form exemplified by the monument of Lysicrates, which is the sole remnant of a temple erected by a Greek artist from Marseilles.

9. Mary Darmesteter: *Contemporary Review,* November 1892.

10. In *Calendal* the poet Mistral tells this same tale of the Count of Orange escaping from the Saracens at the battle of the Alyscamps at Arles: —

> *"Guibour! Guibour! ma gènto damo*
> *Sièu, dis, Guihèn, aquéu que t'amo!*
> *A Guihèn dóu Court Nas, Guibour, véne durbi…*
> *… N'as menti! crido*
> *Guibour…"*

The unfortunate count is only admitted after he has gone back to the fight and chased the Saracens single-handed to the sea.

11. How rarely they came here may be gathered from the legend of that Prince of Orange who visited the home of his ancestors, as it is told in Mistral's "Poem of the Rhone," and of his death by drowning with the beautiful Anglore during a storm upon the river: —

> *"Mai lou verai es que, pèr uno espouncho*
> *Que vèn dóu sang, Guihèn (coume ié dison*
> *Au bèu dóufin de la nacioun flamenco)*
> *Vói trafega lou Rose. Vóu counéisse*
> *Lou nis, lou couvadou, la terro illustro*
> *Que i' a trasmés lou noum preclar que porto*
> *Aurenjo e sa famouso flourieto,…"*

CHAPTER V

The Pacification of Provence

"*E de que tiron glòri*
Toúti li conquietaire li mai trule
Que sus Rose à-de-reng an fan l'empèri,
Li Charle-Magne emé li Bonaparte
Les Annibau e li Cesar de Romo!"
— LOU POUÈMO DÓU ROSE.[1]

IT is a curious thing that the two greatest names of Roman Provence, Marseilles and Narbonne, now contain nothing whatever to which we can point as an undoubted architectural relic of Roman rule. I have determined to say as little as possible of the history that cannot in some degree be traced in stone today; but of Marseilles something must now be said, for its siege was the most important event, during the Civil War, in the Roman Province.

Founded in the age of the Gracchi, Narbo remained a town throughout the Republic, the first burgess-colony proper beyond the sea, but isolated. It was strengthened by Caesar, and under Tiberius was "the most populous city of Gaul."[2] But after the fall of Marseilles, and the rise of Lyons, Arles became the great emporium of commerce in the Rhone valley.

The wealthy Greek mercantile state, which was protected by the standing Roman camp at Aix, was by no means comprised within the city walls of Massalia; it extended along the greater part of the coast, nearly from Montpellier to Nice. But in a political aspect Massalia disappeared after the siege, and became for Gaul what Neapolis was for Italy, a centre of Greek culture and Greek learning, preserving its independence within the modest proportions of a provincial town.

At first the Massaliot envoys desired Caesar to allow them to remain neutral in the quarrel between their two patrons, Pompey and himself.

But their pleasant dreams were soon dispelled by the sudden arrival of Domitius Ahenobarbus (grandson of the first proconsul who made the Via Domitia) with seven swift galleys from the Etrurian coasts; for he immediately put himself at the head of the city's sea and land forces, in the cause of Pompey; a cause which may well have commended itself to a majority of the citizens in an ancient and conservative Greek state, naturally opposed, on general principles, to the incarnation of revolutionary politics which was Julius Caesar.

Being obliged at the moment to cross the Pyrenees, Caesar left Caius Trebonius to command by land and Decimus Brutus to direct the naval operations against Marseilles. The Phocaean city, as it still was, occupied the triangular peninsula between the Old Harbour to the south and a creek of La Joliette to the north-west. The modern Place d'Aix was just outside its eastern boundary, and a curve drawn from the Place de La Joliette, through the Place d'Aix, and round to the "Vieux Port," between the Cannebière and Rue de Noailles, would about indicate the extent of the Greek city.

In spite of the pacific expressions of the ambassadors, the town was well equipped for the siege it must have realised to be inevitable, and military reinforcements had been secured from the friendly Celtic tribe of the Albici, who lived some fifty miles north, between the Verdon and the Durance. Caesar was not slow in taking measures on his side, and the fact that Arles could supply him with twelve warships within thirty days after the trees from which they were built had been felled is one proof of the resources of ancient Arelate. With this unseasoned dozen Decimus Brutus lay at anchor outside the Old Harbour, depending only on the veteran infantry who had volunteered from the pick of Caesar's legions to man them. The very solidity of these new heavy-timbered vessels lent added courage to the landsmen on their decks. As soon as the seventeen warships of Domitius bore down upon them, the legionaries grappled, boarded the enemy, and dispatched their crews. Brutus brought all his dozen safe back to their moorings and six Massaliot vessels with them; three more were sunk; and Domitius had but eight left.

As soon as possible Pompey sent sixteen more ships of war under Nasidius, who anchored opposite the now vanished Tauroenta, some twenty miles to the eastward of Toulon, and summoned Domitius with his old fleet of eight, and nine new vessels built by the men of Massalia to replace their losses. Unfortunately the squadron of Nasidius took to flight almost as soon as Brutus went into action, and the Massaliot ships were fairly easily defeated after making a good fight of it. The crisis of the struggle now shifted to the land, where Trebonius had been working with might and main to undermine the defences of the city. At last he fatally sapped the principal tower of the city wall by means of an immensely strong covered approach, and the besieged, in despair, begged for an armistice till Caesar should return. In the course of this they treacherously attacked the Roman camp and burnt everything in it that would catch fire, after which they withdrew within their walls again, repaired the breaches, and once more bade defiance to the enemy. But the coast-blockade proved too much for them. Domitius Ahenobarbus made good his escape by sea, and Caesar himself, on his arrival, received the unconditional surrender of the city. He spared all lives, took possession of all arms and military engines, all ships and naval stores, the public treasure, and the territories of the State, and quartered two Roman legions upon the city as a garrison. Scarcely a trace of Greek or Roman Massalia now remains.

The fact that Vercingetorix found no successor is almost as great a triumph for Roman diplomacy as was his defeat for Roman arms. The revolts of the Treveri under Julius Florus, in the Ardennes, or of the Haedui and Sequani under Julius Sacrovir, near Lyons, were but a pale reflection of the determination of the Celtic nobility to seize every opportunity of Germanic unrest to try their strength against Rome. But the policy of amalgamation and reconciliation soon did its work of cautiously but completely Romanising every element in the population. Such a deliverance of the Celtic nation as was contemplated by Vercingetorix, or even dreamed of by Sacrovir, was no longer possible in 70 A.D., for already that nation had ceased its separate existence. Its subsequent history was the history of the Roman world, the development of the Romano-Gallic culture founded by Caesar and Augustus.

The beginnings of that foundation are traceable in the last public acts of Caesar in Provence. He gave to the coastwise canton of the Volcae a Latin municipal constitution, with Nîmes, to which the remaining townships were made subject, for its urban centre. Latin rights were given to Roussillon, Avignon, Aix, and Apt; and their burgesses, after acquiring the Roman franchise by entering the imperial army or by holding office in their native towns, stood on a perfect legal equality with Italians. The Roman colony of Lyons (second to Narbo under Tiberius) was the native seat both of all government institutions common to Gaul, and of the Celtic diet of the three Gaulish provinces. What this involved may be seen from the facts that when Rome was desolated by fire in 64 A.D., the men of Lyons sent a subsidy of four million sesterces (£43,500) to the capital, and when Lyons in her turn was burnt out in the next year, she was assisted, not only from the privy purse of the Emperor, but by contributions from the whole Roman empire. It is essential to realise these things if we are to understand the extraordinary amount of traces still remaining in Provence of Roman life and Roman buildings. Just as Christianity took up the legends and heroes of paganism and made her saints and martyrologies from the materials of more ancient faiths, so did Rome keep all the old memories and transform them into greater permanence and strength. The fountain-god of the Volcae and the temple of Nemausus were the centre of Imperial Nîmes. The Emperor Claudius was himself born at Lyons. He married Agrippina, who was born in the camp of her father Germanicus at Cologne. It was but natural that they should each favour the largest possible extension of the privileges of the Gauls. The official language of course became the Latin. But we find Greek inscriptions lingering on for long in Provence,[3] and no barriers were made to Celtic speech on unofficial occasions. At Arles, indeed, most of the dedications so far discovered might have served just as well in Italy; but at Fréjus, Aix, and Nîmes many traces of a prior, indigenous worship have been found.

The results of all this acted and reacted upon both sides. The cavalry of Imperial Rome was recruited from Gaul, and both its manoeuvres and technical expressions were chiefly derived from the Celts. And the soldiers Gaul gave to Rome were repaid by the wine Rome sold to Arles and Lyons. In the Narbonnaise and in Southern Aquitaine there were indeed early beginnings of that Allobrogian vintage which is now our Burgundy, of the Biturigian wines which are the modern claret. But it was not till the end of the third century A.D. that the provinces were really allowed to infringe on the invaluable Italian monopoly of wine-culture. The great highway from Rome to the mouth of the Baetis was repaired in republican times from the Alps to the Rhone by the Massaliots, from thence to the Pyrenees by the Romans. Augustus relaid it, and ample means existed for communication with all parts of Provence, both military and civil, both by land and water. Small wonder is it, then, that this land of olive-yards and fig-trees, even before the general culture of the vine, rose to great prosperity when its agriculture was once solidly encouraged by Augustus, a prosperity which is still reflected in the amphitheatres of Nîmes and Arles, in the theatre of Orange, in the monuments of so small a community as St. Remy, in the public works of Fréjus.

Fréjus, Forum Julii, was, as its name implies, established by Julius as a forum, viz.: an assize centre and market, being situated, as fora usually were, on the high road. It was still a forum when first mentioned in Cicero's *Letters* in the year after Caesar's assassination.[4] After Actium, Augustus made it a naval station and a colony, whence was derived its title of "Pacencis" or "Pacata."

But there is so much Roman masonry at Fréjus that I must give it a separate place to itself (pp. 141-144); and it will only be necessary here to mention that piece of history which connects it with the period just before the reign of Augustus to which we must proceed with what haste be possible.

Mark Antony was the most open champion of Caesarism after Caesar himself had died. Dolabella, the man of the Senate and the assassins, was conveniently shelved in Syria; but the young Octavianus was not to be so easily put off. Claiming his rights as heir to his uncle and father by adoption, he was met by the unwelcome news that Antony had spent most of the four thousand talents (about one million sterling) which the widow Calpurnia had handed over to Caesar's relative and chief representative on the spot. Octavianus therefore at first joined the party of the Senate; but Cicero soon discovered that this was only part of a far deeper plan, a plan remarkably astute for any one, but nothing short of astounding in a youth of twenty.

Defeated near Mutina, Antony was at once pursued by Decimus Brutus, and fled by way of Vada Sabata across the Maritime Alps towards the Esterels. The coast road he chose must have been particularly arduous and difficult for his disorganised forces and undisciplined followers; for there was hardly any food or water on the way. "Antony," writes Plutarch, "was in misfortune most nearly a virtuous man." Overtaken by famine and by distresses of every kind, he set a splendid example of endurance to his troops. "He who had just quitted so much luxury and sumptuous living, made no difficulty now of drinking foul water and feeding on wild fruits and roots. Nay, it is related, they ate the very bark of trees and creatures that no one before had ever been willing to touch." Even when ameliorated by the repairs which the Massaliots were bound to make upon it, the hardships of the road across the deep gorges of the Esterels, choked with impenetrable thicket, killed off a large proportion of Antony's troops, and it was a miserable, starving remnant which presented themselves on the 15th of May, B.C. 43, at the gates of Forum Julii.

There Antony was joined by Ventidius and three legions, and plenty of forage was brought in for the cavalry, while they rested before the meeting with Lepidus, the general in Provence who had assured Cicero so fully of his loyalty to the Senate. There was no fighting. Even if the senatorial general had not decided to choose "peace and politics," the soldiers would probably have preferred Caesarism to the constitution; for many already had traditions of victory behind them as glorious as those of Napoleon's Old Guard, and those traditions were connected with the party represented by Antony. The only victim to the ancient constitution was Laterensis, the senator, who killed himself on the Pons Argenteus from a pathetic loyalty to the hopeless cause of republican institutions. The principles of Plancus, the other Provençal general, were as amenable to argument as those of Lepidus, and he prudently withdrew to Grenoble until Octavianus had shown signs that it would be better to join Antony. This Lepidus immediately did. Decimus Brutus, meanwhile, caught between Octavianus and the rebels, had his indecisions swiftly ended for him by death at the hands of Antony's men. The result of all this shuffling of cards was the Triumvirate which at once beheaded Cicero. Lepidus had to content himself with Africa in the partition that ensued. Antony married Octavia; but for the next twelve years was occupied in dreaming with Cleopatra of an empire in the East. Octavianus quietly consolidated his power with most remarkable success, for the last hopes of the Republicans were shattered with the fall of Brutus and Cassius at Philippi; Lepidus was banished; Sextus Pompeius died in 35 A.D; and the victory over Antony and Cleopatra at Actium left Octavianus alone in his supremacy, and strong enough to justify the title of "princeps," or first citizen.

Wearied out by twenty years of war and anarchy, the Roman communities were glad enough to welcome one, who, if he had not the dazzling pre-eminence of patrician descent, the daring disregard of form, the cosmopolitan tastes of Julius Caesar, yet united deliberate caution and unfailing tact to great administrative capacity and a quiet strength of will, which were especially acceptable in one whose "bourgeois birth" assured his genuinely Italian sympathies. In the years that followed, Rome shared the decline of the Republic. But the provinces grew and flourished under an imperial system, which was seen at its best in developing or protecting an orderly civilisation and maintaining the peace of the world. In the tower at La Turbie and the Tour Magne at Nîmes are to be seen two monuments of that protection as exercised by Augustus.

The colossal monument at Turbie commemorates his final victory over the rebellious Alpine tribes in B.C. 12, which implied the opening of a safe road to traders over the Maritime Alps, and immunity from Alpine raids for the lowland farmers. The modern townlet of La Turbie (which means "the Tower") stands on an inland pass formed behind the mountain walls that rise precipitously from the sea, about two miles from Monte Carlo, and commands one of the finest views upon that splendid coast.

The huge tower that was the triumphal monument of Augustus's victories was built of great blocks of stone upon a square base which supported a circular structure with an inscription in letters of gold: "IMPERATORI • CAESARI • DIVI • FILIO • AUGUSTO • PONT. • MAX. • IMP • XIV • TRIB • POT • XVII • S.P.Q.R." (To the Imperator Augustus Caesar, son of the deified, pontifex Maximus, Imperator for the fourteenth time, invested with the Tribunician power for the seventh time, S.P.Q.R. [The Senate and Roman People])[5] The third portion of the building was a round colonnade, which upheld yet a fourth circle of statues and pillars, the whole being surmounted by the colossal effigy of the victorious Emperor. The imitation, and still more, the exaggeration of the elegant St. Remy monument will at once be noticed; and it is a matter of abiding satisfaction that the better of the two has survived. The later, and decadent example, invited pillage from its mere bulk of masonry, and what ruins were left by the Barbarians were used to construct a fortress during the quarrels of Guelphs and Ghibellines. This remained until it was in turn dismantled by the French in 1706; and very little of the original building can now be seen, for the remnants were as usual employed as a convenient quarry for every building set up near it in the eighteenth century.

Unfortunately the monument at La Turbie was taken as a model by the citizens of Nîmes when in their turn they desired to show their sense of the glories of Augustus; and the Tour Magne, which rises on the hill above the Gardens of the Fountain, is the tribute of gratitude to his valour from "Nemausus, Volcarum Arecomicorum Colonia Augusta," in B.C. 27, and is therefore the oldest building in Nîmes. Octagonal in plan, and chiefly impressive from its size, the Tour Magne is built of rough ashlar; it is hollow, and some hundred feet in height. Below the topmost story a girdle of engaged columns in Roman Doric surrounds the edifice, which was crowned by a terrace supported by the attic. There was possibly a colossal effigy upon this, similar to the one at La

Turbie. It was originally entered by an exterior staircase as far as the top of the first story, and the inner staircase now used is as modern as the lower door. Its present name means the same as the older name of "Tour Lampèse" or "Lamprèse," "the splendid tower," like the "Arc Admirable" at Arles.[6]

I have now completed the list of all the important monuments in our district which may be referred to classical military operations. It will be a more pleasant, and perhaps a more interesting task to proceed in my next chapters with the monuments of peace. In doing so, I shall be following the dictates both of history and of inclination if I begin with Arles.

NOTES

1. "What profit have those conquerors of their greed, those who in turn have held the empire of the Rhone, Charlemagne, and Bonaparte and Hannibal, and the Roman Caesars!"

2. Those who still believe in the artistic tendencies of François I may he interested to know that he built walls round Narbonne with the fragments of mutilated Roman ruins.

3. I have given in another chapter several examples of this. But the most appropriate here is a bilingual epitaph of about the second century, A.D., of which the first line in Latin is followed by Greek hexameters and pentameters.

C.Vibio Liguri Maxsuma mater fecit.
(His mother Maxsuma provided this for C. Vibius Ligur)

Τὸν τάφον ἠργάζοντο γεραιοτέροις· ὁ δὲ Δαίμων
  Νήπιον ἀντεβόλησ᾽ ἑπτάετες κλίματι.
Συγγενέες γενέται τε ὁμοῦ ὃν ἔθρεψαν ἔθαψαν
  Γαίον. ὦ μερόπων ἐλπίδες οὐ μόνιμοι.

(They made this tomb for older men. But Fate
Confronted a child with the climate at seven years of age.
His family and kin together brought up and buried
Gaius. O the hopes of mortals do not endure.)

The reading does not quite satisfy me; but it is obviously a pathetic lament over a boy of seven, who was killed by the climate and buried by his parents. The name Ligur was naturally common in the country of the old Ligurians. On the island of Ste. Marguerite the name occurs again both in Greek and Latin on a votive tablet:—

Ὑπὲρ τῆς σωτηρίας Μάρκου Ἰουλίου Λιγυός.

Pro Salute M. Juli Liguris…
(For the preservation of M. Julius Ligur)

4. This same correspondence has preserved one of the few classical texts which actually mention the presence of Julius Caesar on the Riviera; for Caelius writes to Cicero "bemoaning his bad luck in being sent to Vintimiglia, amidst the snows of the Alps at Christmas time, to quell a riot occasioned by the assassination by adherents of Pompey of one of their citizens for having entertained Julius Caesar on his way to Spain at the outset of the civil war."—Quoted by W. H. (Bullock) Hall in *The Romans on the Riviera and the Rhone.*

5. This inscription continues (according to the reading of Desjardins and the text of Pliny): "QUOD EIUS DUCTU AUSPICIISQUE GENTES ALPINAE OMNES QUAE A MARI SUPERO AD INFERUM PERTINEBANT SUB IMPERIUM POPULI ROMANI SUNT REDACTAE. GENTES ALPINAE DEVICTAE…" (Because under his leadership and auspices all the Alpine tribes from the higher to the lower sea have been brought under the power of the Roman people. The conquered Alpine tribes…) And then follow the names of the conquered tribes.

6. The "Tour Magne" gave rise to the most elaborate pun I know, concerning the romantic adventures of a Provençal courtier named Gal. It runs as follows, and was composed, I believe, by Marc Monnier: "Gal, amant de la reine, alla, tour magnanime, Galamment de l'Arène à la Tour Magne à Nîmes." This is supposed to refer to the athletic lover's feat of carrying his sweetheart on his back from the amphitheatre to the tower.

CHAPTER VI

Greece and Rome at Arles

"Roumo, de nòu, t'avié vestido
En pèiro blanco bèn bastido;
De ti gràndis Areno avié mes à toun front
Li cènt-vint porto; aviés toun Cièri;
Aviés, princesso de l'Empèri,
Pèr espaça ti refouleri,
Li poumpous Aquedu, lou Tiatre e l'Ipoudrom." [1]
— MIRÈIO.

THE Arles of today is, as I explained in my second chapter, very different
in its merely geographical aspect, to the Arelate of Rome; to that
harbour of commerce by river and by sea which Ausonius could
apostrophise: "Pande duplex Arelate tuos, blanda hospita, portus,
Gallula Roma." In the time of the Greeks, and before them, the waters
of the Mediterranean and the Rhone were even a more prominent
characteristic of the place; and many think that the name, which is
neither Latin nor Greek, may be referred to the Celtic word "Ar-lath,"
the place of waters. In the earliest centuries of its history this commerce
must have had its full effect upon the development of the town, and it
soon spread out upon both banks of the Rhone; on the left, or eastern,
side was the official and patrician quarter; on the point of the Camargue
to the west and north rose the business town, the merchants' buildings,
and the barracks; an arrangement which has many close parallels with
that of ancient Alexandria. The maritime character of the town lasted far
longer than we can appreciate today, when the whole country from the
Durance to the sea is over thirty feet higher than it was two thousand
years ago, when the line of the sea itself has retreated several miles, and
when so many of the lagoons that stretched from the deep water of the
Mediterranean towards the shallow expanses nearer Arles have

disappeared. In 418 the Emperor Honorius picked out Arles as a place of national assembly because there were so many means of locomotion: "Velo, remo, vehiculo, terra, flumine, mari." Even in 1101 Roger de Hoveden, describing the course of the English fleet to Palestine, says that it touched at St. Gilles, at Arles, and at Marseilles; all apparently being equally accessible.

Owing to these natural advantages, Arles rose to importance as soon as any foreign traders reached it by sea, and no doubt the Phoenicians had established more than a mere market there even before the Phocaeans arrived at Marseilles. At the end of that period, at any rate, the swift preparation of the galleys already mentioned, which Caesar ordered for the siege of Marseilles, is a convincing proof of the excellence and capacity of the dockyards of Arles.[2] Her prosperity was great enough to last for a long while; for the description given by Flonorius and Theodosius is couched in the most flowery language: "Neque enim ulla Provincia ita peculiaris fructus sui facultate laetatur, ut non haec propria Arelatensis soli credatur esse fecunditas; quicquid enim dives Oriens, quicquid odoratus Arabs, quicquid delicatus Assyrius, quod fertilis Africa, quod speciosa Hispania, quod fecunda Gallia potest habere praeclarum, ita illic affatim exhibetur, quasi ibi nascantur omnia." (For no Province so rejoices in the abundance of its particular fruit, for whatever the rich Orient, the perfumed Arab, the luxurious Assyrian, fertile Africa, beautiful Spain, fruitful France can possess and hold famous is equally manifest in abundance there as if everything originated in this place)

The peace that spread over Provence after the victories of Caesar and Augustus was the opportunity that all the towns of Provence took to decorate their streets with something better than the old defensive works, and more or less solid fortifications. There was just a slight pause between the defeat of Marseilles and the formal colonisation of Greek Arles by Rome. In that pause, Decimus Junius Brutus was appointed governor; and during that interval of rest the theatre was built. Its very ruins still frame a scene that is one of the most beautiful and touching in all France, for they are echoing still with the syllables of a great language that lives no longer, and the air is full of the rhythm and the cadences of tragic verse. "One of the sweetest legacies of the ancient world," wrote an author who was not usually fortunate in his experience of Provence.[3] The two slender columns that rise above the ancient stage stand "like a pair of silent actors" who still dominate an

The Greek Theatre of Arles

audience of ghosts; of tender and appreciative spirits; of gentle wraiths whose living hearts were touched to a tear by the sorrows of Alcestis, or tuned to a smile by the harmonious measures of a dance.[4] Cross northward to the huge arena, and you will see what happened when Rome had planted her mailed foot within the Roman walls of Arles. There the solid and gigantic arches rise in tiers to hold a howling populace that shouts for butchery; there the great oval centre, fenced with tall slabs that look like tombstones, seems still to swim with blood as hecatombs of slaughtered animals are dragged through the darkened gateways at each side, or the gladiators enter, and are slaughtered, for the holidays of Rome.

The theatre produces a very different effect, and produces it even in its ruins, because the art that built it was not the Roman but the Greek. In truth it would be difficult, here in Provence, to recognise that there was a Roman *art* at all. There was a Roman *style,* a Roman architecture built for power and strength, and lasting for eternity; a personification in stone of that material brutality which was an elemental characteristic of their conquering blood and iron; a massive creation of archways and of amphitheatres; of aqueducts that stride relentlessly across mountain, vale, and river. Dominion, durability, Imperial power, these things you may see in every building set up by the Romans in Provence; for in their hands were all the corners of the earth, and the strength of the hills was theirs also. But of the art that loves delicate proportion, that enjoins restraint, that plays in fanciful creativeness with naturally graceful detail—of this you will see nothing that the Romans did not take from Greece.[5]

Ever since Hellas had been ravaged, and her treasures spilt, Greek artists, sculptors, architects, had been travelling slowly through the Roman world. Already more than half Hellenised by their constant contact with Phocaean Massalia, the citizens of Arles were ever ready to welcome the artists from the motherland of Attica. The Maison Carrée is almost the sole trace of pure Greek influence at Nîmes, which is as characteristically Roman as Arles is individually Greek. But the amphitheatre is almost the only building in Arles which is wholly bereft of all Greek influence, and owes its being and its form to the nation which invented amphitheatres and triumphal arches, and borrowed Ionic columns or Corinthian capitals from the more artistic, the less military state. It was a Greek architect who designed the theatre of Arles,[6] and gave at once the dignity of proportion and the beauty of detail which distinguished the original construction. It is built of the same stone as was used for the amphitheatre which so quickly followed it, and there are strong traces of Roman influence, as would be only natural under the governorship of Brutus, in the archways that were the chief, though the invisible, support of the main walls and the external entrances. But the whole effect of the interior is the effect of the theatres still left upon the soil of Greece.[7]

The steps are built into the side of the hill, which slopes from east to west, towards the columns of the stage, and the Rhone beyond it; and the line of the stage is almost exactly north and south, the entry as you come from the amphitheatre being the northern gate of the smaller building. The tower above the southern entrance, known as the Tour de Rolland, is of course of far later construction. There is no huge wall left at the back of the stage as we saw at the Roman building of Orange, and the original wall here was probably very differently treated. The theatre of Arles has suffered sadly, and chiefly at the hands of the religious, for religion seems often to have measured its sincerity by its destructiveness, even from the earliest times. In 446 the Deacon Cyril destroyed every detail of carving his fanatic worshippers could reach, and pulled down every statue; and in 1664 a monastery was built with the materials, and on the actual site of the stage.

It is somewhat difficult to suggest what used to be here without emphasising archaeological details rather more than would be suitable in the present volume. My chief object is to tell the traveller what he can see, to suggest what he may enjoy, rather than to involve him and myself in barren antiquarian discussions which he must look for in pages more austere than mine.

The two beautiful and lonely columns, one from Carrara, the other of African marble, remain the most potent evocation of the vanished splendours of the building, and need least explanation. The eight columns of porphyry and one of verd antique, which were shipwrecked on the Rhone as they were being taken to Charles IX in Paris, were probably once companions of these two, which indicate accurately the background of the somewhat narrow, classical stage. In front of it extended the semi-circular space for the chorus and the dancing, called the orchestra, which was reached from the stage by marble steps at each extremity. Part of the marble pavement of this orchestra may still be seen. Under the Roman Emperors this central space in front, which corresponds to the orchestra-stalls of modern theatres, was used for the seats of distinguished personages, whereas the Hellenic arrangement left it free for the proper development of ceremonial dances. It has been calculated that some sixteen thousand spectators could enter by the great gates, north and south, and find places on seats which were so cleverly arranged that every one could see the stage.[8]

A terribly inharmonious thought is suggested by the fact that throughout the Middle Ages, and up to the Renaissance, the common name given to the sole surviving pair of columns was the "Fourches de Rolland." Modern poets have seen the shape of a lyre in their graceful lines; but if we are to think that "Fourches de Rolland" means "Fourches Patibulaires," we must conclude that the ruin was used as a gibbet on which were hanged those malefactors who had been imprisoned in the "Tour Dominante" above the southern arches, or perhaps in the "Tour de Rolland," which is the highest tower added to the Roman amphitheatre. Such a conclusion, followed as it is by the settlement of a convent upon that desecrated stage, suggests that a spot once consecrated to the drama will never be without its innate possibilities of tragic, as of comic, happenings. The amphitheatre, as I shall point out later, certainly preserved for many centuries the tragic possibilities ingrained in its foundation-stones, as other amphitheatres have done on English soil; for when Judge Jeffreys held his "Bloody Assizes" in Dorchester it was in the "Maumbury" (as they call the Roman amphitheatre there) that the population gathered to see two hundred and ninety persons hanged; and it was again in the middle of those haunted ruins that an English crowd of ten thousand watched Mary Channing strangled and burnt in 1705, on the accusation of having poisoned her husband. Scarcely less terrible are the memories of "Les Arènes d'Arles" in modern centuries.

The Greek character of the whole building of this theatre at Arles is emphasised by the fact that a theatre was as important a part of the life and religion of a Greek town as was its temple; with the result that in the Rhone valley, where there was so much Greek influence, we find one theatre in a small Roman colony at Orange, and another in an important Greek colony at Arles, while in Rome itself there are only the traces of the Theatre of Marcellus, with a diameter seventy feet larger than that of Orange; and in other parts of Italy we have to look in places where Greek influence was paramount, as it was, for example, in Pompeii and in Herculaneum. But even apart from all these general considerations the details of sculpture discovered among the débris of the theatre would alone be sufficient to stamp its artistic origins, even if nothing else survived. The first and most famous of these, dug up during some excavations made by order of the king in 1651,[9] was the exquisite marble statue known as the Venus of Arles, now in the Louvre.

The original may well have been a skilled reproduction of the lost Aphrodite of Praxiteles. The whole of the right arm, and the lower part of the left from the elbow downwards have unfortunately been restored; and this restoration I am compelled to reproduce, though much against my will, for the photograph taken in the Louvre is the only one that gives a just idea of the marble. Whatever else may have been the position of the original arms, we may be certain that the goddess did not hold a ball in one hand and a mirror in the other, as the restorer seems to suggest. Only thirty-six years after the Venus was brought to light, Seguin published an engraving of the marble, which was, by a misplaced loyalty, sent as a present to Versailles, in his *Antiquitez d'Arles*; and this engraving I reproduce with all its defects to show the effect of the modern additions. The Venus of Milo and the Victory of Samothrace have fortunately been saved from similar desecration. It is only when such masterpieces are altered by inefficient workmen that we perceive either the relatively unimportant accident of breakage, or the unsurpassable beauty of the Greek treatment and conception.

The Venus was found by two brothers, whose name was Brun, on the 6th of June 1651. In May 1684 it was brought to Paris by Jean de Dieu, the sculptor of Arles, a pupil of Puget. Michel Angelo refused to restore the lost hand of the statue of Meleager, as he was requested, for

The Venus of Arles in the Louvre (restored)
The smaller figure shows the marble as originally found.

fear his own work might spoil the conception of the ancient artist. M. Girardon felt no such scruples in supplying this Aphrodite with what he thought was needed to complete her, and his execution of the hands seems to me as bad as his idea of their position and use. On April 18, 1865, the statue was brought to the grand gallery of Versailles, and it is now in the "Salle du Gladiateur" in the Louvre.[10] Its colour, a delicate warm brown, shows that the marble (which came from Mount Hymettus) was originally treated with burnt wax, which gives it a soft, sun-kissed patina of mellow gold, and there are slight traces of that tender colouring, in light shades, which are to be found in other examples of the best Greek art. More human than the proud and severely simple goddess from Melos, more dignified than the subtly and delicately sensual Venus de Medicis, this exquisite statue holds a middle place, commands a loyalty all its own. For as it shows the maid just blossoming into the perfect woman, so it exemplifies that moment in the art of sculpture which is after the perfection of the divine and before the frank seduction of the feminine. She is but half unclad. She wears, as is her right, the highest charms of mortal woman, yet she has not quite stepped down from Olympus to the earth. If indeed she be the copy, perhaps even the duplicate, of the Aphrodite of Praxiteles, she is the child of his earliest years when still the influence of Scopas was upon him, before the genius of Phidias was forgotten. There is a copy from the same great original now in the British Museum,[11] which was discovered at Ostia in 1776 by Gavin Hamilton. But the true copies of the Venus of Arles are the Arlésiennes, as Aubanel has sung:—

"O douço Venus d'Arle! o fado de jouvènço!
Ta bèuta que clarejo en touto la Prouvenço
Fai bello nòsti fiho e nòsti drole san;
Souto aquelo car bruno, o Venus! i a toun sang
Sèmpre viéu, sèmpre caud..."[12]

Almost at the same time as the Venus was discovered, a very beautiful Greek head was dug out from among the same ruins of the theatre. Though the face is imperfect it is far better to have kept it in Provence than to have had it restored at the price of losing it in the Galleries of the Louvre. It has been called the head of Livia, wife of Augustus; but, even supposing a statue had been set up in Arles to the deified Empress after her death, this impassive divinity could not have been the portrait of any human original. The nature of the fissure in the marble suggests that we have here the perfect piece as far as it went, and that drapery in some other material crossed the breast from beneath the left arm over the right shoulder. The modelling of the neck and hair, and the perfect finish of the workmanship throughout, have been considered by the best authorities to indicate the great period of Greek art, and the peculiar treatment of the surface has been no less effective than in the case of the Arlesian Aphrodite in the Louvre. The head is placed upon a pedestal which does not, of course, belong to it, but is an altar to the "Bona Dea" set up by her

Greek Bust at Arles

priestess Caiena Attice, the freed woman of Prisca. Of this I shall have more to say in another chapter, and it is only necessary here to point out how much superior is the Greek work at Arles to what little can be attributed to Greece at Nîmes, even if we include the Venus of Nîmes, and such examples of decadent Graeco-Roman workmanship as the bust of Hermes or the Apollo from Ladignan.

There is also preserved at Arles a fine head from the colossal statue of Augustus which once adorned the theatre. Though mutilated and defaced, it still retains the characteristic Roman physiognomy; the low, full forehead, thick lips, and prominent cheekbones. Above all, there is that expression of lofty thought, of almost austere majesty which only the real artist could convey; and the workmanship shows traces of the true Hellenic touch, for it was no doubt carved by some Greek sculptor who had been attracted by the lavish orders given for the later decoration of the theatre.[13] By the same hand, too, are the magnificent imperial wreath, with its broad fillet, which once no doubt formed part of the altar to the divine Augustus; and the separate altar which seems to unite the divinities of the Emperor and of Aphrodite, in the theatre which held so many decorations in honour of them both. This latter is a masterpiece of design and execution in white marble, with swans at each corner, holding a thick garland of laurel in their beaks. The treatment of the silken fillet and of the birds' wings, is especially fine. Augustus, like every member of the Julian house, prided himself on his descent, through

Aeneas, from the goddess Aphrodite; we know, too, from Suetonius, that the palm was his favourite tree, and it therefore appears upon one side of this altar.

As a last example of the sculpture which this treasure house of Hellenic art contained, I may select the statue of a dancing-girl in the Arles Museum, full of graceful life, though so little of the carving has been saved. Her strong yet delicate foot scarce seems to touch the ground as she floats forward amid a gentle sway of billowing draperies. She stood, no doubt, near the steps that led down from the stage to the orchestra, where her living sisters danced the rhythmic steps of Greece. A marble fragment of the proscenium above

The Imperial Wreath of Augustus at Arles

them has been also found, a bas-relief, representing the triumph of Apollo and the punishment of Marsyas.

It should be remembered that although the plans were made, and the building begun, of the Greek theatre at Arles at about the date before Christ which I have mentioned, the decoration of the structure with its elaborate ornaments, and the gradual collection of the statues which adorned it, took at least a century longer, and very probably for some three centuries continual additions of one kind or another were being made. So beautiful and so laboriously perfected a whole deserved better treatment at the hands of St. Hilary's zealous deacon; and it is an ironical commentary on generally received opinions to find that what the early Christians cared not to preserve, and what was either wantonly degraded or sullenly neglected up to the seventeenth century, received the unaccustomed honours of a special guardian from Theodoric, King of the Goths, from his successor Athalaric, and from the Queen Amalasonte, who not only appointed a

Altar to Venus and Augustus at Arles

count of their court to watch over the classical remains, but spent money of their own to save them from destruction. When more modern Arles awoke to the fact that she was the guardian of a priceless artistic antiquity, she could find no better use for her carvings than in giving them away to French monarchs, or Italian cardinals, or to any notability whose passing favour it was important for the municipality to gain. Personally, I can never forgive or understand the transportation of their Aphrodite from her ancient shrine. Yet she is but one example out of many lesser losses. They even include the torso of the colossal statue of Augustus, whose head remains alone in the museum at Arles.

> *"Tout passe. L'art robuste*
> *Seul a l'éternité.*
> *Le buste*
> *Survit à la cité*
> *Et la médaille austère*
> *Que trouve un laboureur*
> *Sous terre*
> *Révèle un empereur."*

NOTES

1. "Rome dressed thee new, City of Arles! built thee true with white stones; a hundred and a score of gates she placed before thee in the Amphitheatre; and like a princess of the Empire, thou hadst the Circus for thy pleasure, the gorgeous Aqueducts, the Theatre, the Hippodrome."

2. An inscription has preserved the name of one of the head workmen in these dockyards, as follows: "CAIUS JULIUS POM...COLLEGA FABRORUM NAVALIUM CORPORATORUM [ARELATENSIUM] CURATOR EIUSDEM CORPORIS..." (Caius Julius Pom... manager of the company of workmen in the dockyards at Arles); and a patron of the same body is also known who is referred to as: "SEVIR COLONIAE JULIAE PATERNAE ARELATENSIS, PATRONI EIUSDEM CORPORIS, ITEM FATRONI FABRORUM NAVALIUM UTRICULARIORUM."

3. See *A Little Tour in France*, by Henry James, who was so worried by the stones in the streets of Arles, and by the photographers of Vaucluse, that his discomfort almost entirely obscures, for the unsympathetic reader, the beauty of the scenes he visited.

4. Associations of Greek actors existed from very early days in Asia Minor and the

East, and travelling companies, under the protection of Dionysus and his worship (whence the word Thymele), were soon organised in various large cities, to which I have referred in the list of Greek actors given elsewhere. One of the presidents of these dramatic and gymnastic brotherhoods was approached for a good troupe by any town that wished to give a special fête. The Naples Brotherhood, with its especially Greek connections, was famous for its good companies, and on one occasion passed an official vote of thanks to Titus Julius Dolabella, a prefect of Nîmes, who either had behaved very generously to some Greek players, or was more probably the agent in Nîmes for the business of the Neapolitan Dramatic Brotherhood. Much the same no doubt occurred in the management of the theatre of Arles, where the existence of a branch of the Dionysiac Brotherhood is even more probable than at Nîmes. The corporation called τὸ κοινὸν τῶν περὶ τὸν Διόνυσον τεχνίτων (the company of the artists of Dionysus) was first known first at Teos and then at Ephesus, where it spread widely both in influence and area. The brotherhoods lasted right on till the sixth century, when ecclesiastical dogmas became strong enough to stop them, and they were replaced by such unedifying functions as the Fête des Fous, or by the Mystery Plays. Augustus is known to have favoured these Greek companies; Caligula brought them to Lyons; Hadrian so much encouraged them, at Naples and elsewhere, that he was called "the new Bacchus"; and his close connection with Nîmes and Arles implies much.

5. The Map of Peutinger preserves the tradition of this influence in the name "Gretia," written on the district between the Durance and the Sea, of which Arles is the centre.

6. There were also many Greeks brought over to perform in the theatres of Provence, as is shown by the inscriptions found at Nîmes; e.g. the stone placed in 1850 near the Porte d'Auguste, which records the patronage of the emperor extended to Greek theatrical art; as we know, from other sources, this was the case with Hadrian. The letters are

.... ΘΥΜΕΛΙΚΗΣ ΕΝ ΝΕΜΑΤΣΩ ΤΩΝ ΑΠΟ ....
.... ΝΕΡΟΥΑΝ ΤΡΑΙΑΝΟΝ ΚΑΙΣΑΡΑ ΣΕΒΑΣΤΟΝ ...

(...of the Thymelic troupe in Nîmes from the...
...Nerva Trajan Caesar Augustus)

which refer to the "Thymelic troupe" at Nîmes patronised by Nerva Trajan Caesar Augustus. Another inscription in the Museum refers to Lucius Samnius, an actor in the "Dionysiac Brotherhood," and three times president of the "Thymelic Confrérie." Another is an epitaph: "Afrodis • Symmele •, Grex Gallicus, Memphi et Paridis..." which not only contains the interesting phrase, "Gaulish troupe of Actors," but mentions a player in the troupe of Memphis and Paris, who may have been the famous actors brought by Verus out of Syria in 165 A.D. Compare with this the inscriptions at Vienne. (1) Scaenici Asiaticiani et qui in eodem corpore sunt vivi sibi fecerunt. (The Asiatic players and those of the same company who are alive made this for themselves) (2) Niciae citharoedo. (To Nicias the cithara-player) (3) Hellas Pantomimus hic quiescit ann: XIIII (A Greek dancer who died at the age of fourteen). At the corner of the Boulevard Gambetta and the Rue de Corcomaire at Nîmes, another inscription refers to the fact that Greek musicians used to play there. The words ΙΟΝΙΚΗΣ ΚΑΙ are decipherable among much that is erased. Most touching of all these dramatic memories is the tombstone found in the ruined circus of Antipolis (Antibes), which was set up to the memory of a boy of only twelve years old, who died after he had twice danced successfully: D.M. PUERI SEPTENTRIONIS QUI ANNORUM XII ANTIPOLI IN THEATRO BIDUO SALTAVIT ET PLACUIT. (To the soul of a boy from the north who twice danced successfully in the theatre of Antipolis)

7. It must not be imagined that the Greek style of theatrical representations ceased with the extinction of Greek nationality. I have already mentioned the support given by Hadrian to the Dionysiac confraternities. Antoninus Pius was equally enthusiastic, and the connection of his paternal stock with Nîmes ensured the benefits of that enthusiasm for Provençal theatres. The crocodile and the palm-tree on the ancient coins (and the modern escutcheon) of the city of Nîmes recall the fact that its original colonists were veterans from Egypt, who would also be likely to have brought Greek theatrical fashions from Alexandria. A very instructive inscription preserved at Athens fixes without further doubt the connection of Hadrian and Antoninus with the Dionysiac brotherhoods. It runs as follows: "Decretum sacrae Hadrianiae Antoninae thymelicae peripolisticae magnae synodi eorum qui ex toto orbe terrarum circa Bacchum et imperatorem Caesarem T. Aelium Hadrianum Antoninum Augustum Pium novum Bacchum sunt artificum." The title of "novus Bacchus," given to Hadrian and Antoninus Pius, was continued to Caracalla, and implied a double significance in the priesthoods under the protection of both the god and the divine emperor. Later on we find a treasurer or procurator, appointed by the emperor, who managed the dramatic funds, with the title of "logista thymelae." His functions were necessitated by the fact that every performance had a competitive element, and prizes were awarded to the best players, for tragedy, comedy, flute playing, and poetic composition. Honourable titles were borne by actors who had been thus rewarded at various famous performances. One Valerius Eglectus is known to have won prizes in Greece, Italy, Syria, and almost all the ancient world, and cities vied with each other in bestowing titles upon him, and raising statues or monuments in his honour.

8. There were thirteen small chambers hollowed out in various places beneath the rows of seats, containing a large bronze urn, or a vessel of pottery, which were supposed to aid the acoustic properties of the theatre as a whole. The building was about one hundred and three metres in diameter, with an opening span of some forty-two metres for the stage.

9. Seguin says, "excavations made for a cistern in the courtyard of the convent," which in his day (1680) was on the site of the stage.

10. Just as the masterpieces of Phidias and Praxiteles were at one time to be seen close to the ancient fetish-stones which represented the earliest conception of Divinity, so, in Provence, there has been found at Antibes an oval fragment of diorite of the fifth century B. C., which represents the ancient fetish-stone before the Aphrodite of Arles had been created. It bears an inscription to Eros (for in that way I construe Τέρπων) as follows Τέρπων εἰμι θεᾶς θεράπων σεμνῆς ᾽Αφρο-δίτης τοῖς δὲ καταστήσασι Κύπρις χάριν ἀνταποδοίη.. (I am the one who gives delight, servant of the holy goddess Aphrodite. May the Cyprian Aphrodite bestow her grace on the inhabitants) No doubt it is a remnant of the Phocaean colonists of Marseilles.

11. Our Museum has also secured an exquisite statue called the Diadymene of Vaison, one of the marbles which once decorated the theatre there.

12. Aubanel's graceful lines, written for Paul Arène, are too long to quote in full, and are of a delicate savour which would evaporate in translation; but I have included one of their suggestions in the verses that preserve, elsewhere, some of the impressions that Aphrodite's statue made upon the writer of this book.

13. In Bernoulli's *Bildnisse der römischen Kaiser,* in the volume on the Julian and Claudian houses, the author says of this bust at Arles (which is No. 60 on his thirty-eighth page), that it is "vom Typus der Statue von Primaporta im Vatican." The bust, numbered 1877 in the British Museum, may be compared with it.

CHAPTER VII

Of Ancient Religions in Provence and Greek Art at Nîmes

"...Per omnia quasi superstitiosiores vos video.
Praeteriens enim et videns simulacra vestra
inveni et aram in qua scriptum erat IGNOTO DEO."

(I perceive that in all things ye are too superstitious.
For as I passed by and beheld your devotions, I found an altar
with this inscription, TO THE UNKNOWN GOD.)

THE building of the theatre of Arles marks the end of an era distinguished by the gradual intermixture of various racial elements, chiefly Celtic and Hellenic, upon a favourable soil. After the reign of Augustus, this composite population was profoundly modified by Roman ideas and Roman modes of life; yet it retained certain characteristics which have never been lost; which retarded its union with an alien Paris until very late in its history; and which preserved its individual and peculiar flavour until the present day. This is not the place for ethnological discussions; but I may at least venture to suggest a few of the constituents into which the living unity of Provence can briefly be analysed in its progress through the ages, especially those which so profoundly modified its early years that maturity has never lost their influence; and I can do so best by reference to what remains of its most ancient faiths.

The earliest nurse of Gallic culture was no doubt the religion called Druidic, which taught the doctrines of metempsychosis and of a future life, mingled with much nature-magic, and the use of the moon for the divisions of the calendar. On the sixth day of the moon was cut the mistletoe, which symbolised the new life flourishing upon the old oak of the past; and at the ceremony two bulls were sacrificed. These rites did not tend to unite a population still widely disseminated in many small groups all over the country; and it was the necessity for self-defence, when every man's hand was against his neighbour's, that produced the clans and tribal associations. The tribe of the Allobroges were gathered into Vienne; the Tectosages, a tribe of the Volcae, into Toulouse, Carcassonne, Béziers and Narbonne; the Arecomician tribe of the Volcae into Nîmes, which preserved the name of Nemausus, their fountain-god. These attributions cannot invariably be shown to be accurate; but they indicate quite fairly how remarkably similar the divisions of the ancient peoples remained after the Roman conquest to what they had been before it.[1]

This extraordinary persistence in racial characteristics continued after Gaul had changed her religion, her customs, her language, and her laws, as far as public life went, for those of Rome. One reason is that the actual infusion of new blood, Latin blood, was not very great in proportion to the indigenous mass of population. Of relatively few "colonies" can this infusion be proved beyond doubt, and be traced in the official name given. That of Narbonne suggests the importation of the veterans of the tenth legion. The sixth legion had a similar connection with Arles, called "Colonia Julia Paterna Arelate Sextanorum." The Latin colonists, sent to Vienne in B.C. 46, were nearly all expelled later on by the original inhabitants. Lyons was but small, as a Roman town, and represented no large previous settlement in spite of its high-sounding name of "Colonia Copia Claudia Augusta Lugudunum." Béziers was colonised by veterans from the seventh legion, Fréjus from the eighth. Even if Desjardins's estimate of three hundred families as forming a "colony" be too exiguous, we shall not be justified in increasing it too far, and in nearly every case it could only influence to a given extent the agglomeration of tribal inhabitants already on the spot. Even then it must also be recalled that many of Caesar's veterans had been recruited in Cisalpine Gaul and in the Narbonnaise.

After all these considerations it would be very difficult to formulate any precise desire on the part of Rome to "assimilate" the Gauls. Tacitus seems to indicate the process in describing the policy of Agricola, but in its essentials the idea itself is entirely modern. Rome certainly broke down the old barriers of tribal and city exclusiveness; but it was not at her will that the Gauls changed so much. It was at their own.

The Aquitanian Julius Vindex, the Haeduan Julius Sacrovir, the Treviran Julius Florus; these men, who rebelled against Rome, bore the names bequeathed to them by fathers or grandfathers who had been made Roman citizens by Julius or Augustus. Innumerable instances of the same thing occur in the inscriptions, some of which I shall mention later on; and examples of such Gallic names as Smertulitanos, Comartiorix, or Dubnacus are rare enough to stand out as obvious exceptions to the general rule, and almost entirely disappear by 200 A.D. The reason, no doubt, is that the Gauls rapidly recognised the advantages of Roman citizenship, and took the name of the man to whom they owed their rights, just as a liberated slave was described as the freedman of his former master. When, for example, a Gaul named Cabur had been given his citizenship by Caius Valerius Flaccus, he called himself Caius Valerius Caburius, and his son was known as Caius Valerius Procillus. The transformation was complete; and in this case, too, before 50 B.C.

From the condition of subjects, such men as these had aimed at membership of the Empire, and they could rise step by step in the official ranks until, at last, even the highest place was theirs. The price they paid was that instead of calling themselves Gauls they gloried in the name of Roman; by that name Gregory of Tours describes them in the fifth century; and their ancient patriotism insensibly became the love of Rome. As one of their own poets has said, apostrophising the capital of his Empire: "Fecisti patriam diversis gentibus unam" (Out of different people you made a single fatherland). It was not Rome who tried to gather these men into her bosom. It was they who were not content till they had been gathered in, for the sake of the legal protection of person and of property, of recognised sale and purchase, of marital or paternal authority. From the unstable, external, shadowy position of a "peregrinus," they reached the acknowledged status of a citizen. They asked no better reward for their services in the field, as was seen when the five thousand Gauls who were in Caesar's famous Transalpine legion, the Alauda, were at a stroke given their citizenship. They expected no other recognition from Augustus and his successors, for their public work or political activity, than this same citizenship, which had much the effect, though far more than the significance, of the modern list of honours which appears on various important dates at the present day; and, in precisely the same way the rich, by degrees, asserted and maintained their right to the same favours.

It would not be correct therefore to imagine that Gaul was oppressed, enslaved, and desolated by the Roman Conquest.

Populations which had never previously coagulated into even the nominal unity which may be called a nation can hardly be said to have bewailed their "loss of nationality." With very few exceptions they were allowed to retain their own organisations, their own family life. The trifles a man thinks so essential to his personality were untouched. The only radical changes made were those necessitated by the administration of Roman law and life over large districts, and the rapid approximation to Roman ways of living in those districts was the free and subsequent expression of individual desire. Men whose outlook was bounded by their own concerns would notice very little change at all in every detail of private existence. The Vocontii, for instance, in Gallia Narbonensis, retained their tribal integrity, but with this weighty difference: that instead of constant inter-tribal feuds they now enjoyed continual peace: the "Pax Romana" of the Empire they soon grew to love.

For these same reasons such ancient faiths of theirs as Druidism were not persecuted out of existence. They merely ceased to exist. The same modern fallacy must be avoided here as we noticed in transferring modern notions of "assimilation" to Imperial Rome. The missionary is a modern development, and wholesale religious persecution is chiefly posterior to the formulation of various modern creeds. The need for some kind of spiritual belief is innate in man, if human history has any meaning since its earliest records; but the forms of that belief have changed and are changing since the beginning. Nor is it possible to assert that Druidism was the religion of the Gauls.[2] It was rather a sacerdotal cult imported from more northern peoples, and its highest mysteries were the monopoly of a priestly hierarchy. It grafted itself upon an older, more natural faith, and gradually imposed its ceremonies everywhere; but the people had their gods, and Julius Caesar recognised very little difference except the names in the divinities which represented to them his Diana (Arduinna), Mercury, Jupiter, Mars (Camul), Apollo (Belen), or Minerva. The consequence of this was that the only change observable after the coming of Rome was that Druidical intervention ceased. The Druidical corporation came to an end when the conventions for tribal government ceased with the substitution of another government. Its magic rites were forbidden by Tiberius, its human sacrifices by Claudius. It departed, in fact, to its old home in the British islands; and only an unconsidered remnant lasted on a few more centuries in the wilder forests of Provence.

Once more it will be fair to see the exercise of Gaulish freewill rather than of Roman constraint. The tribes saw that nothing to outrage their established customs was suggested, and of their own accord they gradually gave up what they would have eagerly defended, had it been openly attacked. As the Latin language grew more and more popular, the Gallic gods added the Latin names to their own ancient appellations. Divinities more aged still, and brought from other lands, were worshipped also: Isis, and Mithra, for example; for under the Roman rule religion enjoyed nearly always the greatest freedom, except when it took on a dangerous political complexion, as was sometimes the case with Christianity. No nationality at any rate was recognised in the many divinities of the world. Greek, or Egyptian, or Asiatic gods were worshipped in Italy; Italian gods in Gaul.

As an example of this tolerance of ancient faiths, we find that the Arecomician tribe of the Volcae were first attracted to Nîmes by the beautiful spring which gushes out from the last low buttresses of the Cévennes, and the tribe continued to give honour for the foundation of their "colony" to Nemausus, the fountain-god who gave the town its name, long after the Romans had established their dominion. Inscriptions were set up by Gallic inhabitants with the words: "Deo Coloniae Nemauso," "Genio Coloniae Nemauso." The Gallic shrine was carefully preserved by the Romans, who built the more enduring temple to the same divinity, which may yet be seen; and sometimes a Celtic worshipper dedicated his altar both to his own and to the Roman deity; sometimes both races made their separate offerings to their ancient gods.[3]

Besides the local religions of the Celtic inhabitants, and the Greek rites of later colonists, there existed for long in Provence, and especially in Arles, the memory of Eastern rites which were different from Hellenic faiths; and of these rites we can still see traces in the worship of the "Bona Dea" or Cybele, which had come west in the third century B.C., and of Mithra, which was subsequent to the Roman conquest. In the polyglot and miscellaneous rituals of Rome, even in the purer, nobler ceremonies of Periclean Athens, there remained traces of a more ferocious, Oriental past, which was the shadowy mother of all ritual and all symbolism. Dionysus or Bacchus was more an Asiatic or an Indian type than he was either Greek or Roman. In the orgies over which he officially presided the Oriental taint is manifest; and in nearly all rites which included "mysteries" the same Eastern survivals may be traced. In exactly the same way the Mysteries of the "Bona Dea" and the cult of

Mithra lasted on among the rites of Arles until the sturdy Christianity of the fifth century seems to have dispelled them finally.

Mithra was the God of the Sun and of Fire, the supreme divinity of Zoroastrianism, the incarnation of Ormuzd, the regenerator of the world. Some of the earliest representations show him as a young, heroic god, slaying a bull, and the Taurobolic rites preserved that memory. But there was an esoteric presentment of him also, showing all the mighty symbols of his power; and of this kind is the strange statue in the Museum of Arles. The lion's head has vanished. Round the torso a serpent winds its splendid scales, and between its coils are carved in relief the constellations of the Zodiac. This strange and interesting fragment of antiquity was discovered in 1598 on the left bank of the Rhone near the old Porte de la Roquette, and in 1723 was bought for twenty-seven livres by the consuls of the town, who were under the erroneous impression that it was an Egyptian effigy of Esculapius. The inscription recording this mistake still exists. The lost lion's head represented the strength of the sun when it entered the constellation Leo; the serpent symbolised the ecliptic course apparently taken by the sun as it moved through its yearly path across the sky. The mysterious nature of these tenets ensured them a long life. Especially to the poorer classes did the sacrifice known as "taurobolia" appeal, and the memories of it are preserved on altars with carvings of oxen's skulls, and the inscription "DEO SOLI INVICTO MITHRAE." (To Mithras, the unconquered god of the soil) The ritual consisted in the digging of a pit within which stood the worshipper. Above him, supported by planks, was placed the bull chosen for sacrifice, and its blood was poured upon his body through the interstices of the wood over his head.

Far less repulsive was the worship of the "Bona Dea," the Good Goddess, that Mighty Mother of the universe whom the Greeks sometimes called Cybele, who was worshipped in the Eleusinian Mysteries, and whose cult goes back to Phrygian and Phoenician shrines. As Rhea, Demeter, the Idaean Mother, Astarte, Ceres, this same divinity appeared in various forms, and in her honour also were held those nocturnal dances and debaucheries which accompanied the rites of Cybele. The altar to the Bona Dea in the museum at Arles is a square block of Carrara marble, about four feet high. Upon the front is carved a beautiful wreath of oak leaves, within which are placed two ears,[4] as if to indicate that though no one might carve the face of the divinity, yet she was ever present, and ever listening to her worshippers. Above the wreath is the inscription: "BONAE DEAE CAIENA PRISCAE LIB. ATTICE MINISTRA," which signifies that the altar was set up to the goddess by her priestess Caiena Attice, the freedwoman of Prisca. The elegant ewer carved on one side, with an olive branch upon it, is especially worthy of notice; and the whole style implies a time not much later than Augustus.

This altar is, somewhat inappropriately, used as the pedestal for the marble head of the goddess "au Nez cassé," with which it has no connection whatever. It was found in 1758 beneath the chief entrance to the church of Notre Dame la Major, which was first built near an old pagan temple in about the sixth century A.D. The male head, with ram's horns carved on one side, represents the sun in Capricorn, and suggests the union of Cybele with Jupiter Ammon, of the spring sunshine with the earth it fertilises.

The carelessness which the majority of the inhabitants of modern Nîmes and Arles display towards the extraordinary collections in their museums is only equalled by the difficulty with which the local authorities surround every effort to discover or to reproduce them. Several of the interesting statues kept in the Maison Carrée at Nîmes were photographed for the first time in April 1904,[5] owing to my determination that my readers should be able in some measure to form their own opinion about these practically unknown treasures. The majority it will be more appropriate to mention later on, in my sketch of Roman life in Provence, but all of them have a deep interest from the fact that they are among the very relics of an age that comes after the best period of either Greek or Roman art, and before both were swept away by northern or by Saracenic invasions. They are not the work of skilled artists; but they show how the old ideals were preserved by inhabitants of the towns, and even the villages, of Provence, long after the expression of those ideals in stone had lost its first perfection; and three among them I may take as symbolising that especially Graeco-Roman form of art which it is the purpose of this present chapter to emphasise.

One of them is an Apollo. The photograph is before me; but I have hesitated to reproduce it because I think the zeal of the rustic restorer has placed the head from a similar statue of Aphrodite upon the male figure of the god, which throws the whole work out of proportion. But Reinach, who mentions this statue *(Repert. de la Stat. Grec. et Rom.,* vol. ii. p. 94), does not notice the substitution of the head, and considers the pose is typical. The little statue still preserves its elements of charm, and deserves more than the notice it obtains. It was found at Ladignan. Rather better, both in style and workmanship, is the small bust called the Hermes that was found at Nîmes. The hair is bad, the cap is an addition, but the face itself is original. It is only down to the join of the neck that we have the rest of the original marble, but this is more than enough to convince the sympathetic spectator of its genuine value as the Greek portrait of a Roman boy.

Bust called the Mercury of Nîmes

More important than all is, of course, the graceful figure known as the "Venus of Nîmes." She cannot be compared to the Aphrodite at Arles, either in treatment or in workmanship, as was only to be expected from the more distinctively Roman surroundings among which she first appeared. But, though decadent, she is still Greek, and the true inspiration is still evident even after the numberless misfortunes to which the hapless marble has had through many centuries to submit.

Less than thirty years ago, some workmen had dug a trench for the purpose of repairing gas and water pipes, in what is now the Rue Pavée, in a poor quarter outside the boulevards, which was once the centre of Nemausus, near the Maison Carrée. At two metres below the surface, which is exactly the level of the Roman city, they found a hundred and three pieces of marble in a fairly compact mass. Luckily M. Irénée Ginoux recognised certain traces of the human form in these pathetic fragments, and he had them all brought in safety to the old town library. Some time after this the sculptor Prosper Maurin set to work to fit them together, aided by finding that the feet, the bosom, the top of the head and the lower part of the face were still recognisably intact.

The Venus of Nîmes

He finally reconstructed a statue in white marble, one metre thirty-five in height, a little shorter than the celebrated Venus de Medicis. The right arm alone had disappeared. Luckily he placed neither an apple nor a mirror in a new arm of his own, but left to the imagination the gracious curves of wrist and elbow that once half veiled and half discovered the beauties of a breast now bare.[6]

The head-dress is Greek in its simplicity, with a plain "sphendone" to keep the hair in place. The left hand that partly veils the body also lifts up the draperies above the knee; and perhaps the less said about this drapery the better, though there are certain affinities with the treatment of the folds at Arles, which will be obvious after any careful comparison. I cannot, I confess, imagine this to be a goddess. She is neither nude nor draped, neither girlishly modest nor divinely unabashed. She is but a pretty model, carved as she stood, a somewhat saucy baggage, it may be feared, without a trace of idealisation either in herself or in her artist. Yet there is undeniable attractiveness in the work. It is the work of a clever and a facile hand that has forgotten the old dignity of a greater art. The girl was thinking she was pretty, and the sculptor was thinking of the girl, and I cannot imagine either of them giving much thought to the goddess. The result is that mixture of purity and provocation which has inspired the role of the ingenious *ingénue* in every decadent studio since art began. If she was indeed a Venus, she was a "Vénus du Quartier," and I seem to see this "gueuse parfumée de Provence" in the hall of some fat merchant, who shows her off to his commercial partners after dinner, rather than in the sanctuary of a temple. She has the air of that frivolously fashionable religion which amuses the irreligious patrons of an unbelieving art, which makes you see, in the conscious divinities of Versailles, the more or less undraped acquaintances of the eighteenth century sculptor and his elegant young friends. Still, she is the product of a time which has left us scarcely any trace of its existence; and she would have her value were you but to see, from looking at her closely, the reason why her sister of Arles, still more her sister from Melos, are so immensely her superiors. And she is the best that Nîmes can show.

Of the four other carvings from the Maison Carrée Museum, which I shall reproduce later, three are obviously Roman portraits of about the beginning of the third century A.D., and the fourth is a priestess of Ceres whose Roman origin becomes conclusive when she is compared to the Apollo and the Venus just described. Judging from the head-dress (see p. 167) she was made about the time of Domitian, and very likely for the decoration of the Nymphaeum. The Venus, too, is very like the type of those fountain-goddesses often found in Italy, and, whether carved with that idea or not, she may very well have been considered as an appropriate decoration of the Fountain of Nemausus (see Reinach, *op. cit*, p. 357). I have drawn more attention to these carvings than, as far as I know, has been done before by any other writer, because they represent an age which has been singularly barren in art-products hitherto, and therefore possess a value entirely apart from their individual excellence.

In a most interesting note on the statues lately discovered in the wreck off Cerigotto (see the *Journal of Hellenic Studies,* vol. xxiii.), Mr. K. T. Frost has shown that the famous bronze Hermes, then so miraculously retrieved, though inspired by the Praxitelean school, was not the handiwork of either Praxiteles or Scopas. The cargo, in fact, was that of a wrecked Graeco-Roman merchantman, consisting of clever, shop-made copies and artistic adaptations of great originals which still remained in Greece up to the time of Pausanias. They are, therefore, admirable examples of the "art-furniture" of the period from 200 B.C. to 300 A.D., just the period of the classic art of Arles and Nîmes; and I believe that most of what I have reproduced as Graeco-Roman from these Provençal sites may be referred to a similar origin, with the exception, of course, of such admitted masterpieces as the bust with the broken nose at Arles, and the Aphrodite of Arles, which, if not originals, are such fine copies, carved in Greek marble, that they may well be duplicates from the hand of the master himself.

Though the details of the temple of Nemausus of the Fountain are thoroughly Greek in treatment and conception, the whole style and workmanship of the fabric are so characteristically Roman that in this chapter I must pass on at once to the most Hellenic work of art in Nîmes, the temple so absurdly called the Maison Carrée, which, as the now vanished inscription once declared, was dedicated to Caius and Lucius, those sons of Agrippa and Julia whom Augustus adopted as his heirs. "As for Caius and Lucius," writes Suetonius in the translation by Philemon Holland which I shall invariably quote in these pages, "Augustus adopted them for his owne children at home in his house, having bought them of Agrippa their father by the brazen coine and the ballance. Whom being yet in their tender yeeres he emploied in the charge of the common-weale: and no sooner were they consuls-elect, but hee sent them abroad to the government of provinces and the conduct of armies." Caius died in Lycia, Lucius at Massilia, and the empire passed to Tiberius, son of the third nephew, Agrippa; but Provence remembered the two "Princes of the Imperial Youth," whom Augustus had so dearly loved, one of whom had died within her borders, while the other was official patron of the colony of Nîmes; and it was to their deified memories that this temple rose, before Augustus died.[7]

From the five centuries of Roman imperial rule in Gaul we have records in medals, inscriptions, monuments, and tombs, besides actual written evidence. In none of this do we find hatred of the Empire expressed by the inhabitants. Emperors might personally be criticised in Gaul, as they were by Tacitus or Juvenal in Rome; but the Imperial system was as highly honoured there as here. Even when Gaul had the choice of her own destiny in the third century, apart entirely from Italian influence, she chose an emperor. Nor were the inhabitants ever disarmed. The thirty legions of the empire could never have controlled so many millions unless their political ideals had gradually become identical. The monarchy, as a system, was universally beloved, for the simple reason that men found their interest and profit in it, without a thought either of moral reasons or of logical justifications.

This affection was reflected in such titles addressed by provincials to various Emperors as "Pacificator of the World," "Preserver of the Human Race" "the Patron and Father of the Peoples." It was reflected also in the numerous dedications by individual provincial worshippers of a temple, an altar, or a monument, in honour of such Emperors as Caligula, Domitian, or Marcus Aurelius, whom they could never have even seen at any time. From this it was but a slight transition to that religious cult which made divinities of the Emperors themselves. Near Lyons, at the confluence of the Rhone and Saône, sixty tribal federations joined together to consecrate a common shrine to Rome and to Augustus. Though this form of worship was officially established by Augustus, it is a suggestive and interesting fact that the rites near Lyons were served by prominent Gauls who had held office in their own country, and who were publicly thanked for their devotion to the common altar.[8]

This universal deification of the Emperor, with its resulting priesthoods and temples, was far from implying mere servility during the three centuries it lasted. The palace of the prince was almost the only spot in which it could not be found. All Rome elsewhere, and all the Empire beyond it, worshipped him as the embodiment of beneficent institutions, and hence it was that the Christian faith at first incurred the suspicion of political significance. Until the time of Diocletian this worship was spontaneous and sincere, though afterwards it may have degenerated into forms and formulas. In the second century A.D. religion held a far larger place than it ever will again in ordinary life. The outburst of spiritual enthusiasm which built the twelfth and thirteenth century cathedrals is the only parallel to it; and before we despise it we must ask ourselves the value of any substitute with which we may have endeavoured to replace it. In those ages of the early Empire, divinity was immanent everywhere, and superstition was the only alternative. There was "no divine right of kings," but there was a head of the Empire; and the representative of so beneficent an institution, of so world-wide a power, was adored as divine whatever was his personality, as the principle of that authoritative monarchy which filled and satisfied the minds of all men.

Though the "Maison Carrée" had nothing to do with "Caesar-worship," among all the temples in the provinces of the Empire, that erected to Caius and Lucius Caesar at Nîmes is by far the most beautiful that survives, and in the opinion of many it is the finest outside Hellenic territories[9] and one of the most elegant in the Roman world. Small in size, for it is only forty-five feet by eighty-five, the beauty of what must now be called the Maison Carrée depends on its exquisite proportions and tasteful Greek decoration. It is hexastyle, with eleven Corinthian

Roman Temple called the Maison Carrée at Nîmes

columns on each side, three of which stand free and support the portico, the remaining eight being attached to the walls of the cella. Counting the columns at each end there are thirty in all, and the structure is built on what is known as the pseudo-peripteral plan, the true peripteral temple having all the columns separate from the cella, as in the case of all famous Greek temples, except the huge edifice at Agrigentum, in which the interstices of the columns are built up with walls.[10]

The Nîmes building was therefore ordered by Romans, who had definite ideas about the plan they considered appropriate; but it was set up and decorated by a Greek architect of the Augustan Age, who knew how to give the best effect to his work. Mérimée talks a good deal about "the evidences of decadence" which point to the architecture of the Antonines. Proofs of this he selects in unequal spacing of the columns, and unequal number of modillions on opposite sides, and other "irregularities." He made a singularly bad choice. It is just its subtle divergencies from mathematical exactness which make the Parthenon so beautiful and so unapproachable. It is just because the Madeleine in Paris is a strictly mathematical enlargement of the Maison Carrée that the modern building is so dull and unsuccessful.[11] People are apt to think that a straight-lined, symmetrical modern copy of an ancient masterpiece of architecture is likely to reproduce its beauty; and when they find this is not the case, they say the older structure gets an unfair handicap from "the kindly hand of time," "the mellowing finger of antiquity," and so forth. The real causes lie far deeper. Beauty is not a matter of mere lineal reproduction, it is a question of essential differences; of subtle variations, not of machine-made uniformity. Only in 1810 did Cockerell establish the entasis of the columns of the Parthenon. Only in 1851 did H. Penrose publish the *Principles of Athenian Architecture*. The vertical lines of the Parthenon had been supposed to be perpendicular, the horizontal lines to be level, and therefore straight. To discover an exact mathematical ratio in its proportions was the main effort of the archaeologist; that he did not exactly and everywhere succeed was supposed to be rather his fault than that of the Greek. Suddenly Penrose proved that no two capitals were of corresponding size, that the diameters of columns were unequal, that the columns were irregularly spaced, that the metope spaces were of unequal width, that apparently vertical columns lean towards the centre of the building, that the architrave and frieze lean backward, while the pilasters at the angles lean forward, and finally that the main horizontal lines of the building are constructed in curves, which rise in vertical planes, but are never parallel. This means that there was an unquestionable intention of avoiding exact ratios or mathematically exact correspondences wherever such an avoidance was calculated to produce a certain effect. It was also clear that these deviations were not the result of error in the workmen, or of accidents by time or vandalism; for irregularities which would be easily detected or obtrusively conspicuous were avoided and where accuracy was necessary it was so finely achieved that the maximum deviation of the Parthenon in lines intended to correspond (as at the two ends) is as little as the fiftieth part of an inch; while the refinement of joining the masonry is so great that the stones composing the huge steps have actually grown together beneath the pressure of the columns they support. Nor must it be imagined that the intentional differences are large. The columns which lean towards the centre of the building would only meet if prolonged to a height of five thousand eight hundred and fifty-six feet above the pavement.

Though Penrose proved the measurement of those divergencies in the Parthenon, it was John Pennethorne who discovered their existence after he had seen the undoubtedly convex constructive curves in the Theban Temple of Medinet Habou. The same discovery was made concerning the constructional curves of the Maison Carrée by Professor W. H. Goodyear in 1891. That these subtle irregularities should have remained unnoticed, even longer than those of the Parthenon, is not remarkable. The superiority of Greek art implies a superiority in eyesight too. Nowadays we *look* but we very rarely *see*. The effects produced, too, by these variations, tend to obscure the underlying causes. We are pleased without knowing why. We wonder, indeed, that a modern line, reproduced from a Greek line, does not attract us so much as the original. We have not yet realised that this is because modern lines are straight, and the Greek were not. Neither are the lines of the Maison Carrée. Professor Goodyear's measurements establishing this fact were assisted and approved by Eugène Chambaud, architect of the city of Nîmes, and by his colleague A. Augière. These gentlemen have proved that, for example, the curves of the cornice, wholly due to masonry construction, are in horizontal planes convex to the position of the spectator, and measure about five inches; the side walls, in fact, bulge outward to that extent, at about the middle of their highest point, and the stylobate beneath them shows slight corresponding curves.

This was done not merely to give apparently increased dimensions to the building when seen from a point of view facing the centre of either side, but also to give it a life and beauty far superior to the monotonous and cold effects of mathematical exactitude. The line of the horizon, "Nature's great and only horizontal line," is in fact a delicate but not inappreciable curve. The sides of this temple at Nîmes are in fact also delicately, though now not inappreciably, curved, because all curves in plan convex to the line of vision produce an effect of curves in elevation. At an angle of forty-five degrees a curve of five inches in plan, when not perceived by the eye, will produce an effect of five inches curve in elevation. In the Parthenon the curve is under four inches in two hundred and twenty-eight feet. At Nîmes it is nearly five inches in less than a hundred feet. At Medinet Habou it is as much as eight inches in about the same distance. The fact that no curves occur in the entablature of the pediments at Nîmes shows that the side-curves were independent of these, instead of a complement to them, as Penrose considered was the case in the Parthenon, and we have here therefore a case not of deliberately correcting an ordinary optical illusion, but of deliberately creating an optical illusion with a definite purpose.

From Egypt then, from Periclean Athens, and from Roman Nîmes we have traced a definite theory of curves, of divergencies, of differences, which has now been lost, chiefly owing to a division of labour which has lowered the capacity of the individual artisan, and to a machine-made work which has accustomed the eye to inartistic uniformity of ornamental detail, and destroyed its proofs of delicate structural effects. But it was some time before this loss occurred. From Roman buildings the true tradition was handed on to Italo-Byzantine, Byzantine- Romanesque, and Gothic structures, and only fell into abeyance when a Renaissance which forgot the vital principles of classical workmanship reintroduced the barren elements of classical style. But in the cathedrals these curves can still be traced. Mr. Julian Moore has shown that the walls in the nave of Westminster Abbey are bent inwards at about the height of the keystones of the arches and outwards above and below this point, and they are structurally sound unto this day. In the same way the piers and upper walls of the nave of St. Mark's in Venice lean outwards to an extent of eighteen inches, a deviation which, if accidental, or subsequent to their original making, would have ruined the mosaics and destroyed the building. The same divergencies may be seen in the choir of Sant' Ambrogio at Milan, and in Sta. Maria della Pieve at Arezzo. I may perhaps explain the difference as something of the difference between an architectural drawing done with compasses and rulers, and an artist's painting of the same building done with a free hand and with just those "inaccuracies" which give it life and beauty. But I must linger no more upon an essential principle which, known to Greece and known to the builders of the Maison Carrée, is one of the chief reasons why this little temple is the greatest treasure of classical architecture north of the Alps.

Apart from all constructional questions, the detailed carving of the cornice and the frieze is worth the most careful examination, and no one has really seen this temple who has not walked carefully all round it with a pair of field-glasses. Its interior is now used for the housing of a small collection of antiquities, not to be compared with the Museum of Arles, and not so rich in varied detail as that called the Musée Lapidaire in the old Lycée of the Grand' Rue at Nîmes, but still full of interest, and, as I have already said, not half appreciated or understood by its possessors. I shall have to return to its contents later on, so it will be only necessary here to say that the present use of this building is by far the best to which it has been put since the religion for which it was erected passed away.

From 1050, when it was partly disinterred from excrescences of masonry all round it, the temple served as a kind of Hôtel de Ville until 1540. At the latter date a certain Pierre Boys bought it, and lived in it with various architectural arrangements to suit himself. One would imagine that by this time it had been forgotten altogether; so it is refreshing to find that the Intendant of Languedoc actually refused to let the Duchesse d'Uzès buy it to make a family mausoleum. However this refusal can hardly have been based on artistic considerations, for it was eventually bought by Felix Bruyès, Seigneur de St. Chaptes, who made a stable of it, filed away the pillars to give wider passage to his carts, and built haylofts in the roof. Once more the eccentric Intendant of Languedoc puts in official objections; this time to the idea of the Augustinian monks turning it into a church. But they secured permission from a higher court in 1672, and the long-suffering temple became a church, which had probably been its first, though unknown, destination in the early centuries of Christianity. Not content with building chapels, a nave, a choir, and stalls, the monks buried their dead in the vaults beneath the portico, and the building was in this state when the remaining houses still adhering to it were finally cleared away. The Augustinians remained till 1789, when the structure was put to vague municipal uses, and afterwards served as a granary and a public market. But in 1823 it was saved at last. A museum was established in it, dedicated to Her Royal Highness the Duchess of Angoulême. Further clearances have since been made, which give a better view of this exquisite little building; and it may be hoped that it will now be left at rest.

The stones of the solid walls of the cella come from the Sernhac quarries near the Gardon. The bases of the columns are of the same used in the amphitheatre. The columns and entablatures were chosen from yet a third source, beyond the village of Fonsoutre-Gardon, from the quarries at Lens. Originally it formed the central sanctuary of a large covered colonnade, with long lateral porticoes, and buildings for many various purposes behind them.

With the Maison Carrée we have come to an end of all the material traces of Greek life in Provence. The influence of Hellas lived on, however, as long as the Roman Empire lasted; and in what I have now to say of life in Provence under the Roman rule, it will be seen that though I can only illustrate my pages with Roman buildings and with Roman handiwork, the Greek spirit has left traces intangible, yet no less valuable, in many and various directions.

One of these traces is to be found in language, a very different thing from that Hellenistic attitude towards literature and art, which is of more general application. There is a Gallic inscription preserved at Nîmes which not only shows this linguistic survival, but is also appropriate to the chief subject of this chapter, the more ancient of the religions of Provence. It runs as follows:—

... ΑΡΤΑΒ ... ΙΛΛΑΝΟΤΙΑΚΟΣΔΕΔΕ
ΜΑΤΡΕΒΟΝΕΜΑΤΣΙΚΑΒΟ ΒΡΑΤΟΤΔΕ [12]

which means that Karta, of Bedilhan, dedicated this altar to the Mothers of Nîmes by their order. The cult of the Mothers is one well known elsewhere in Gaul, and may perhaps in this instance be connected with that of the "Proxumi," already noticed,[13] as specially favoured by the Arecomicians of Nîmes.[14]

At Arles, of course, the Greek idiom is likely to have lasted much longer than it did elsewhere, and indeed in 540 we find St. Césaire inviting the congregations of the diocese of Arles to sing their anthems in Greek while waiting for the service in church. Two hundred years before that the funeral oration of the younger Constantine was pronounced in Greek before the same population, and something of the beauty of the Arles speech at the present day may perhaps be owing to traces of Hellenic syllables. M. Martin has, for instance, published a long list of Provençal words derived from the Greek, especially those used in the Marseilles district with reference to the sea, and to fishing, and to simple articles of food and of ordinary life.[15]

In matters of Hellenic cultivation, the Gauls were of course still more ready to copy their Roman friends. Having no models of their own, for the Druids left neither temples nor statues, and the cromlechs can hardly be called architecture, the Latinised Gauls sought artistic training where the Romans had found it; and it was to Greece that they looked for types of beauty in the various arts, or of philosophy and scholarship in educational matters. Their local schools were as much a question of voluntary effort as the majority of their local public buildings, and the expense was borne partly by their own rich families and partly from the public funds. This is the true reason why, under the aegis of the Roman Peace, civilisation spread so swiftly and so deeply, upon Greek and Roman models, among the peoples of Southern Gaul, that on the soil of Provence more evidences have survived of what life meant under the Roman Empire than is the case in any other equal space beyond the boundaries of Italy.

As Cicero expressed it, the peoples of Provence had "two fatherlands, one of their birth and the other of their citizenship." With the "Jus Suffragii" went the "Jus Honorum," under the Empire, if the recipient had the "latus clavus." Under Augustus we find already a Spanish consul in Rome. Eventually the provinces supplied the Emperor himself. The "fatherland of birth" had insensibly become merged in the "fatherland of citizenship," and, as is so often noticed in similar cases, the provincials became "more Roman than the Romans." A very similar process, under very similar conditions, is going on in British India at the present day, with the exception that the highest offices are not open to the Hindu.

If the Romans quickly appreciated that Massilia, like their own Campania, was a centre of Hellenism,[16] the Gauls in their turn were not slow to travel across the Alps in the opposite direction, even when their fame had not preceded them. It was from Hellenic motives that, in the Augustan age, a Vocontian historian (Pompeius Trogus) began his history of the world with Alexander the Great, and only included Roman affairs within that Grecian framework of the first "Universal History." It was Gaul which gave Rome her Roscius; and Petronius Arbiter, born near

Marseilles, who gave the world our first romance. Varro Atacinus, from near Carcassonne, and Cornelius Gallus of Fréjus, the friend of Virgil, were not unworthy of their poetic rivals on more classic ground. In oratory the genius of Southern France established itself even more decidedly. Caesar and Cicero themselves were indebted to the rhetoric of Gnipho. Votienus Montanus from Narbonne was called the Ovid of Orators in the late Augustan age. Caligula had two eloquent Gauls among his personal friends: Valerius Asiaticus of Vienne and Gnaeus Domitius Afer of Nîmes, who was consul in 39 A.D. Favorinus, of an esteemed burgess family in Arles, was a Gaul by birth, who wrote in Greek, and was a distinguished scholar in all branches of science under Hadrian. The pupil of Dion of Prusa, the friend of Plutarch and Herodes Atticus, the master of Aulus Gellius, the opponent of Galen in one direction and of Lucian in another, Favorinus was not only an author, a philologist, and a rhetorician, but a philosopher of the sceptical, Aristotelian school, and one of the most brilliant examples of the cultivated man of letters of his time. Marcus Aurelius himself was the pupil of the Gaulish rhetorician Cornelius Fronto.

Under Caesar and Claudius, Gaul had provided Rome with senators; under Caligula with a consul. It was to the Aquitanian, Vindex, that Nero owed his fall; Galba, his supremacy. It was Agricola, the Provençal, who subdued Britain to Domitian.[17] It was Nîmes which gave the Empire one of its best Emperors, Antoninus Pius, who succeeded the two Spaniards, Trajan and Hadrian, and adopted a third in Marcus Aurelius. Caracalla, born in Garil, was Syrian on his mother's side, African on his father's. The spread of civilisation now produced a mixture of races, and a community of ideas, which went far to break down all the conventional barriers of geography. Provence, for instance, became as "Roman" as any spot in Italy. The proofs of this are in the buildings and the inscriptions I shall discuss in the next chapter.

NOTES

1. Preserved at Avignon is an inscription in which Hirschfeld sees the only trace now left of a supreme magistrate of Nîmes (between the fall of Marseilles and the Principate of Augustus), who was still called Praetor of the Arecomician tribe of the Volcae. It runs as follows: T. CARISIUS. PRAETOR. VOLCA. AR. DAT. (T. Carisius, Praetor of the Arecomician tribe of the Volcae)

2. Too much stress has been laid, in this connection, on the passage in Suetonius's life of Claudius, which runs in Holland's translation: "The religion of the Druidae among the Frenchmen, practising horrible and detestable cruelty, and which under Augustus, Romane citizens onely were forbidden to professe and use, he quite put downe and abolished."

3. *E.g.* (1) "Deo Nemauso Valeria Procilla," (Valeria Procilla to the god Nemausus) inscribed on a bronze votive tablet. (2) "Jovi Optimo Maximo Heliopolitano et Nemauso Caius Julius Tiberii fiius Fabia tribu…" (Caius Julius, son of Tiberius of the Fabian tribe, to best and greatest Jupiter of Heliopolis and to Nemausus) inscribed on a votive altar with a sword and buckler carved on one side, and on the other the statue of "Jupiter Heliopolitanus," to whom Antoninus built the gigantic temple at Baalbec, the only known example of such a statue of this god, who was widely worshipped throughout the Empire at the end of the second century A.D. (3) "Jovi et Nemauso Titus Flavius Hermes Exactor Operum Basilicae Marmorarii et Lapidarii votum solvunt," (Titus Flavius Hermes, inspector of the works of the basilica, and the marble-workers and stonemasons fulfil their vows to Jupiter and Nemausus), a votive inscription of thanksgiving from the inspector, and the marble- and stone-workers for the safe erection of buildings at Nîmes in the Augustan period. Inscriptions also occur to Mars, as "Augusto Marti Britovio,'" "Marti Augusto Lacavo." (4) "Laribus Tertius Lesbii Filius Minervae et Nemauso Votum Solvit," on a votive altar to the Lares, Minerva, and Nemausus. (5) "Nemauso Augusto Censor Jugarius …" inscribed on the base of a portico in honour of the fountain-god. In the "Proxumi" we find some special domestic divinities of the Arecomicians, female, and privately worshipped. *e.g.* (6) "Proxumis Suis Cornelia Cupita," (Cornelia Cupita to her closest gods) (7) "Proxumis Bituka Votum Solvit." (Bituka has fulfilled her vow to her closest gods) Other old worships are suggested in (8) "Rufina Lucabus Votum Solvit Libens Merito" (Rufina Lucubus has willingly fulfilled the vow), an altar to the sacred groves, in (9) "Junonibus Montanis Cinnamis Votum Solvit" (Cinnamis has fulfilled the vow to Junos of the hills), an altar to various personifications of Juno of the Hills, sometimes called "Matronae." (10) "Titia Savinis Ornatrix Fecit Hisidi Votum…" inscribed on an altar dedicated by Titia, a lady's maid, to Isis. These are all (except the first) chosen from inscriptions which may be seen at Nîmes, and were published in 1893 by Eugène Germer-Durand. On an epitaph at Nîmes is preserved the fact that Tettia, wife of Marcus Gesicus, was a priestess of Isis; "ISIDIS SACERDOS." One of the most curious of all these religious fragments, and in its way unique, is the monument set up at Nîmes to the Fates by Valerius Tatinus, "in accomplishment of a vow made according to the orders received in a dream": PER SOMNIUM IUSSUS VAL • TAT • PARACABUS • V • S • L • M.

4. The ears are mentioned in the inscriptions, though unknown in other carvings; for Gruter quotes a dedication (lxxxix. 6) "Aurihus Bonae Deae." (To the ears of the Good Goddess) The combination of the cult of the Bona Dea with the Taurobolic offerings appropriate to Mithra is observable at Vence: IDAEAE MATRI VALERIA MARCIANA VALERIA CARMOSINE ET CASSIUS PATERNUS SACERDOS

TAURORIPOLIUM SUO SUMPTU CELEBRAVERUNT. (Valeria Marciana, Valeria Carmosine and the priest Cassius Paternus performed a sacrifice of bulls to the Idaean Mother at their own expense) And at Riez—MATRI DEUM MAGNAEQUE DEAE L. DECIMUS PACATUS ET COELIA SECUNDINA [EIUS OB] SACRUM TAURORUM FECIT. (Decimus Pacatus and Coelia Secundus made a sacrifice of bulls to the Great Goddess, the mother of the gods)

5. By Raphael Royer, 3 Place d'Assas, Nîmes.

6. Compare the famous torso at Vienne, known as the "Vénus Accroupie de Vienne,"evidently a Greek work in Parian marble, naked, and bending forward upon her right leg in the well-known provocatively pudibund attitude. She, too, has more of the human than the divine, and all the charms of the Hetaira are realistically rendered with the same skill of the connoisseur that might have inspired the chubby sirens of a Rubens.

7. The inscription was deciphered, from the holes left by the lost bronze letters, by Séguier, as follows: C. CAESARI AUGUSTI F. COS. DESIGNATO PRINCIPIBUS JUVENTUTIS. (To the Prince of Youth, C. Caesar, son of Augustus. Consul) This dates the occasion of the inscription as A.D. I; but I am not sure that this should be taken as the exact date of the building. To Lucius, of whom there were no doubt once traces in Marseilles, this is the only inscription I know in Nîmes. But of Caius, its patron, there is undoubted trace elsewhere in the inscriptions on a long stone found in 1810 near the amphitheatre, which records: "C. Caesar Augusti filius consul designatus patronus Coloniae Augustae Nemausensium xystum dat." C. Caesar, son of Augustus, Consul-elect, gives the colonnade to the Colony of Nîmes)

8. Some of their names survive: Vecundaridub, the Aeduan, Losidius, the Nervian, and others; and inscriptions record their honours: "C. Servilio Martiano Arverno sacerdoti ad templum Romae et Augustorum tres provinciae Galliae"... "Losidio Quieti filio sacerdoti ad aram Caesaris nostri ad templum Romae et Augusti inter confluentes Araris et Rhodani tres provinciae Galliae." (Three provinces of Gaul... C. Servilius Martianus Avernus priest at the temple of Rome and the Augusti... three provinces of Gaul to Losidius Quies son to the Nervian priest at the altar of our Caesar at the temple of Rome and Augustus netween the Saône and the Rhone) There were also special priests for the temples of the Emperors set up in each provincial city, and these men were each known as "Flamen of Augustus," which is quite distinct from the "Flamen Romae et Augusti," recorded at Nîmes in an inscription. Half a century after the death of Claudius we find a "Flamen Divi Claudii" elsewhere. Though the erection of these temples was fashionable, it was certainly not compulsory, and the freedmen also took their share in these same rites, presided over by six "Seviri Augustales," who held annual office, wore the toga praetextata, and had lictors before them. Many names of these "Seviri" occur in inscriptions at Nîmes.

9. Vienne is, as I have said, outside my district; but it is full of interesting parallels to which I shall have occasion to refer; foremost among them being the beautiful little temple DIVO AUGUSTO OPTIMO MAXIMO ET DIVAE AUGUSTAE, which is almost the same size as the Maison Carrée, being about fifty feet by eighty feet, with six Corinthian columns in front. Though not so fine in detail or proportion, it is more technically Greek in construction than the Nîmes building, for there are six detached columns on each side, and only two pilasters at the end of each side are attached to the cella.

10. The Parthenon, which measures a hundred and one feet across by two hundred and twenty-eight long, has octastyle porticoes, but within them are porticoes of six columns like that of the Maison Carrée. This screen of free columns all round the cella, which is a characteristic of Greek architecture, was probably planned to protect the frescoes on the walls from rain. In Rome the plan was modified. The Ionic temple of Fortuna Virilis in Rome, mutilated as it is, shows clearly the arrangement of six free columns of the porch and the twelve engaged columns round the cella. The Temple of Antoninus and Faustina, also in Rome, which measures seventy-two feet by a hundred and twenty, has six pillars in front of the porch like the Maison Carrée, and ten in all are free, the rest being engaged and looking more like pilasters. Any arguments about the Nîmes style being the product of Antonine art must surely have omitted to take this Roman temple into account.

11. I can only here suggest the elements of a theory that is more fully worked out elsewhere. See chap. vi., *Spirals in Nature and Art.* London: Murray, 1903.

12. This would be Καρτα Βιδιλλανονιακος δεδε Ματρεβο Νεμανσικαβο βρατουδε, being the Greek letters for the Latin form: Karta Bidillanoviacus dedit matribus Nemausicabus ex imperio. (The Karta of Bedilhan dedicated this to the Mothers of Nîmes by their order) The last word in the inscription (as translated by Pictet) is, I confess, new to me, though frequent at Nîmes; but the rest is clear enough.

13. P. 193 *note.*

14. There are other Gaulish inscriptions in the same letters, such as that of Cassitalus (who writes ΚΑϹϹΙΤΑΛΟϹ), and of the altar found in the little chapel of Notre Dame de Laval. But three more Greek inscriptions will be sufficient to quote to show the survival of the language among various races. The first was found on the Avignon road, a mile out of Nîmes, and runs as follows:—

ΘΕΟΙϹ—ΔΑΙΜΟϹΙΝ	Θεοῖς δαίμοσιν	To the Divine Manes
ΙΟΤΛΙΑ ΦΕΙΔΑ	Ἰουλίᾳ φειδᾳ	And to Julia Fida
ΤΙΤΙΑ—ΜΗΤΡΙ	Τιτια μητρὶ	Titia to her
ΓΛΤΚΤΤΑΤΗ	γλυκυτάτῃ	Sweet mother.

The second is of special interest, because, though fragmentary, it evidently refers to another fountain-god, worshipped, as was Nemausus, by the Celts. It was found between Orange and Vaison, and contains (among others) the Greek letters ΓΡΑϹΕΛΟΥ ΒΡΑΤΟΥΔΕ ΚΑΝΤΕΝΑ, which refer to the god of the Spring of Grosel, a source which has many affinities with that of Vaucluse. At Marseilles the signboard of a grammarian who taught Latin to the Greeks long before Augustus's reign has been discovered: ΑΘΗΝΑΔΗϹ ΔΙΟϹΚΟΡΙΔΟΥ ΓΡΑΜ ΜΑΤΙΚΟϹ ΡΩΜΑΙΚΟϹ. For many generations such Greek names survived as Eupor, Nice, Athenais, Hellas, Attica; such funereal greetings as ΘΕΟΙϹ, or Εὔπλοὶ, or the letter Θ, the beginning of the name of Death. Gaulish inscriptions, it should be noted, use Latin characters in the north and centre of France, but Greek letters in the south. The third and last example I need give is as follows: ϹΕΓΟΜΑΡΟϹ ΟΥΙΛΛΟΝΕΟϹ ΤΟΟΥΤΙΟΥϹ ΝΑΜΑΥΚΑΤΙϹ ΕΙΩΡΟΥ ΒΗΛΗϹΑΜΙ ϹΟϹΙΝ ΝΕΜΗΤΟΝ, in which the word "Nemetum" for a sacred place is to be especially noticed. The words are "Segomaros Villoneos, magistratus Nemausensis, effecit Belisemae hocce fanum."

15. Such as:—

	Provençal	Greek
Bread	artoun	ἄρτος.
Gluttonous	boufaire	βουφάγος.
Basket	canasto	κάναστρον.
Axe	destraou	δεξτραλιον.
Small boat	esquifou	σκάφη.
Foolish	matou	μάταιος
Hearth or home	oustaou	ἑστία.

I have not mentioned the evidence of the language of the New Testament, but it should be added that all official letters to the Bishops of Gaul were written in Greek; that the responses in the liturgy were for long written in both languages; and that the indestructible traces of this remain in such French religious words as hymne, psaume, liturgie, homélie, catéchisme, baptême, prêtre, évêque, église, and others.

16. It may be noted that the coins of Nîmes in the Augustan period show the Crocodile of Egypt and the Alexandrian numbering of the years, which is not solely to be put down to the settlement of Alexandrian veterans in Nemausus, but also to the fact that the city itself showed no inveterate opposition to the Hellenism traditional in Marseilles.

17. Enthusiastic Provençal poets have explained to me that this was the first of three victories over perfidious Albion. For if Agricola conquered Britain, so did William the Conqueror, the son of Arlette; and who, they ask, was Arlette but a girl of Arles? And then what about the Prince of Orange already mentioned?

Chapter VIII

Life Under the Roman Emperors

Part I: Above Ground

"...Aedificemus civitates istas; et vallemus muris;
et roboremus turribus et portis
et seris donec a bellis quieta sunt omnia..."

(Let us build these cities and fortify them with towers
and gates and bars until all is at peace
and free from war...)

"...Et erit fortitudo eorum in direptionem,
et domus eorum in desertum;
et aedificabunt domos, et non habitabunt..."

(And their strength will be ravaged
and their house deserted; and they will build houses
and they will not live in them)

To step from Greece to Rome, in Arles, it is only necessary to walk from the theatre to the "Arènes." The one is the flower of that Greek culture which had its nearest centre in Marseilles; the other is the symbol of those public pleasures which were the hall-mark of the Roman Empire; of those buildings, erected for amusement only, which have long outlasted subsequent edifices that owed their origin to the religious beliefs, to the municipal energies, or to the private necessities of a society less broadly based, less proudly conscious of its eternal significance and merit. Rome has no greater relics of her glorious antiquity than the

Coliseum and the Baths of Caracalla. Beside them the remnants of the Forum, of the temples, of the triumphal arches, fade into insignificance. In the same way, it is the amphitheatre that bulks still the largest both at Arles and Nîmes, as it does still at Fréjus, at Verona, at Pompeii, at Pozzoli, at Capua. In all these places you may read, in those now silent stones, the story of a lustful Roman mob. It is not always a pleasant story; but some of it we may profitably listen to in these pages.

The reason for these enormous public pleasure-places is very like the reason for the beauty of the Gothic cathedrals. The ordinary middle-class population of the thirteenth century lived under circumstances of restraint and poverty; the poor, in surroundings of the most abject squalor; only the richest, the strongest, the very few had habitable and spacious homes. There was no middle term between the palace and the hovel. And as the cathedral was the poor man's palace, the one building which opened wide its doors to every Christian of the lowliest degree; and closed them to the sinner of the highest; so the amphitheatres were among the few buildings in which pauper and patrician of the Roman Empire might enjoy themselves together, over the brutalities of the spectacle which appealed to both. The days had long passed when citizens, absorbed in wars or politics, found their common meeting-place in the Forum. With the accession of Augustus neither of these things remained attractive to the multitude. Peace abroad was accompanied by apathy concerning local issues. The loss of public liberty was lightly masked in the vast increase of individual freedom for dissipation. Already Julius Caesar[1] had realised that the chief preoccupation of the Dictator would be to feed the people and keep them amused. Every Emperor after him remembered it. At length it might fairly have been imagined that the Roman only left the luxurious idleness of his public bath to enjoy the carnage or the debauchery of his public pleasure-houses.

The Roman ruins in Provence nearly all owe their origins to this deliberate programme of "Panem et Circenses." The magnificent baths at Nîmes, the amphitheatres both there and at Arles, the "spina" of the Roman circus, the theatre we have just been visiting at Orange, are but indications of a luxury of life that has departed from all but individual existences today. The theatre, the circus, and the palaestra the Hellenic world had known. But the amphitheatre was distinctively Roman; and as it is in the Coliseum that you may best realise the meaning of imperial Rome, so it is in the similar and more perfect buildings at Nîmes and Arles that you will best imagine what life meant in the provinces under the Roman Emperors. Their type remains the same in all. Only the dimensions vary. The Coliseum's walls were over fifty metres thick all round its huge arena, and within their massive stone recesses, below the public corridors, were vast caves for the wild beasts, the prisoners, the countless servants, and the gladiators. More than ninety thousand persons could sit upon its stone and marble benches at each performance; and it was always full, for it gave the most pompous and the most cruel tragedies ever seen in the world, in which the blood that flowed was real, the men and beasts and women really died, the game of public murder went on as merrily and as continuously as the prattle of our pantomimes at Christmas. For four centuries the world was ransacked "to make a Roman holiday." Whole populations, taken prisoner, were butchered for the delectation of society. Whole nations were ground down with taxes to provide extravagantly gorgeous details for the spectacle. Whole tracts of country were laid waste to supply the animals that furnished jaded epicures with novel forms of death, or fiercer appetite for carnage. Unequal combats were not enough. Defenceless families were cast to the lions to be publicly devoured, on the excuse of having professed a religion that was considered politically dangerous.

It is difficult to believe all this even among the sinister shadows of the Coliseum. At Arles it seems impossible. Yet the fashions of Rome were the fashions of the provinces; the difference was in quantities alone; and there was not a fragment of that huge building where the public circulated which was not in some way given up to the gratification of their passions—sometimes the vilest. After a brilliant sketch of what went on in Rome, Montaigne (III. vi.) concludes that men in his own time were far less virile, less inventive, than in those hot-blooded, breeding days, when the fertility of invention was only equalled by the unbridled extravagance in execution which attended it.

Did they wish to represent a hunting of wild beasts, they tore up huge trees by the roots and planted them in the centre of the arena, filling this quick-grown forest with a thousand ostriches, a thousand stags, a thousand fallow-deer, a thousand wild boars. The next day showed a massacre of a hundred lions and lionesses, two hundred leopards, and three hundred bears. By the younger Gordian, searching for unknown delights, two score of zebras were brought over, ten elks, and as many giraffes, together with thirty African hyaenas, and ten Indian tigers. Among them moved the savage bulk of the hippotamus and rhinoceros; and the patient unwieldiness of two-and-thirty elephants. While all these were being slaughtered, nothing was omitted that might delight the other senses of the cloyed spectators. An ample canopy protected them from sun or rain, yet left the free air of the sky to ventilate that seething crater of fresh bloodshed. Fountains played among the marble columns, scented with aromatic herbs. The nets that guarded the audience from the frantic struggles of the beasts in the arena were made of gold and silver wire. The porticoes were gilded. The cord that divided the various ranks of spectators from each other was studded with precious stones. The walls were clad in marble; the pavements shone with multicoloured mosaics. And it is thus we must imagine the first century of the amphitheatre at Arles.[2]

Under Domitian, though the games began soon after the rising of the sun, the day was not long enough for the troops of African, Thracian, and German gladiators to finish all their combats. Line upon line of torches rose in flaming circles from the arena to the topmost tier of stone, to light up the scenes of bloodshed that went on far into the night, while the populace were fed (and even clothed) without leaving the huge building. St. Jerome, in his chronicle of Eusebius, speaks of three whole days and nights having been passed in this way on one

The Amphitheatre of Arles as Originally Built
(Reconstructed by Jacques Peytret)

occasion. During the celebration of the triumph of Aurelian over the Queen of Palmyra, the forum, the streets, the shops, and houses of Rome were deserted. The whole population was in the public pleasure-buildings. Arles at its height of splendour, when a Roman Emperor lived in his palace within her walls, must have sometimes seen sights like this. To the sound of the long trumpets, the combats of the gladiators closed. After them came the boxers. Whole processions of victorious soldiers would celebrate their triumphs by marching through the arena in full armour to the plaudits of the multitude. Then two animals, of different kinds, but bound together by a chain, would be thrust out upon the sand to fight each other, or to be attacked by various weapons. The corpses were dragged out, one after another, by the busy hooks, and there was scarcely any pause between one item of the entertainment and the next. Even the edicts of the Christian Constantine could not wholly eradicate a passion so deeply seated in the Roman heart; and Honorius, when the Goths were beating at the gates of Italy, only exchanged the amphitheatre for more effeminate and just as inexcusable amusements. Professionalism in football is rapidly developing the same proportion of lazy and insatiable spectators in England. Already the difference between it and the gladiatorial games is rather in favour of the Romans.[3]

I have already said that the Greek theatre in Arles was built during the short period of the governorship of Decimus Junius Brutus, which gave its Greek inhabitants time to set up their characteristically national monument. But by 48 B.C. the definitely Roman "colonisation" of Arles was provided for by Julius Caesar, who sent Tiberius Nero with the veterans of the sixth legion, at first to hold the military position, and then by that process of civilisation already described, to give the population every opportunity of thoroughly Romanising themselves. These necessities prescribed the order of the public buildings which soon sprang up, and their position may roughly be realised by looking at any good map of the town.

Modern Arles is shaped like a right-angled triangle, St. Honorat des Alyscamps being at the right angle to the south-east, while the longest side follows the left bank of the Rhone. Roman Arles was much smaller, in the shape of an irregular pentagon, the western angle of the river-wall beginning more than a hundred yards higher up stream than the present Pont de Trinquetaille, and only extending about four hundred metres up the Rhone along the Quai de la Gare,

Ruins of the Roman Amphitheatre (Exterior) at Arles (1903)

the "Pons Navalis" being outside its northern angle. From that northern angle the Roman walls moved south-east to the arena, then went on towards the Route d'Avignon, turning sharply southwards round Notre Dame la Major, which was the Roman temple to the Bona Dea. From this eastern angle, the southerly line past the "Porta Romana" to the angle tower at the extreme south-east can still be traced, on the opposite side of the road to the cemetery.

The south-eastern angle was formed by the Roman temple of Diana, and is still marked by a ruined tower near the old abbey of St. Césaire, from which the walls passed westward to the south side of the Greek theatre, and from there in a straight line past the Porta Pretoria (or "Aquaria") to the south-eastern angle, which was close to the present Place du Marché Neuf. From this angle the walls went straight north to the river bank. They were two metres twenty-five thick, made of small and easily worked stones.

The Celtic settlement of Arlath began at about the point of the present bridge, while the docks and the circus were still further down stream, close to the river bank.

It may be well to say that the obelisk now set up in the centre of the Place de la République, opposite the western door of St. Trophime, was originally discovered near the Rhone in 1389, among the ruins of the Roman circus, of which it formed the "spina."

Fifteen metres in height, without the base, it is the only granite monolith from European quarries which can compare in size with the obelisks of Egypt, and it was brought from the gorges of the Esterels. Left for a long time with only its extremity emerging from the soil of a private garden, it was dug out during the visit of Catherine de Medicis and Charles IX, and Henri IV jovially suggested that it should be planted in the middle of the amphitheatre. At last MM. de Boche, Romany, Agard, and Maure, consuls of the town, raised it on the masts of eight stout sailing barques, to the sound of trumpets and firing of cannon, and it was solemnly dedicated to Louis XIV, with a globe of azure on the top and a disc to represent the Roi Soleil; the whole was rested on a pedestal inscribed with fulsome compliments to the monarch, which are now only preserved in the antiquarian volumes of his reign. This was replaced by four bronze representations of the Lion of Arles early in the nineteenth century, and by these appropriate emblems it is still upheld.

Within the first Roman walls of Arles the public offices and barracks were placed to the north, near the river; and the huge space needed for the amphitheatre was only obtained, about the middle of the northern line, by incorporating about a hundred metres of the wall built by Caesar's soldiers within the substructure of the vast arena reared at the end of the reign of Augustus, who built a temple in Arles during a two years' visit to Provence which he divided between this city, Fréjus, and Aix. The principal axis of the oval arena does not go from east to west as was thought usual, but from north to south; and its slight deviation to the west of north was no doubt arranged, not only to take advantage of the old town-walls,

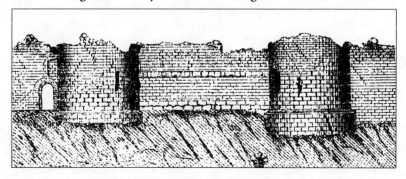

Ruins of the Porta Romana at Arles

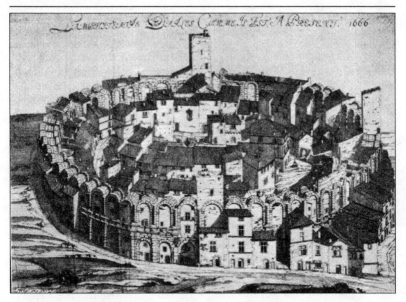

The Roman Amphitheatre at Arles as it appeared in 1666

but also to make a correct alignment with the head of the Roman bridge across the river to the Camargue, the exact point also reached by the great road from Milan across the Cottian Alps, upon which (near the same spot) rose the famous arch called "Admirable," of which I have spoken elsewhere.

The increase of palaces and of public buildings within a restrained area soon necessitated the migration of many of the manufacturing classes and business men across the river to the island of the Camargue, on much the same spot where now is the Faubourg of Trinquetaille. Here, favoured by both branches of the river, by two bridges which took the road across the Rhone from Arles to Nîmes, by a long extent of docks and quays, and by the protection of the fortifications so near at hand, the business-suburb flourished exceedingly. Thus did Arles, the double city, "duplex Arelata," live within her towers and ramparts on the double Rhone, for more than two centuries, until Gallus, on the Ides of October, 254 A.D., celebrated the peacemaking with the Goths by magnificent entertainments in the amphitheatre.

The building was worthy both of that and of its many previous triumphs. By the middle of the third century Arles had already heard the warning of her fall. One last aftermath of splendour, one Indian summer, she was still to see before she fell. And she enjoyed life to the full while she had it. Her amphitheatre held places for thirty thousand persons. In Italy only Pozzoli, Capua, and the Coliseum held more; only Poitiers, in France.[4] It covered a space of over eleven thousand square metres, having a large diameter of one hundred and thirty-six metres, and the smaller one of one hundred and seven. From north to south the thickness of the walls from outside to the line of the arena is thirty-three and a half metres, and a trifle more from east to west (across the short axis) in order to give space for arranging the chief places. The arena today has two thousand one hundred and sixty-six square metres of free surface, and is sixty-nine metres long, but that space was not wholly available when it was in full use in the first century of its construction, soon after the death of Augustus, a date which is also suggested by the noble sobriety of design, the absence of trivial ornament, and the trabeated archways of the grand gallery, one instance among many of that just eye for proportion and correct appreciation of massive values which was the privilege of the early builders of the first century A.D., when the true principles of Greek construction had not yet been lost.

Of the founders and the date of the foundation no documentary evidence exists. The only inscription that can refer to structural work is the fragmentary letters which record that C. Junius Priscus paid two hundred thousand sesterces (about £1500) for the restoration of certain arches and stairways.[5]

The amphitheatre of Arles may be considered as an immense polygon with sixty sides formed by projecting pilasters. Upon vast substructures, which are continued throughout the whole space covered by the building, rises a stage of Doric architecture, above which is another tier of arches with Ionic columns. The square towers now to be seen over the main entrances are of course later, mediaeval constructions, set up when the place was used as a fortress long after the days of the Saracens. The attic story, also of Ionic architecture, and probably a reduced copy of that still visible at the summit of the Coliseum, has disappeared from the Arles building, partly owing to its continued use as projectiles against an attacking enemy beneath, partly owing to deliberate destruction in order to give room for those battlements dear to the heart of the mediaeval military architect. But there is no doubt that this attic existed to hold up the great awning, and there are traces of steps which went up to the highest tier of seats, now vanished, in which the spectators were the only ones who had their backs against the actual outside wall.

There are twenty-four great staircases and twelve passages leading to the seats of the patricians, alternating with sixteen other passages that lead to the higher places. The thirty-seven tiers of seats were probably divided into four divisions, the lowest, for the patricians, containing four ranks; the next, for the knights, with ten; eleven more for the freedmen; and the uppermost twelve for slaves and common people. The most perfect of these now remaining are the four lowest, with their larger seats slightly divided one from the other, just above the podium, or arena-wall. Beyond these are also traces of the balteus which divided the senators from the knights, especially on the west side, on the right of the Imperial box, which was placed at this extremity of the short axis to secure a perfect view, and probably extended straight back from the parapet of the arena to the balteus of the knights behind. Opposite to it was the box for local magistrates, also with its own special entrance and other constructive conveniences. No doubt the Imperial box had also a private way of communication direct from the palace in the town behind it.

I have reproduced various views of this remarkable building, and among them I would draw particular attention to the extraordinary engraving made in 1666. Among the views of the outside and inside of the amphitheatre, I have tried to include a series which would show its various aspects as the centuries progressed; its new original, its seventeenth-century debasement into a mass of houses, its present noble ruins. As is so often the case in ancient buildings, which have preserved even in their dilapidation a charm which modern exactitude can never reach, this amphitheatre is even more full of mathematical irregularities than we found to be the case in the Maison Carrée, for there is hardly a single one of the external round arches which is of the same height or width as its neighbour.

This arena was never flooded with water for the presentment of those mimic naval battles which were frequently the joy of Rome. The crowds of horsemen and charioteers who so often began the day's entertainment were gathered in the great corridors on each side of the north and south doors. The gladiators waited at one or other of the side entrances. The wild beasts and those who fought with them were collected in the great passages beneath the arena. At the signal of the Emperor, or the chief magistrate present, the trumpet would be blown to call each of these various troops of men and beasts from their own

Ruins of the Roman Amphitheatre (Interior) at Arles (1903)

quarter, and to the roar of thirty thousand voices they marched in to fight and die. The sound of that applause seems still to echo in the silent building when the shadows fall in a clear line across its white stone seats from the burning blue above. It is a sound that was in my ears whenever I entered the amphitheatre—a cruel roar of lusty encouragement as the fighting lines drew close a sudden hush as in some separate corner of the arena a death-struggle went on: the shout of partisans from this side and from that, the deep-drawn sob of agony from some strong man, wounded to the death, the scream of tenderer victims as they felt the sullen stroke of steel or claw… It is all over now; but the place is as full of ghosts as some great battlefield, and must have claimed, ere all was done, as many dead and wounded.

Some few details of the gladiators who fought here I have reproduced on p.153. But this is the right place for the inscription set up to his favourite pupil by Olympus, the captain of the gladiatorial team at Arles. It runs as follows: L • GRANIO L • FILIO TERETINA ROMANO M • JUL • OLYMPUS NEGOTIATOR FAMILIAE GLADIATORIAE OB MERIT • L • GRANII VICTORIS AVI EIUS MERENTI POSUIT. (M. Julius Olympus, manager of the company of gladiators, set this up for L. Granius, son of Lucius, of the Terentine tribe, from Rome, who deserves it because of the merit of his victorious grandfather L. Granius)

Exterior of the Roman Amphitheatre at Nîmes

Traces are also to be found at Arles of the place allotted in the amphitheatre to various persons. Near the Imperial box was carved the inscription reserving places for the trumpets: "Chororum Tibicinarum Gradus." Opposite were placed the rhetors: "Loca Scholasticorum." In other parts of the building are certain seats set apart for citizens who had merited this distinction by some public service: "Loca data decreto Decurionum XXX." An actual ticket of admission, found among the débris, was preserved by M de Romieu, with the words: "CAV. II. CUN. V. GRAD. X. GLAD. VELA," which not only mark out the seat with minute exactness, but even promise that it shall be shaded by the "vela," or awning, which was spread from the now vanished attic story

At Nîmes, where inscriptions have been far more carefully preserved than at Arles, these traces of the various arrangements made for the amphitheatre are more numerous. The epitaph exists of C. Veratius Trophimus "curator ludorum," one of the "managers" of the games. In the ruins of the arena were found inscriptions reserving twenty-five places for the boatmen of the Ardèche and the Ouvèze; and forty seats for the boatmen of the Rhone and the Saône.[6] These are carved on three long stones five and a half metres long in all, found at the foot of the north-western wall of the arena boundary. Ball games are also known to have been played, for the word SPHAERISTERIA has also been discovered.

The amphitheatre at Nîmes is not so large as that at Arles, nor has the original work in its interior been so well preserved, though the whole has been far more fully restored, and many of the topmost rows of seats remain intact, showing that there was no attic story in the original building. The exterior, which is in a far better state of preservation, and still shows the fine cornice which finished off the skyline, was composed of two superimposed arcades of sixty arches, with square pilasters on the ground-tier, and engaged Doric columns above them. The consoles and holes that received the masts to hold the awning may still be traced round the top, but the circle in which they occur is not large enough to be dignified with the appellation of a separate story. The vela had to be there, and the arrangements to support it were added to the second tier of archways, helping to emphasise the bold shadows thrown by the cornice. There are traces of sculpture here and there. Two bulls' forequarters are placed above the north entrance, and there are also carvings of two gladiators, and of the Roman wolf. Only the ornaments of the western division were finished off, the remainder being left in roughly blocked-out stone.

As was the case at Arles, this building has suffered more from man's brutality than by the ravages of time. It has been a fortress. It has been filled up with earth. It has been crowded with mean houses. There has even been a church in its upper gallery, which bricked up two of the archways, and the little Romanesque window with its twisted column may still be seen among the huge masonry of pagan Rome: The whole building measures over three hundred and sixty-four metres all round the outside, and the cornice at the top is over twenty-one metres from the ground. There are five concentric galleries in the thickness of the great circular walls, which unite the passages at various stages, and are themselves approached by massive staircases.

The breaking of the long sweeping curve of the entablature over every column is, to my mind, a defect in design when compared with the magnificent effect of these unbroken, flowing lines on the outside of the Coliseum at Rome. Like the amphitheatre at Arles, and most of the other great Roman buildings, this huge arena is constructed of massive materials, built without cement, and bound together with solid stone lintels and arches. The stones were quarried at Barutel, seven kilometres from Nîmes, on the Alais road, and are frequently a cubic metre in size. The letters "T. Crispius Reburrus fecit," found in the débris of the arena, may possibly refer to the original architect, whose plans are now being very considerably modified by the restoration of the monument which has steadily been going on since Revoil began it in 1858. It will soon be completely ready for spectators again, and it is often as crowded as that at Arles, though it never looks so picturesque, on the occasion of what are known as "bull-fights" in Provence. Some authorities consider that water could be introduced into this arena for "naval" displays, and that the walls of the podium were too low to admit of the larger wild beasts in the arena, though the teeth of wolves and wild boars and the antlers of stags have been found among the débris. But both these conclusions lack precise proof. The only thing that can probably be said is that the building is later than that at Arles, and may date from about 100 A.D. Its thirty-four rows of seats are divided, in the same way, into four tiers for the senators: ten for the knights, ten for the freedmen; and ten for the slaves and menials. And, as is the case with all these constructions, the rapidity with which the whole audience could either enter or leave the building is one of its most remarkable features. It may be better appreciated and understood by an examination of the excellent models of the arenas of Nîmes and Arles, and of the Coliseum in the town museum.

I first saw the amphitheatre at Nîmes by moonlight on one of those perfect spring nights of April in Provence. The arches, as we approached it, showed like giant eyebrows over darkened eyes that peered out of abysses of the past. Within, the shadows lay deep-blue upon the long stone seats. Ringed round by that gigantic cup of masonry, all white and grey, the sky itself, with all its ancient constellations, was the one external thing that we could see; the one thing, too, that was unchanged as long, and had a longer life, than that ellipse of stone which was the moment's perfect microcosm. Beyond those walls the life of old Rome might still be stirring in its sleep for all we knew. Here, and on the same spot at Arles, you may put back the hands of Time. His wings are motionless; his scythe is stayed. When Rome fell, it seems, his task was done. There was no more to chronicle.

At Fréjus there are far more dilapidated ruins of an amphitheatre which was once almost as large as that of Nîmes, for its external length

Interior of the Amphitheatre at Nîmes (1903)

was nearly one hundred and fourteen metres, by over eighty-two metres broad, and the arena measured sixty-seven metres by thirty-nine; but there could only have been seating accommodation for some ten thousand spectators. All the Roman public buildings at Fréjus are built in the same way, of the same materials, and in rather smaller stones than usual, without a trace of ornament.

By Tacitus, who was associated with it as the birthplace of his father-in-law, Agricola, Fréjus was called "Claustra Maris." To Caesar it was "Claustra Galliae"; and its western gate still bears the title of the "Porte des Gaules." It was the "Caput," or place of measurement for that section of the Via Aurelia which ended at Arles, having started from Rome to Vada Volaterrana, and so by way of the Var to Forum Julii, keeping along the coast almost the whole way from Rome to Arles. Like pearls along that route, the flourishing seaboard and inland towns were threaded. Cannes and Antibes had theatres like Fréjus; Clausonne and Vallauris had their aqueducts as well; Vence and Grasse, their temples to the twelve great gods. But in her best days Fréjus was the equal, if not the superior, of them all; and among her many Roman ruins, that of the amphitheatre remains the most imposing. Some ancient walls and towers were pulled down when the Route d'Italie was laid out, which comes from the west straight into the Place des Herbes, and there turns to the north-east. The first Roman construction just outside the town, west of the Église St. François and the Place Agricola, is the semicircular bastion with a tower at each end of its diameter of fifty-five metres, known as the "Porte des Gaules," near the station. After this the Roman wall continued west by north, along the bottom of the sloping ground, to the amphitheatre, which is clearly visible from the railway, on the east or left bank of the Reyran; and, like that of Arles, was built at an angle of the city walls; but its north-eastern corner is supported by a slight hill which avoided the necessity for substructures to hold up the lowest rows of seats at that point, though it also necessitated a certain clumsiness of construction which lessens the perfection of the building. The view from the Butte du Moulin à Vent, just above the amphitheatre, is particularly beautiful, and gives a good idea of how much larger and more important was the Roman Fréjus than the modern town, and how different were the geographical conditions of two thousand years ago.

Nearly two kilometres to the north-east from the amphitheatre are the ruins of the theatre, and no doubt the patrician quarter of the Roman town lay between them. The walls, however, went further north than the theatre, and follow the lines of a rocky hill until they turn south and east again towards the point where the arches of the aqueduct (eighteen metres high) enter their enclosure close to the "Porte Romaine," and the line of the modern "Grande Route d'Italie." As soon as the aqueduct had reached this point, the water was carried along the same line as the ramparts we have just passed, which thus served a double purpose. The meeting of these two constructions is still distinctly traceable near the Porte Romaine, and is a most imposing mass of solid masonry and lofty arches. The furthest point east to which the old walls extended was the platform above the hill to the south-east of the Porte Romaine, and it should be remembered that the sea washed the base of this hill two thousand years ago, and that the coastline went south from there to the east of the Chapelle St. Roch. Within the platform are certain subterranean constructions, difficult of access, which were probably huge cisterns or reservoirs, like those of the famous Abbey of Vézelay. The pattern of the external brickwork is especially noticeable.

The "Porte Dorée," just north of the railway-line, and at the south-eastern corner of the modern town, is more carefully built than anything in Fréjus, and originally formed part of far larger constructions on the same spot. It is one of the most remarkable relics of antiquity on the Riviera. From this gate the fortifications extended to cover the Butte St. Antoine southwards, and at least as far as the Tower called "La Lanterne" to the east, which was the landmark of the Roman harbour, and is just south of the railway-line. Within that harbour, now almost completely dry land, Augustus moored the ships he took from Antony at the battle of Actium, and desired to add the title of "Navale Augusti" to that of "Forum Julii." Just what we saw had happened at the mouths of the Rhone has happened again here in the valley of the Reyran and the Argens, which have filled up the old coastline with alluvial deposits and driven back the sea. In vain was Fréjus made a naval headquarters in 1555. By 1663 its port was already dangerous even for light barques of just over fifty tons. In 1704 it had become little more than a pestilential swamp that had lost communication with the sea. A demand made in 1847 for the excavation of the old harbour was followed in 1859 by its complete disappearance beneath the embankments of the railway from Toulon to Nice, and its locomotives are now rolling to and fro where once the galleys of Antony were moored. Fréjus had suffered the fate of Ravenna, of Ostia, of Narbonne, of Aigues-Mortes.

I have already spoken of the defection of Lepidus at the bridge over the Argens, and I need only add that this historic stream rises close to Tegulata (La Grande Pégière) on the victorious battlefield of Marius. The gulf through which it reached the sea was once fifteen kilometres further up the valley, and even in Roman times the port was not on the sea itself but on the salt lagoon, which has now in turn been filled up, and which was not entirely healthy even in classical days, if the tomb of C. Vibius Ligur (see p.88) may be taken as an indication.

In considering the possibilities of the Roman port, the light weight and small size of Roman warships must of course be realised. They were nearly always pulled out of the water at night: "Trahuntque siccas machinae carinas." The legionaries fought on them with military tactics that savoured very little of nautical evolutions. Fleets were only a disagreeable necessity imposed by a long coastline; and it was as the naval arsenal of the Narbonnaise that Fréjus was added to her elder sisters at Misenum and Ravenna.[7] She rapidly rose to importance as a civil and military colony, though never of very large size; and her buildings are a most remarkable evidence of the rapidity and uniformity with which the official stamp could be put upon a colony by the use of masses of men, easily-worked material (very different to the huge blocks at Nîmes and Arles), and simple processes of structure, in which every natural advantage in the way of rocks or hills was promptly seized upon, covered with bricks and worked into the plan. Judging from the amphitheatre and the walls there could never have been more than thirty thousand in the Roman population.

The ruins on the Butte St. Antoine are especially worth visiting, just south of the canal, and to the east as you go out of the railway station; and the remains of the high lighthouse, which was copied from the famous Pharos at Alexandria, are a particularly imposing type of the careful and solidly-built constructions with which the Roman port was guarded, and in which arms or provisions for the fleet were stored. These are the only buildings (with the mole and the quays) which are quite different from any other constructions in the Roman provinces. They stamp its essential naval character on the town. But it is the aqueduct which, to my mind, is one of the most interesting things to trace along the valley of the Reyran, as its arches stride across the country bringing water to Fréjus from Siagnole, fifty kilometres away. Here and there all traces of it disappear; suddenly you come upon gigantic masses of masonry again; and each surviving section has its own name among the peasants: Arcs Serraillier, Arcs Bérenguier, Arcs de Gargalon, Arcs Bouteillière (the best of all), Arcs Escoffier (which are double, as are those called Sénequier), Arcs de Grisolle, and several more. I can conceive no more interesting journey than one, with a good guide, which follows the whole line of these arches on their way from the Siagne. The different modes of construction employed to meet the various difficulties of the route, and keep the water at the right level, are a revelation of Roman persistence and ingenuity, which thought as little of piercing mountains as of bridging valleys.

For the finest Roman aqueduct, not only of Provence, but of the world, we must return, however, to Nîmes; for the famous Pont du Gard is certainly the most impressive construction in this or any other district. It is situated in a beautiful gorge of the valley of the Roman river Gardon, rather more than twenty kilometres out of Nîmes, and can be reached by carriage along the Avignon road, or by train to Lafoux, which is about half an hour's distance on foot through interesting country.

This colossal piece of engineering was built more than nineteen hundred years ago, and still remains as gigantic and as enduring as when it brought the spring-water of the Eure from Uzès to the Roman baths and public buildings of Nemausus. Its solid yet elegant arches span the whole ravine with masonry that rises from the bed of the stream to the lip of the hills on either side, a height of one hundred and sixty feet. The lowest tier of six arches, which span the river like a bridge, are built with four distinct courses in the breadth of the structure. They support a second row of eleven arches, which in their turn hold up the highest tier of thirty-five small arches, eight hundred and eighty-two feet in length, upon which the actual conduit is laid. All three tiers are built of enormous blocks of stone from a neighbouring quarry, fitted without cement, and the two upper arcades have three courses in the breadth of their structure. The waterway is five feet high and two feet wide, lined with strong Roman cement that is still sound and good, and covered with immense flagstones, which the Goths themselves were unable to carry away. The calcareous deposit of the water left so thick a layer in the channel, after many centuries of use, that many houses near are built of thirty centimetres of sediment found in it, and the village church of Bezonce was entirely constructed out of it.

It must have been chiefly with the idea of cleaning out this conduit when necessary that projecting blocks of masonry were left on the flanks and under the arches to hold up any scaffolding that might be required; and it is no trifling indication of the builder's faith in the eternal duration of the Roman Empire that he should have made such careful provision for the repairing of a structure so titanic in its proportions and its strength. The name "Veranius," placed within the eighth arch (counting from the right bank) of the second tier, is probably that of the architect. The carving, which is called "Le Lièvre du Pont du Gard," is probably not a hare at all, but very possibly represents one of the same symbols of nature-worship which are to be found in the amphitheatre. There is also an inscription at Nîmes which may refer to an early example of those guilds of bridge-builders, of which I shall have more to say at Avignon; but it is more likely to be one of the many altars set up by the gratitude of classical antiquity for springs of good fresh water.[8]

Those who recall the aqueducts of the Campagna will remember that those lines of brick arches are devoid either of ornament or of architectural design, in spite of that quality of impressiveness which they retain in common with all Roman work of the kind. Roman engineering was as free from the transitional element as it was from all the affectation of style which occasionally weakened their public buildings of a different class. The engineers knew what they wanted, and they went directly for it, achieving their purpose with a massive simplicity of strength and fitness which gives attractiveness even to the wonderful substructures of the Appian Way. In such an aqueduct as the Pont du Gard this quality is especially conspicuous. The three tiers of arches, as Fergusson points out, produce the same effect as an entablature and cornice upon a long range of columns, with the additional and stupendous feature that the whole structure spreads out wider and wider as it rises in height from its foundation. The full beauty of the work is therefore only appreciable from a little distance down the valley where the sloping hills above the stream add their supporting lines to a picture which combines the majesty of nature with the daring skill of man. From here you realise how the Roman converted a merely utilitarian structure into an architectural screen of unrivalled beauty without the introduction of a single ornament or a single useless feature. A comparison with the double tiers of the aqueducts at Segovia or Tarragona, or with the single arches of the Bridge of Trajan at Alcantara, will bring out the architectural supremacy of the Pont du Gard by comparison with the best works of the kind. By such buildings as this did the Romans acquire the constructive skill and magnificence of proportion which enabled them fearlessly to plan buildings so vast in size, and to vault spaces so huge, that the impress of their maker's power has lasted while the rock on which they built them has endured. As I have frequently pointed out in other cases, another reason for the particular charm of the Pont du Gard lies in the fact of its irregularity. The arches are unequal in span. The structure itself is bent in its length. It is not mere machine-made measurement, but the strong handiwork and giant eyesight of a conquering race; and the orders for it may well have been given by that Agrippa, son-in-law of Augustus, whose mighty monuments at Rome had earned for him the title of "Curator perpetuus aquarum."[9]

In the sixteenth century the Duc de Rohan, who was engaged near Nîmes in manoeuvres necessitated by the Wars of Religion, cut through a third of the thickness of the archways on the second rank in order to give room for his cannon to be transported along the space upon the first row of arches. Further mutilations did not improve the strength of the original masonry, and, after some repairs had been made, the estates of Languedoc restricted the traffic to men on foot or on horseback. But the increase of intercommunications, and the frequent floods which blocked the ford beneath, soon necessitated a more commodious bridgeway; so between 1743 and 1747, M. Pitot, the Director of Public Works, built a new bridge, carrying a road along the eastern flank of the lowest arcade; and from this bridge a close examination of the Roman masonry is possible.

The drive to the Pont du Gard takes you along a broad white road, of the best, too spacious to be dull, too flowing in its curves to be monotonous, through a mild and sunlit plain of olive-trees. You see the arches for the first time when you are close to them, and it is not until you move down into the gorge itself that it is possible to realise how exquisite a choice of setting was made by the old builders. As has happened to so many Provençal ruins, these stones are of light golden-yellow, which is particularly rich in tone in all its shadows. They spring out of the green-clad slopes on either side, and through their noble frames the blue of the infinite air looks deeper and more full of memories than it does in the free space above; as if some intimate community had been established between the present that we know and the past that has been captured by some far-off spell, some strong enchantment of a builder who builded more wisely than he knew.

But if there is here so strong a shadow of the everlasting Roman name, the image of their vanished world is reflected even more clearly in the dark and cool and ever-changing scenes of the Roman baths at Nîmes. Beneath the Pont du Gard it is difficult to believe that a monument more lasting than any modern London has to show was built but to carry the water of a pair of springs to a provincial town, and was but a single portion of an aqueduct that assured the passage of good water for more than forty kilometres. In the gardens beneath Mont Cavalier, even more than in any spot at Nîmes, it is possible to realise how large a part fresh water played in Roman life. If cleanliness be luxury, our eighteenth century was one of the most ascetic in our history; and even yet we are but faintly approaching the state of civilisation, which was familiar to every Roman until the Empire fell, and to every inhabitant of a Mohammedan city for many centuries afterwards. The Roman baths of Nîmes and the temple to the Fountain-god Nemausus are a typical example of one pleasure—and that the simplest—which every Roman town enjoyed of right.

Opposite to the Maison Carrée is the modern theatre, and from its north-western corner the Rue Antonin runs straight to the long military canal called the Quai de la Fontaine. As you walk westwards along this you soon see the long straight Boulevard de la République, which leads in a mathematically correct line to the Jardin de la Fontaine, with its iron gateway and its concierge complete. It is one of the most delightful public gardens in provincial France, and though eighteenth-century architecture has done much to alter its original appearance, there is still much left that has the true flavour of Imperial Rome. It will be well to begin with the ruined temple that is the least changed of all the old constructions, the shrine raised by the Romans upon the earlier Celtic temple to the fountain-god.

Fortunately an inscription has been found, and deciphered, which throws a great deal of light both upon the building itself and upon the original disposition of its surroundings, and the wording of this inscription shows that the title of "Temple de Diane," which persistently survives, may well be a tradition of one of the divinities to which the Roman temple was dedicated as follows:—"To the God Nemausus, and to the Goddess Diana, the Commonwealth of Nîmes has dedicated this Fountain of the Nymphs, constructed, with its marble columns, its statues, and all its ornaments, by the munificence of the Emperor Augustus, consul for the tenth time, consul designate for the eleventh time, and there were built in addition to it this portico and temple."[10]

The Temple of Nemauses near the Roman Baths.
(In the Jardin de la Fontaine at Nîmes)

This valuable and interesting inscription, the original of which I reproduce, according to Germer-Durand's reading, in the footnote, was found on a magnificent fragment of a frieze and architrave of Corinthian architecture dug out of the soil on the south side of the square Roman basin. Sufficient fragments were re-united to form a façade, which had originally eight columns, with a colonnade at an angle, and rich carvings. The square basin, south of the actual pool of the spring, is the "Nymphaeum" which Augustus first constructed in B.C. 24 (his tenth consulate), and which appears with its eighteenth-century urns and cherubs, in my illustration. Eight years afterwards (B.C. 16 and 15) he built the town walls, the finest remnant of which is the "Porte d'Auguste"; and the Nîmes medal, showing the palm-tree and the crocodile, was no doubt struck to commemorate a fortification which would be intimately connected with the veteran soldiers from Egypt who had been settled in the town. The "portico" was a splendid colonnaded entrance to the baths, and was added to the constructions of Augustus by the free township, or Commonwealth (Res Publica) of Nîmes, which also built the "temple" that is still standing. No doubt the portico connected this temple with the Nymphaeum. In A.D. 121 Hadrian restored all these buildings, and the inscription recording their foundation by Augustus, and by the city, is chiefly written in letters of Hadrian's date, for that Emperor was always careful (as Spartianus records) to preserve the ancient founders' names and inscriptions on all the many buildings he restored.

Ruined and dilapidated as is this little temple, it retains the charm that is due to the locality and the interest that is inseparable from anything unique; for in its way this fountain-temple is unique, though some have compared it with the "Nymphaeum" built by Augustus at the spring of Egeria, in a lonely field some three miles out of Rome; and others see in it considerable resemblances to that temple to the Heliopolitan Jupiter, built by Antoninus at Baalbec, which is suggested by the inscription on an altar to that deity found in the Nîmes fountain, and already referred to in these pages (pp.108 and 148).

The façade was originally formed of three irregular arches, and there are traces indicating that the centre entrance once had a porch in front of it. The actual space now covered by the "cella" is fourteen metres eighty, by nine metres fifty-five and of the two side galleries (two metres fifty broad), that to the right of the entrance alone remains, the whole of the south side having been irreparably damaged. The existing gallery provides an extremely interesting example of barrel-vaulting, the roof being arranged in three separate parts which permit the light to enter, but overlap each other sufficiently to keep out the rain, and accompany the rising steps, as it were, towards the window in the façade which originally lighted them. But the vaulting of the "cella" itself is an even more picturesque example of the strength and skill of Roman masonry; for here you may see the naked ribs soaring upwards and across, apparently in defiance of every law of gravity and weight, without a trace of mortar to support them. This roof was evidently first built over with a series of twelve thick arches, or transverse ribs, and the space between them was then filled in with a plain wagon vault or flags of stone. This structure had undoubtedly a great influence on the first vaulted churches of Provence; and it is a very curious coincidence that it was also adopted in the construction of the early Christian churches of Syria, for in referring once again to the altar dedicated to Jupiter Heliopolitanus, and found on this spot, I find that the Tiberinus who set it up was a native of Berytus, which is close to Heliopolis in Syria. The construction of the early Christian churches in Syria has been carefully described by Count Melchior de Vogüé, and it is so extraordinarily like that of the early churches in Provence that, if this temple at Nîmes had not existed, we should be obliged to believe the method had been brought here from the East by the monks of the eleventh century, who visited Palestine while it was in the hands of the Crusaders.

This Roman temple is on the site of a far older shrine to the fountain-god, set up by the Celtic tribes. Close to the same site has been found an altar to Isis. The twelve well-designed niches within the temple no doubt contained the statues of as many different divinities, and the especial care taken to protect this structure from damage either by settlement of the soil, or by floods, is very remarkable, resulting in elaborate substructures and drainage arrangements, which have provided antiquarian problems for centuries. The wall of the façade alone is no less than three metres thick. This is just as well; for the temple was altered by the Benedictine monks who owned it till it was used as a granary by a sixteenth-century farmer. Then it was almost destroyed by fire in 1576, and suffered even more by the wanton violence of the townspeople in the next year, who wished to prevent Marshal de Bellegarde holding it for the Catholics in the

Religious Wars. In 1622 it was still further weakened by being pillaged for stonework for the fortifications of the town which passed not far off and included the Tour Magne (just above, on Mont Cavalier) in their circuit.

The Baths themselves are somewhat difficult to reconstruct beneath the Italian-Formal-Garden that now almost conceals them. The strange column now kept in the right-hand passage of the temple originally served as one of the supports of the velarium that shadowed the central block of masonry in the square bath; and beneath it the Roman ladies reclined in the sun after they had bathed, or waited for their turn to "take the waters." The pattern of this column is worth notice, for an acanthus-leaf is carved upon its base, which must be almost a unique instance of such a position. It was but one among many of the adornments which originally made this place worthy alike of the fountain-god and of the Emperor; and, as may be seen from the inscriptions preserved in the Museum, it was the pride and pleasure of the inhabitants of Nîmes to contribute to its beauty with votive-offerings of carved capitals, of altars, of fine marbles, and of pillars. There were also statues of famous citizens placed round its borders, and the names of some of them have been preserved. Quintus Solonius Severinus, for example, had held high office, civil, religious and military, in Rome; he had been pontiff at Nîmes; and he was "patron" of the city of Fréjus, which sent his statue here for the decoration of the Baths. Lucius Sammius Aemilianus was another Roman knight, the prefect of an auxiliary cohort, and an office-holder in the province of Narbonne. His statue was placed here by a freedman who was at the head of that Dionysiac dramatic brotherhood in Nîmes which was so warmly supported by Hadrian. Caius Aemilius Postumus, a military tribune, was decreed the honour of a statue by the town. Quintus Cominius Aemilianus, headman of the city watch, was awarded a statue by the Gauls of Nîmes. To Quintus Soillius Valerianus the three cities of Cavaillon, Avignon, and Fréjus had united in erecting a statue in these same gardens. To complete the rough idea of Roman luxury these various details will gradually permit you to imagine, it is only necessary to remember that on the east side of Mont Cavalier, within easy reach of the Baths, are the vestiges of a little theatre, and several of the inscriptions referring to its actors I have already quoted in connection with the theatre of Arles.

For the rest, no further merely problematical archaeology is necessary to enjoy the impression of cultured pleasure still conveyed by the "Jardin de la Fontaine," changed as it is in nearly every essential since its first foundation. The spring itself, with its semi-circular stone borders, is probably the least changed of all its features, and remains the most beautiful. The garden terraces are now arranged very much after the formal Italian manner common near Tivoli or Albano; and apart from the temple, little of the original Roman structures remains except some of the columns that stand in the water in the square basin beneath the eighteenth-century balustrade. The urns and cupids do not spoil the effect. They are so obviously different, and the setting of the whole picture is on such a large and generous scale that a blended harmony of line and atmosphere is achieved with far greater success than any written description of the place could ever suggest to the untravelled reader.

With the Roman Baths of Nîmes I have now completed the list of those larger monuments of Roman life and luxury which reveal so much of what Rome did for Provence in the four best centuries when her influence was paramount. In Italy itself the very multitude of ruins somewhat obscures the significance of each; but in the Rhone valley, each Roman relic has a value of its own. The Maison Carrée of Nîmes, the amphitheatre of Arles, the triumphal monuments of St. Remy, each has the value of an ordered, spacious setting; each, too, as it seems to me, is preserved in an atmosphere of more kindly antiquity, and more appropriate grace, than is the case with many similar examples in a modern Italian town. They are not surrounded by the bustle and the tramcars and the electric lights of modern Rome. They are not preserved within the living tombs of Herculaneum or of Pompeii. They seem to be the appropriate setting for the mild dignity and the unhasting commerce of a Provence that has never lost her memories of classic Greece and Rome.

Before I pass on to the Middle Ages, by way of St. Trophime at Arles, I propose to touch on a few of those smaller personal details of Roman life and Roman individual character which history must sometimes omit, and art can only now and then suggest. From some of the smaller portrait statues, from a few inscriptions, from the wonderful tombs preserved at Arles, it will be possible to picture for ourselves a classical antiquity that is not wholly out of the pages of our school-books; that is a little more intimate in its revelations of a common humanity, a common joy, a common sorrow. Before we say good-bye to Rome, it will be well to realise what we shall have lost; that so, with a somewhat better grace, we may pronounce our "Ave atque Vale" above the ruins of her decline and fall.

NOTES

1. As Plutarch says of Caesar, in the English of Sir Thomas North: "When he was made Ædilis he did show the people the pastime of three hundred and twenty couple of sword-players, and did besides exceed all other in sumptuousness in the sports and common feasts which he made to delight them withal... he so pleased the people and won their love therewith that they devised daily to give him new offices for to requite him."

2. On p. 101, I have given a list of some Greek actors and others known to us. I will add here some names of gladiators from the inscriptions at Nîmes. (1) In the Museum at Nîmes is a terra-cotta medallion found at Cavillargues in the Gard, which represents a fully armed man fighting a lightly-dressed soldier, who carries a buckler and a trident. Behind them are two men in togas, one holding a small wand, and four others sit in a tribune, who have spared the lives of both combatants, for the inscription says "Pugnantes Missi," and the names of the gladiators are given as Eros and Xanthus. (2) An epitaph setting forth that a stone was put up by Optata, his wife, to Lucitis Pompeius of Vienne, a retiarius who fought with net and trident, and was nine times crowned. He died at twenty-five. (3) His widow married again, and again survived her husband, Aptus of Alexandria, who fought in the Thracian manner, and died at thirty-seven. (4) Sperata, his wife, put up an epitaph to the myrmillo (a fully armed gladiator) Columbus, who was an Aeduan, and member of Serenus's troupe of fighters. He died at twenty-five. (5) Another Thracian fighter was Quintus Vettius Gracilis, born in Spain, who was crowned thrice. His trainer, Lucius Sestius Latinus, put up a tombstone to him at his death at twenty-five.

The "Myrmillo" fought with a short and sharp-pointed sword, defended by a helmet a brassard, greaves, and square-ended buckler. The "Retiarius" wore nothing but a waistband and a brassard, aiming to envelope his enemy in a net, and slay him with a trident. The "Thracian" carried a small round buckler, and his right arm was fully protected. He had a plumed helmet, and fought with a curved cutlass.

3. The inscription numbered (23), in the list in Appendix I gives a particularly engaging view of the character of one of these gladiators. It is the epitaph set up to a young man by his trainers and his sister, and may be roughly translated as follows: "Stay thy steps, I pray, thou young and pious traveller, to learn from these lines the jealousy of fate. For nineteen years I lived, pure, and doing no harm to any one, and my character won me the esteem of all. Eager to learn the lessons of youth, I was well trained for the amphitheatre. I was the famous Pulcher; and with various weapons I appeared in combat against the wild beasts. Besides that I knew somewhat of the art of Medicine. I was a colleague not only

of those who had charge of the Bears, but also of those who slew the victims at the public sacrifices, and who decorated the statues of the Gods with garlands at the first of every spring. The inscription tells you my right name." This was set up by Sextus Julius Felicissimus and by Sextus Felix to their unrivalled pupil; and to her brother, by Felicitas.

4. A few comparisons in size will be of interest, the measurements being exact, the estimates below the mark.

	Audience	External-Diameters	Thickness of walls	Area of Arena
Coliseum	90,000	187 x 155 metres	51 metres	3611 metres
Capua	62,000	169x139 metres	46.5 metres	2740 metres
Arles	30,000	I36x107 metres	33.5 metres	2166 metres
Nîmes	22,000	133x101 metres		2092 metres
Pompeii	20,000			

5. This may be compared with the inscription preserved at Pompeii in honour of the duumvirs who restored the amphitheatre there after the damage done by the earthquake of February 63, in which it is recorded how Celer, a magistrate appointed for the games, paid for entranceways and a block of seats; how Saginus and Marcellus did the same; how passages and stairways only were put in by Cicinius and Rufus.

6. " N • RHOD • ET • aRAR • XL • D • D • D • N," which is: "Nautis Rhodanicis et Araricis (loca numero) XL Data Decreto Decurionum Nomausensium." (40 places granted to the boatmen of the Rhone and the Saône by the Decurions of Nîmes)

7. Lenthéric quotes Tacitus: "*Italiam utroque mari duae classes, Misenum apud et Ravennam proximumque Galliae littus rostratae naves praesidebant, quas Actiaca victoria captas Augustus in oppidum Forojuliense miserat, valido cum remige.*" (Two fleets, at Misenum and Ravenna, defend Italy on each coast and the coast nearest Gaul was protected by beaked ships, which Augustus had captured at the victory of Actium and sent to the town of Fréjus with powerful oars)

8. AUGUSTIS LARIBUS CULTURES URAE FONTIS. "To the Lares, the worshippers (or perhaps the guardians) of the spring of the Eure." Four lines of somewhat incorrect elegiacs found at Uzès preserve a more naïve admission of the benefits of the spring. They run as follows:—

"*Sextus Pompeius…cognomine Pandus
Cujus et hoc ab avis contigit esse solum
Aediculam hanc nymphis [posui] quia saepius ussus [?]
Hoc sum fonte senex tam bene quam juvenis.*"

(Sextus Pompeius Paulus, who inherited
this land from his ancestors, set up this shrine

for the nymphs because he often enjoyed this spring
as an old man as much as in his youth)

9. An inscription mentioning his name was found at Nîmes in 1742, and I am inclined to attribute it to a commemoration of Agrippa's work at the finishing of the aqueduct from the Pont du Gard within the town itself, perhaps near the celebrated baths. His third consulate was in B.C. 27, and he was in Provence again in B.C. 19. The words are: M. AGRIPPA LUCII FILIUS CONSUL III COLONIAE DAT." (M. Agrippa, son of Lucius, Consul three times, gives this to the colony)

10. The original inscription, found near the Roman basin of the fountain in 1739, runs as follows, as deciphered by Germer-Durand:—DEO NEMAUSO ET DIANAE SANCTAE RES PUBLICA NEMAUSESIUM NYMPHAEUM CUM COLUMNIS MARMOREIS SIGNIS CETERISQUE ORNAMENTIS SUIS EXSTRUCTUM MUNIFICENTIA IMPERATORIS CAESARIS DIVI FILI AUGUSTI CONSULIS X DESIGNATI XI ADDITIS PORTICU ET AEDE DEDICAVIT.

I may add here some other inscriptions found in these same gardens.

(1) NEMAUSO Q. CRASSUS SECUNDINUS QUAESTOR COLONIAE. (Q. Crassus Secundius, quaestor of the colony to Namausus)

(2) C. ANDOLATIUS NEMAUSO VOTUM SOLVIT LIBENS MERITO. (C. Andoliatus gladly fulfils his vow to Nemausus)

(3) NEMAUSO SACRUM RENICCI FILIUS CAPITULUM DAT. (The son of Reniccius dedicates a capital to the shrine)

(4) PAETUS ET RENICCIUS VOTUM SOLVUNT. (Paetus and Reniccius fulfil their vow)

(5) NYMPHIS AUGUST1S SACRUM TERTIUS BAEBII FILIUS L. DECUMIUS DECUMANUS L. POMTINUS MARTIALIS L. ANNIUS ALLOBROX DE SUO. (L. Decumius, son of Babbius and tax-collector, L. Pomtinus Martialis and L. Annius Allobrox make an offering to the august nymphs at their own expense)

(6) NYMPHIS AUGUSTIS SACRUM LICINIA SEVERINA V.S.L.M. [See No. (2)]. (Licinia Severina fulfils her vow to the august nymphs)

(7) NYMPHIS. (To the nymphs)

(8) LARIBUS AUGUSTIS MINERVAE V.S.L.M. (Vow fulfilled to the august tutelary gods of Minerva)

(9) VENERI AUGUSTAE. (to the august Venus)

(10) JOVI OPTIMO MAXIMO HELIOPOLITANO ET NEMAUSO...[et cet, v. supra, p. 192 note]. (To the greatest Heliopolitan Jupiter and to Nemausus...)

(11) JOVI ET NEMAUSO TITUS FLAVIUS HERMES EXACTOR OPERUM BASILICAE MARMORARII ET LAPIDARII VOTUM SOLVUNT. (Titus Flavius Hermes, manager of works of the basilica, and the marble-workers and stonemasons fulfil their vows to Jupiter and Nemausus)

Part II: Beneath the Surface

"...Edebant et bibebant; emebant et vendebant;
plantabant et aedificabant... usque in diem qua veni
diluvium et perdidit omnes..."

(They were eating and drinking; they were buying and selling;
they were planting and building... up to the day when the
flood came and destroyed them all...)

So much might be said about the Romans in Provence from the time of
Augustus up to the invasions of the Barbarians, that I shall confine
myself to selecting those typical suggestions which the traveller may
confirm for himself by studying what he can actually see upon the spot.[1]

The Nymphaeum and the Temple of Nemausus may well serve as the
starting-place for our brief consideration of Roman life, inasmuch as his
baths were one of the most important functions in a Roman's day. Many
bathed twice; and the demands of luxurious effeminacy were occasionally
responsible for as many as seven or eight baths in the twenty-four hours.
The price of admission was low enough to enable every section of the
population except the lowest of the slaves to enter, and there was a
portico (filled with notices and advertisements) in which people waited
their turn when the rooms were full. From here every one passed into a
dressing-room which was also a cooling-room, in which arrangements
were made for hanging up clothes, or placing them on shelves. Its walls
were yellow, the ceiling panelled in white with red borders, the pavement
of common white mosaic, and stone benches ran round the walls.
Ground glass was used (as at Pompeii) for the window placed under the
vault of the roof. The decorations usually represented some such subject
as a pair of tritons carrying vases and surrounded by a shoal of dolphins
with cupids playing among them. Out of this apartment opened the door
to the cold swimming-bath, shaped like a circle, with four alcoves
framing it in a square, and a walk all round of about a yard wide, the
whole in white marble, beneath a domed roof painted blue. The walls
were yellow, with certain green branches painted on them, the alcoves

being blue or red. Eight feet from the floor a decorated frieze of stucco-work ran round the walls, representing a chariot race.

The monument erected to the memory of Antistius (see No. (9) of the epitaphs) shows that there was a doctor at Nîmes, for he is described as "Medicus." His profession was one that was only honoured in Rome at comparatively a very late period, for the "chirurgi" and "iatraliptae" of Greece were at first looked upon with a distrust which rapidly ripened into aversion. Only by the reign of Tiberius did any division into special departments occur in this profession; but I have no doubt that the use of hot baths, and of perspiration generally, was one of the earliest remedies the doctors suggested with any certainty of credence owing to the immediate visibility of "results." Bathers therefore who, either by their doctor's advice or from natural indolence, preferred warmth, used a dressing-room with an open charcoal stove at the end of the room, and bronze seats all round. Here the walls were crimson, and the cornice was supported by terra-cotta statues which separated the available space into recesses. Here the number of fragrant oils in which the Romans delighted were applied, from the oil of saffron (or "crocus") beloved by Elagabalus to the "nardinum," with which the hair was anointed before festive

The Roman Baths at Nîmes.
(In the Jardin de la Fontaine)

garlands were placed on it. The rich carried their own perfumes to the baths in precious boxes; the poor, who used meal of lupins instead of soap, were supplied with cheaper odoriferous powders. Opening from this was an apartment; like the hot room of the modern Turkish bath, and used for the same purpose; which was kept at the right temperature by a kind of universal flue which surrounded floor and ceiling and all four walls with a column of heated air from a central furnace. At one end was a large "labrum" or tazza, of basalt, granite, porphyry, or alabaster, with a lion's head in the centre, from which a spray of water rose to cool the bather before he moved into less heated apartments. There was also a large circular marble bath, full of hot water, so constructed as to contain eighteen or twenty bathers at once in a comfortable sitting posture round the edge. The only seats here were of wood, and everything in the apartment was naturally warm and dripping. There were windows in the domed roof which could be closed or opened at will. The floor rested on small pillars throughout to ensure the proper distribution of heat, as described above, and the walls were hollow for the same reason.

It will easily be seen that great magnificence could be displayed in the ornamentation of these buildings; and very varied amusements were contained in the largest of them. A library, for instance, was considered fashionable from the days of Claudius onwards. Though at first the property of private speculators, the baths at Rome soon became as free to the people as the amphitheatre or the circus, and remained so, while the older, private institutions still survived beside them. There were separate baths for the ladies; though it is a well-known fact that a good deal of disorder was occasionally created in Italian cities by persons who objected even to this temporary separation; and on certain festivals, for instance the Kalends of April, the poorer classes first celebrated the cult of Fortuna Virilis, and then their richer sisters did honour to Venus Verticordia, by bathing with the men, a kind of solemn "lustration" involving the wearing of myrtle. Women were especially fond of the worship of Fortuna, whose dedication-day (now that of St. John the Baptist) was exactly at the summer solstice, and whose symbols were the wheel, the rudder, and the globe. On the eleventh day of that same month of June was the festival of Matralia, at which the goddess Mater Matuta was worshipped with sacred cakes cooked in old-fashioned earthenware. She may well have been only another form of the Bona Dea, whose altar was described on p. 109, whose temple on the Aventine had been first dedicated on the 1st of May, and was ever afterwards cared for exclusively by women, as was the case with the Athenian Demeter Thesmophorus, another feminine personification of the earth-goddess, of the fructifying power which was shown also in the child-bearing of women. Her appropriate sacrifice was a pig, and this was offered by the women on the night of the 3rd of December, with rites which continued to be perfectly decorous until at least a century after the famous sacrilege of Clodius in 63 B.C.

With that sacrifice, as with the spring festival of the Parilia, the Vestal Virgins were associated at Rome. Their chief ritual consisted in the visitation of barefooted matrons on the 7th of June, praying for blessings on their households. While sacred cakes were offered plucked from the earliest corn, the bakers and millers all kept holiday, their mills were garlanded, their donkeys wreathed in flowers. In Provence we find also, as was only to be expected, that women were as closely connected with the public religion as they were in Italy. At Arles we have seen the altar of the priestess of the Bona Dea. At Nîmes one of the most conspicuous tombs in the courtyard of the museum is that of Licinia, a priestess of the Augustal rites, and of her husband beside her. She is represented, not in her priestly dress, but as an honourable Roman matron, her hair dressed in rows of tight curls above the forehead, with a long plait hanging down to the breast on each side of the face. Her epitaph is "D.M. Liciniae Lucii Filiae Flavillae Flaminicae Augustali." Above the two heads the sculptured dolphin at each corner refers only to the happy voyage of the beloved dead towards the Blessed Isles. They have no reference either to her own or to her husband's profession. The importance to which these priestesses of the Imperial divinities might rise, and the wealth they might possess in a career which did not depend at all upon their husbands, may be estimated from the inscription found on the podium of the amphitheatre at Vienne, which records of a lady who held the same office as Licinia that she gave gilt-bronze tiles for the roof, statues of Castor and Pollux on horseback, and of Hercules and Mercury, besides other ornaments at her own expense for the decoration of the building (Allmer. Inscr., Vienn., No.191).

Licinia's husband, whose sturdy face is carved next to her own, was Tribune of the Sixth Legion, called the Victorious; one of the four chief magistrates of the town; and a pontiff—no small official record. He is represented in the cuirass, which shows his military rank, and on each side of the carving are the fasces, or ceremonial rods, terminating in laurel leaves, which typify his magisterial functions. It is interesting also to note that the man who reached these high honours in the township of Nîmes before the reign of Septimius Severus was undoubtedly of Gallic blood. His epitaph runs as follows: "D.M. Sex. Adgennii Macrini Tribuni Legionis VI. Victricis Quattuorviri Juredicundo Pontificis Praefecti Fabrum." Curiously enough the stone which probably commemorates the names of the children of Licinia and Adgennius is still to be found in what must have been its original position, and on it may be read the words: "Sextus Adgennius Solutus et Adgennia Licinilla Parentibus."

Tomb of Adgennius and his Wife Licinia at Nîmes

From the little sketch of family affection and justifiable pride which these inscriptions give us, it is an easy transition to the various epitaphs, still preserved at Nîmes and elsewhere, which throw light on some of the ordinary avocations and proceedings of the Roman citizen. On two tombs are recorded the deaths of gardeners (numbered (1) and (2) in the list in Appendix I). The first, named Cornelius, had his dibble and his favourite billhook carved above his epitaph; and on the tomb of Nundinus there also appears the wheel of the well that gave him water for his vegetable-beds in a thirsty land. Restricted to the flora of the country in which he happened to be living, deprived of all those far-fetched blooms which are the exotic glory of modern horticulture, the Roman citizen had to make the most of what he had; and he very naturally developed a style of formal gardening and clipped shrubbery which might well have anticipated the French eighteenth century on the one hand and the English box-borders on the other, and was very probably copied from Oriental examples. Among the trees and flowerbeds was a broad regular pathway, in which the owner took exercise in a litter; and in larger gardens the "hippodrome" for private horse-and-chariot racing was a distinctive feature, set apart by groves of laurel and box, of myrtle, and the rosemary, which grows much higher in Italy than with us. Among the flowers they loved were the rose and violet, the crocus, lily, and narcissus, the iris, hyacinth, and poppy, of which it was the bright red damask-rose that was most frequently employed for garlands. By the time of Martial something[2] which closely corresponded to the modern greenhouse or conservatory had come into use for winter grapes and early melons as well as for lilies and roses,[3] which were not only forced in Rome, but also imported from Egypt in winter. Among their fruit were apples, pears, plums, cherries, quinces, peaches, pomegranates, figs, chestnuts, almonds, medlars, and mulberries, besides the grapes and olives, which were the most important of all; and we may be sure that in a town so near St. Remy as is Nîmes, in a climate where flowers and vegetables grow luxuriantly in the mild sunshine, the gardeners whose epitaphs I have quoted had not much difficulty in supplying all their patrons wants, when once the water question had been satisfactorily solved, as the Pont du Gard had solved it.

Vine-growing was a rather different matter. For a long time the monopoly of the wine-trade had formed the staple of Italian commerce with Mediterranean coast-towns, and it was only by slow degrees that the Romans encouraged those vineyards in Southern France which were in later centuries to produce the best wines in the world. It is known, for instance, that Domitian (in 81 A.D.) tore up the vineyards of Provence; but it is also known that Probus (in 276 A.D.) restored and encouraged the culture of the vine; Martial calls Vienne "vitifera"; and there was certainly much vine-growing near Nîmes before the Romans left it, for Quartina (see No. (3) in the epitaphs) set up a monument to her "excellent brother Vallo," and carved upon it the pruning-knife which may still be seen in every vineyard near the Southern Rhone. From Vallo's grapes, no doubt, was made the "ordinaire" served in the little wine-shop commemorated in another inscription (see No. (4) of the epitaphs), which was kept by an innkeeper with the sounding name of Lucius Trebonius Nicephorus Patillus, a bachelor apparently, whose tombstone was provided by his good friend Epaphroditus.[4] We are apt to forget that inns are not entirely the invention of the modern traveller. In the Roman Empire the hostelry, as opposed to the wine-shop, was a necessary result of the "colonising" of various centres, of the movements of officials between their "homes" in Italy and their "situations" elsewhere, and of the commercial activities engendered by the growth of luxury. Even in our own little Roman Silchester, our unknown ruins just ten miles south of Reading, there was a hotel within a few yards of the southern gate. The inn of Nicephorus was far from being the only one of its kind at Nîmes. It may have been a little wine-shop like that so well known in Pompeii, where the stone counter still shows the circular holes of various sizes cut to receive the "amphora" of good Falernian, of mellow Massic, of costly Caecuban, or of the thick, sweet wines of

Greece. It was possibly just like one of the inns which Horace so wittily describes in his poem about the journey from Rome to Brindisi in the train of Maecenas. At Forum Appii the water was bad; another inn made his eyes smart with the smoke of the fires; several were obviously started by owners of villas on the road to sell off the wine grown on their own estates. As "Caupo" (the title on his epitaph), Nicephorus would technically be a retailer of food and wine, which was sold in his "caupona" or "taberna," but might be consumed elsewhere. People generally made use of inns to sleep in only in the country districts, which accounts for the universal contempt shown for innkeepers in Rome itself. At Nîmes these feelings were less prominent; and though the "social reunions" of the modern "public house" were there to be seen more frequently at the Baths than anywhere else, it is evident that Nicephorus had made his mark; for his epitaph is the only one of the kind that has come down to us.

Besides pure wine, the Roman affected a drink called "mulsum," in which four-fifths was composed of "must" and the rest of honey. Hot spiced wine was well known in winter. Beer, or something very like it, was better known in Gaul and Germany than in Italy; and one customer of Nicephorus who may have asked for it was Saturninus the sheep-shearer (see No. (5) of the epitaphs), whose tombstone shows the blunt-ended shears and the rough comb of his trade. Some of the bronze drink-vessels and wine-coolers which have survived in our museums from the days when Nicephorus first filled them were no doubt made by that Sextus Spurius Piperclus (see No. (6) of the epitaphs), whose trade is clearly stated on the monument he set up before his death to himself and his good wife Secunda. Music there must have been in the inn too, occasionally upon feast days; and the instruments were made by Avidius Secundus, who had a shop at Nîmes and a wife called Festa (see No. (7) and (8) of the epitaphs). Some of these instruments, a seven-tubed Pan-pipes, and a kind of hand-organ, are carved at Arles upon the tomb of Julia Tyrrannia, a lady whose artistic culture was evidently only less than the sweetness of her natural disposition: "Quae moribus pariter et disciplina ceteris feminis exemplo fuit." Though couches were usual at feasts at home, chairs were also in common use for visitors; and one can imagine that some of those made for the audience at Nicephorus's concerts came from the shop of Julius Albus, the chairmaker (see No (10) of epitaphs) to whom his widow Euplia set up a monument. For women the more comfortable "cathedra," with a broad and sloping back, was used; the men's "sella" had straight back and sides, with elegantly carved legs and small foot-boards attached. Many in the Pompeii paintings are strikingly like modern articles of furniture. They were generally of wood, sometimes veneered or inlaid with ivory.[5]

Garlands were an equally necessary adjunct in the Roman's "happy day", and a particularly seductive inscription (see No. (11) among the epitaphs) preserves the charming sentence on a signboard, announcing that here dwelt a merchant who sold "Garlands for Lovers only"! Romance flies out to us at once from these letters that so many Roman lovers read; and I should like to think that among this crafty shopkeeper's customers was a certain "viveur" from Vienne, whose epitaph still secures those good wishes for his jovial soul which his delightful personality had drawn so readily from all his friends in life. "Marcus Magius Sotericus"—it does not sound a jaunty name at first (see No. (12) of the epitaphs), but listen:— "a lover of his friends who was nicknamed 'the Cheerful.'" Cannot you see him rolling through the streets of Nîmes, on a holiday; his eye, alert for every pretty face, caught by that subtle sign-board; leaning across the counter and chaffering with the lady behind it for the most fashionable garland in her stock? His conquests must have often given a toast to happy revellers in that amorous valley of the Rhone. His epitaph he wrote himself, asking that happy shouts of greeting might follow him even beyond the tomb—"ut esset memoriae bonum iter vocibus 'Feliciter.'"[6] Not only in the days of garlands did Sotericus, we may be sure, enjoy himself. Every 17th of December, after the public sacrifice at the altars of Saturn, the citizens of Nîmes, of Arles, or of Vienne sat down to feast together, shouting "Io Saturnalia!" as they dispersed. Early the next morning every one met again at the baths, and each man on his return home made the family sacrifice of a sucking-pig. There followed visits to every friend in town, congratulations, games, and such light gifts as wax candles or small earthenware images. Here and there the slaves were sitting in their masters' couches, and the masters gaily ran about with jars of wine and pasties; for the goodwill of the holiday had levelled every rank.

Of ladies, just as ready for a revel, there was no lack. Some of their names still sound delightful even on a tombstone—"Attiolae Dulcissimae"... "Lucilla lucet Secundilla salve"... "Mariae Nemausinae Maria Marituma Liberta." Who was this freedwoman whose name was "Mary of the Sea"? It is the strangest classical foreshadowing of later Christian nomenclature, and all the stranger that it hides an actual death. (See Nos. (17), (16), (15) of the epitaphs.)

There is one very curious inscription of this epoch, written in a pair of verses, of which the hexameter scans (to our ears) as badly as the pentameter (see No. (13) of the list), and they give us the last words of one Aetherius upon his deathbed: "Let earth, our common mother, hold the body which she gave." This is from Ste. Colombe. The epitaph of the young boatman of Marseilles, which I have quoted in No. (21) of the list at the end of this chapter, reveals yet another system of philosophy of great interest. It runs as follows: "Traveller, stay thy steps beside this tomb. A young man calls you, one dear to the God, and having now laid aside mortality, unmarried, and of the age of those divinities of Amyclae who watch over sailors. A sailor myself, I delighted in the waves of the sea. But in this tomb, which my devoted parents gave me, I am delivered from all disease and toil and sorrow and labour; for these evils during life the flesh endures without respite. The dead, on the other hand, are divided into two bands, of which one is borne hither and thither on the earth, while the other joins the dance of the celestial bodies; and of this army am I one with the God as my leader."[7] Vienne provides again a cheerier outlook (see No. 14): "Here Mercasto rests in peace, who flourished during sixty years, and led a happy life through all of them." No hesitation here; an unabashed Epicurean to the last. Vienne, if all these indications may be believed, must have been a gay little town in its best days. That jovial poet, Martial, was naturally full of sympathy with the place,[8] and boasted of the popularity of his rhymes in it; and this very fashion in "pretty Vienne" throws a very characteristic light upon the town of Sotericus. Curiously enough, the inscriptions of Lyons reveal quite a different state of things. The chastity of the home, the sanctity of the marriage-tie, are their almost invariable note. At Arles and Nîmes it was the same. Vienne was evidently the Capua of the Rhone. One of the few Roman paintings surviving in Provence is to be seen there, a fresco in water-colours on thick plaster, arranged in rectangular panels of bright green, framed in red. On a background of brilliant black are drawn arabesques, garlands and birds, vine leaves growing russet in the autumn sun, with golden yet transparent grapes in clusters, and branches of cherry laden with sparkling red fruit. Above the foliage and the twisted patterns rise two figures, one a bacchanal, the other the goddess Fortune on a globe.

In Nîmes, though there are no pictures left, there are some good mosaics. The largest is a rectangle of some fifty metres square, representing the marriage of Admetus, who drives up to the palace of his future father-in-law in a chariot drawn by a wild boar and a lion, followed by two soldiers, and received by Peleus and Alcestis. Elsewhere in the composition a very clever geometrical arrangement of various figures fills up the ground, with winged cupids, dolphins, and fish playing amongst them. Perhaps the best workmanship is that of the Acanthus, which is particularly well modelled and coloured, the foliage being filled with animals of every kind: dogs, hares, leopards, lions, tigers, antelopes, partridges, frogs, serpents, snails, and others. Not so large in size, but finer in execution, is the Nîmes mosaic, representing the sleep of Endymion, who slumbers naked on Mount Latmos, pillowed on his cloak, his right arm above his head, his left arm near his body, still holding his shepherd's crook, while his Spartan sheep-dog watches by his side. The goddess is not seen, but it is to her, no doubt, that the little winged Cupid beckons; and when we have passed on, she will approach. The border of lotus-flowers is richly worked in very small marble cubes, which have enabled the artist to express himself far more subtly than is usual in this material. There are other examples of mosaic at Aix, especially a figure of Orpheus with his lyre charming the animals, but none are as good as the mosaics of Nîmes.

Houses with such treasures within their walls might well, it may be thought, have looked beautiful from the streets. But those familiar with the streets of Pompeii will know better, for those ancient thoroughfares are lined with blank walls wherever a temple or a great public building does not interrupt and beautify them. This was because in nearly every case the living-rooms were turned towards the central courtyard, and the level surface of the outside walls was only broken by small shops, which were crowded into any suitable recess, and sometimes seemed to go right back into the house behind, though in that case the shop-room was entirely shut off from the rest of the building.

It will perhaps scarcely be believed that we have in England itself many of those traces of Roman life which have enabled me to reconstruct so much of it from what is left in Nîmes and Arles. But an Englishman will always prefer to visit Provence or Italy, even if he can see much of what they hold in his own country; so it is from no fear of comparisons that I recall the Roman town of Silchester, with its baths, its forum, its temples, its amphitheatre, its walls; or the Roman walls and amphitheatre of Dorchester; or the Roman epitaphs and the magnificent fortifications on the north and east of Chester, which was once a seaport with sailing-ships upon the watery expanse of what is now the racecourse on the

Roodee. Now it is only the highest point touched by the sea-tides up the Dee, and its harbours are as desolate of maritime adventure as that sea-gate of Pompeii, which was once at the water's edge, and now is on the road from Naples, separated from the Mediterranean by the whole width of the railway to Salerno and the expanse of cotton fields. Then, too, from Newcastle to Carlisle we can still see the traces of that mighty wall which Hadrian first founded, after he had restored so much in Nîmes, to keep out the northern raiders. But at Bath we have an even closer parallel. There is the old shrine to the native fountain god, Sul, as the shrine was first built to Nemausus. Above it, as above the Provençal altar, rose a Roman temple; here, to Minerva. Some fourteen feet below the modern level is a Roman bath, eighty feet long by forty feet across, larger than that in Pompeii, larger than I have suggested even for Nîmes; and in it bathed the soldiers from the legions of the Rhine who caught the rheumatism in our British climate. Here, too, is a separate round bath for ladies, and, strangest parallel of all, the ruins of a Corinthian facade, forty feet high, just like that portico which the township of Nîmes added to the Nymphaeum of Augustus. The Rhone valley was far enough, in those days, from Rome. But Britain was infinitely further. Yet in each, we find the Roman living as he loved to live. In each we find the original inhabitants deliberately choosing to copy his way of life, his ways of worshipping, his very language.

It may be suspected that the old Roman, who at first knew no glorious gods in human shape such as the Greek divinities, tried to make up for his vagueness as to their individuality by a remarkable formality in ritual, which for long remained the chief characteristic of his religion. Augustus recognised this when he tried to bring back the flavour of the pristine days of virtue by reviving the old minutiae of worship, by extending them to the cult of the Emperors, by restoring (as he tells us himself) no less than eighty-two of the old temples by his own orders, and by carefully emphasising the connection between their worship and the general prosperity of family life both in town and country. His most delightful poet is careful to echo a view at once so statesmanlike and so sure of popularity:—

"Jam Fides et Pax et Honos Pudorque
Priscus et neglecta redire Virtus
Audet, apparetque beata pleno
Copia cornu." (Carm. Sec. 57.)

(Now Faith and Peace and Honour
and our previous Decency and
neglected Virtue dare to return
and blessed Plenty appears with full horn)

Or, again, Horace points out the results of this return to simple faiths:—

"Tutus bos etenim rura perambulat,
Nutrit rura Ceres almaque Faustitas,
Pacatum volitant per mare navitae,
Culpari metuit Fides." (Carm. IV. V.17.)

(And now the cattle stalk about the land in safety,
Ceres and sweet Fortune nourish the land,
The sailors fly back and forth over a sea at peace,
Faith shrinks from all possibility of blame)

I have reproduced in these pages a little statuette of a priestess of Ceres, found at Bouillargues, and now preserved in the Maison Carrée. It is not of the best period, and from the arrangement of the hair it may be argued that it was carved in the reign of Domitian, as may be seen from the bust of his wife, which is No. 1892 in the British Museum. It is roughly carved, and in bad proportion here and there. But the sway of the body is well rendered, and it is a valuable and interesting relic of a decadent age which has left few works of art, and of a small Roman village which could never have boasted skilled artificers. The festival of Ceres was on the 19th of April, when her temple was first founded at the foot of the Aventine, and from its very beginning was closely associated with the common people; for the famine from which they were then suffering was only relieved next year by importations of corn from Etruria, Cumae, and Sicily. That association lasted

Priestess of Ceres from Bouillargues
(now in Maison Carée at Nîmes)

while the worship of Ceres survived, and as the goddess of the fertility of the earth she was worshipped by its labourers:—

"Fertilis fragum pecorisque Tellus
Spicea donet Cererem corona."
(Carm. Sec. 29.)

(Let the Earth fertile with fruits and flocks
Bestow a crown made of corn on Ceres)

In the spring her favour was invoked upon the sowing; in the autumn both she and Tellus were prayed to bring the crops to their maturity at the "Feriae Sementivae" or "Paganalia." There were offerings of cake and a sacrifice of a pregnant sow, and the oxen which were to serve in ploughing were decorated with garlands.

If there was one person to whom a cry of gratitude must have gone up from all Provence for the peace that had given beauty to her cities and plenty to her lands, it was Augustus, whose bust is in the Museum at Arles. His personality is worth looking at a little more closely. It is described in careful detail by Suetonius, and I can do no better than quote Philemon Holland's version as it was published in 1606, for there is a flavour of intimate antiquity in his Elizabethan periods that our modern speech has either vulgarised or lost. Augustus, then:

"was of an excellent presence and personage and the same throughout all the degrees of his age most lovely and amiable; negligent though hee were in all manner of picked-nesse, for combing and trimming of his head so carelesse as that he would use at once many Barbers, such as came next hand, it skilled not whom; and one while hee clipped; another while hee shaved his beard; and yet at the very time he either read or else wrote somewhat. His visage and counte-nance, whether he spake or held his peace, was so mild, so pleasant and lightsome, that one of the Nobles and Potentates of Gaule

Bust of Augustus at Arles

confessed unto his countrymen he was thereby onely staied and reclaimed...Hee had a paire of cleere and shining eyes ...but in his old age he saw not very well with the left eye, his teeth grewe thinne in his head, and the same were small and ragged the haire of his head was somewhat curled and turning downeward; and withall of a light yellow colour. His eyebrowes met together: his eares were of a meane bignesse: his nose both in the upper part (toward his forehead) bearing out round, and also beneath somewhat of the longest. Of colour and complexion hee was betweene a browne and a faire white... Hee was five foote and nine inches high. .... In his left hucklebone, thigh and legge hee was not very sound, insomuch as many times for griefe thereof he halted on that side: but by a remedie that he had of Sand and Reedes he found ease and went upright againe. Also, the forefinger of his right hand hee perceived otherwhiles to be so weake that being benummed and shrunke by a crampe upon some colde, he could hardly set it to any writing, with the help of an hoope and fingerstall of horne... In winter time clad he went against the colde with foure coates, together with a good thicke gowne, and his Wastcoate or Peticoate bodie of woollen, well lapped also about the thighes and legges. During sommer he lay with his bed-chamber dores open, and oftentimes within a cloisture supported with pillers, having water walming out of a spring, or running from a spout conduit... Even at home hee never walked up and down in the aire without a broad brimd Hat (or Bond-grace) upon his head. He travailed in a licter, and never lightly but in the night."

Yet the man whose bodily infirmities were thus apparent probably knew the truth about the inhabitants of a greater extent of Empire than was ever under one control until our own Victoria ruled her seven seas. He was, as we know, for some time, and on several occasions, in Provence; and at Arles is preserved a touching memory of one of those tragedies from which not even the lives of emperors are free.

In the museum opposite St. Trophime is a bust of Marcellus,[9] son of Octavia, the sister of Augustus, whose daughter, Julia, the young prince married in B.C. 25, when he was eighteen, and when Horace wrote of him:—

"Crescit occulto velut arbor aevo
Fama Marcelli micat inter omnes
Julium sidus velut inter ignes
Luna minores."

(As a tree grows by unmarked lapse of time,
So grows the glory of Marcellus:
The Julian star shines among all others
like the moon
Among lesser fires)

Within two years he died. "Shortlived and unfortunate were those to whom the Roman people gave their love." His brilliant promise, and his early death seem to have touched every poet even in that age when sudden death had grown so common. They inspired one of the most beautiful passages in Virgil which closes with the famous lines:—

Marcellus
(from a drawing by Jane E. Cook of
the bust at Arles)

"Heu miserande puer! si qua fata aspera rumpas
Tu Marcellus eris. Manibus date lilia plenis:
Purpureos spargam flores..."

(Alas, pitiable boy! If only you can break the bonds of your harsh fate,
You will be Marcellus. Give me lilies with full hands:
Let me scatter purple flowers...)

The pathos of those mournful cadences shows still in the boyish face at Arles; a face, I can but think, which Augustus himself may have brought there, as a proud reminder of the prince whose power should follow his. Mutilated as it is, uneven as its workmanship may be, this bust is to me more touching in expression than many a more ostentatious statue that was meant to typify both splendour and catastrophe; for here the boy who has hardly yet realised the one seems already impressed with the impending sorrow of the other.

"Egregium forma juvenem et fulgentibus armis
Sed frons laeta parum et dejecto lumina vultu."

(A young man of handsome form and with shining weapons
But his face was not happy and his eyes were downcast)

Very different are the memories aroused by three other portrait-busts, which are here reproduced for the first time from the little collection in the Maison Carrée. They represent the Emperor Caracalla in his youth; the woman who was most intimately associated with the horrors of his subsequent career, his mother, Julia Domna, and her niece Julia Mamaea.[10] The brutalised and heavy features of Plantilla are to be found there also, but they are better known.

About the year 186 AD., Septimius Severus had lost his first wife, while he was acting-governor of Provence. An African by birth, Severus successfully concealed his real and daring ambition during his gradual ascent of honours until he was in command of the Pannonian army. When the news reached him that the Praetorians had foully murdered Pertinax and then sold the throne to a vain old senator, the wealthy Didius Julianus, he felt that the discontent of Rome would justly be diffused throughout the frontiers of the Empire. Unfortunately two other generals were also filled with equally righteous, and perhaps equally selfish, indignation. From Britain, from Syria, and from Pannonia, the legions of Clodius Albinus, of Pescennius Niger, and of Septimius Severus hurried to punish the assassins in the capital; but Severus was in the most advantageous situation, his province extended to the Julian Alps, and he was but fourteen days' march at most from Rome. His army, stimulated alike by honest vengeance and by strictly business principles, hastened to salute him as the Emperor, and surrounded his person with a picked bodyguard of six hundred men throughout the march, which ended almost bloodlessly; for its only victims were the actual assassins, whom the other Praetorians cheerfully betrayed, and the wretched Julian, who was beheaded in the baths of his palace. The other competing generals were crushed one after another, and Byzantium alone held out a three years siege in loyalty to Niger. Peace and a measure of prosperity were by degrees restored to the distracted provinces. It was time for the Emperor to choose a second wife.

Addicted, as was every African, to magic and divination, Severus picked out a young lady of Emesa, in Syria, whose first recommendation was her "royal nativity"; but Julia Domna, throughout her long life, proved that she was well worthy of all the stars could promise her, and there are indubitable traces of the beauty of her youth in the bust that represents her in maturer years at Nîmes. The combination of a lively imagination, a firm mind, and a strong judgment had seldom been visible in a woman who united to it so many amiable qualities; or whose love of letters, philosophy, and art was only equalled by her disregard of those conventions which are usually supposed to bind even the most exalted of her sex. She was the mother of Caracalla and of Geta; and if her prudence was sole support of her son's authority, her moderation was also the unique correction which his wild extravagance received. The constant quarrels of the young princes had early divided the court into two factions, which were as sharply hostile as those of the circus or the theatre; nor was the situation improved when their anxious father bestowed on each the titles of Antoninus and Augustus.

*Bust of Julia Domna
(from the Pont du Gard, now in
Maison Carrée at Nîmes)*

Hearing in 208 A.D. that Britain had been invaded by the Barbarians of the north, Severus welcomed the opportunity, though he was a gouty old man of over sixty, to take his two sons with him on a punitive expedition beyond the Wall of Hadrian, which only subdued the stern and wild Caledonians while the obstinate legions were still actually fighting on their territory. In 211 A.D. the Emperor Severus died at York, and his veterans immediately hailed both his sons with the august title of emperor. The brothers retired, with every sign of mutual suspicion, to the capital, where the vast estates of the Imperial Palace were scarcely large enough to separate the sinister ambitions of a mutual hostility. Only in the presence of their mother, Julia Domna, were they ever seen together; and by her passionate intervention alone was prevented the formal separation of an empire whose wide extent had hitherto remained inviolate. Caracalla at once prepared a swifter solution of the problem. While Julia Domna was striving to reconcile her sons, his centurions rushed in and despatched the wretched Geta in his mother's arms, and she herself was wounded in her unavailing efforts to protect her firstborn from assassination. An enormous donative rapidly placated the uneasy soldiers, but nothing availed to give the imperial murderer forgetfulness. Even his weeping mother he compelled by threats of instant death to welcome him with simulated smiles of approbation. Some twenty thousand others, less able to protect themselves, he condemned to death on the sole plea that they reminded him of Geta. Papinian, the Praetorian Prefect whose memory is immortalised in the annals of Roman jurisprudence, suffered the usual fate of an honourable refusal to condone his master's crimes. That little carving in the Maison Carrée represents the youth of one who became, in Gibbon's just and striking phrase, "the common enemy of mankind." If it be difficult to trace the future we now know in the lineaments that do not yet bear the stamp of senseless and universal villainy, it is at least possible to look with a new understanding at the firm lips, the deep-set eye, the strongly-marked and characteristic profile of the unhappy mother of that prodigy of vice. The end of Caracalla came in another assassination as he was on a pilgrimage from Edessa to the Temple of the Moon at Carrhae. It is a strange coincidence that to this precociously cruel and iniquitous despot was owing the important edict which conferred the name and privileges of a Roman citizen upon every free inhabitant of the Empire; and this apparent liberality would be entirely unintelligible were it not the direct result of his desire to increase by a more widespread taxation those funds which he so rapidly exhausted in gratifying the dictates of an insatiate extravagance. The Provincials soon found that any distinction which had formerly attached to their new title was rapidly obscured in the burdens of a complicated and intolerable tribute.

The dangerous honours of the imperial throne passed to Macrinus in 217 AD., who at once attempted to strengthen his position by bestowing the highest titles on his ten-year-old son Diadumenianus; and amidst the growing tumult of the disorderly army in Syria Julia Domna saw herself obliged to descend from the position of Empress-Mother to that of subject; and her proud spirit found release in voluntary death.

Her sister, Julia Maesa, meanwhile retired to Antioch with an immense fortune, and with two daughters, Soaemias and Mamaea, each a widow, and each with an only son. To her grandson, Bassianus, she soon managed, by intrigues and bribes, to transfer the affections of the soldiery. Macrinus and his son were conquered and destroyed. In twenty days the East was hailing the advent of a new Emperor, of Asiatic blood; and the Senate of Rome was

Bust of the Young Caracalla
(In Maison Carrée at Nîmes)

reading soon afterwards the astonishing tidings of Macrinus's fall. It was not long before Elagabalus, as the new Emperor called himself from the sun god of Emesa, was celebrating extravagant and impious rites within the walls of Rome and defiling the Eternal City with every circumstance of unrestrained debauchery and licence. Julia Maesa had no sooner foreseen his downfall than she had provided a successor in his cousin Alexander, the son of her other daughter, Julia Mamaea, the princess whose singularly frank and pleasing girlish countenance is preserved in the last bust I reproduce from the collection in the Maison Carrée. On the 10th of March A.D. 222, the Praetorians assassinated Elagabalus, his mother, and his favourites, and raised Alexander Severus to the throne under the guidance of his mother, Julia Mamaea, who virtually ruled the Empire, without attempting to secure those outward manifestations of majesty which had ruined her sister Soaemias, and which were invariably repellent (in a woman) to the majority of the Roman state. She preferred the substance to the pageantry of power; but she would brook no interference between herself and her son, and his wife she banished with ignominy to Africa. By means of a special council of sixteen senators, headed by the wise and celebrated Ulpian, she strove to fashion the

growing strength of the young Emperor for good. The story of his education and his life is the best testimony to the real worth of Julia Mamaea. Her fame would have remained unsullied but for the pardonable weakness which led her to demand from her son's riper years that minute obedience which had so much assisted his inexperienced youth. The imputation of effeminacy could never be eradicated, and all the devotion of his mother did not save her son the Emperor Alexander from assassination by the partisans of the rough Thracian soldier, Maximin. She perished with him, and would no doubt voluntarily have given up a life which had then lost its dearest object.[12]

Bust of Julia Mamaea in Youth (From Ste. Colombe, now in Maison Carrée at Nîmes)

Far off as were these tragedies from the valley of the Rhone, the certainty that Nîmes was not unaffected by them is preserved by the presence of these busts among the ruins of her Roman past. With good reason a modern monument recalls the benefactions Nîmes received in earlier years from Antoninus Pius. The public works of Augustus, and of Hadrian on the same spot, have been already mentioned. There is no doubt that for a long time after the confirmation of Augustus in his power the vices of his successors fell upon the capital alone, and it was the blessings of their ordered rule that were enjoyed by Provence. Even the bloodshed and disorder that followed the death of Marcus Aurelius did not prevent the prosperity of Arles from continuing for another sixty years. But it is significant that the magnificent gladiatorial shows provided in her amphitheatre by the Emperor Gallus in the October of 254 A.D. were given to celebrate a successful treaty of peace with the Goths, whose leader, Crocus, eventually pillaged the city and destroyed many of its monuments only six years afterwards. It was entirely due to the favour of Constantine that she ever recovered. The greatness of her Roman existence rose, indeed, to its highest point under the reign of that enlightened Emperor, whose palace is still represented on the banks of the Rhone by the ruined tower called La Trouille. From his time began a more intimate connection between Provence and the Emperors than had ever been before, a connection which was no doubt the beginning of that lasting prestige which made the city of 879 the capital of an independent kingdom. Valerius Paulinus, the imperial "Procurator" of Provence, had assured the loyalty of Gaul to Vespasian. The Emperors Carus, Carinus, and Numenan were all natives of Narbonne. But the Emperor Constantine, at the beginning of our fourth century, made Arles his chosen seat of power, and was confirmed in his affection by the birth there of his eldest born, the son of the Empress Fausta.

By the munificence of Constantine, the public and the imperial buildings of Arles rose to a greater splendour than had ever been seen before; and with him the Christian religion had become the religion of the throne. Even when the Emperor himself left it, the city was made the seat of the Praefecture of Gaul, including Spain, Britain, and a part of Germany within its jurisdiction, and it was often visited by his successors. Already the first great council of the Church had been summoned by Constantine, and attended by the Bishops of York, Trèves, Milan, and Carthage, and many more, under the primacy of the Bishop of Arles. By Saturninus, another Bishop of Arles, the Arian heresies favoured by the Emperor Constantine were supported in a second Council. By Honorius in 418, Arles was picked out as the meeting-place of the seven provinces of Gaul; and there, too, in 455, Avitus was proclaimed Emperor in the Alyscamps, while Theodoric and his Goths looked on. The Court of Majorian, established in 458 in the palace of Constantine (which was carefully described by Sidonius), was the last flicker of independent Roman power. Arles was captured, after an eight months' siege, by the King of the Visigoths in 468. Rome in Provence had died. We have only to look at a few of the tombs of Roman dead in Arles before we pass on to other centuries, and other forms of civilisation. Nearly all which I shall here describe are to be seen in the museum opposite St. Trophime.

A mighty hunter was evidently buried in the sarcophagus, which is carved with details of the chase. In the left-hand corner a wild boar, standing at bay, is despatched by a spearman. In the middle a pair of stags are endeavouring to escape. Out of the meshes of a net in the right-hand corner a hare slips away to safety, and above rides a huntsman in a Gallic hood. The workmanship is vigorous, though rude, and may well have been executed for one of those Gallic nobles whose country life in the vicinity of Nîmes Sidonius described in the fifth century. In the morning they played tennis in the "sphaeristerium," while the idler visitors read profane Latin authors in the library, leaving religious volumes to the ladies. They sat down twice in the day to a table spread with hot meat (boiled or roast) and wine. They hunted or rode on horseback at their pleasure, and used the hot baths on their return before the dinner-hour. Whoever the dead man may have been for whom this tomb was made he was certainly not a Christian, but this does not alone prove to me that the tomb itself is prior to the reign of Constantine. A far finer "hunting tomb" than this represents the slaying of the Boar of Calydon by Meleager, and was given by the town to Alphonse du Plessis Richelieu in 1640. It is now in the Museum at Autun.

A magnificent example of the work of the best classical epoch is the tomb of Cornelia Lacaena, which she set up in her lifetime to be cared for by her heirs. Finely carved rams' heads adorn each corner, and are also placed at each end of the heavy garlands of fruit that fill the space on each side of the tablet. It is a well-proportioned and well-executed piece of sculpture; and its reticence is typical of the Roman ideas of what was appropriate to a funereal monument. Another epitaph, numbered (18) in my list, shows that in early centuries a Roman husband and wife could record their sorrow for the death of a promising son of seventeen

Tomb of Cornelia Lacaena at Arles

in language as touching and as dignified as that (No. (20)) in which Donatus of Cologne deplores the loss of a baby three years old at Nîmes; and in this Museum at Arles exists the most outspoken expression of sorrow I have ever seen on a pre-Christian tomb. It is inscribed over the body of Julia Lucina (No. (19)), the beloved daughter of Parthenope. The grief felt for a loss of the opposite nature is well expressed in the Greek epitaph quoted in No. (22) of the list given in the Appendix, and taken from the tomb set up by his young son at Marseilles, to a father untimely dead. "This is the tomb of Glaucias, which was set up by the filial love of his young son, who showed, small as he was, this reverence towards his father. Ah! unhappy father! Thou didst not live long enough really to see thy child, who should have grown up to give thee sustenance instead of building thee a tomb. But envious Fortune was all too hard upon thee, dealing out tears to thine aged mother, widowhood to thy wife, together with orphanhood for thy unhappy son."

A most striking difference, both in treatment and in subject, is to be found in the early Christian monuments which form the most interesting part of this unparalleled collection of Roman sarcophagi. The pagans approached death cheerfully. They carved upon the dead man's tomb an agreeable recollection of the happiest scenes of life: the vine-gatherings, the olive-plantings, the hunting excursions that had filled his days; or they gave a frank and free expression of the best art they considered appropriate to his memory. The grace of these conceptions vanishes in early Christian work. It is replaced by saints and mourners, whose expression reveals an intensity of conviction that makes you forget their enormous hands, their unwieldy heads, their disproportionate limbs and bodies. Where the Roman took his happiness from the past, the early Christian fervently looked forward to the future that was the integral factor of his passionately trusted creed. One of the largest of these Christian tombs was made to hold two bodies, that of the husband and wife who are shown in the plain round medallion in the centre, dividing the two lines of horizontal sculpture which cover the front of the sarcophagus. In the upper division on the left are shown the stoning of St. Stephen and the sacrifice of Abraham. On the other side Moses (nearest the circle) receives the tablets of the Law from God; Susanna, standing between two trees, is watched by two old men; and in the right-hand corner Pontius Pilate washes his hands. Beneath him, on the lower line, are seen the Israelites escaping after the passage of the Red Sea, which is shown engulphing Pharaoh's horses under the central medallion. On the left are carved Shadrach, Meshach, and Abednego; and Daniel in the Den of Lions.

Scarcely less full of Scriptural allusion is the tomb on which the central medallion, holding the portraits of husband and wife, takes the form of a shell. Again there are two lines of carving. In the upper one, beginning on the left, is God receiving the sacrifices of Cain and Abel. This is followed by the seizure of Christ in the Garden, the Jews being given the form of headdress common to their sect in the fourth century. Further on is shown the healing of blind Bartimaeus, and the reception of the tablets of the Law by Moses. These subjects are closely crowded together with as little regard for space as for chronology. On the other side of the shell is again the sacrifice of Abraham, followed by the miracle of the loaves and fishes. The left-hand corner of the lower line is another representation of Susanna in the Garden, spied upon by only one old man. The miracle of the water which became wine is interposed between her and the story of Jonah, whose boat is represented beneath the shell, while on the left side the whale devours him, and on the right it vomits him on shore again. Next to this is the tree beneath which he slept, which the Lord withered. Further on are Adam and Eve with the devil as a serpent coiled round a tree; and the last group depicts Daniel in the Lions' Den.

A remarkable Christian tomb is that which shows the Cross, above which two of the Twelve Apostles represented, are holding a laurel wreath. At the foot of the Cross are two kneeling soldiers. It may well be that the soldier on the left represents Constantine when he saw the sacred signal in the heavens; and if so, this carving represents a very interesting transition from pagan to Christian art, a transition which would be further emphasised by the thoroughly pagan treatment of the medallions and winged children on the cover above it, if that cover can be proved to have originally formed part of the same tomb. In no case can the monument have anything to do with that son of Constantine and Fausta who was born at Arles in 316, as has sometimes been imagined.

The last Christian tomb I need select for special mention is that which represents the figure of Christ standing between two lambs in the central arch of an arcade with six Corinthian columns. Christ hands to St. Paul, upon his left, the Gospel which he is to preach to the Gentiles; St. John stands a little further on. St. Peter and St. James are carved upon the other side. In the corner, to the spectator's left, Christ washes Peter's feet. In the other niche is the scene of Pilate washing his hands at the Condemnation. The arcade upon this tomb is especially worth notice for the style of architecture it reveals. It is supported on columns with composite capitals and bases, and shafts like those of the early mediaeval cloisters, ornamented with spirals and flutings. The archivolt has become an architrave with leaf-encirclement carried round the arch, and filled in with a scallop shell, which shows very distinctly how the late Roman architects dispensed with the straight architrave, and adopted the arch springing directly from the capitals of the columns; so that we get here not only the transition from the Greek trabeated style to that of the Roman builders, but also a very valuable indication of the mode in which Roman art was continued into Christian times. The steps by which Provençal architecture bridged the gap between her great Roman ruins and her twelfth-century churches and castles will be suggested in later pages. But the example of this tomb was too good to be omitted here; and from it we may pass on, knowing a little of what is soon to come, to that avenue of tombs which leads to the holy fields of Arles, the Alyscamps; for there we shall find the beginnings of modern history in Provence.

NOTES

1. Part of what I have to say is sufficiently illustrated by the pictures reproduced in these pages. Other points may he studied from the original inscriptions, and a list of those which I have chosen will be found in Appendix I , numbered thus "(I)," for convenience of reference from the text.

2. "*Hybernis objecta Notis specularia puros*
   Admittunt soles et sine faece diem...
   Quid non ingenio voluit nattira licere?
   Auctumnum sterilis ferre jubetur hiems."

(The glass facing the winter winds lets in
pure sunshine and perfect daylight...
What is nature unwilling to grant to intelligence?
The barren winter is ordered to bring autumn)
[These quotations are given by Becker]

3. "*Dat festinatas, Caesar, tibi bruma coronas:*
   Quondam veris erat, nunc tua facta rosa est."

(The winter grants you, Caesar, garlands hastened into bloom:
Once it belonged to the spring, but your rose is ready now)

4. Mommsen quotes a dialogue from an ancient bas-relief which I will leave the antiquarian to translate, the price list being of great interest in its comparison between various items:—
Guest. A. *Copo computemus.* (Innkeeper, let us work out the bill)
Host. B. *Habes vini sextariom unum: panem, assem unum: pulmentariom, asses duos.* (You've had a pint of wine, a pennyworth of bread, two pennyworth of relish)
A. *Convenit.* (Fine)
B. *Puellam, asses octo.* (The girl, eightpence)
A. *Et hoc convenit.* (That's fine too)
B. *Foenum mulo, asses duos.* (Hay for the mule, twopence)
A. *Iste mulus ad me factum dabit.* (That mule will ruin me)
A bill of something over sixpence certainly deserves no more than the gentle irony of the last sentence. Its charges would certainly not appeal to the modern representative of Nicephorus at Nîmes.

5. At Arles, as elsewhere in every part of the Empire, there was a regular guild of carpenters and builders, as is shown by the following inscription:—"*Tit. Fl. Tito. Corp. Fabror. Tignarior. Corp.* (The guild of carpenters and builders of Arles for their patron Titus Flavius)

6. Others read "reducibus" instead of "vocibus."

7. The letters L. P. S. at the end of the inscription probably mean "Libertis Posterisque Suis." The "divinities of Amyclae" are the Dioscuri, the twin brethren, sons of Leda, and friends of seamen.

8. "*Fertur habere meos, si vera est fama, libellos*
   Inter delicias pulchra Vienna suas."

(If the report is true, fair Vienne is said to consider
My little books among her amenities)

9. Compare this head with the statue of Marcellus in the Candelabra gallery of the Vatican, and see Bernoulli (*op. cit.*) p. 124.

10. A careful comparison of the three busts I have reproduced here with others in the British Museum, and with coins, and with the volume of Bernoulli dealing with the reigns from Pertinax to Theodosius, has convinced me that the attributions here given are correct. The way this face of the young Caracalla changed as he grew older may be studied in Bust No. 1917 in the British Museum. In the coin department there is also a charming "'aureus," showing his youthful face with that of Geta, and another wilth Caracalla alone, showing just the type of this bust at Nîmes. The very characteristic face and headdress of his mother, Julia Domna, are also unmistakable. See Bernoulli (*op. cit*), p.40, No 14, and plate xvi, which shows the deep-set eye so conspicuous in the Nîmes carving. The only doubt I had was concerning Julia Mamaea, whose face in the Vatican (illustrated in Bernoulli's plate xxxii) has a decidedly aquiline nose, and strong, proud features, more like what we should expect in one who virtually ruled the Roman world. The only likeness to this head at Nîmes is in the thin underlip and the upward turn of the corners of the mouth. The "aureus" of Julia Mamaea also seems to show a more aquiline nose; and, when I had examined bust 1905 in the British Museum, I almost concluded that the bust at Nîmes represented the wife of Marcus Aurelius. But I am now convinced that this is indeed Julia Mamaea in her youth before her marriage, before power and responsibility had hardened her features; and in this I have the valuable support of Bernoulli, who says (*op. cit.*, p. 110, No.15) of Julia Mamaea's portraits: "Kopf im Nîmes, mit hohem Untergesicht, *doch vielleicht richtig benannt.*" The Caracalla was found at Nîmes, the Julia Domna at Pont du Gard, and the Julia Mamaea at Ste. Colombe. The bust of Julia Mamaea in the British Museum is labelled No. 1920, as "the mother of Alesander Severus, died 235." It is later than the one at Nîmes, which was probably sent there by her aunt.

11. These busts were photographed for me by R. Royer of Nîmes.

12. There is an inscription preserved at Aix, concerning Julia Mamaea, part of which I give here because it is curious to find both these lines and the bust in Provence. This inscription was first brought from St. Cannat to King René's chapel in Aix, and was bought by St. Vincens in 1798. Kaibel thinks it must have originally come from Ostia, or rather Porto. It begins as follows: ὕπερ σωτηρίας Μάρκου Ἀυρηλίου Σεουήρου Ἀλεξάνδρου Ἐυτυχοῦς Ἐυσεβοῦς Σεβαστοῦ καὶ Ἰουλίας Μαμαίας Σεβαστῆς μητρὸς Σεβαστοῦ Διῒ Ἡλίῳ μεγάλῳ Σεράπιδι καὶ τοῖς συννάοις θεοῖς Μ. Ἀυρήλιος Ἥρων νεωκόρος τοῦ ἐν Πόρτῳ Σεράπιδος ἐπὶ Λαργινίῳ βειταλίωνι . . . . κ. τ. λ.

(On behalf of the preservation of Marcus Aurelius Severus Fortunate Pious Augustus and of Julia Mamaea August mother of the Augustus to the great god Helios Serapis and to the other gods of this temple M. Aurelius Heron, temple warden, on the authority of Larginius Vitalion...) The original is in Uncial letters divided into very short lines.

CHAPTER IX

The Churches and Cathedrals of Provence

Part I: The Alyscamps and the Kingdom of Arles

> "Si come ad Arli, ove Rodano stagna
> ...Fanno i sepolcri tutto il loco varo...
> ... Qui son gli eresiarche
> Coi mr seguaci d'ogni setta, e molto
> Più, che non credi, son le tombe carche...
> "Qui con più di mille giaccio:
> Qua entro è lo secondo Federico
> E il Cardinale."...
> —DANTE, Inf. ix. x.

DEEP as we may bury the Roman Empire, we cannot hide it in the valley of the Rhone; for its bones pierce through Provençal soil in many places as though that giant grave were still too narrow for the skeleton of a past that can never wholly die. Rome herself, Eternal City though she be, held but for a relatively short period the heart of that colossal, civilising force. Provence herself was but one district in the enormous tracts of Europe, Asia, Africa, which can still show the strength of Roman walls, still listen to the decrees of Roman law. At St. Remy and elsewhere we have seen the beginnings of that Empire which lasted even after the cataclysm of 476, through evil fate and good, until Charlemagne was crowned in Rome;

until the Holy Roman Empire rose again with Otto the Great in 962; until the title handed on from Hohenstaufen to Hapsburg was resigned for the last time by the House of Austria, and the heir of all the Caesars laid down their crown in August 1806. Napoleon Buonaparte added to the Act of the Confederation of the Rhine the fateful sentence that Francis II "no longer recognises the existence of the Germanic Constitution"; and in 1806 the last formality perished of an institution which had ceased to have any vital influence after the death of the Emperor Frederick II in 1250, but which lasted more than a thousand years after Leo the Pope had crowned the Frankish king, and nearly eighteen hundred and sixty years after Caesar had conquered at Pharsalia.

Yet it is by no mere allegory of a poetical imagination that Rome, and all Rome stands for, has been called the "Eternal City"; for while the world lasts Rome can never die; and unless the mediaeval theory of the Roman Empire, and its continued existence, be thoroughly understood, the significance of mediaeval European history can never be realised. The course of events in the British islands has indeed been scarcely modified at all by conditions which left almost their sole trace in the title of Richard, Earl of Cornwall, and King of the Romans, who, like his brother, our own Henry III, married a princess of Provence, the sister-in-law of St. Louis and of Charles d'Anjou. But neither the story of Provence, nor that of any part of Europe, can be explained, up to the fourteenth century, unless we realise the belief of such a man as Dante, for instance, as to the government of the world he knew. To him it was a matter of right that there should be a universal monarch of the world; that this monarch should be the Roman Emperor, the successor of Augustus Caesar; that the chosen of the German electors was, of eternal right, as that successor, the Lord of the World. That this largely remained a theory, rather than a fact, in no way diminishes its importance; nor is it less essential to remember, concerning this idea of a universal Christian monarchy, that the Roman Empire and the Catholic Church were two aspects of the one Society ordained by the divine will to spread itself over the world, with the Roman Caesar as its temporal chief, and the Roman Pontiff as its spiritual head. This was an impracticable dream; but it was none the less magnificent; and it had that enormous effect on practical politics which the unrecognised forces of deep-rooted sentiment invariably exert.

For the Mediterranean coasts the first sway of Rome meant chiefly peace. Far from those scenes of terror and humiliation which surrounded the immediate neighbourhood of the Emperor's person, the upper classes of Provence lived in the enjoyment of their wealth and liberty until the first shock of the Barbarian invasions; and the motto of the Roman Empire seemed to be the proud lines of her greatest poet:—

> " *Tu regere imperio populos, Romane, memento;*
> *Hae tibi erunt artes; pacisque imponere morem,*
> *Parcere subjectis, et debellare superbos...* "

(Remember, Roman, that you are to rule the peoples with your empire.
These will be your arts: to impose the custom of peace,
to pardon the defeated and vanquish the proud)

Even when the separation between East and West became necessary, Rome seemed but to have left her older throne that she might Romanise the world more thoroughly; her power became a natural and undying attribute of life and time, above the chances of mortality:—

> *"Quod bibimus passim Rhodanum, potamus Orontem,*
> *Quod cuncti gens una sumus. Nec terminus unquam*
> *Romanae ditionis erit..."*

(Because everywhere we drink the wine of the Rhone and the Orontes,
because we are all one family. Because there will never be a boundary
to Roman domination)

The Christianity which Constantine took to be the religion of the Empire was already a great political force. The union was inevitable. The Church at once began to reproduce the imperial system for herself, to set before the eyes of men the visible Catholic religion, uniform in faith and ritual, to which the life and feelings of the people might for ever firmly be attached.

No better symbol can be imagined of that union in Provence than the Alyscamps of Arles; for among those tombs around St. Honorat we can see both the death of old Rome and the rise of that new Empire which was to last into the nineteenth century, of that new faith which was still to inspire the twentieth. And Arles herself is typical of that Holy Roman Empire, alike in its rise and its decay. The latter lasted on until, as Voltaire said, it was not Holy, it was not Roman, it was not an Empire. Of Arles, it may be said with equal truth that, when her imperial splendours faded, she refused all lesser sovranty, and has ever since been slowly dying, amid the pathetic remnants of her past magnificence. No longer are her walls for soldiers, her palaces for statesmen, or her quays for merchants. She has become a shrine to which the artist and the poet may make pilgrimage; she has become the tomb of a whole population, of a city buried, like the warrior chiefs of old, with all her jewels and her gold and gods around her.

The words *Campi Elysii* have given rise to two place-names about as different in the associations they arouse as any names could be: the Champs Elysées, that central artery of Parisian life; and the Alyscamps, the Avenue of Death at Arles. There is perhaps a significance in this which will he worth our notice; for it is profoundly true that nothing so clearly reveals the attitude of every generation towards Life as the monuments which it has raised to Death. This is so because we must envisage the Unknown to ourselves in terms of the Known, and because Art can only represent the meaning of the end of life by using the materials of a life that has not yet passed away; by expressing regret for what is left behind, or happiness in hope of change; by laying stress upon the little circle of individual affection which is lost, or upon the greater world of those uncounted multitudes who have but gone before.

The finest tombs of the Alyscamps, as works of art, are either in the Arles Museum or in the Louvre; but like those that fringe the sides of that sad avenue of poplar-trees which leads towards St. Honorat, all of these are empty. Sometimes even the names of their dead are wanting. But any consideration of sepulchral architecture brings out at once the fact that we have already lost one great pre-occupation of antiquity, the building of our own tombs. The Pharaohs must have filled up large portions of their lives with it; many of the Roman Emperors made it their highest and most serious task; the busiest of the Popes found time for it; the least important princeling of a tiny state never forgot it. When this fashion seemed slightly passing away the sculptors and the architects revived the same vanity in a different form. For ten whole years Pollaiuolo chiselled the tomb of Sixtus IV; almost as long were Cousin and Jean Goujon upon that of Louis de Brézé;[1] twenty-nine years' work was represented in the monument of Philip the Bold, thirty-five in that of John the Fearless and Margaret of Bavaria, eighty in that of Maximilian. Life must have seemed almost smothered by these labours in the praise of Death.

The Alyscamps

Greek art showed the living figure on the tomb of the dead man. Graeco-Roman and early Christian art preserved that living attribute although their sculptors made less of it. In the early Renaissance and the best of the middle ages the dead lie still, but ready; the helmet near their uncovered head; the gauntlet near their hand; their good sword at their side. At the sound of the trumpet they will arise, ready for the battle they have been dreaming of so long. The sequence of Papal sepulchres in the Lateran and St. Peter's at Rome shows a strange change as time progresses. The once prostrate figure raises himself upon one elbow, looks about him; at last he kneels in prayer, or sits enthroned upon the sepulchre, with outstretched hand to bless or ban. A wave of sinister memories seems in the sixteenth century to have overwhelmed the dead. The warrior asleep has become the *Pensieroso*, sitting, thinking over the melancholy of life. Beneath the knight in armour, mounted on his warhorse, lies the naked corpse, the unveiled horror of the charnel-house. By the eighteenth century life seems to have tried to triumph. Marshal Saxe, his baton in his hand, marches in all the pomp of military etiquette towards an official and respectable interment. Yet it is a sad and sorry farce. He is far more lifeless than the sleeping warriors of the Gothic churches; for they seem ready to awake, helmeted, and sword in hand, and robed in all their heraldry; their greyhounds up and straining at the leash, and clouds of sympathetic cherubim above them. So, in this strange development of art, that early Christian work which we chiefly associate with St. Trophime, St. Honorat, and the Alyscamps, reveals the hunger of these first disciples for the reality of Christ, for the literal and true exactness of the Scriptures. Miracles, and parables, and stories of the saints filled every corner of the stone and marble in these holy plains to which the Rhone brought down upon her waves the bodies of the Christian dead.

> *"...Dis Aliscamp lou cementèri*
> *Plen de miracle e de mistèri*
> *Plen de capello emai de cros*
> *E tout gibous di mouloun d'os*
> *Se relargavo..."*[2]

Here was the true necropolis of Gaul, consecrated, as the legend runs, by the blessing of the Christ Himself, who appeared to St. Trophime upon this sacred spot, and by the chapel dedicated to the living Virgin... "sacellum dedicatum deiparae adhuc viventi." At first a Roman burial-place, this cemetery gradually became the chosen bourne of every man who wished his body to await in peace the coming of the resurrection. By the twelfth century it was sufficient to place the corpse of some beloved dead, from Avignon or further, into a rude coffin, fashioned like a barrel, and to commit it to the Rhone, which brought its quiet charge in safety to the beach of La Roquette. No sacrilegious hands were ever laid upon that travelling bier; for once a man of Beaucaire had robbed the coffin that was floating past his bridge, and straightway the corpse remained immovable in the current of the river, and stayed there until the thief confessed his crime and put the jewels back.

Here, until the translation of the relics to the cathedral, lay the body of St. Trophime,[3] and at the end of the seventeenth century Seguin saw in the vaults the tombs of "St. Genet, St. Roland, Archbishop of Arles, St. Concorde, St. Dorothea, the virgin-martyr who was born at Arles, and the two archbishops Hilary and Virgil."

The archway near the present entrance is one of the original gates of the ancient cemetery, and the building to which it is attached is called the chapel of St. Accurse, which was built in 1521 at a time when the arch formed the gateway to the convent of St. Césaire, who was one of the very early bishops of Arles in the sixth century. It commemorates a fatal duel which was fought in the Parvis of the convent between a bully named Antoine de Quijéran, Baron de Beaujeu, and the young Accurse de la Tour, who was slain in a quarrel that was pressed upon him for a trifle. He died with the hilt of his sword upon his heart, and the name of his betrothed, Etiennette de Laval, on his lips. The blood-fine of two hundred crowns of gold paid by de Beaujeu was devoted to the building of this chapel, where Masses were said every day for the soul of the young lover, whose tomb may still be seen close by the archway. It is a fitting introduction to a place where the Angel of Death seems so near at hand that you may almost hear the beating of his wings.

The cemetery itself was the scene of that fight between William of Orange (known as the "short nose") and the Saracens, which is described in a thirteenth-century poem. A hundred thousand fought on either side, and when the Rhone ran red with blood the Count of Orange fled back to his lady, Guibour, who refused at first to let him in as I have described elsewhere. In the church of St. Honorat itself is the tomb of the only Frenchman who escaped from the horrors of the Sicilian Vespers, one of the Porcellets. Elsewhere, among the scattered tombs is the little unregarded pyramid that was set up in memory of some of the bravest men who were ever buried in that historic soil, the Consuls of Arles in the year 1721, the year of the last great plague.

I must stop by it for a moment, in defiance of chronology, to tell you what those consuls did, for they suggest one of the most terrible pages in that long history of Arles, of Provence, and of the Empire, which lies buried in the Alyscamps. Their names were Guillaume de Piquet, Jean François Franconi, Guillaume Granier, and Charles Honorat, and they were elected to take the place of others who had fallen in the same honourable cause, devoting themselves to the salvation of their fellow-citizens from the pestilence.

From 1226 to 1721 there are many horrible instances of the decimation of the people of Arles from this one hideous cause. Two-thirds of them were swept away by the Black Death of 1348, which crammed the cemetery of St. Maclou in Rouen, and devastated Europe. One notary alone in Arles remained at his post throughout a pestilence which was not confined even to the city walls, but stalked abroad through the parched fields of the countryside. From March to August in that fearful year his registers contain nothing but the record of testamentary depositions; not a sale, not a single marriage-contract, had to be written down. Following hard upon the plague came a massacre of the Jews, who were the more easily supposed to be its authors, because the majority of the citizens were indebted to them. Four times again in that miserable fourteenth century did the plague return. By 1416 the grass was sprouting in the streets, and weeds were growing in the fields. The houses were nearly all deserted. Scarcely had the unhappy city begun to recover from the shock than, in 1429, another pestilence came down upon the weakened population; and men and women had to be tempted to take up their residence here from other parts of France by promises of special exemptions from taxation. In 1456 two magistrates fled from the town, Jacques de Massio, and Jehan de Porcellet, whose name had never had to bear so deep a stain before. But their burgess comrades, Julien Doume and Pierre Borel, stayed nobly at their posts and carried out the duties of their perilous office. Repeated visitations of the same sickness in the sixteenth century led to the establishment of a plague hospital beyond the city walls in 1579.

In 1640 some soldiers from Languedoc, where the contagion was still rife, brought the germs of the plague into that seething cauldron of close-packed and poverty-stricken humanity which the amphitheatre had by that time become. Abandoned to base uses ever since the Romans had departed, in turn a citadel, a dungeon, and a thieves' kitchen, that vast arena had gradually become choked with the hovels of the poor, or the dens of the criminal. Every archway held its nest of human outcasts. From stone to stone they cast their rotting beams and plaster and burrowed into the very entrails of the enormous building to seek a safe shelter for their hideous iniquities, a secure retreat from the pursuit of the officers of the law.

A man murdered his enemy in the market-place of Arles, carried his corpse to the Arena, and was tracked there by the avengers. But after they had thought to trap him in the four walls of some dark recess, he vanished utterly. In another moment the pursuers were themselves cut off; and as the great stone behind them rolled into its place they caught a glimpse of the hell-mouth beneath them. From its pestiferous recesses rose the noisome exhalations of a crowded airless pit. The smoke of fires swirled fitfully from every corner, and cooking-pots swung heavily above them. Here and there, in wide stone ledges circling upwards, the gable of some temporary tottering shed shone livid in the torchlight as men moved to and fro about their hideous business. A stir of indescribable ferocity, of smothered vice echoed from the cavernous vault. One of the pursuers escaped, but only lived to tell what he had seen, then died in madness.

Such was the place in which the plague broke out in 1640. Already cut off socially from the rest of Arles, the inhabitants of "Les Arènes," as they were called, were now shut off from all communication. A cordon of militia was drawn up at a safe distance outside, and orders were given to shoot without pity any who attempted to escape. There was no means, within that fatal circle, of burying the dead, of getting fresh water, or of procuring medical assistance. Day by day, the corpses were seen, beneath the walls, of women who had cast themselves down at night to easier death than they could find inside. Morning by morning the soldiers shot down one child after another who tottered out towards the fresh air and the water of the town that had never before refused him either.

Meanwhile booths were being set up as quickly as possible in a remote faubourg of Arles, and in some of them the plague-stricken, in others the still healthy inhabitants of the amphitheatre, were to be bestowed. At sunrise on the 20th of May the barricades were opened, with a strong guard in attendance, and the first file of volunteers moved into the Roman amphitheatre. The survivors who could still walk, now that they were offered an escape, refused to move from the hovels in which they had hitherto had to be imprisoned by main force. The dying were left beside the dead. The rest were ruthlessly torn out. By midday the passing bell began to toll from the church close at hand, and the hideous procession made its way slowly through the great north door, between a double line of soldiers with their hallebardes lowered. At once the whole population of the city rushed to the spectacle. Some few had acquaintances, even relations, in that plague-stricken band of phantoms; and here and there a woman would struggle through the soldiers to catch a wasted hand she once had loved, or a child—and there were very few of them—would slip beneath the weapons of the guards and run into the crowd of citizens behind towards a well-known face. A long wail of distress and agony went up from every side as the line grew longer and the crowd that pressed upon it grew more passionate. A charitable rain of offerings fell from one quarter and another upon the sick and weary prisoners—garments, bread, fruit, and wine—some of it only to fall unheeded and be trampled in the mud. Here and there the men from "Les Arènes," leaving the provisions of which they stood so sore in need, were seen to be fighting with the last remnant of their strength for the coins that richer citizens had thrown in misplaced kindness; for they could buy nothing.

Suddenly a man died; died in horrible convulsions among the muddy cobblestones of the main street and, as if some dread signal had been given, five more fell dead beside him. Those in front stopped, trembling. Those behind refused to move. For a moment panic seemed about to break loose, and a quick order was given to the arquebusiers. From all sides of the road the soldiers hemmed in the procession, blew on their matches, and prepared to fire into the wavering ranks. But the immediate danger passed. As soon as the leading files had passed the city gate and felt the fresh air blowing from the fields, a merciful balm seemed to have been laid upon their favoured brow. The relics of St. Roch had been brought out and laid upon an altar by the wayside. With one accord the multitude, plague-stricken and whole alike, fell upon their knees. Above them on a rocky eminence, protected by their guards, the archbishop and his clergy raised the chants of Holy Church, and blessed their stricken people. Headed by the reliquary of the saint, the procession went on with new faith and new hope, and as they disappeared into the places set apart for them, the people on the walls of Arles were singing:—

Ora pro nobis, beate Roche,
Ut mereamur preservari a morte.

(Pray for us, blessed Roch,
That we may deserve to be saved from death)

The plague of 1720 was the only repetition of these fearful sufferings that can ever be compared with them, and the last which Provence had to bear. Brought from Marseilles in March on board a ship from the Levant, the contagion was carried into Arles by a Tarascon pedlar, who had bought some of her infected cargo, and sold it to a tradesman who was found dead in the town. His children, his wife, his mother died soon afterwards. Sanitary committees were immediately formed by the civic authorities, and every ordinary precautionary measure was at once enforced. The poor, and all without homes or means of support, were sent into isolated camps at Trinquetaille. The monastery of St. Honorat in the Alyscamps was one of several buildings set apart as special hospitals. Enormous trenches were dug in the nearest shores of the Camargue in which to bury the dead, who soon fell too quickly for any funeral rites to be still possible. All this had not happened until

November, and at first it seemed as if the quick precautions born of cruel experience had been sufficient to check all but the first outburst. Then came news that the plague had once more broken out in the Amphitheatre. The fearful memories of eighty years before had not yet died out, and the same stern measures of seclusion were again adopted. Then men waited, as though on the verge of a volcano.

In March 1721 Arles was cut off, by royal orders, from all communication with her neighbours, and mills were put up on the banks of the Rhone to grind the flour that had formerly been imported. In the month of May only one hundred and thirty persons perished. The inhabitants begged M. de Caylus to be allowed to reap their harvests, in fields which lay outside the line of isolation. But the eyes of almost the whole of France, terrified at what might happen, were upon him; and he refused. The scum of the streets, and the more reckless citizens, chafed against a severity they misunderstood, and riots arose in which the town's small stock of grain was looted, wasted, thrown away. Three thousand ruffians, followed by their women and children, forced the bridge of the Crau, and scattered over the countryside. Within the town barricades were immediately set up by the authorities, and the whole place put in a state of siege. The archbishop, heroically endeavouring to restore order, went in person to Trinquetaille, where most of the rioters had gathered, and exhorted them, by every means of persuasion, to remember their duty to their city and to Provence. Three of the ringleaders were publicly shot by de Caylus's guards, in June 1721, and a compromise was arrived at by a slight extension of the lines of isolation. But the evil had been done. In that one month the plague claimed three thousand five hundred and twenty victims.

Those who ventured out of doors were hurled into the hospitals on the least sign of weakness, and when the hospitals were crammed to overflowing, the sick were left untended in the streets; those who stayed in their homes died, alone amid the wealth they tried so fruitlessly to guard, untended by servants, by relations, by their own sons. Neither fresh linen nor serviceable drugs were to be found any more in the whole town. The bakers closed their ovens, and no more bread was made. The butchers left their shops, for there were no more beasts to slaughter. Nîmes, Beaucaire, and Rheims did what they could for the unhappy city by sending generous alms; the Bishop of Castres and the Archbishop of St. Trophime sent their whole stock of plate and linen; the monks of the monastery of Montmajour sent all their money: in the very worst of the disorder M. de Jossand, major in the Régiment de Noailles, came from Tarascon to take command of the Arles garrison, after the death of M. de Beaumont. It was from him that hope at last began, and safety came a little nearer. By his energy a vessel was sent up the Rhone with medicines and curatives of all kinds, and barges were started along the river, laden with grain and loaves, from Tarascon and Beaucaire, All through August the harvest of hideous death went on;—

> "...La Mort, segant la farandoulo—
> Hoù! Hou! la Mort-peleto idoulo —
> S'esperlongon alor en lènto proucessioun
> Li rengueirado vierginenco
> Li Penitent dins si bourrenco
> E dins si raubo purpurenco
> Lou Parlamen illustre, e vint coungregacioun. "4

For a time no practical measures, no religious fervour, no patriotic charity seemed able to stem the strength of the pestilence, or to alleviate horrors which were doubled by the inevitable outbreak of brigandage and every form of crime. In the convent of St. Césaire by the Alyscamps the courage and persistence of the abbess alone stamped out the disease before it had entirely devastated her flock. But the consuls were driven from the Hôtel de Ville, and had to meet elsewhere to transact their business, in a town where the very churches had to close their doors for fear of the contagion of the congregations. All four of them died, and their dangerous office was taken up by the four men whose tomb I have mentioned in the Alyscamps. With eight others they now formed a sanitary commission which had originally numbered sixty. Each survivor had to do the work of five. The heat and drought of that awful summer lent the last touch of fatal virulence to the disease. The registers were so crammed with entries that margins and even bindings were inscribed with dead; for four thousand and twenty-five had died within a month.

In their despair, men and women, weak themselves but still untouched, began processions round the town; carrying the relics of St. Roch before them. At last the worst was over. The devoted efforts of the consuls in every quarter of the town—almost in every house—began to bear fruit. The deaf ears of the Deity seemed at last to open to the agony and the supplications of His worshippers. It was again possible to send armed patrols through the streets to enforce the sanitary ordinances.

Great fires were lit in the open spaces, and cannon were fired down the streets. In August only three hundred and forty-one deaths were registered. By the end of September the pestilence was over. The enfeebled population were allowed out into their lands to reap what little harvest there was left. The town was saved at last; and in their work of saving her the consuls died. That little pyramid in the Alyscamps alone preserves the names, and the heroic efforts, of Piquet, Franconi, Granier, and Honorat—four of the noblest of the citizens of Arles.

The church of St. Honorat at the end of the long avenue of tombs is a building that seems overcome by the desolation and decay of which it has for so many centuries been the guardian. The raised choir is built over a crypt, as at San Miniato, and its sturdy, round pillars look so squat because the soil has gradually risen above their bases until nearly half of every shaft is buried. It is a very ancient foundation, which has been frequently restored; but the west doorway with its zig-zag carving is evidently of the twelfth century, as is the very beautiful and peculiarly shaped belfry which surmounts the whole, with the most unusual feature of the dome that covers it.

The St. Honorat to whom this church in the Alyscamps was dedicated was born in Toul. He founded on one of the Iles de Lérins, between Antibes and Fréjus, an abbey which became the Thébaïde of Provence, and now bears his name, next to the Ile Ste. Marguerite. This little island, for it is the smaller of the two, and lies beyond the other, still contains fragments of almost every style of building known in Provence from the time of the Romans. It had been deserted by their latest garrisons when St. Honorat first reached it. Probably nothing of his time remains. But the chapel of Ste. Trinité, at the eastern point of the island, is one of the earliest structures in Provence. The original had a triapsal choir crowned by a small dome, and above the old walls the Spaniards built up a square platform for guns in the sixteenth century. The interior, however, retains features of construction which may well go back as far as the seventh century; and it deserves comparison with the ancient crypt beneath the church of St. Gervais at Rouen, which was built in 406 by St. Victrice, and is the oldest relic of its kind in France. The eleventh century church was replaced by a new church in 1876; but the old original cloister, built in the simple Cistercian style, still remains, with its circular vault strengthened by transverse ribs. The monastery, however, was a far more important building, and the castle which protected it still shows the great square crenelated towers which were finished in 1190. In

St. Honorat des Alyscamps, Arles

the eastern division of this monastic keep is an open cloister, which was once three, and is now two, stories in height, and is reached by a narrow passage from the entrance in the north wall. It was probably begun in 1315, and completed, after an interval in which nothing was done, before 1422, probably soon after the body of St. Honorat was brought here from Forcalquier. The upper and lower cloisters together form one of the most interesting architectural features to be seen in Europe.[5]

I have mentioned this monastery here partly because St. Honorat, its founder, afterwards became Archbishop of Arles, and partly because such foundations as his, or that of the Abbey of St. Victor at Marseilles, by Cassian, may be taken as typical of that extraordinary religious situation with which the invading Barbarians came in contact. These uncultured and untaught soldiers were suddenly faced by the stupendous and massive edifices erected for Rome's pleasure or dominion, on the one hand; on the other they found the crowding worshippers, the already stately ceremonies, of a Christian faith as different from their own rude sacrifices as was the Coliseum from the hovels and waggons of their roving communities. The double influence went on in other directions as well. If the skill of a well-trained Roman official was indispensable to princes who were suddenly called upon to rule wide lands and scattered populations, so the aid of the Christian bishops, the intellectual aristocracy of these new subjects, was equally invaluable both in guiding their own policy and in conciliating the vanquished. From these considerations arose the association of the Empire with the Church, and the belief in the eternal universality of both.

"His ego nec metas rerum, nec tempora pono;
Imperium sine fine dedi..."

(I shall impose no limits to their power through the ages;
I have granted them an empire without end...)

If the Empire had grown somewhat weaker, its work had been taken on by the Church, until the two became indissoluble, and the sanctity of one was endued with the strength and the traditions of the other; for indeed no power has ever since been based upon foundations so sure and so deep as those which the Roman Empire laid during three centuries of conquest and four of undisturbed dominion. There are many who see, in the deep-rooted belief of the French people, that to them it naturally belongs to lead the policy of neighbouring states, a survival, for good or evil, of that imperialist spirit of Rome which was so deeply ingrained in her constitution and her soil during the centuries when Rome was ruling in Provence.

Yet, if it had not been for Christian churches as well as Roman laws, it is doubtful whether Rome herself could have lasted through the chaos out of which the empire of Charlemagne was finally evolved.

The first kingdom of the Burgundians, founded in 406 from Dijon to the Mediterranean, was wrecked by the sons of Clovis in 534, and survived weakly through the Merovingian dynasty in shrunken borders. Arles had already suffered many a siege when the Franks succeeded to what Burgundians and Goths had held. Yet through it all she kept to Roman customs, and remained a centre of religious legislation. In 570 the Lombards fell upon her, and though they no doubt brought certain principles of the art of those Comacine "Freemasons," whose work we shall see at St. Trophime, yet they devastated once more, with fire and sword, a Provence that must have wellnigh reached the limit of endurance. Her greatest name, in those terrible years, was that of

Mummolus, who held back the invaders as well as he could, assisted by the military bishops of Gap and Embrun. But even he could not survive the intestinal struggles which desolated Provence from Marseilles northwards, and which originated among those who should have combined for her defence. As if human dangers were not enough, earthquakes began to shake the tortured soil, and plague broke out along the valley of the Rhone.

Amidst all these accumulated horrors, Childebert founded the famous Abbey of Montmajour on the hill just outside Arles, which was then surrounded with so much water that it is called in ancient deeds an island; "insula S. Petri quae nominatur a monte majori," as is written in the Act of Exchange by which "the Chapter of St. Stephen of Arles" gave it up for other property in Provence in the ninth century. In 974 it passed into the hands of the Abbot Mauringus by consent of Manassès, Archbishop of Arles. Its lands were almost at once largely increased, and by 1019 Abbé Rambert was asking another Archbishop of Arles to consecrate the chapel of Ste. Croix on the eastern slope of the hill; and the close connection kept up with the metropolis is once more evident in 1040 when the Archbishop Raimbaud secured to Moutmajour some lands endangered by the powerful monastery of St. Victor at Marseilles. By Count Raymond-Bérenger, the fishermen of Arles were ordered to take the first sturgeon caught between Fourques and the sea to the Abbey of Montmajour, a privilege which provided numerous causes for quarrel from 1193 to 1740. The abbot's rights to his own gibbet and justice, brought into question in 1336, were confirmed over the lands of Montmajour and Castellet in 1417. On several occasions the same man had held both the dignities of abbot of Montmajour and Archbishop of Arles before his death. Such were Louis d'Allemand, Cardinal Pierre de Foix, Philippe and Eustache de Levis, and Nicholas Cibo. The Pardon of Ste. Croix, which had attracted a pilgrimage of nearly 150,000 persons in 1409, was given a still higher reputation by the bull of Pope Julius II; and in 1502 the independence of the monastery was finally assured by Alexander VI. The foundation-stone of the latest buildings was laid by the Archbishop of Arles in 1703, after a magnificent plan suggested by the Benedictine monks of that time; and these are the strangely modern-looking rooms which may still be seen in ruins near the old towers and shrines. The mass of architecture may be easily visited on the way out of Arles towards Fontvieille and Les Baux, and presents a very clear epitome of the history just sketched.

The Abbey of Montmajour

I first saw Montmajour as one stage in the most beautiful drive Provence, or perhaps any country, can show, the journey that begins at St. Remy, passes through Les Baux, and so, by way of Montmajour, reaches the town of Arles. The guide pays no attention to historic sequence in showing the visitors a mass of architecture which resumes at least five different periods of Provençal building. But the heart of the whole is the smallest, lowliest, structure of them all, the rough and rock-hewn sanctuary in which St. Trophime is said to have preached the Gospels to the first Christian catechists who burrowed in the very bowels of the rock for safety. This ancient and sacred hiding-place was later on converted into a chapel and enclosed with an arcade cut in the rock. Over this again an outer wall was added to form a chapel dedicated to St. Peter. At its east end are the three rude chambers, hewn in rock without any architectural features except a rude seat cut all round the inner side and the apse. One of these cells was the confessional of St. Trophime. At the west end is a space forming a kind of narthex. Its external buttresses are the lowest feature in the whole mass of buildings, at the eastern end, as you look at them from the garden to the south.

Above this ancient site, on the upper part of the rock, was built the monastery, protected by fortified walls, and by a huge oblong donjon-keep, erected in 1369, by Pons de l'Orme, of square-dressed stones with the surface left rough. The whole forms a parallelogram of forty-eight feet by thirty-two feet, with a slight projection at the south-west angle to hold the spiral staircase which leads to the top, where a magnificent view of the surrounding country can be obtained. The impression of military strength obtained as you slowly pass one fortified room after another, and finally reach the platform upheld by its machicolated battlements, makes a very strong contrast with the purely religious character of the buildings round it; and this combination of religious with military architecture is one that we shall find to be particularly characteristic of the churches of Provence.

The church of the monastery is in the severe Provençal style of the twelfth century, without aisles; for though it was begun in 1016 it was not continued for two hundred years, and it has never been completed. Both the church and the huge crypt beneath it are in the form of a Latin cross, and the upper building forms one great hall with a transept and apse and extremely short nave; the choir too is very short, as is usual in Cistercian churches. The enriched Gothic chapel was added to the north transept in the fourteenth century. The cloister is equally simple, and in this, beautiful as are its proportions, it offers a strong contrast to the richly-chiselled decorations of St. Trophime. The bodies of Geoffrey, Count of Provence (d. 1066), and of Adelaide, widow of Count William I (d. 992), were buried here. Its arcades are formed of segmented arches springing from solid piers and fluted pillars, and each large arch is filled with three smaller ones resting on pairs of light shafts with sculptured capitals. The original lean-to roof, covered with stone flags, and provided with large gargoyles and corbels, is here preserved, and will show what the cloister of St. Trophime must have looked like when it was first constructed.

The most interesting structure after this is the separate little chapel of Ste. Croix, which stands by itself beyond the east end of the main mass of buildings. This is a very remarkable church, which seems far more appropriate to the east than to any western home of religion. Its four apses are arranged in the form of a Greek cross, crowned with a square dome. At the west end is a square porch, which will remind you of the entrance to Notre Dame des Doms at Avignon.[6] The triangular pediments and cornices, of egg-mouldings and modillions, and the circular arch of the doorway, are all reminiscent of late Roman work, while the ornamental cresting and other details are thoroughly Byzantine. The inscription which mentions Charlemagne is a forgery, and Mérimée showed that the date of the building was 1019. It was probably a mortuary chapel, and the excavations outside it, at the west and at the south-east, are meant to represent the graves of martyrs, which were supposed to lend additional sanctity to the burial-place.

Of the inextricable mixture of eighteenth-century work on the hill, and various other unimportant details on the "Island of Montmajour," I have deliberately said nothing, for the place is only mentioned here to give one more instance of the religious activity that was so remarkable among the Benedictines and other religious orders, who were almost the sole guardians of scholarship and culture in an age of ignorance and violence. The taste which guided the builders of Montmajour, not in their architecture only, but in their choice of so noble and impressive a site, is but one indication of the ideals which they upheld so worthily. Desolated, ruined far more by man's brutality than by the kindlier hand of time, these abbey walls preserve an undying memory of all that is represented by their past, a past which began to show its promise only when the Saracens had been finally vanquished; and it is a singular example of that difference in geographical conditions on which I have so often had to insist, that the invading Mohammedans were able to reach "the island of Montmajour" by boats from the Mediterranean.

Though Charles Martel crushed the Saracens near Poitiers when they attempted to attack the very heart of France, the southern provinces within reach of the Pyrenees remained at the mercy of the infidel invaders from Spain, who had begun to sack and pillage the buildings of Provence as soon as they crossed over. It was more than a century before they were driven out with any prospect of finality; and it was the Franks who cleared Provence of them, for the Goth who held the seigneury of Nîmes, Maguelonne, Béziers, and Agde found himself powerless to overcome them without help. The long and agonising struggle for existence which their ruthless warfare had involved—a warfare against carvings of men and women as bitter as against the population itself—had one good result out of all the evil which preceded it: for Church and State, those two great entities that were gradually rising out of the chaos of individual ambitions, were slowly welded together in the conflict of both against the Mussulman. The Church had taken Rome; Charles, the Frankish king, took the Emperor's crown, and between them the Holy Roman Empire came into being. The only sovereign of the time who could compare with Charlemagne was the famous Haroun-al-Raschid, who, as the head of the Moslem world, sent the Keys of Jerusalem to the head of the Christian world, besides a striking clock, an ape, and an elephant; things which impressed the imagination of those times as typifying that Charlemagne had been invested with the sovranty of Jerusalem and the lordship of the world.

The dream did not seem so far off now, the noble ideal of the unity of God and of the religion of all nations. For it was on their religious life that the permanence of nations had ever seemed to depend as far back as nationality could be predicated at all; and the brotherhood of man, depending as it did upon the common worship of so great a section of humanity, seemed likely to unite the tribes which had been divided by their various creeds, just as strongly as the common language and the common law of Rome had welded together the diverse tongues and customs of so many various populations. By Clement, by Alcuin, by St. Benedict, by Paul Warnefrid, by Theodulf, by Agabart, the results of that unification were brilliantly proclaimed, and it became the central governing fact of the world's progress, indissolubly connected with the Church.

A terrible shock was, however, given to this new system, which in the reign of Charlemagne had arisen almost too swiftly, almost too perfectly, by the renewed attacks of the Barbarians when Charlemagne's empire was divided at his death. But that division was rather the result of exaggeration in extent than of intrinsic weakness of quality. However high might be the ideals of all in spiritual matters, many little material difficulties had yet to be adjusted, many irresistible individualities of race and tradition remained to be reckoned with. One result of this partition of the boundaries was the foundation of the two kingdoms of Burgundy: the upper, called Burgundia Transjurensis, founded by Rudolf, and recognised by the Emperor in 888, included the north of Savoy and all Switzerland from the Reuss to the Jura; the lower, called the kingdom of Provence, founded by Boson, brother-in-law of Charles the Bold, in 879, included Provence, Dauphiné, the southern part of Savoy, and the country from the Jura to the Saône, and its kings were crowned at Arles. But all this had not been accomplished without the sad but certain proof having been given that the Church, mighty as had been her influence in civilising and unifying mankind, could not defend the nations from their enemies; and men whose life in this world had been wholly wrecked were not yet ready to accept, as perfect consolation, her promises of happiness in the world to come. Provence, for instance, had seen Roland, Archbishop of Arles, besieged by the Saracens in his own abbey of St.

Césaire on the Isle of the Camargues; she had seen the invaders bought off with difficulty by huge ransoms in money, stuffs, and slaves; she had seen the corpse of the archbishop, attired in all his sacerdotal splendour, carried over a Saracen ship's side and derisively returned to the care of his fellow-countrymen who had paid so heavily for his release. It was evident that some new machinery for solving the practical problems of life had to be devised; and that machinery was found in the feudalism which lasted until the continued absence of the barons at the Crusades gave the free communes a chance to seize their liberty, and to found, upon the shoulders of the people, the true powers of the king.

Of the feudalism that filled, for a time, the gap so well, Boson, King of Provence, was one of the first and the most powerful champions, and he was elected by twenty-three bishops of the south and east of Gaul in council assembled. His kingdom, as such, has almost vanished from history; but it held the land between the Rhone and the Alps, and in modern geographical terms it included Provence, Orange, the Venaissin, Dauphiné, Lyons, Bresse, Bugey, Franche Comté, Savoy, Nice, and a large part of Switzerland. With the Rhone and Saône to the west, the Alps to the east, and the Mediterranean to the south, its natural boundaries seemed as well marked out as those of any kingdom of France; and all its inhabitants (save a few in what was to be Switzerland) spoke the Latin speech. There was, indeed, no valid reason, in the nature of things, why the kingdom of Arles, instead of the kingdom of France, should not gradually have absorbed all the territory that eventually became French; just as Saxony or Bavaria might have risen to the place which was eventually held by Prussia in the German Empire of 1871.

The dominion of the Frankish kings of the house of Clovis corresponded neither to ancient Gaul nor to the territory of modern France, and did not extend much further than the Loire. Charlemagne was indeed the Lord of Western Christendom, gathering Saxony, Bavaria, Lombardy, and Aquitaine under his rule, and wearing—as a Teutonic king—the diadem of Augustus bestowed by Rome herself. But to him Paris was only the provincial town occasionally visited by the lord of Rome and Aachen, who spoke his native Teutonic; and though be also acquired the Latin, and could understand the Greek, he could neither speak nor understand the French, if indeed any French language could yet be said to have existed.

Boson was Count of Bourges, of Lyons, and of Vienne, Duke of Aquitaine, and Abbot of St. Maurice in the Valois, one of the richest abbeys of the Empire. He was therefore well equipped to take up the responsibilities of the kingdom of Arles and no doubt the ecclesiastics who elected him fully understood his value as a protection against the attacks of the Saracens and other invaders. He was succeeded on the throne in 887 by his ten-year-old son, Louis Boson, who was under the regency of the widow Hermengarde, and was once more confirmed in his rule by the election of the Church. That these elective powers surpassed any hereditary principle became clearer still when Hugh, son of Count Theobald, succeeded to the regal power of Louis Boson, who, after a vain attempt on Lombardy and Italy, had been blinded by his enemies, and had languished away in Vienne; leaving much of his wealth to the monasteries and churches of the Rhone. Hugh, more attracted by Italy than by the lands he had a right to rule, only deserved well of Provence by destroying the Saracen stronghold of Fraxinet from which the infidels had been accustomed to ravage the Mediterranean coast, where their memory is preserved in the name of the Montagnes des Maures. But he lost all his popularity and power by eventually making a treaty with the Mohammedans which left them far more advantage on French soil than was either natural or right, and after having given up the greater part of his dominions he was at last forced to abdicate the throne of Arles itself. The Saracens were not finally driven out until the time of Count William I, who succeeded to Provence in 968.

By 962 Otho the Great had been crowned Emperor at Rome; and the last emperor whose suzerainty the French kings admitted was the first to found again the real strength of that Holy Roman Empire which Charlemagne began. In 987 the kingdom of modern France may be said to have begun with Hugh Capet, to whom Lotharingia, Provence, and Burgundy belonged as little as did England, and Aquitaine was virtually independent. Provence had practically fallen by this time into the hands of the territorial magnates, and a thorough realisation of their own powerlessness drew the Counts of Provence who called themselves kings of Arles, to seek the definite protection of the Emperor Conrad II, the first monarch of the great Franconian line, who entered into possession of "the Arelate" in 1032, seven years before he died. Its acquisition was of importance to the Empire, for it was a Romance land; it made the Empire look less German; for several generations it put off the tendency to union between Burgundy and France; and it guarded the Italian frontier. After 1032 it is only as counts, as men who must do homage to the Emperor for their fief, that one can speak of the rulers of Provence;

and after that date too we find that the Emperors, as Kings of Arles, were often crowned there, as well as at Rome, at Aachen, and at Monza.[7] And though they may not all have attached as much importance to Arles as to their other ceremonial visits, the Emperors began to recognise the value of Provence as a bulwark against France in 1350 when they lost Dauphiné; and the union of Provence with France, in 1481, proved a serious calamity to them, for it brought the French nearer Switzerland and opened to them a tempting passage into Italy.

What Boson of Provence had represented in feudalism, that was Raymond de St. Gilles, Count of Toulouse, in the Crusades which were preached under Pope Urban II, in 1095. The religious fervour of the people had been stirred at first by the sufferings of their own land from the Saracen; then by the universal terror of the year 1000, which was supposed to be the end of the world; and finally by an outburst of almost fanatical enthusiasm for the call to free the Holy City from the defilement of the infidel. The words of Peter the Hermit fell like flames upon the stubble, and there was a mighty upheaval from one end of France to the other. Not one of the great feudal princes who started for Palestine was so wealthy or so powerful as the Count Raymond of Toulouse, of Rouèrgue, and of Nîmes and Duke of Narbonne; and all the south land followed him.

The character of the Provençal, as it appeared in Count Raymond's army, has been preserved for us by a contemporary eyewitness,[8] and it is worth transcribing here as an instance of the tenacity of national characteristics: "The Provençal is as different from the Frenchman as a duck from a chicken, in customs, character, costume, and food. Not very warlike, if the truth be told, but their prudence during the time of famine was more useful than all the courage of more military races. Without bread they were content to eat roots or the stalks of vegetables, and carried a long iron rod with which they probed the earth for eatables. Hence came the proverb: 'The Frenchman for fighting, but the Provençal for victuals.' But they were not always honest, for they sometimes sold dog for hare, and donkey for goat's flesh, and were not above killing a stray horse or mule when they had the chance, which they did in a secret manner of their own that much surprised the ignorant; and they were usually offered the carcase by the astonished owner, who was as sorry for their apparent starvation as they were amused at his evident stupidity." Their constant liveliness and loquacity is observed by another historian; and it is clear that with some of the civilisation of the Greeks they had absorbed a little of their cunning; while the industry of their commercial habits was not unmixed with a large share of chicanery; and the whole was leavened by a freedom of thought and life reflected from the many eastern customs with which they had already come in contact.

But there are better associations than this between Provence and the Crusades. In 1080 a citizen of Martigues, Gérard Tenque by name, founded the Hospital of St. John at Jerusalem, which afterwards became the great order of the Knights of Malta; and the husband of Gerberge, Countess of Provence, who was called Gilbert the Good, brought back many relics from the Holy Land which were afterwards to be seen in the churches of Arles and all its district. One of his daughters, as we shall learn later, was wedded to a Seigneur of Les Baux; the other, with the pretty name of Douce, married Raymond-Bérenger, Count of Barcelona, and therewith began a dynasty of Catalan Counts, on the eastern bank of the Rhone Under this Raymond-Bérenger the many fiefs into which Provence had been divided were gradually brought into a closer union: Forcalquier, which included Avignon, Cavaillon, Gap, Embrun, and other places, besides the County of Venaissin; the Viscounty of Marseilles, which included Toulon, Trets, Hyères, Fos, and Martigues; the barony of Guignan; the county of Sault; and the strongest of all, the barony of Les Baux. Raymond-Bérenger died in a hospitallery of the Knights Templars, who were then at the height of their power, and was succeeded in 1130 by his second son, Bérenger-Raymond, in Provence. The house of Les Baux, seconded by the galleys of the Genoese, now made continuous efforts to secure the sovranty. They were repulsed for a time by the help of Barcelona, and eventually the second Raymond-Bérenger was firmly fixed in the Provençal dominions by the same puissant aid; but not until Hugues des Baux had been driven out of Arles and conquered, in 1161. The politic marriage between young Raymond-Bérenger and Richilda, niece of the Empress, seemed about to settle him firmly, and for long, in his domains, when he was slain, in 1166, beneath the walls of Nice in a vain attempt to extend the boundaries of the realm he had but just acquired with so much difficulty.

Only twelve years afterwards the house of Les Baux inherited the county of Orange through Bertrand, brother-in-law to Raimbault the troubadour, and thus acquired the title of Prince, conferred by Frederick Barbarossa as he passed through Orange to Arles. Bertrand's son was granted the kingdom of Arles by the Emperor Frederick II, and throughout the thirteenth century Orange did homage to Provence, which in turn was itself a fief of the Empire, and as such was done homage for, to the Emperor, by its counts, until the time of Charles d'Anjou (d. 1285).

The houses of private citizens of this time are so rare that I must now draw particular attention to the Romanesque house at Arles, with the parapets above it, drawn for me by Mr. F. L. Griggs, with that round-arched doorway which will remind us of the decorative arches of St. Trophime; and at St. Gilles is an even finer example of a Romanesque dwelling, which stands up a by-street opposite the great west front of the cathedral, and is now used as the dwelling of the curé. In this was born Pope Clement IV (1265-1268), and the house itself probably dates from about the middle of the twelfth century; and though the outside was preserved by Prosper Mérimée as a "monument historique," not much is left of the splendours of the interior except the chimney piece on the second floor. It was dedicated as the habitation of the priest in 1877.

With the middle of the twelfth century I have now reached the period of the building of the church of St. Trophime, for amid all the changing fortunes that have been already sketched, it will be seen that very little opportunity for building can have occurred; and it is most significant that the art which resulted in the wonderful portal we shall now examine appears to have begun to flourish just when the city of Arles proclaimed itself a Republic, a form of internal government which it preserved from 1131 to 1251.

It was therefore within the walls of St. Trophime that the Emperor Barbarossa was crowned in 1178, and that his son was crowned King of Burgundy after him. But no better instance could be given of the almost inextricable entanglements of suzerainty at this time than the fact that homage for Arles was done to the Emperor Henry VI (who was crowned in 1190) by Richard Coeur de Lion of England; a transaction which represented the fact that Richard had handed over England to the Emperor, and received the fief of Arles in exchange, thus being enabled, as a prince of the Empire, to vote at the election of Frederick II.[9] The kingdom of England was also, of course, graciously returned to Richard, as a fief of the Empire; but the policy involved in the grant of Arles was no doubt that of expressing hostility to France by the most vivid and picturesque means at the Emperor's command.

The review of history that has been suggested to us by the cemetery of the Alyscamps ends, therefore, as it began, with a greater realisation

Romanesque House at Arles

of the meaning and the power of the Church, as the vital expression of the Holy Roman Empire in Provence. For, after the year 1000 had passed away without the sounding of the trump of doom, the Crusades began a development of liberty which was, in its final source, directly attributable to the Church. Feudality had had its reasons; but it left a feudal overlord, who turned into the tyrant of his countryside. But when he had armed his serfs and vassals, when he had led them to Palestine, when he had suffered hunger and thirst and wounds with them in war against the infidel, their relations became entirely changed. The poorer men who went to fight came back with broader views on many subjects; the poorer men who stayed at home took the opportunity of their lord's absence to live in greater freedom, and to frame the first idea of the first Communes. The absence of the barons had strengthened the king as much as it had helped the people; and these two extremes found each their own benefit in the rise of the other, being warmly assisted by the bishops and clergy, who were ready to accept anything rather than the continued power of the feudal overlord.

In the north it was Church and King which rose: in Provence it was the people and the Church. The Republic of Arles and the Church of St. Trophime typify the social evolution of the country in the middle of the twelfth century; and perhaps the most illuminating example of the change wrought in men's minds is to be found in the process which developed "Gothic architecture" (as it is so wrongly called) in the north, and which evolved the Romanesque cathedral of the south out of the primitive basilica.

NOTES

1. See *The Story of Rouen,* by T. A. Cook, chap. xii. p.292.

2. "The cemetery of the Alyscamps was outstretched, full of miracles and mysteries, full of chapels and tombs, and bossed with heaps of bones..."—*Nerto.*

3. His epitaph was copied in 1687 by Seguin, as follows:—

Trophimus hic colitor Arelatis praesul avitus
Gallia quem primium sensit Apostolicum.
In hunc Ambrosium Proceres fudere nitorem,
Clavigerer ipse Petrus, Paulus et egregius.
Omnis de cujus suscepit Gallia fonte
Clara salutiferae dogmata tunc fidei.
Hiuc constanter ovans cervicem Gallia flectit,
Et matri dignum praebuit obsequium.

(Trophime is venerated here, ancestral prelate of Arles,
who was the first to be recognised as bishop by France.
On him ambrosial glory was poured by the great,
By St. Peter with the keys himself and by the illustrious Paul.
From his fountain all France received
The clear doctrines of the faith which brings salvation.

From this time France constantly bowed her neck in prayer
And offered worthy service to her mother)

4. "Death with his scythe sweeps down the dance, his hideous skeleton howling—
and then the slow procession of the virgin ranks begins, the penitents in black or
purple robes, the senators, and congregations by the score."—*Calendal.*

5. For a description fuller than I can give in this place, see MacGibbon's *Architecture
of Provence and the Riviera,* pp.324-340.

6. See note on p. 316.

7. A notary of Frederick's household, quoted by Mr. Bryce, gives the list of these four
coronations as follows (*Holy Roman Empire,* p.193):—

> "*Primus Aquisgrani locus est, post haec Arelati,*
> *Inde Modoetiae regali sede locari,*
> *Post solet Italiae summa corona dari...*"

(The first place was Aachen, afterwards Arles,
Next the royal throne was placed at Monza,
After that the highest crown was granted to Italy...)

8. Quoted in Michelet, *Hist. de France,* vol. ii, p.277.

9. Hoveden (quoted by Bryce) says: "*Consilio matris suae deposuit se de regno Angliae
et tradidit illud imperatori Henrico Sexto sicut universorum domino.*" (On the advice
of his mother he deposed himself from the kingdom of England and handed it over
to the Emperor Henri IV as supreme lord)

Part II: St. Trophime and St. Gilles

"Ansin la nav de Sant-Trefume
Que longo-mai l'encèns perfume
Amount se bandiguè cenacle esperitau
Di primat d'Arle e di councile;
Ansin la glèiso de Sant-Gile
Emè li Sant de l'Evangile
Que vihon aplanta sonto si tres pourtau
E sa viseto qu'en mourgeto
Es perfourado...
...Erias li Franc Massoun! La tiblo,
Aplanarello irresistiblo,
Coume un lume de nive brihavo... "[1]

WITHOUT some clear realisation of the disorders of the Middle Ages, it is quite impossible to understand their passion for the unity typified by the Roman Empire and the Roman Church. Few and slight as must necessarily be—in a book of this kind—the indications of the violence, the uncertainty, the manifold terrors of the centuries between 500 and 1150, they have been, I hope, sufficient to explain that frenzy of obedience, that unquestioning submission to dogma and to sacerdotalism which was one inevitable result of all that had gone before. Phrases, which have now degenerated into the mere catchwords of a mechanical and unmeaning liturgy, were then filled with a vital and profound sincerity. Unable, still, to rise far above material feelings, men realised, with a thrill that was as full of awe as of belief, the visible Church militant upon earth; and into language which was equally insistent and intelligible they translated the doctrines of a triumphant Church in heaven, or of a kingdom of the damned in hell. They willingly surrendered all their individual opinions to one comforting body of belief; which was the constant companion of their thoughts, and which was brought practically into contact with their lives from the first morning Mass to the last vesper hymn at evening, from their first entry into being at baptism to the last consecration of their ashes after death.

By degrees the signs and symbols of this unseen life so multiplied in number and in strength that it seemed even more real than the phenomena of their own senses. The Church became, not the portal merely from this world to the world to come, but the very incarnation of them both; for if she hallowed and sanctified the one, she visibly displayed the other; and this is the true key to the architecture of the centuries from 1100 to 1400, as it is also the true, and only, reason why that architecture can never reappear. For the state of mind and conditions of life which evolved its best expression can never be reproduced.

Here, in these pages, we have comparatively little to do with that style of architecture called "Gothic" "Opus Francigenum," the art of the Île de France, of which England's pointed style is a younger, a less perfect, though still a very beautiful sister. But if that architecture meant anything—and I am not speaking now of technical details such as the pointed arch, but of the inspiring spirit of the whole—it meant an embodiment of the life around it, a life full of ardent faith, composed of elements which are now as obsolete as the sincerity which animated them. That is why a nation which only half believes, which has lost nearly all its handicrafts, which is debased as much by wealth as by machinery, and as much by breathless impatience of delay as either, can never reproduce the "Gothic" cathedrals. When a "Renaissance" followed on the exhaustion of the "Gothic," it was necessarily to the perfection of classical models that the new teachers had to go. That perfection happened, in its architectural expression, to be capable of reproduction in its essential details, much as the society by which it was developed was capable of some faint imitation by the princes and courtiers of the Renaissance. But in Provence we are in a different age; and it is only one more example of the separation constantly observable between Provence and France, that the greatest instances of Provençal architecture

A Choirstall at Albi

are entirely different from the greatest achievements of the more northern French. Above the line of the Loire, the rise of king and people produced a style which reached perfection in the "Gothic" cathedrals on the one hand, in the Renaissance châteaux on the other. Here, down the valley of the Rhone, the rise of Church and people produced the perfection of the "Romanesque," because in Provence Rome had never been forgotten, and the Roman Church was but another manifestation of the spirit of the Roman Empire. The Christian Church was the direct descendant of the Roman basilica; and though the turmoil of Western Europe in the years between Justinian and Charlemagne left scarcely any buildings of that time still standing, the Eastern Empire encouraged, throughout all that period, the full splendour of architecture and of the arts. Thus, then, we can realise a little better why Provençal architecture has something Eastern as well as something Roman in its composition, and why it differs from more northern work in sentiment, in structure, in decoration, and in style. I do not propose to be more technical than is necessary for the better enjoyment, by the casual, cultivated traveller, of the things he sees; and the various features in St. Trophime at Arles will provide me with quite sufficient material for my purpose. When the best of the other churches in my district have been added as illustrations to the various subjects thus suggested, I shall have mentioned all that is essential to the understanding of some of the most interesting structures on the soil of France.

There was a church on the site of the present St. Trophime in the earliest centuries of Christianity in Arles; within it was held the important council of 314 which condemned the Donatists, and the later councils of 442 and 451. Within it also was consecrated St. Augustine, the apostle to England. It was probably dedicated to Stephen, to whom St. Virgile is known to have consecrated the church he erected on the same site in 606. That building has entirely disappeared, and though some good authorities wish to find remnants dating before 1100 in the present structure, it would, I think, be dangerous to date any of the work we now see as much before 1152, the year in which the body of St. Trophime was brought from the Alyscamps to a more imposing shrine.

Very possibly building was begun sufficiently previous to 1152 to ensure a safe resting-place for the saint's remains; but since the bell-tower, the western porch, and the north walk of the cloisters are the oldest parts, and are all of the same period, it is tempting to suggest that they were begun very soon after the sculptor Brunus had signed his work upon the marvellous façade of St. Gilles, completed in 1150, so near at hand; and it may well be that the portal of St. Trophime was not finished until 1180. I am only now giving a general idea of the chronology of the whole edifice, without discussing details, so I may add at once that the portal is older than the wall behind it, as is the case at Notre Dame des Doms at Avignon, and Ste. Marthe at Tarascon, for the nave is in the Cistercian manner of what may be called the second Provençal style, severely plain, without ornaments. As you look down it from the western entrance, this nave seems closed in at the eastern end by a blank wall which comes down apparently from the roof until it almost shuts off any good view of the choir. This wall is really the bottom of the tower, which rises over the crossing and the line to which it descends gives the height of the original church for which the tower, porch, and north cloister-walk were built. When the nave was rebuilt, and raised higher than any other Romanesque vault in the south of France, it was impossible to raise the arches at the crossing on which the bell-tower rested, so they were left untouched, with the result just mentioned.[2]

The present choir and apse were built in 1430 by Cardinal Louis d'Allemand in the style of northern "Gothic," and the transepts have a great deal of seventeenth-century work.

Almost the first noticeable peculiarity about these structures, whose various dates have now been given, is that the main structural features of the church show the pointed arch, while for such decorative elements as the portal, cloisters, and windows, the round arch is employed. This use of the pointed arch in Provence is the most remarkable divergence from the usual Roman model in which, of course, both vaults and arches were invariably round. Now it cannot be too often emphasised that the pointed form was adopted, not from aesthetic, but for constructive reasons; it was more easily built at first, it exerted less thrust on the side walls, and it suited the slope of the tiled roof. Besides this, the pointed arch could be used with greater flexibility, as the northern builders found out later with such surprising results, because, by its means, intersecting vaults could be erected over spaces of any form, either square or oblong, and the apex of all the vaults could at the same time be kept at any desired height. This gradually led to its employment by the "Gothic" architects for all the openings of their building as well, so as to secure uniformity in construction. But the Provençals kept their round arch for decoration even when they found themselves obliged to use the pointed arch for construction; and it is singular to observe that as their skill increased, they gave up the pointed arch even in construction, just at the time when the northern builders finally abandoned the round arch altogether, in the middle of the thirteenth century. This is one reason why such cathedrals as Carcassonne or Narbonne, of purely northern design, have the imported look of an exotic plant, and are quite inappropriate to their southern surroundings.

It is often thought that the pointed arch is the chief differentiation between the "Gothic" and other styles. This is not the case; nor was it to "Gothic" architects that we owe the invention of the pointed arch, if indeed its "invention" can ever be discovered anywhere. It has been found in constructions of 2000 B.C. in Latium, in the tomb of Atreus at Mycenae, in the subterranean gallery at Antequere in Mexico, in several subterranean aqueducts near Rome, in the mosques of Caliph Omar in 638. These may be perhaps considered as either accidental or ornamental, or at any rate singular instances. But the form is freely used in an Armenian church at Ani in 1010, and the important development of ribbed ogival vaulting was employed at Durham Cathedral, one of the most marvellous structures in the world, between 1093 and 1104. The first pointed arches in Italian churches are generally said to be in St. Francis's at Assisi (1120) and St. Antonio at Padua, five years later; but pointed arches occur among the round, in 981 and 1053, in two little churches annexed to the monastery of Subiaco on Monte Telaso, and the ribbed vaults of St. Ambrogio in Milan were certainly built before 1129.

The most casual glance at the interior of St. Trophime will do more to show the difference between "Romanesque" and "Gothic" than volumes of learned disquisition, for it will reveal a building with pointed vaults that is the very reverse of such a nave as that of Chartres, or Rheims, or Beauvais, or any other of the great cathedrals of the Île de France. That Provence, wedded as she was to Rome and to Byzantium, and to the traditional dogmas they implied, should have boldly adopted for herself the simple pointed style of construction introduced by the Cistercians in the twelfth century, is one of the greatest debts which architecture owes her; for from that style was developed the noblest art of building in the world. But Provence returned, as she was bound to do, to the style of architecture natural to the south, and to the traditional dogmas so deeply ingrained in her soil by all her history; and in the sombre nave of St. Trophime you can see how this came about.

That nave is only lit by the small round-topped windows, let in over each bay in the eighteenth century; for owing to the system of building the aisles in relation to the nave, very little light could reach the middle of the church from them, because the central vault had to be held up by the half vaults of the sides. In a "Gothic" building, the thrust of that central vault would have been conveyed to flying buttresses strengthened by pinnacles, with the immediate result that the side walls instead of being thick and heavy, with small windows, would become so much thinner that at last they would be transformed almost completely into great sheets of coloured glass, divided only by the ribs and pillars that held up the vaults. This vital relation of the vaulting to the window-openings, accompanied as it was by the construction of ribs at the intersections of cross-vaults, is one of the essential characteristics of the "Gothic" work of the Île de France, where a rainy, cloudy climate necessitated sloping roofs, and plenty of light, and thus developed that amazing system of balanced thrusts which is the triumph of northern architecture. In the hot sunshine of Provence, thick walls pierced with small windows seemed natural and convenient, so we find shadowy churches whether the pointed arch is used or not.

The whole difference between the social developments of the north and south is clear in this one feature of their respective architectures. The first is full of vigorous life, on which the light shall stream in its full strength from heaven; the second, earnestly, passionately imbued with a profound belief in ecclesiastical traditions and teachings, prays in a darkened building, and fills its porches and its cloisters with the innumerable symbols of the priestly dogma, with the most fantastically imagined yet wholly reverent details of an austerely authoritative faith.

It has been thought that much of the constructive detail in Provençal masonry was derived from those early Syrian, Graeco-Roman churches between Antioch and Aleppo, which were from 1098 to 1268 in the possession of Crusaders who brought over the principles of their architecture to the valley of the Rhone. This link in the development of the art of building I have already mentioned in speaking of the Temple to Diana in the Roman baths of Nîmes. But I do not think it is necessary to go so far for an explanation of Provençal architecture in a country which is still so full of Roman remains that a whole system could be reconstructed from their stones alone. The Syrian churches had none of the statuary and figure-sculpture which is so characteristic of the valley of the Rhone; but the Graeco-Roman remains throughout Provence provided innumerable models of such work, and when the Byzantine carving began to arrive from the Levant, "Roman" was already in a fair way to become "Romanesque."

How slow and visible was the transition may be seen from a consideration of such a façade as that of St. Gabriel near Tarascon, which might almost have been built during the "Lower Empire," if you judge from its fluted columns, its Corinthian capitals, its high-pitched pediment, and such essentially classic enrichments as the "egg and dart" pattern, which is a conspicuous motive in its decoration. At St. Trophime as at St. Gilles, at Tarascon as at St. Gabriel, the thoroughly Roman idea of an architrave between the columns and the arch has been faithfully preserved; and the notion of placing small columns on the top of flat pilasters no doubt originated in a desire to preserve the old classic rule of proportion in those columns. The Corinthian pilasters on the upper story of the Bell Tower of St. Trophime are another instance of direct development from classic style, very different from the later "Renaissance," which implied a long disuse. So also in the porch of St. Trophime, we can see the classic enrichments, the thoroughly Roman character of the sculpture, which is more freely treated than that in the earlier St. Gilles. This Roman feeling is just as prominent in the mass as is the Byzantine treatment of its detail in jewels and ornaments, or the thoroughly Romanesque modillions supporting the cornice. The beauty of sane development and growth could scarcely be better exemplified than in such buildings; and even in the classical St. Gabriel we find the pronounced buttresses which indicate that the transition towards the Provençal Romanesque is already well on its way. Of the actual borrowing of such Roman materials as columns and carvings made for far earlier monuments, and of their incorporation in later buildings, I need say nothing. The process is especially obvious when the differing heights of the transplanted columns have necessitated bases of varying sizes. It is the influence these details had upon the spirit of the whole which is the most important thing.

Only one more element in this organic, architectural compound remains to be mentioned here: it is that contributed by the Lombards, who built the detached columns at Ancona, Genoa, Modena, and Verona so like the portals of St. Gilles and St. Trophime. Lombardic architecture has been traced back to the ancient guild of the Comacine Freemasons. In Rome the remains of Comacine architecture, buried almost as deep as the classical buildings, are to be traced in panels of complicated "Solomon's knots," or in the spiral columns, or in the crouching "lions of Judah," which were the chief sign and seal of the old guild ever since the beginning of Freemasonry. As the link between the classic "Collegia" and the art and trade guilds of the thirteenth and

Porch of the Church of St. Gabriel near Tarascon

fourteenth centuries, the Comacines were called "Freemasons" both in England and Germany because they were builders of a privileged class, absolved from taxes, and free to travel about in times of feudal servitude; and this freedom was preserved when Como came into the possession of the Lombards. The edict of King Luitprand, signed in 713, and called "Memoratorio," is an indication of the close connection between the Comacines and Lombardy, which led to their being given the general name of Lombard architects for some time afterwards. Another decree, signed by Otho at the request of the Empress Adelaide in 962, confirms the liberty of "the inhabitants of the Comacine Islands," the place of refuge of which Junius Brutus and the younger Pliny had once been prefects, where once Catullus lived, and whither the guild of architects fled for safety after Rome herself had been destroyed by the Barbarians.

The Comacine masters were pre-eminently sculptor-architects, but their armament was more than mere decoration; it was an eloquent part of their religion, with a meaning for every leaf, for every animal, for every figure; and by degrees it reached the perfect height of symbolism,

Porch of St. Trophime

in which lies its great difference from the "Gothic" northern work; for "Gothic" work is a direct transcript of what the sculptor saw, and its "grotesques" are very different in conception and in meaning from the mystical figures of the south.[3] For the Comacines, animal symbolism represented to the unlettered masses the signs and parables of a mystical religion; and what seems to us "grotesque" is really the earnest expression of a difficult conception by an artist who has not yet got full command over his materials. Already Dionysius the Areopagite, who was consecrated by St. Paul, writes that "only by means of occult and difficult enigmas is it given to the fathers of science to show forth mystic and divine truths."[4] And again the same writer says, "...for this end are chosen many-footed beings or canine creatures with many heads; canine images or lions or eagles with curved beaks; flying creatures with threefold wings; celestial irradiations, wheel-like forms, variously-shaped horses, the armed Sagittarius, and every kind of sacred and formal symbol which has come down to us by tradition." So on the façades of St. Michele or St. Stefano at Pavia we find the huntsman and his dogs, to symbolise the faithful Christian driving out heresy; or the fisherman-priest casts his line for souls out of the ocean of sin. Pavia gives one good example, but Milan gives even a better, in the old pulpit of St. Ambrogio, supported by a truly Comacine variety of pillars, round, hexagonal, short, and long. Upon the capital of one rests the lion of Judah supporting the round arch, the original position, before later Romanesque put the column above the lion as in the porch of St. Trophime. The frieze of sculpture above the arches in the pulpit, filled with the mystic symbols of evil, dragons, wolves, and serpents, bound in a knotted scroll of foliage, again suggests the carvings of Arles, as do the quaint animals of San Donato in Polenta, where Dante worshipped, and where Paolo and Francesca may have kneeled to pray.[5]

The round arch, which I have noticed in the decorative openings of St. Trophime and beneath the old pulpit of St. Ambrogio, may very possibly have reached Saxon England with those "Liberi Muratori," who were sent over by Pope Gregory with St. Augustine in 598 A.D., and who revived in Britain the "collegia fabrorum," established there by the Emperor Claudius, and preserved in Como by the "Freemasons" after they had fallen into disuse elsewhere throughout the Roman Empire. The well-known "Whalley Cross," attributed to Augustine's comrade, Paulinus, is certainly Comacine work of the early seventh century, of the same character as may be seen on the crosses at Kirkdale, Newcastle,

Ruthwell, Crowle, and Yarm; and the carving on the Saxon font in Toller Fratrum church, Dorset, shows exactly the same pattern as the eighth-century well-head at the office of the Ministry of Agriculture in Rome. The church built in the monastery of Hexham by St. Wilfrid (674-680) was copied from Comacine churches of that period elsewhere, and the Saxon towers, there and elsewhere in England, have clearly a Comacine origin, especially in the treatment of the windows and their colonnettes. The beautiful little Saxon chapel of St. Laurence at Bradford-on-Avon should also be noticed in the same connection, for it has now been entirely dug out of its surroundings, and stands free in its own garth. It was built in 708 by Aldhelm, second Abbot of Malmesbury, of large and carefully fitted stones. The arcaded panelling on the outside is like the later chancel at Wing, in Buckinghamshire; and on the whole the Bradford chapel is a most important relic of the oldest style of English architecture introduced by the Comacine architects of Pope Gregory. But Normandy had probably received and practised the best doctrines of the Comacine masters before any really great architecture had developed in England at all; and this becomes clearer when we consider one of the oldest of the churches which the Normans built in London, St. Bartholomew the Great, in Smithfield, which shows Comacine influence in all its early masonry. The curious affinity of Norman architecture in Sicily rather with Italian forms than with French is also explicable on the same theory, that it was due to Comacine builders; and there is very little doubt that the same builders had the chief influence in the building and decoration of the earliest church of St. Trophime, as may be seen from the lion-supported columns of the central porch, and the frieze of sculpture above.

This sculpture deserves more detailed explanation, considered, as it must be, in the architectural setting designed for it. The first element in that design is the fine flight of steps which at once gives dignity to the portal and removes the church entrance from the vulgar bustle of the market-place outside. I never see those steps without thinking of Mistral's beautiful poem in "Lis Isclo d'Or":—

> *Davalavo, en beissant lis iue*
> *Dis escalié de Sant Trefume…*[6]

At the top of the steps the portal opens, shaped like a triptych, filled with carving as an illuminated manuscript is filled with pictures, the frontispiece to that great Book of Faith which was the Church, the welcome to the entering believer, the warning to the wicked passing by. Fully to appreciate the balance of the masses, the distribution of light and shade, and the clever way in which the plain pedestal gives value to the carving above, as a large margin shows off a delicate engraving, you must stand a little distance away, and thus grasp the central idea of the architectural composition.

At the top, beneath the topmost circle of the central arch, amidst the swinging choirs of cherubim and all the heavenly hosts, sits the Eternal Father with the four figures that typify the four Evangelists on either side of Him. The rest of the scheme falls into three lines: the highest, beneath the Father in glory, is the procession of the Blessed and of the Damned; in the centre are the great figures of the Saints, with a frieze of smaller scriptural subjects above, and flat pilasters with low-relief carvings dividing the larger statues; at the bottom are the lions of Arles, and pedestals with symbolic scenes from Biblical history. The whole is set against a tall and simple wall almost barren of ornament, the "mounting" for the splendour of the porch. Above the main arch, which conveys a faint suggestion of a point, but no more, at the centre of its semicircle, is a flat gable with a cornice resting on large corbels crowned with the lion, the ox, the eagle, and the angel of the Evangelists, and with other animal heads and large acanthus leaves.

The main idea of the portal, at the very summit of which the archangel blows the trump of doom, is a magnificent conception of the Last Judgment, with all that shall lead up to it, and all it will involve; and, having now realised its splendid framework of architectural line, we can go nearer and examine its detail, the detail which Dante was later on to elaborate in his Purgatorio, his Paradiso, his Inferno.

All the evangelistic figures, except the eagle, hold a book, upon the tympanum in the topmost centre; and these carvings project boldly beyond the line of the containing mouldings in high relief. These mouldings are themselves richly decorated with Roman patterns, the outermost being a Greek fret. Immediately beneath, and above the central pillar of the door, are the Twelve Apostles, seated on a bench, each holding a volume of the Scriptures, the whole cleverly arranged in little broken groups of two, with a good deal of individual expression and far more skill than is sometimes observable in the treatment of a line of similar figures.

On either side of the Apostles is unrolled the story of the human race, from the Alpha to the Omega of existence, from the Fall of our first parents on the angle at the extreme left, to the torments of hell which are its consequence, on the extreme right. In the carving that begins this story on the long line of the main frieze, to the left, the serpent of evil, coiled round the Tree of Life, is represented as having plucked the forbidden fruit; he gives it to Eve who persuades Adam to share it with her. This is an interesting variant on the more usual theme which deserves notice. The scene is immediately followed by the beginning of the Procession of the Just, on the right hand of God the Father. Furthest to the spectator's left are the women; then comes a line of men, all clothed in the same formal garments; the whole of these fourteen figures being in the straight line above the three front columns. The procession continues round the angle, to be headed by two kings each wearing his crown. On the inward return is a magnificent angel; and it is observable that the transition from the body to the soul takes place just at the very step which leads into the church; for this angel holds a soul, represented as a naked child, towards, Abraham, Isaac, and Jacob, who sit on thrones encrusted with gems, each holding two souls in his lap. On the other side of the arch, after the Apostles, stands St. Raphael with a sword guarding the gates of Purgatory, which stand ajar, with a mysterious hand issuing from the clouds above them. In Purgatory several figures are represented clothed, among whom are two bishops in their mitres. Still further along to the spectator's right begins the miserable cohort of the naked damned, bound with a cord, and walking through flames of fire towards hell itself (on the return angle) crammed with souls in torment, already half-consumed. The theme is completed with two separate large panels beneath, showing the weighing of the souls of the dead at one end, and at the other the torture of the lost by Satan, a hideous prince, naked as his subjects, and revelling in the torments he inflicts.

It should be added that the noble seated figure to the left of the Apostles, and next to Abraham, Isaac, and Jacob, is supposed to represent the New Dispensation, crushing beneath him the prostrate form of the apostate Emperor Julian.

Above the large statues, and beneath the frieze of the Last Judgment which I have just described, is a line of carvings which show the least skill in actual sculpture of any part of the portal. But they are full of life and interest, and represent the Dream of Joseph, the Annunciation, the Nativity, the angel bringing good tidings to the shepherds, the Presentation and Purification in the Temple, and the story of the Magi, which is told in charming detail. It begins by showing all the wise kings, asleep in the same bed with their crowns on, suddenly roused by the voice of the angel. On the horizon gleams the Star of Bethlehem. They ride to Jerusalem and reach the palace of Herod, who receives them surrounded by his guards, with his sword upon his knee. They pass on to the sacred end of their journey; and are finally shown making adoration to the Divine Child. The Massacre of the Innocents and the flight into Egypt closes this series, and the band of carvings is filled up (on the right) by a weird collection of zoological curiosities. These little carvings are just the height of the capitals of the columns behind which some of them are seen and the columns themselves, gracefully poised on delicate and differing shafts, show varied carvings both in capitals and bases.

Humanity under the law of Moses is the chief theme represented on these carved pedestals. A man half-clothed in the skins of wild beasts, and holding a crook, signifies the pastoral state of our first ancestors, and his lost immortality is typified by the ox's skull, the well-known pagan symbol of death. On the next pedestal a group of hideous monsters, ready to devour him, signify the vices he must soon encounter on his earthly pilgrimage. The mortal weakness of his nature is shown, further on, in the story of Samson and Delilah, whose undraped bosom is the invariable sign, in all such carvings, of her unchaste life. On the other side of the portal is set the consolation for this fall; for there is carved the triumph of Daniel in the lions' den; thus showing that even as such wondrous human strength as Samson's can turn to weakness by the judgment of the Lord, so also can the weakness of a man, cast even into a den of lions, be made strength by the support of the Almighty. Yet another group of tangled monsters, fighting ferociously, is meant to typify the internecine disorders of mankind before the Coming of the Gospel of Peace. The series is closed with two signs of the zodiac, the Archer, and the Lion of Arles.

I have left till the last the splendid series of the saints who stand behind the columns against the main wall of the doorway, forming a line of panels separated by richly-carved bands. The two end panels represented the two scenes from the Last Judgment already mentioned, one at each extremity of the porch. The others contain, counting from the left, the statues of St. Peter, St. John, St. Trophimus, St. James the Less, either St. Bartholomew or St. Thomas, St. Paul (on the right of the door), St. Andrew, the stoning of St. Stephen, St. James the Great, and St. Philip. The two most conspicuous positions are given to St. Stephen on the right, to whom the first church on this site was dedicated, and to St. Trophimus, who holds a position of equal importance in the cloister.

Each figure bears an inscription; and on that of St. Trophimus, to whom the present building was dedicated when his body was brought from the Alyscamps, is written (in vertical syllables on the pallium): CERNITUR EXIMIUS VIR XTI DISCIPULORUM DE NUMERO TROPHIMUS HIC SEPTUAGINTA DUORUM (Here you may see Trophimus, one of the seventy-two disciples of Christ), a distych which lays stress on the old tradition that this Trophimus was one of the original seventy-two apostles sent out to the Gentiles.[7] With Tychicus, also of Asia, and others, Trophimus was one of those who waited for St. Paul at Troas (Acts XX. 4), and were with him when Eutychus was restored to life during the week's sojourn there, and went on with him until the parting at Miletus, where Trophimus was stayed by sickness. On the stole of St. Stephen is written: PRO CHRISTO PROTOMARTYR ANIMAM SUAM POSUIT STEPHANUS. (St. Stephen, the first martyr, gave his life for Christ) The inscription for St. Peter runs as follows: CRIMINIBUS DEMPTIS DESERAT PETRUS ASTRA REDEMPTIS (His sins forgiven, let Peter depart to heaven). The motto of St. John is: XPI DILECTUS IŌÆS EST IBI SECTUS. (John, beloved of Christ, is carved there) On the phylactery of St. Paul are the words: LEX MOISI CELAT PAULI SERMOQUE REVELAT NAM DATA GRANA SINAI PER EUM SUNT FACTA FARINA (the law of Moses conceals; the word of Paul reveals. For the grain given on Sinai was made into flour by him), an obvious reference to the old story of the "Gospel-Mill." The statue which is attributed either to St. Bartholomew or to St. Thomas remains doubtful, because the names of both are placed upon the pages of the book held by the figure. Beneath the feet of the Apostles are the crushed monsters of the heresies they have overcome, and these monsters are represented as devouring the men who embraced the errors which they symbolise. Among them a bird of prey endeavours to devour the egg from which its own progeny should emerge, typifying the matricidal fury of the heretic who struggles against Mother Church.

Scarcely less famous, and certainly as fine as the portal, are the cloisters of St. Trophime, which are reached by some steps in a small passage out of the south transept of the church. The rectangle is charmingly irregular, and presents an epitome of Provençal architecture, the west being the oldest side, which passes along the main church wall, and is called the northern walk. This is of the same date as the portal, though some authorities consider it may be older than the twelfth century. The eastern walk, to which this leads, is slightly more modern,

The Cloisters of St. Trophime, Arles

but cannot be later than the end of the same century. Still further to the right, the south walk is a restoration towards the end of the fourteenth century, and the last, or western walk, is frankly "Gothic," probably built at the beginning of the fifteenth century, though some historians have placed it later still. The entrance door brings you to the corner where the northern and the western galleries meet, and in the middle of the first pier you see the statue of St. Trophime.

Nothing finer than this northern gallery exists in the early decorative style of Provençal architecture, and it deserves the most careful examination. As I did in the case of the portal, so here I will describe the structural setting of the place before I go into its innumerable details. In this northern walk, and in the eastern, which turns to the right at the end of it, solid piers of masonry are built at each corner, and at regular intervals along the gallery, with round arches resting on coupled columns in the intermediate spaces. The piers give room for large statues and for broadly decorative fluted panels, which are sometimes also used for sculpture. At the angles these piers are designed to receive the springing of three transverse ribs, one at right angles across each of the adjoining galleries, and one diagonally under the line of the junction of the two barrel-vaults; and the way this complicated piece of masonry is thought out and constructed is most interesting. In the older galleries it will be noticed that the statues they bear have been cut out of the solid stone of the structural mass, while the Gothic statues carved from separate stones have disappeared from the more modern galleries. The intermediate piers which are not at the corners are strengthened with an external square buttress, towards the cloister-garth, which is fluted and carved with a Corinthian capital, after the classic manner, and may well have been taken from the theatre or some other classic monument of Arles. The arcades between these piers consist of three wide bays, each containing four small round arches on coupled columns, both piers and arches standing on a broad continuous base; and the delicate round or octagonal columns have capitals of grey marble like themselves, which are superbly carved, with an almost bewildering wealth of imagination, each pair cut from a single block, with an abacus which is generally decorated as well with wreaths and foliage.

The walks are roofed with a rounded tunnel-vault, that is stopped on the enclosing walls at a higher level than its origin over the arcades, giving an elliptical or segmental section, strengthened with boldly moulded transverse ribs thrown from a projection applied to the piers between the bays, on one side; to large corbels or consoles, on the other; and these corbels, carved with grotesques and foliage, form part of a plain string at the origin of the vault upon the inner wall. This arrangement is probably due to an alteration of some older construction which existed before these galleries were elaborately carved, and which was probably of the same kind as that already described at Montmajour (see p. 199). The original old roof no doubt was made of tiles laid outside the vault and leaning against the church, and the change in the segment (resulting in the use of the consoles) was necessitated by the raising of the outer wall sufficiently to form a fairly level promenade, with stone seats, upon the roof of the gallery. The height of the original outer wall can be seen by the hollowed ledge which was the gutter of the old construction, and now runs along the outside, as you look from the cloister-garth, just above the capitals of the external, fluted pilasters. The slits in the wall are made to allow the water to fall from the higher level into the original gutter. There is not much to notice in the inner walls, which have been considerably restored and altered. The entrance from the cathedral is featureless, but the wall of the church next to the north cloister-gallery contains a beautiful little Romanesque arcade with fluted pilasters. One other thing is also noticeable. As you pass the end of the north walk, above a door on your left is the eagle which commemorates the crowning of Frederic Barbarossa in St. Trophime in 1178, when the carvings of these cloisters were in all the freshness of their first creation.

My simplest plan in dealing with this extraordinary mass of sculptured detail will be to describe the carvings that a visitor will find on his right hand as he goes round the galleries, entering at the door from the cathedral, and beginning with that angle pier in which St. Trophimus forms the central figure, as the patron saint of the building. The inscription beneath[8] has no reference to the statue, but was placed there by some ecclesiastic connected with the church in 1188, after the carving had been finished. On the right of St. Trophimus is St. Peter, and on the left St. John. Between the statues of St. Trophimus and St. John is a panel representing Mary Magdalene, Mary the mother of James, and Salome; so that the legend of the three Marys is intimately connected in the carver's mind with St. Trophimus. Beneath them are the disciples at Emmaus. Between St. Trophimus and St. Peter is a carving of the Resurrection, with "SEPULCRUM DNI" on the open tomb in the centre, from which the winding-sheet is hanging. The next capitals represent the raising of Lazarus, the sacrifice of Abraham, and Balaam's ass. The middle capital shows Abraham walking with Isaac on one face, the angel arresting the sacrifice on another, and the ram laid upon the altar on the third. The story of Balaam is similarly divided into various episodes, of which Balak forms the first, and the camp of the Israelites the last. On the pier which follows are three statues, St. James of Compostella between two pilgrims, a Christian, and a Moor of Spain. On the next capital is Abraham fetching an ox for his angel-visitors at Mamre, which is succeeded by St. Paul before the Areopagus; the third capital has no figures carved upon it. Three statues, as before, are found upon the next pier. In the midst, Christ shows His wounds to St. Thomas on His right; on the other side is St. James the Less, holding a book inscribed with his name. Only the first of the ensuing three capitals have figure-subjects; and on this Moses is shown receiving the tables of the Law. On two other sides of the same capital are carved the burning bush and Moses shepherding his flock.

Epitaphs on the internal wall, which is decorated with arcading, show that a monk named Gavallerius died here in 1203; that Canon Poncius de Barcia was head schoolmaster in the twelfth century; and that Canon Poncius Révoil died in 1183. These are chiefly interesting as indications of the date of the wall on which they are placed;[9] and the last name fixes the "clerk of the works," or the canon responsible for architectural upkeep, whose name "Rebolii" I have ventured to translate as *Révoil*, for the sheer pleasure of adding that we owe the present preservation of the fabric to that famous modern architect, M. Révoil, who certainly inherited the spirit, if not the name as well, of his ancient predecessor.

Having now reached the end of the north walk, we find another large angle-pier at the junction of the northern with the eastern gallery; and in the place of honour is St. Stephen, to whom the first building on this site was consecrated, and whose skull is preserved within its "treasure." His name is carved upon the book he holds. Between him and the statue of St. Paul, who holds the roll of the law, is a panel carved with the Ascension of Christ upon the Mount of Olives. The other panel, between the centre statue and St. Matthew; represents the stoning of Stephen the Martyr. The arrangement of the rest of this east walk follows the plan of the north walk with as great fidelity as did the corner pier.

On the capitals of the coupled columns are represented the Mysteries of the life of the Virgin, and the first capital shows her birth. St. Anne is in bed; an angel cares for the child; the father stands between two columns. Then is carved the Annunciation by the Angel Gabriel, followed by the salutation of Elizabeth, and the infant Jesus is shown in His cradle above, with the ox and the ass near Him. Over the arches are carved the symbols of the four Evangelists. The second capital is decorated with four eagles and an angel. The third contains the figures of the shepherds to whom the angels bring the tidings of the birth of Christ. The carving of the flagellation has disappeared from the centre of the next square pier; but on one side of it may still be seen Judas carrying his blood-money, and on the other is a soldier wielding a scourge. Above is Godefroy de Bouillon fighting a bear, a subject we shall find again upon the façade of St. Gilles. The story of the infant Christ is continued on the next three capitals. On the first is the Massacre of the Innocents; Herod stands in front, and Rachel at one side. On the second the Virgin with her Son is seated on an ass, which Joseph leads, on their journey into Egypt, accompanied by two angels. On the inner side of the column are the three kings asleep, receiving the angel's warning in a dream. On the third, King Herod is in front; at one side of him are the Magi with their presents, and their horses behind; at the other are the king's priests and scribes and courtiers; above the pier which follows are carved the lamb and cross of John the Baptist. The statues on the pier itself represent King Solomon and the Queen of

Sheba. The adoration of the infant Christ by the Magi is the subject of the first capital afterwards; and the next shows, on the inner side, the Entry of Jesus into Jerusalem, and on the outer, the Conversion of St. Paul, who falls off his horse beneath a little tower carved full of faces. The last capital represents the preaching of the Gospel to all the world by the Apostles. Over the last two arches are sculptured the wise and foolish virgins with their lamps. The last large pier, at the angle of the eastern and southern galleries, has an ancient well in front of it, and is formed of the base of some old Roman pillar, with channels cut in it to direct the cords of the bucket. The chief statue on the east side of the pier is that of Gamaliel, as is shown by the name on the book he holds. The centre is occupied by a shell for holy water supported by another statue. As before, there are two panels filled with carving on the pier: the first (to the east) representing Christ washing Peter's feet; the Last Supper; and the kiss of Judas in the Garden of Olives; the second (to the south) showing first the baptism of Christ, and then the three temptations of Christ by the Devil; in the desert, on a pinnacle of the Temple, and on a high mountain.

On the internal wall of the east gallery are two more shields with the imperial eagle of Barbarossa, which was taken later on as the arms of the chapter of St. Trophime, and three epitaphs to Canon Durand, who died in 1212; to William of Miramar, buried in 1239; and to William Boso, died in 1180. These are the last of such an ancient date, and as you turn into the southern gallery the change to more modern work is very obvious.

The south walk was begun by François de Couzié, Archbishop of Arles in 1389 and 1390, and was finished by his successor, Jean de Rochechouart; and the style differs accordingly. The arrangement of the columns and arches is different from that in any other walk. Columns and piers are arranged alternately, the piers being in turn alternately disposed into threefold pilasters, with a "baldaquin" above, from which the statues have disappeared. The best sculpture is to be found on the capitals of the double columns, which are again in a single block, but the subjects of the carvings are generally taken from ecclesiastical history of the first century, or from later symbolism, rather than from the Biblical stories of the two earlier galleries we have just examined. On the first, Jesus Christ is preaching to the people; on the second, the Virgin and Child are worshipped by the faithful; on the third, Christians in bonds are praying to the Christ in glory, while their executioners wait behind;

on the fourth, the martyrs, bound in chains and surrounded by the torturers, kneel to receive the Holy Eucharist even at the price of death; on the fifth, other Christians are being hanged and tortured, while the providence of God (represented by a hand above their heads) is fortifying them to bear their pain; on the sixth and last the bishop is represented administering the consolations of the Church to more martyrs who have been chained by the executioners near them. At the west end of this gallery is a seventeenth-century altar, restored by Jean-Baptiste de Grignan, whose arms are on the wall near it, and used for the funeral Mass of the monks buried in the cloister-garth. On one side of it is the name Galantier, and the date 1749, which records the death of a priest who fell lifeless as he was celebrating the Mass.

The newer style, and the pointed vaulting of the western gallery, are even clearer than was the case in the south walk. Colonnettes and pillars alternate all the way, and the thicker piers are plain, without decoration. The capitals of the double columns are carved with the stoning of St. Stephen, Samson, St. Martha, and the Tarasque—Mary Magdalene in the house of Simon the Leper, the Annunciation, the crowning of the Virgin, and the descent of the Holy Spirit at the Feast of Pentecost. The inner wall contains the epitaph of Bertrand de Athillanus, a canon who died in 1221, which shows that all the cloister-walks were originally built at much about the same time, and that only the north and east walks remain as they were built.

I should add to the description of these carvings something of the ecclesiastical treasures preserved in the church, of which a record was kept in a book of accounts, drawn up in 1478, containing a list of architects and workmen, and of the liturgical chants used up to 1544, the whole written in a mixture of Provençal and Latin before the age when the national speech had become definitely crystallised. The terrible famine of 1709 resulted in a transformation of much of the church plate of St. Trophime into bullion; but there still remain a fine cross in rock-crystal, the oliphant of St. Trophime, a bishop's staff, and a beautiful little ivory coffer. The reredos in the chapel of St. Trophime is a painting which preserves the form of the original archbishop's cross, together with an interesting view of the Greek theatre. But there is no trace, even so slight as this, of the crown, the sceptre, and the hand of Justice which were borne before the Emperors at their coronation. Perhaps the most remarkable relic of this kind is the leathern belt and buckle of St. Césaire, bishop of Arles, in the sixth century, which is in the "Treasure" of the Church of La Major. The ivory buckle represents two soldiers asleep before the Holy Sepulchre, in the Byzantine style.

The only church in Provence, or indeed in France, which can be compared with St. Trophime, is St. Gilles, which well deserves a visit, though practically nothing of its original splendours is left except the unique and gorgeous façade, the magnificent crypt, and the spiral staircase of the ruined choir. The best way to go there is by the little railway across the plain from Nîmes.

In Greek the name of St. Gilles is Αἰγίδιος, and the holy man is said to have been born in Athens in the middle of the seventh century, "with the blood of the Greek kings in his veins." He reached Arles in 663, but went further up the Rhone into what was called the Flavian Valley, where Wamba, King of the Visigoths, who had just reduced Nîmes, was out a-hunting in the spring of 673. The stag took shelter in an anchorite's cell, and the javelin hurled after it by one of the Visigoths transfixed the hand of St. Gilles, its protector, to whom the generous Wamba immediately gave a large tract of the surrounding country, as some consolation for his wound, adding a sufficient sum of money to begin building a monastery, of which the saint was the first abbot. He visited Rome to hand over the whole property to the Pope, and in the Bull of April 28, 685, Benedict II formally took over the monastery of St. Gilles under the protection of the Holy See,[10] a protection which unfortunately availed little to save it from worse ravages than almost any other church of its importance in the Rhone Valley.

The first danger to the infant community was the attack of the Saracens in 719, before whom St. Gilles fled to Orleans, taking with him the holy vessels and relics. Charles Martel sheltered them all under his own personal care until those perils were overpast; and it was given to St. Gilles to die in peace, in the monastery he had founded, in September 721, to be succeeded as abbot by Atticus, and to be made a saint by two bulls of Pope John VIII in 878.

In the eleventh century the crypt beneath the present church was constructed to receive the tomb of St. Gilles, and the high altar was consecrated by Pope Urban II in 1095. It extends beneath exactly the same amount of ground as is covered by the modern reduced building. Since the religious wars of the sixteenth century both tomb and crypt had disappeared. The Protestant army conquered the Counts of Suze and Sommerives in a battle near the town of St. Gilles on September 27, 1562, and proceeded immediately to celebrate their victory by massacring the priests, who were slain, with the choir boys, and their bodies cast into the well that may still be seen within the crypt. The constant sieges the town had to undergo from that year until 1575 completed the ruin of the building, which was alternately desecrated by the reformers and used as a fortress by the churchmen. Henri de Rohan ordered its complete destruction in 1622. The Byzantine bell-tower was cast down, the whole of the choir was dismantled and destroyed; the crypt, robbed of its holy tomb, was filled with rubbish; and the façade itself seems only to have been left standing in order that its carvings might the more openly be debased and mutilated. In 1650 a new sanctuary was built by the zeal of the faithful at the end of the ancient nave where the transept had originally stood, and this is the rounded apse with plaster walls which you may see today, joined to the old façade by an interior which is entirely different from the magnificent constructions at its eastern and western extremities. The Revolution of 1790 nearly completed the degradation of a façade which even the religious wars had to some extent respected, and the ruins of the old choir were almost entirely levelled, though much of the disposition of its walls and pillars can still be traced. On the arches of the dishonoured crypt some pious hand traced the pitiful record of that barbaric devastation: "Les siècles à venir sauront qu'en 1793 l'église ci-dessus fut totalement ravagée et toutes les saintes images brûlées sur la place."[11]

The new régime began with M. Clavière as curé in 1795, and the seventh curé, M. Achille Goubier, who succeeded to the position in 1864, was moved to excavate the crypt in the hope of rescuing some of those treasures, hidden but never forgotten, which the sacrilegious fury of the past had apparently destroyed. At last his zeal was rewarded by the discovery of a large tombstone bearing the inscription "IN. H. TVML. Q. C. B. AEGD." It was the tomb of St. Gilles. Within it were some bones. The necessity for establishing their authenticity became imperative. In 1562 a portion of the relics of the saint's body had been taken for safety to St. Sernin in Toulouse, by the Sire de Pouzilhac, who desired to save them from the reformers. In 1817 a small portion was returned to the church of St. Gilles by the care of M. Bonhomme of Nîmes and the Bishop of Avignon. In 1862 the Bishop of Nîmes, a see which invariably seconded the legitimate desires of St. Gilles, secured yet another portion of the Toulouse relics, which were brought back to their old home that July and placed in a worthy shrine. By making careful examination of the relics already at St. Gilles, of those still remaining in

Toulouse, and of the bones brought to light by M. Goubier; it was possible to announce with certainty that the complete skeleton of the saint was at last accounted for. The Abbé Goubier at once proceeded to complete his work by the restoration of the crypt, which was magnificently carried out by M. Révoil, the state architect of "Monuments Historiques," and to these two men is owing the recovery of one of the most interesting ecclesiastical buildings in France.

The well, which is connected with such sad associations in the massacre of the religious wars, stands to the south, near the cloister door, and is traditionally said to have been supplied with water by the spring which refreshed the anchorite Aegidius in the seventh century. It was the first part of the crypt to be cleared out. The tomb of St. Gilles was made the central point of the whole building, and was placed upon a mosaic pavement within an iron screen, with candelabra at each corner. At the head of the tomb is the old altar used by St. Gilles for saying Mass. From it are steps rising to the ancient choir. The crypt is lighted by five low windows, but is naturally very dark, and can only be visited when the sacristan descends with a candle from the nave of the upper church. The original staircase by which the monks descended to celebrate the office can still be seen to the south-east, but is not yet connected again with the building above, and serves merely as a kind of retreat in which various fragments of carving have been placed for safety. It is a place in which you realise the possibilities of an earnest sincerity in faith, and it is here that I should chiefly recall the energy of the Abbé Goubier, who revealed the very existence of this crypt itself, and the zeal of the Abbé d'Everlange who wrote the history of St. Gilles after he had been made its curé in 1873. The good Abbé journeyed to the parish of St. Giles in London to receive the blessing of Cardinal Manning, and to be sent on by him to John Archer Houblon in order to visit the beautiful little Gothic chapel of St. Giles at Hallingbury. It was a pious pilgrimage; and it deserves the return which every English visitor to the Valley of the Rhone can make, if he will not only see the great façade of St. Gilles, but will also walk across to the old Romanesque house where its present curé lives, and help him to keep up that magnificent relic of Christian devotion and of Christian art that is now almost unknown in the little village of which it is the precious jewel.

The town of St. Gilles stands on a little hill above the river, and the walk from the station through an avenue of trees, then to the left up the long main road, and so round towards the great church is full of unexpected interest. To your left of the façade, a small street goes

West Front of St. Gilles

upward, past the locked door of the ruined choir, and through the buildings of the Mairie. Once beyond them you come suddenly upon the brow of a great cliff, that falls sheer down towards the river and the plain; and ancient stone seats are placed upon the very brink for you to rest and look upon the view. The landscape, thoroughly Provençal in its every feature, seems full of the history that once gave the town a far nobler place in the Valley of the Rhone than it has now, and enriched the great church with a far finer setting than the few squalid streets which are all that remain today.

St. Louis was particularly well affected towards the town of St. Gilles, because his favourite private secretary, Guy de Foulkes, who afterwards became Pope Clement IV, was born there, and now lies buried in Viterbo, where he died in 1268. On the base of one of the columns of the church is a rough carving of King Louis, and beside it is the name of Joinville. A more tragic memory, which connects the place with the fearful outrages of the Albigensian Crusades, is that Pierre de Castelnau, legate of Pope Innocent III, was murdered here in 1208; and of the horrors which began with that assassination we shall hear more at Carcassonne. Fifty years earlier the carvings on the façade of St. Gilles were finished.

This marvellous portal is fitly framed between two low towers on each side, with a string course drawn straight between them above the arch of the central doorway. It is approached by a splendid flight of steps along its whole length. Each of its three round-arched entrances has a separate tympanum, with enriched vaults, the centre arch resting upon a small projecting cornice, supported by four carved consoles on each side. A fluted pilaster stands in the middle of the door, supporting the carved tympanum, whose extremities rest on two other fluted pilasters, crowned by an eagle and a bull. The arrangement of detached columns in front, on each side of the centre door, no doubt suggested the more elaborate, but less splendid porch of St. Trophime. The northern tympanum, which bears evident traces of painting, represents the Virgin with her Son, who blesses the three Magi. In the right-hand corner an angel is appearing to St. Joseph. The central tympanum is carved with Christ in glory, seated between the four animals of the Evangelists. The southern tympanum shows the Crucifixion of Christ. John and Mary are at the foot of the Cross. Mary Magdalene and another woman are near them. Beside St. John is the prostrate figure of a woman hidden in a cloak, representing the downfall of the Synagogue. On the frieze are other carvings of the life of Christ. He is teaching His disciples, while one of them throws his cloak over the ass on which the entry to Jerusalem is to be made. Thirteen disciples follow Him on the way into the city, which is represented in the distance with its battlemented walls between two towers. Two men throw branches and garments in His path, and other spectators look on from the boughs of the palm-trees. Upon the fluted part of the frieze is shown the story of the prodigal son. A representation of the Temple divides this from the scene in which Christ is driving out the merchants from the sanctuary. Further on is shown the resuscitation of Lazarus. In the next portion is the scene where Peter denied his Lord and the cock crew, and above the principal door the carving on the lintel begins with the washing of the Apostles' feet, and the Last Supper. On the return-angle, St. Peter cuts off the ear of Malchus; then comes the kiss of Judas (which the revolutionary Vandals seem to have thought alone worthy of protection); followed by the flagellation, and the bearing of the cross, which completes all that can here be deciphered until the last archway on the right is reached, where the frieze begins, in the angle, with the council of the Pharisees, and Christ before Pilate. After this Mary Magdalene wipes the Lord's feet with her hair in the house of Simon the Pharisee. On the lintel are shown the holy women buying aromatic herbs from the merchants and approaching the Sepulchre of Christ surrounded by the sleeping soldiers, while an angel with a sword shows them that the tomb is empty; and in the last carving the women tell the great news to the Apostles, while Jesus is seen rising to the skies.

The whole of this splendid frieze rests upon a kind of prolongated abacus, which stretches from one capital to another above the columns, and is thickly sculptured with hideous figures of wild beasts typifying the evil passions of mankind. On the main wall behind these columns are the Twelve Apostles, stretching from the right side of the north door to the left side of the south entrance, each with his appropriate inscription, except the four last, who would be SS. Andrew, Matthew, Philip, and Simon. The statue of St. Jude, the first on the left between the northern and the central door, bears the inscription BRUNUS ME FECIT, and no doubt this same sculptor did all the six on the left of the centre. The façade itself reposes on a solid base, part of which is fluted; and all round the central door it is filled with carvings in low relief. On the right the marble bases of the detached coupled-columns contain the carving of David playing on his harp among his flocks, with an angel appearing to him. The corresponding bases represent David slaying Goliath. Other carvings show two monkeys roped together, a camel and a prostrate man, a lion holding down his victim, the sacrifice of Cain and Abel, and Balaam with his ass. Medallions, surrounded by circular frames, contain centaurs, stags, chimeras, and lionesses. Beneath the feet of the Apostles are magnificently carved lions, representing, as at Arles, the heresies which have devastated mankind.

The time taken by the completion of this wonderful portal may be judged from the fact that the date just quoted from its carvings is 1150, while the date given on a lost inscription which was once carved on the old wall near the cloister is 1116[12] the year in which the church was begun by Alphonse Jourdain, son of Raymond, fourth of the name, Count of Toulouse; and another interesting fact is that the unequal heights of the columns of the portal show they were taken from some previously existing classical edifice, as was so often the case elsewhere. From the lions carved round the doors, the abbot, who sat in the gate to render justice, between them, often dated his charters "Inter Leones."

No visitor should leave the church without gaining admission to the enclosure in which the ruins of the original choir can be studied, for in no other way can an adequate idea be gained of the splendour of the first structure. The most fascinating relic for architects in this enclosure is the

Detail Carving from the Church of St. Gilles

extraordinary little spiral staircase at the north corner of the sanctuary in a separate tower. Known as the Vis de Saint-Gilles, it is famous all the world over for the skill and perfection of its stone-cutting. Imagine that the round arch of the door is hung by its left-hand pillar to a tall central shaft in such a manner that it can slowly revolve round that shaft and rise while it turns, and you may perhaps begin to realise the delicacy of measurement and workmanship involved in the vault that covers the ascending steps. The masonry can be closely studied at the very top, where the breakage of the crown reveals the twisted stone courses.

Few people, as yet, have taken the trouble to visit St. Gilles from Nîmes, yet it is one of the journeys most worth while in this land of wonderful excursions, and if you start early enough in the morning, so as to have the morning sunlight, you will be able to go on to a still more extraordinary, though far less elaborate church, at Stes. Maries, which I mentioned at the end of my third chapter.

The building is a very remarkable relic of the twelfth century upon the site of a far older shrine destroyed by the Saracens, consisting of a single nave of seven bays, roofed with a pointed barrel vault, and surmounted externally with a crenelated and machicolated parapet, which has all the effect of a fortification with a donjon keep at the east end. In this tower is the apse, which contains three chapels, one above the other. In the lowest is the tomb of Sarah, the middle is the choir of the church, and on the topmost level are the relics of the holy women who came over, as the tradition says, in the boat from Palestine to Provence.

The time to visit Les Saintes Maries, if you wish to see its most characteristic sight, is on the 24th of May, when the great double ark is let down slowly from its shrine in the roof, and the faithful sick are healed, who will wait there all that night as they have waited all the night before. Long processions pour in and out of the little town for three days from every part of Provence. On the 25th, the Archbishop of Aix accompanies the little model of the Holy Boat and the Marys down to the seashore, and into the waves, which brought the Mother of Christ to these lands so long ago. The railway will of course spoil the simplicity of a religious fête which was once the most sincere and impressive in all France; and not the least interesting part of the ceremony was the fervent adoration of the shrine of Sarah by the gipsies.

In structure the church of Les Saintes Maries is typical of many other of the fortified churches in Provence, which give the country one of its most striking peculiarities. No doubt the style originated in the constant

Church of Les Saintes Maries

alarms of the Saracens, the Albigensian wars, and the corsairs. At Narbonne, Béziers, and Fréjus are good examples of the way in which the spiritual shrine was turned into a temporal salvation; and in the Palace of the Popes at Avignon we shall find the principle carried to its extreme in one of the strongest fortresses ever built within a walled town in Europe. A still later example of these ecclesiastical crenelations is shown in the drawing made for me by Mr. Mallows of the door of Albi Cathedral, and one of the most imposing instances is to be found at Agde. But there are many more which every traveller will notice for himself, and with these few examples of fortified churches I must leave the subject and pass on to the fortresses themselves.

NOTES

1. "Thus was thrust up to heaven the nave of St. Trophime, and ever may it be perfumed with incense, that holy meeting-place of the councils of the Church and the Archbishops of Arles; thus mounted towards God the church of St. Gilles, with the saints of the Gospel who stand and watch beneath its triple portal, and its little spiral staircase was wrought out... Ye Freemasons, its builders, hail! Your trowel that levelled every difficulty shone like a lamp in the dark night..."—*Calendal.*

2. Some authorities are of the opinion that the tower was built at the same time as the nave was raised, and that the arches upholding it at the crossing were deliberately

made lower to bear its weight, as at Vaison, Sisteron, and St. Paul Trois Châteaux. But I cannot agree with this view, for the blank wall of St. Trophime is scarcely likely to have been deliberately designed; it was an inevitable accident of reconstruction.

3. For some further explanation of this Gothic spirit, see *The Story of Rouen*, by T. A. Cook, chap. vi., and especially p.125.

4. See *Sti. Dionisii De Theologia Simbolica*, ep. I, ad Titum Pontificem. Quoted by Leader Scott, *Cathedral Builders*, p. 76.

5. Carducci's verses describe these carvings well;—

> ...*Da i capitelli orride forme intruse*
> *A le memorie di scapelli argivi,*
> *Sogni efferati e spasimi del bieco*
> *Settentrione.*
> ...*Goffi sputavan su la prosternata*
> *Gregge: di dietro al battistero un fulvo*
> *Picciol cornuto diavolo guardava*
> *E subsannava.*

6. As I believe *La Coumunioun di Sant* has not been translated yet, I will venture here to render its rhymed cadences into simple English prose: "Down the steps of St. Trophime she walked with lowered eyes. The first of the night was falling and the vesper-candles were growing dim. As she passed the stone statues of the saints within the doorway they blessed her, and their eyes followed her as she moved homewards from the church. For she was good and wise; young she was and lovely too. In church no one had ever seen her laugh or talk; but when the organ played and the psalms were sung she thought she was being borne by angels into Paradise. So the stone statues of the saints, watching her day by day, as she lingered last of all beneath their splendid portal and walked adown the street, those holy ones, in the goodness of their heart, showed a compassionate loving-kindness for the girl, and spoke of her in the quiet of the evening air through the still autumn weather. 'A white nun she should be,' said Saint John, 'for the convent is a haven from the stormy world.' 'Doubtless,' said St. Trophime, 'but I have need of her within my temple; for there must be light in darkness, and the world needs such good examples.' 'Brothers,' went on St. Honorat, 'to-night when the moon is shining over pools and fields we will go down from our columns for the festival of All Saints. The holy table will be spread to do us honour, and at midnight our Lord Christ will say the Mass within the Alyscamps.' 'Now if you will believe my word,' said St. Luke, 'thither will we lead this young virgin, clad in a mantle of blue over a white dress.' So, on that word, the four saints moved away as softly as the evening-breeze, and they took the soul of the girl, as she passed by, and led it with them... Early the next morning that lovely maid awoke, and spoke to all who met her of the festival she had attended, of how the angels had passed down the sky when the holy table was laid ready in the Alyscamps, and how St. Trophime had read the responses there while the Lord Christ Himself had said the Mass."

7. As the bishops wrote to Pope Leo after the death of St. Hilary, "*Prima intra Gallias Arelatensis civitas missum a beatifico Petro Apostolo Sanctum Trophimum habere meruit sacerdotem.*" (The city of Arles was the first in France to merit having as priest St. Trophimus, sent by the blessed apostle Peter) It was Trophimus, a Gentile and a native of Ephesus, who, accompanied by Titus, journeyed to Corinth with St. Paul's Second Epistle. His longer journey into France is naturally placed by tradition as in the sacred boat which brought the three Marys to Provence (see first volume), and this explains the traditional dedication, "in her lifetime," of the chapel to the Virgin Mary in the Alyscamps. Mistral has described *(Miréio,* xi.) the coming of St. Trophime and his holy companions to Arles, and the scene they saw in the Greek theatre: "A flight of young girls moved to the sound of music, and loudly sang its chorus as they danced and leaped round the marble statue of Venus 'Let us sing to Venus, the great goddess who giveth happiness and joy, to Venus queen, the mother of the land and of Arles!' and above them in the clouds of incense the goddess seemed to lift her brow in pride beneath her laurel diadem. Then the old saint Trophimus broke out in indignation, and called in a loud voice: 'People of Arles! Listen to my words, listen in the name of Christ!' He spoke no more, but when he frowned the marble idol shivered, and with a groan fell headlong from her pedestal amidst her fainting votaries. A thousand blades flashed in the air, a thousand voices cried 'Death' upon the intruders, and the place was filled with shouting and with tumults. But when they crowded nearer, they saw the salt of the sea encrusted on the garments of the saints; they saw as it were a halo above the calm face of Trophimus; they saw the Magdalen all bathed in tears and lovelier than their fallen goddess; so they stood back, and Trophimus spoke to them again 'Listen, and then slay me if you will. The power that broke your goddess into pieces was not mine but that of God, of God who hath no temple, but whom Night and Day behold in heaven, and who hath made the earth, and the sky, the sea, and the high mountains. Looking down from above lie beheld the misery of the slave and the triumph of the sinner, and to wash away the sins of man He sent His only son, to be born of a pure Virgin in a manger..."

8. ii. Kal. Oct. Jordan. Dec. Sci. Trophimi Anno Dni MCLXXXVIII.

9. In the order given the epitaphs are: (1) *iii. Non. Februarii die fesitvitatis Sancti Blasii aggressus est viam universe carnis Gulielmus Gavallerius anno Domini Incarnationis MCCIII. Orate pro eo.* (Gulielmus [William] Gavallerius went the way of all flesh on 3 February, the feast of St. Blaise, in the year of our Lord 1203. Pray for him) (2) *vi. Id. Oct. Obiit Poncius de Barcia caput Scholae et canonicus regularis Sancti Trophimi anno MCI...* (On 10 October 1101 Poncius de Barcia, head of the school and canon regular of St. Trophime, died) (3) *vii. Kal. Jan. anno Domini MCLXXXIII obiit Poncius Rebolii sacerdos et canonicus regularis et operari ecclesiae Sancti Trophimi. Orate pro eo.* (On 26 December 1182 Poncius Révoil died, priest and canon regular and clerk of the works of the church of St. Trophime. Pray for him)

10. The Bull begins as follows: *Gratia Dei summus Pontifex Benedictus omnibus fidelibus Beato Petro Apostolo obedientibus salutem a Domino et Apostolicam*

benedictionem. Cum omnis Ecclesia eidem a Domino sit commissa, sunt tamen quaedam monasteria sic in nostra manu posita ut nemo illis dominetur nisi nos et successores nostri: cum quibus monasterium venerabilis viri Aegidii noviter ab ipso nobis est traditum... maneat semper locus ipse liber et quietus, cum omnibus sibi pertinentibus, sub protectione Beatorum Apostolorum Petri et Pauli et hujus Sedis Apostolicae.—Datum Romae in Laterensi Palatio, per manus Lini, Archidiaconi, vi. Kal. Maii Bened. II. PP. (Benedict, by the grace of God supreme Pontifex: Salvation by the Lord and the Apostolic blessing to all the faithful who are obedient to the Blessed Apostle Peter. Although the whole Church has been entrusted to us by the Lord, there are, however, certain monasteries placed in our hand on such terms that no one may have authority over them except us and our successors. Among them the monastery of the venerable Aegidius has recently been voluntarily entrusted to us... let this place remain always free and at peace with everything belonging to it under the protection of the blessed Apostles Peter and Paul and this Apostolic seat. Given out at Rome in the Lateran Palace by the hand of Archdeacon Linus, on 22 April in the second year of Pope Benedict.)

11. The succession of abbots up to 1532 (after which the monastery was laicised) contains a list of names, among which may be selected those of Rangefroi, afterwards Bishop of Avignon (940); Pierre de Situlvero, afterwards Archbishop of Narbonne (1139); Jean III de Mareuil, Bishop of Uzès (1472); Julien de la Rovère, Cardinal-Archbishop of Avignon, and afterwards Pope Julius II (1483); Théodore Jean de Clermont Taillard, afterwards Bishop of Senez and Vice-Legate of Avignon (1532). From then to the Revolution occur, amongst others, the names of Martin de Beaune, chevalier de la reine, and Bishop of Puy (1562); Guillaume V de Noset, Archbishop of Seleucia and Vice-Legate of Avignon (1622); Claude de St. Bonnet de Toiras (1625); Antoine Denis Cohon (1642), and Jean VI de la Parissière (1732), who were all three Bishops of Nîmes; François IV de Béringhen, Bishop of Puy (1738), and Louis François Vivet de Montclus, Bishop of Alais (1743).

12. It runs as follows: *"AD. 1116 hoc templum sancti Aegidii aedificare cepit mense Apr. Feria 2A in Octava Paschal."* (AD1116 the building of this church of St. Gilles began in the month of April on the Monday on the octave of Easter)

CHAPTER X

The Fortresses of the South

Part I: Les Baux

"*O princesso di Baus! Ugueto*
Siblio, Blanco-flour, Bausseto,
Que trounavias amoun sus li roucas aurin,
Cors subre-béu, amo galoio
Dounant l'amour, largant la joio...

L'auro que rounflo encaro, forto
E ponderouso, entre li porto
E dins li tourre à brand de si viei casteu rout,
L'auro d'ou Rose dins si veno
Revolunavo..."
—MISTRAL.[1]

As types of the fortified towns of feudalism there are no finer examples in the world, within so short a distance of each other, than Les Baux, Carcassonne, and Aigues-Mortes. I place them in that order with no idea of comparing their merits, but rather to indicate that Les Baux suggests the greatest age, in the insistent mortality of its irretrievable decay; while Aigues-Mortes, where prisoners were languishing within the Tour de Constance during the eighteenth century, has modern associations in spite of an the Crusading galleys of St. Louis, to whose son it owes the towers and ramparts which remain, untouched, as Boccanegra built them after the model of captured Damietta. Carcassonne I have added, because, though not strictly within the geographical limits of Provence, its most heroic history is inextricably associated with the horrors of the Albigensian crusade of which we have just seen traces at St. Gilles; and also because no excuse is needed for reminding the traveller in Provence that he is within reach of the most magnificent fortress in Europe, which has been held in turn by Visigoth, by Frank, and Frenchman, and is now restored, by a very miracle of tasteful knowledge, to all the primitive splendour of its rugged beauty, its isolated strength, its marvellously complex architecture.

Of Les Baux we shall never know either the real origin or the primeval glories. But it is the tomb of many mighty memories, of warriors who were princes of Cephalonia and Neophantis, of Orange, Tarentum, and Achaia, Counts of Spoleto, Avelin, and Montecoglioso, Podestats of Arles, and Milan, even Emperors of Constantinople; whose royal alliances were counted in the houses of Provence and Barcelona, of Poland, France, Savoy, England, Nassau, and Brunswick; and who traced their descent and took their arms (the star with sixteen rays) from that Balthasar, the wise King of the East, who came with his two comrades to worship the infant Christ in Bethlehem[2]. Their motto was of evidently later origin; but they lived up to it until the last one died—"Au hasard Balthasar!" It is significant, too, of much that went before, that the last descendant of that race of reckless fighters and fair women was a woman, the Countess Alix, at whose death the star that had watched over the fortunes of her house came down to shine within her chamber, and vanished into night for ever as her last breath left her body. The latest discovery within those ruins that are haunted by so many restless souls was a woman's skeleton, with all her wealth of golden hair still perfect. It was found in a vault of the church, beneath the oldest Romanesque nave on the south side, under a stone bearing the date 1471. The dead hands held a Book of Hours, which fell into dust when they, too, vanished at contact with the outer air. But the long, light golden hair, of the colour Titian loved to paint, was saved, and is now in the "Museon Arlaten," which Mistral founded in the town of Arles to preserve all that was characteristic of the Old Provence that will so soon be changed.[3]

The "Cabelladuro d'Or" may perhaps have been the hair of some Italian girl who came to Les Baux, while it was the property of Jeanne de Laval, wife of the good King René, as the betrothed of the seneschal, and who died just before her marriage; for her tresses were bound with a slight ribbon of light blue, and she was buried near the Altar of the Virgin. If so, it would have been the Princess Strella of Florence.

It is a squalid little village that nestles today in the centre of the old

Door at Albi

robber-stronghold, "like a rat in the heart of a dead princess," feeding, apparently, on "Gaulish tibias, skulls of Roman soldiers, dead cats of the Stone Period, and a miscellaneous assortment of rusty iron."[4] The place is a confusion of ruins, grown fragmentary and deserted through the gradual withdrawal of the population from a site destroyed by

Richelieu's soldiers, and dishonoured many a century before—a mediaeval Pompeii, a Herculaneum without its lava, set among the scarred boulders of the Alpilles, in a melancholy landscape all of cinder-grey, as might be imagined in some far-off and extinct planet of the frozen inter-stellar space.

Some thirty-six hundred souls is all this rugged site could ever have contained in normal circumstances, and if there were ever more its numerous sieges must have kept the average down. Yet the extent of the ancient fortress-château of its barons must have been at least as great as that of the vast Castle of the Popes at Avignon; and its ruins have an effect of nightmare exaggeration even in broad daylight. Huge masses of grey stone lie scattered here and there, indistinguishable from the thick walls and towers which were themselves hewn deep within the living rock. Staircases wind upwards to end in gaping caverns. Cellars yawn hungrily for food beneath. The shattered columns tremble on the verge of shaking walls. The fierce wind of Provence seems to have revelled in its task of utterly demolishing what was left; for the walls and rocks are honeycombed and worn so deep with the fury of the blast that the very earth seems ready to give up its dead through every crack and crevice in its wounded surface.

I have driven to Les Baux both from Arles and from St. Remy. The first excursion makes too long a day, and usually involves covering the same ground twice, though it is worth seeing how the gorge of limestone, which shuts in each horizon soon after leaving Montmajour, gradually narrows into a mountain pass lined by fantastic boulders, which leads precipitously upwards to the fortress-town. You feel at last as if a blood-stained band of mediaeval cut-throats were lurking behind every crag, or slowly retreating, as you mounted, to lure you on to final, irremediable fate.

From the Hôtel de Provence in St. Remy it is, however, much wiser to hire a light carriage that will take you at about nine o'clock on a bright spring morning past Les Baux and Montmajour to Arles. The best road to travel by does not lead past the "Plateau des Antiquités," as might be imagined, but by way of the Hôtel Dieu (along Route Nationale No.99, de Montauban et Tarascon à Aix) along fields of flowers bordered by olive-trees and cypresses to the Café Massane at the corner of a road where there is a children's school. From here the way turns sharply to the left, southwards, and you come in sight of an old ruin, called the "Tour du Cardinal," opposite a grove of mulberry-trees, which is followed by the rows and rows of pansy-blossoms, grown by a rambling old farm that nestles in the shelter of the low spurs of the Alpilles. The red earth, that was so strong a colouring in the landscape from Tarascon to St. Remy, is still visible, but now the limestone begins that will soon swallow up all the rest and spread its uniform grey tint across the landscape. But there are still some lovely little wild flowers visible here and there, and suddenly, in a narrow cleft of rich ground, ringed in by hills, appears a tiny vineyard, almost the last sign of cultivation before the shouldering buttresses of mountain close in completely as the road winds slowly up.

Wild lavender and thyme and yellow gorse still fringe the road a little further, with here and there an almond-tree; but soon the road begins to cling to one side of a cliff, with a sheer drop on the outer edge, guarded by lines of scattered stones. Then a wild, desolate valley opens out to the east, and the guardstones of the winding road crowd close together like the battlements upon a fortress, while the steep mountain-sides burn blue and gold with countless tiny blossoms set among the scanty green. Alone and bare, and straight ahead, a gaunt crag of wind-swept limestone marks and bars the valley's end. The road, now built upon a wall, crosses over to the northern side, and the stone-carts from the quarries above begin to swing down with their first freights for the day. Quite unexpectedly the horizon opens out towards the plains of Orgon and Cavaillon on the east, and westwards to Tarascon and Beaucaire. Above the rocky amphitheatre from which the road seems to have emerged the silver line of the Rhone shows like a glittering thread in the morning sunlight, just where the elephants of Hannibal crossed it so long ago, just where Nicolete first saw Aucassin coming downwards from the castle gate. Through towering walls of white, a way has been cut for the carriage road sheer down into the limestone, and quarries begin to gape on every side, until suddenly upon the right a little slip of green valley pushes its way into this rocky desolation, and from some hidden building in it a bell rings slowly, like the dirge for a dead world that has already turned to stone.

Fantastically grouped, and weirdly shaped, the rocks lie here and there on the roadside; some like bleached, giant skulls; some perching, like monstrous reptiles of the prime, upon the edge of an abyss that is their den; some shaped in form of menhirs or of dolmens—all with that strange look of charmed silence which makes you momentarily expect some sudden crash, some ghoulish trump of doom, that shall arouse this hideous medley of grotesque creations to a fearful wakefulness, and call

Les Baux

the sleeping warriors from their dusty tombs, to mingle in the final Armageddon for which the scenery is ready. I can conceive no more eerie place by moonlight, and it is a fit setting for the tragedy of the mountain-citadel of Les Baux.

Of the traces left near this wonderful site by the Romans, I have already spoken, and the carvings known as "Les Trois Maries"[5] are the first things the visitor should ask to see. Even older than the campaign of Marius is the tradition of the "Kabre d'Or," that fabulous hidden treasure which was left by the Phoenicians when the sea washed the crags of Les Baux, and which has never been discovered yet. Older, too, is that "Fairy Grotto" near the "Gorge of Hell," in which the sorceress Tavèn healed Mirèio's sweetheart; for it is probably a Celtic cavern, and may have been used by even remoter prehistoric races, who were sheltered in the very bowels of the earth when they returned from hunting in the foothills. But the first link of Les Baux itself with history is at the time, soon after Euric, the Visigoth, had taken Arles in 480, when his son Alaric drove out the Christians from the capital of Constantine, and they took shelter in this rocky fastness of the Alpilles, much as the Catholics fled from here to Arles a thousand years later during the Religious Wars, when Jehan de Manville was Seigneur under Charles IX. From this lofty eyrie the refugees could look down from

Mont Ste. Victoire on the east to Aigues-Mortes on the west; from Mont Ventoux on the north to the sea beyond the Crau and the Camargue, southwards. Even the amphitheatre of their native Arles was visible on a clear day before rain, beside the blue ribbon of the Rhone, ever widening in its long, slow course towards the lakes and the Mediterranean. The escarpment on which Les Baux was built is not much more than nine hundred metres long by some two hundred broad; and though its position gives an idea of inaccessible solitude, it is in reality less than a thousand feet above the sea, and is formed of compact masses of calcareous limestone, still full of fossil shells, deposited by the prehistoric waters of the Mediterranean, and now covered with small, aromatic plants, and scanty, coarse grass.

The first Count of Les Baux, whose name alone we know, was Leibulf, at the end of the eighth century, whose son Pons, or Poncius, owned large lands in Argence. This latter name suggests a possible origin from overseas; but we are still in a merely conjectural atmosphere, and there are no documents to guide us until the name of Pons the younger, of Les Baux, is mentioned in a deed of gift to the Abbey of Montmajour by Boson of Arles in 971; in another, by Pons himself, to what is now St. Trophime, in 975; and in a third, by the same, to Montmajour in 981. This last definitely speaks of land "near the château called Les Baux," and it is the first claim of the site to a historical position, noteworthy chiefly from its connection with religion, a connection that needs to be borne in mind in judging fairly of the far from saintly aspect of so much that follows.[6] By 1024 we find a bull of Pope Benedict VIII giving the names of Hugues, Seigneur of Les Baux, of Montpaon, and of Meyrargues, and husband of Emaur, the daughter of the Vicomte de Cavaillon. His possessions were extensive in Marignane, in Martigues, and elsewhere, and he was evidently one of the most important of the feudal barons who rose to power during the weakness of the Kings of Arles. His son, Guillaume-Hugues, followed his friend Raymond, Count of St. Gilles and of Toulouse, to the first Crusade in 1095, and there distinguished himself alike by courage and by strength, being chosen as witness to Count Raymond's will, which was made shortly before his death in Palestine.

His son, called after his friend, Raymond, succeeded him, and with him the house of Les Baux begins to take a larger place in the history of Provence. Possessing no less than seventy-nine towns, châteaux, fortresses, or estates, in what were known as the "terres Baussenques,"

Raymond des Baux could count the Bourg-Neuf at Arles, Berre, Myremas, Meyrargues, Castillon, le Castelet, Salon, Pertuis, St. Remy, Aix-en-Provence, and Montdragon, among his many possessions. Some of these, but comparatively few, came to him through the important marriage with Stéphanette, daughter of Count Gilbert of Provence, the last of the dynasty of Boson, who died in 1109, with grave suspicion of murder. Stéphanette's sister, Douce, contracted an alliance, even more fruitful of consequence, by her marriage with Raymond Bérenger, the Count of Barcelona, who already owned part of Provence as Count of Forcalquier. In 1113 Douce added the other part, as her dowry from her mother, and it seemed as if the whole of Provence were about to pass into foreign hands. But for the moment Raymond des Baux concealed his natural resentment. The Saracen corsairs were harrying the coasts from the Balearic Isles, and as Admiral of the Provençal galleys he assisted the Count of Barcelona in repelling the enemy and taking possession of Majorca. Two years afterwards, in 1116, this was recognised by a gift, from Douce and the Count of Barcelona, of the important Seigneury of Berre, and other lands seized from the murderers of Gilbert of Provence, whom the Count of Les Baux had vigorously attacked and punished.[7]

In 1122, with Guillaume de Sabran and another, Raymond des Baux showed his restless spirit by attacking and plundering the Abbey of St. Gilles; for which he and the Count of Toulouse were duly excommunicated by a bull of Pope Calixtus II, until the stolen property had been restored. Still, nothing was done in the important matter of Provence itself, and the inequality of the division of Count Gilbert's property between his two daughters still rankled. The death of the Count of Barcelona, and the marriage of his son, Bérenger-Raymond, with Béatrix de Melgueil, in 1135, gave the signal for that revolt for which Raymond des Baux had so long bided his time. Sixty-six Provençal knights joined his banner, among whom were the Count of Toulouse, a relation of Raymond des Baux, who claimed the guardianship of Béatrix de Melgueil; the Count of Forcalquier; Rostang and Guillaume de Sabran; Arnaud, Ponsodol, and Bertrand de St. Remy; Hugues and Guillaume de Porcelet; Rostang-Raymond, Isnard, and Rostand de Tarascon; Gantelme de Ventabren, Hugues des Arènes, Pierre Garcin de Trinquetaille, and Pons Aicard. But the defenders of Douce were just as powerful; and many families were divided among themselves in this internal struggle, which for long desolated Provence.

The help given to Douce's son by the Count of Barcelona and the Genoese mercenaries was at first most valuable. But the latter proved fickle allies, for they soon betrayed Bérenger-Raymond, and killed him in a sea-fight off Melgueil in 1144. His son, who bore the same name, was left the heir at only seven years old. His widow, Béatrix, married the Seigneur d'Alais, and took her dowry with her. But the Count of Barcelona, who was also King of Aragon, at once made up his mind to face the situation, and his vigorous measures soon forced the rebellious barons to make oath of allegiance to his young nephew, Raymond Bérenger (II), at the Assembly of the Three Estates, held at Tarascon, in 1146.

Raymond des Baux, thinking his opportunity had come at last, had done homage to the Emperor Conrad III, King of Arles, for the whole county of Provence, in which his rights were recognised by a prince whose interests were fully served by the quarrels of the Provençal nobles, and the weakening of the feudal barons. As a consequence, Raymond des Baux went on fighting even after the disastrous surrender of Tarascon, and only in 1150 was he forced to give in his own submission. His proud heart broke, and he died in Barcelona, leaving four sons by Stéphanette: Guillaume, who entered the Order of St. John; Gilbert, Hugues, and Bertrand. Hugues succeeded to the Seigneury of Les Baux; and by his mother's direct assistance a treaty was made in Arles, between Les Baux and Barcelona, which ended for the time this internecine strife, on a basis of total amnesty for the past, and the cession to Barcelona of the châteaux of Trinquetaille, Meyrargues, Aix, Berre, Méjanes, and other lands, together with promises of homage and fealty.

As might have been expected after so one-sided a treaty, Hugues des Baux soon grew dissatisfied. He was encouraged by the recognition of his rights, in 1156, by the Emperor Barbarossa, who followed the same artfully disintegrating policy as that of Conrad; and, supported by his cousin, the Count of Toulouse, and other friends, Hugues refused to give up Trinquetaille. War broke out again at once. The local seigneurs, headed by the Count of St. Gilles and the Viscountess of Narbonne, intervened; and peace was patched up in the church of St. Trophime, on the basis of taking everything from Les Baux except the citadel itself, Castillon, and Vitrolles. Very naturally, Trinquetaille held out as obstinately as ever. This roused the Count of Barcelona to furious reprisals: he besieged and sacked Les Baux and all its territories; and finally beset the town of Arles, and after a tremendous struggle, which has remained legendary in the Rhone valley, he took Trinquetaille by means of a bridge of boats, and levelled it to the ground. Soon afterwards died the gallant princess Stéphanette, and her son Hugues once more broke his treaties, and was again besieged and conquered. The Count of Barcelona, seeing that fire and sword were powerless against his indomitable foe, tried the more fatal snares of policy, and by the marriage of his nephew, Count of Provence, with Richilda, niece of Barbarossa, secured the revocation by the Emperor of all previous recognitions of Les Baux, and assured the sovranty of Provence to his own family. Even so, the Seigneury of Trinquetaille went back to its old masters; but the power of Les Baux was for the moment gone. Hugues would not stay and see his lands diminished. He left Les Baux to his brother Bertrand, and went off to Sardinia to found a new family.[8]

The destinies of Les Baux in Provence were safe in the hands of Bertrand, Princess Stéphanette's fourth son; for not only were his lands restored him by the Count of Barcelona, as the price of formal submission, but by his marriage with Tiburge, he became, in 1175, Prince of Orange on her brother's death, and was granted all those privileges of coining money, and of marching through the country with his flags flying, which the Emperor Barbarossa bestowed upon that house, and which it enjoyed until the union of the principality with France in 1700. He was assassinated in 1181, and his estates went to his three sons: Les Baux to Hugues, Berre to Bertrand, and Orange to Guillaume.[9]

The new Hugues des Baux faithfully followed the traditions of his house, in their hatred of Barcelona, by revolting against Alphonse, Count of Provence; and he was only delivered from the consequent imprisonment at the united request of many Provençal noblemen, who paid ransom for him. Some considerable financial difficulty followed, which was partly solved by the sale of the vast lake of Valcarès, in the Camargue, to the Republic of Arles, of which he was a "Consul" in 1206. But Hugues held firmly to Castillon, and Les Baux itself, and by marriage with Barrale he became Viscount of Marseilles, with large lands near the city. The Albigensian Crusade, however, soon threw the country into still further disorder, and it is with some surprise that we find a member of this stormy house in the character of peacemaker, a role apparently filled with such success by Hugues des Baux, between his friend the Count of Toulouse, and his rival the Count of Provence, that most of the possessions of Les Baux had found their way back to him before his death in 1240.

His son Barral, who married Sibylle d'Anduze, niece of the Count of Toulouse, incurred the excommunication of Pope Gregory IX for holding the heretic Comtat de Venaissin safe in its allegiance to his uncle by marriage. He was equally firm in holding all his possessions near Arles, and especially the much-disputed fort of Trinquetaille, for which he did homage to the archbishop in St. Trophime; and when this wily political prelate was seen to incline too much to the side of Charles d'Anjou, who was now Count of Provence, and very much determined to humble those sturdily independent towns of Arles, Avignon, and Marseilles, Barral des Baux was joyfully acclaimed Podestat of Arles by the citizens in defiance of their ecclesiastical superiors; and Archbishop Daussan had to retire in high dudgeon to Beaucaire, in 1249.

Soon afterwards Charles d'Anjou landed at Aigues-Mortes from the Crusades, followed by the Count of Poitou. Their strength was too much for Barral, who abandoned Arles, and became Podestat of Avignon instead, which was the deathstroke of the Arlesian Republic. By 1251 he was compelled to make peace with Charles, and to sue for the remission of the interdict from the archbishop; in order to save anything of the Comtat Venaissin, he gave up Avignon as well. The star of the Counts of Provence,[10] now passing to the mighty house of Anjou, was in the ascendant. Barral wisely continued his friendship with the strong, by putting down a rebellion in Marseilles for his overlord; and in 1254 he followed Charles d'Anjou to Italy, when the Pope called him in to conquer the kingdom of Naples, which was to prove so fatal to France for centuries afterwards. Barral's son, Raymond, in command of the advance-guard against Manfred in the battle of Benevento, was rewarded by the county of Avelin; his brother Bertrand received a revenue of four hundred golden crowns and twelve castles in the Abruzzi; and these two were the first knights chosen for the hundred companions Charles d'Anjou selected for his proposed duel with the King of Aragon. Their father became Podestat of Milan, and was Grand Justiciary at his death in Italy in 1270.

Barral's sons distinguished themselves later on, as might have been expected from so brilliant a beginning. Their sister Cécile was so beautiful that she was known throughout Provence as "Passe-Rose," and she married into the house of Savoy. Raymond became Grand Seneschal of Provence, taking command, in turn, of the cavalry and of the fleet in the Italian campaign; but he was cut off in a night surprise by the King of Aragon's troops, and slain by his own men in the tumult. His brother

Bertrand succeeded him as Baron of Les Baux, Count of Avelin, Seigneur of Pertuis, and Baron d'Aubagne. He married Philippine de Poitiers, and his fine fighting in Italy resulted in the peace of 1290, after he had himself been ransomed from captivity by the Comte d'Artois. His personal strength and prowess in the tournament were particularly remarked by his contemporaries. These expensive pastimes, added to the continuous drain of the Italian war on his resources, soon compelled him to raise ready money by the sale of his lands; and among these, the famous château of Trinquetaille was sold to the Archbishop of Arles. He ended his days in Palestine in 1304, after visiting the Tomb of the Apostles in Rome.[11] He was succeeded by another Raymond, who was Captain-General of the kingdom of Naples in 1308, and Grand Seneschal of Provence seven years afterwards. His son, Hugues-Raymond, followed him in this latter office, and in 1343 he married Jeanne de Chateauneuf, and as Grand Seneschal, he received the homage of the knights of Provence for the famous Queen Jeanne, who made him her Grand-Admiral.

But his patriotism was stronger than his loyalty to that extraordinary woman; for when public opinion openly accused her of the murder of her first husband, Andrew, of Hungary, and after she had made her second marriage with Louis of Tarentum, he seized her and threw her into prison until the Pope himself had given his assurance that she would not give up Provence. When the Italian estates were attacked, he went, apparently with the object of assisting her, to Naples, with ten Provençal galleys; but he was flying for higher game. He arranged a truce with the avenging King of Hungary, in 1351, on the basis of marrying his own son Robert to Marie, sister of Queen Jeanne, who first married Charles, Duc de Durazzo, and had also lost her second husband, Philip of Tarentum, through whose mother, Catherine, she had become titular Empress of Constantinople. As soon as the first part of this magnificent plot had been safely carried through, and he had put Queen Jeanne and her husband on shore at Gaeta, he set sail for Provence with the Empress, as his daughter-in-law, on board. But an unlucky delay near Gaeta, on the way, proved fatal. Louis of Tarentum, helped by the treachery of the crews, boarded his galley and stabbed him to death with his dagger. His sons, Robert and Raymond, were imprisoned, and the Empress "kept in safety" by her sister.

The tragedy was not over yet; and long negotiations ensued, in which Pope Innocent VI tried in vain to secure the liberty of Robert des Baux. At last, in 1354, the Empress herself, in despair at her anomalous position, forced her way into her husband's prison, with four armed men, watched them assassinate him, and threw his corpse out of window upon the seashore.

Queen Jeanne at once showed her displeasure; but the pompous funeral she gave the murdered man did not remove the suspicion of her own complicity. In the next year Louis de Durazzo was fighting through the kingdom of Naples, while his brother Robert, helped by the Seigneur de la Garde, attacked Provence, and actually took Les Baux. Raymond des Baux, the Grand Seneschal, at once roused the country against the marauders, and besieged the Duc de Durazzo in Les Baux. Raymond came to his own again chiefly by the help of a huge military machine, probably a balista, for hurling rocks over the walls; and in memory of their deliverance the inhabitants set up the "Croix de Machine," which still may be seen on the left of the path that leads down to the "Tremaïe" and the "Gaïe," on the road out of the north side of the village. The invader surrendered in August.

All these alarms and excursions had naturally a lamentable effect on public safety and the well-being of Provence. A band of brigands and discharged soldiers, reaching the alarming total of four thousand, began to ravage the Comtat Venaissin under Arnauld de Cervoles, Seigneur de Castelnau; and unfortunately for the reputation of Les Baux, a member of that turbulent house was with them. The "Archiprêtre," as de Cervoles[12] was grimly nicknamed, was bought off at a high figure by the Pope, and the Seigneurs of Les Baux promptly took advantage of his armed rabble to intimidate the rest of Provence, assisted by still further levies of the same haphazard character under the appropriate leadership of a renegade priest from Salon, named Galapascum. Provence at once became again the theatre of fratricidal strife, and Count Jean d'Armagnac was called in to the help of Marseilles. He promptly attacked Les Baux, and the family itself became divided in the struggle which followed, for the house of Orange was opposed to its parent stem, now chiefly prominent in Antoine des Baux, who devastated Aix and its territories with fire and sword, heartily assisted by the "Archiprêtre" and all his gang of cut-throats. Their reign of terror was only ended by Antoine's death in 1371; and the Pope did his best to annihilate even the memories of past disorders, by granting complete amnesty and absolution to the survivors.

The last in the direct line of Les Baux was Alix, daughter of Raymond and of Jeanne de Beaufort, born in 1367, soon after her father's death. She was placed under the guardianship of Guillaume

Roger de Beaufort, Vicomte de Turenne, whose harsh and self-willed nature seemed to thrive and flourish in congenial soil, as soon as he was in the "Robber's Nest" upon the strong heights of his ward's castle of Les Baux. Two members of his family had reached the papal throne, Clement VI, in 1342, and Gregory XI, in 1370. He married Éléonore de Comminges, sister of that Cécile whose influence over the Pope arranged the alliance and the transfer of the title of Turenne. Their son, Raymond de Turenne, was perhaps the worst enemy Provence ever had (except Anne de Montmorency). The death of Louis d'Anjou, King of Naples and Count of Provence, in 1384, gave him his first opportunity of making trouble; for many towns united in revolt against Marie de Blois, the widow of Louis, and joined the party of Charles de Durazzo, who also claimed the possessions of Queen Jeanne. The Vicomte de Turenne had spent certain sums of good money on Les Baux and its territories, as much for his own sake as for his ward. He proposed to get his interest back, and something more, and with that object he forced Alix des Baux, when she was only thirteen, to marry Adon de Villars. But the bridegroom, who had merely been called into existence as a convenient vassal to be squeezed for money, proved quite recalcitrant. Pitying, as we may justly surmise, the forlorn state of his child-wife, he stoutly espoused her cause against her guardian, and asserted their combined independence against his control. Turenne burst out at once, only too glad of the pretext of a quarrel; and though the Pope immediately advised Marie de Blois to treat for an armistice of two years, Turenne forthwith began to devastate the country.

It may be surmised that the visit of Jean Lefèvre to Alix, in 1382, to purchase for the Duke of Anjou the rights of the Seigneurs des Baux to the empire of the East, did not tend to diminish Turenne's appreciation of his ward's value. The army of bandits which he raised earned for themselves the name of "Tard-venus"; and the cruelty of their leader, Ferragus, when he seized and sacked Les Baux itself, was sufficient to be conspicuous even among those scenes of cruelty and high-handed violence. Like a swarm of vultures, these daring ruffians defiled the eagle's nest, and from the safety of their rocky fastness carried destruction far and wide, plundering and burning towns and villages, and sparing neither age nor sex from their brutality.

The city of Aix roused its militia in self-defence. The Pope sent armed men to the help of Alix and her husband. Turenne replied by rousing the corsairs of the Mediterranean, and ravaging the coasts of the country he was depopulating. Attempts at bribery completely failed. A meeting with the royal ambassadors at St. Remy proved equally ineffectual. In 1393 Les Baux was besieged, and Marie de Blois acknowledged the help given by Arles to her forces, and to those of the Pope, before its walls. But Les Baux held firm. In the next year the Pope tried excommunication. Turenne only laughed, saying that a thousand florins would get him more soldiers than seven years of plenary absolution from the Holy See; and his boast held good. The Pope it was that died.[13]

For so great an emergency a great remedy was needed; and it was forthcoming at the hands of Marshal Boucicaut, who had been sent down by King Charles VI of France to besiege Benedict XIII, enthroned, contrary to the royal wishes, in his castle of Avignon. The Pope fled promptly to Chateaurenard,[14] and the town of Avignon surrendered. Boucicaut was then able to turn to his next task, the pacification of Provence. For this he seemed very fortunately qualified, not merely by his high and honourable reputation as a soldier, but by his recent marriage with Antoinette, the only daughter of Turenne, and one of the loveliest women in all France. He soon found, however, that his father-in-law was not going for a moment to listen to any sentimental arguments. The Vicomtesse de Turenne, approached by a friend at Meyrargues, refused all attempts to negotiate. By slow degrees the attack developed. Les Baux, Roquemartine, and Vitrolles were simultaneously besieged, and Pertuis was taken. Three thousand partisans of the traitor were cut off from the Rhone by the Seneschal of Beaucaire, under direct orders from the king, and at last Turenne, compelled by famine, came to terms in 1399. Boucicaut drew up the treaty, which delivered Provence at last, and was rewarded by the gift of large lands from the queen, and of the body of St. Roch from the grateful Provençals, a relic which he eventually handed to the Religieux Trinitaires of Arles, who passed it on to St. Trophime after the Revolution, and in that church it still remains.

One final effort at revolt Turenne made, in defiance of the treaty, but was forced to take refuge in Tarascon, where he was surrounded, and was finally drowned by falling out of his boat as he tried to escape by the Rhone in 1400. At last the "Fléau de Provence" was dead. So long had this deliverance been vainly prayed for, that the proverb "Aco es long coumé la mort de Tureno," still preserves the execration of his memory in the Valley of the Rhone.[15] Two years afterwards, Alix des Baux, then a widow of thirty-five, married Conrad, Count of Fribourg and Neuchâtel, adding to her title of the Countess of Avelin, those of Alais and Beaufort, and the

Viscounty of Turenne. Louis de Châlons, who had become Prince of Orange through the marriage of Marie des Baux, the heiress, with Jean de Châlons in 1386, received by her will the rights to the Turenne estates; and at her death, in 1426, Les Baux passed with the county of Provence into the hands of Louis d'Anjou, King of Jerusalem and Sicily.[16]

I have deliberately here collected more details concerning this extraordinary family than would be suitable elsewhere in a book of this kind, because the story of the house of Les Baux is so little known, and the site of their fortress-town is so remarkable as to be unique, of its kind, in Europe. It can never again be repopulated, and its appropriate denizens are the ghosts of its once famous rulers, those sturdy robber-barons whose policy was friendship with Toulouse, and hatred for Barcelona, and whose unyielding feudalism fell only before the gradually growing strength of the Counts of Provence, and the great house of Anjou; before, in fact, the royal family of France. The democratic spirit of the rising communes may have helped their downfall; but it was only to the Fleur de Lys that the star of the sixteen rays ever openly acknowledged that its light was dimmed.

That house of brave men was a home of fair women also; and from the inventory made for the Crown, on the death of Alix des Baux, we may still glean some faint notion of the gentler life they sometimes lived amid the turmoil and the bloodshed that so constantly surrounded them.

The entrance-courtyard of the château lay to the south. The Chapel of Ste. Marie, with its vaulted roof, was in the rez-de-chaussée, near several large reception-rooms, with kitchens, bakery, larders, and cellars beneath them. Above were fifteen more out of the thirty-five rooms. That in which Alix died was situated in a tower, beneath a granary. It was furnished with two candlesticks of silver, with plate of silver and of gold, with many lengths of tapestry, and with fine Eastern rugs. In the oaken chests were robes of silk and velvet, of cloth of gold, and "vair"; furs, belts, eight rosaries set with pearls, prayer-books, and books of hours, bound in red cloth of gold, with clasps of silver-gilt. Within the "Chambre de la Rose" were more books of prayer, bound in cloth of gold and pearls, and set in a case of stamped leather, bound with a silver band all gilt with fleurs de lys. The chapel and its vestry were filled with rich ecclesiastical garments and plate, chalices, patens, candlesticks, and reading-desks, in gold and silver-gilt, enriched with gems, enamel, and embroidery, a number of illuminated liturgies, and a set of tapestries, showing the adoration of the Magi, with Balthasar, the traditional ancestor of the house. In other rooms were tables with huge legs enriched with carving, long seats that opened to form linen-chests, sideboards in solid worked wood, cupboards let straight into the stone, and lined with cedar. In the larders and cellars were tuns of wine, both white and red, great store of nuts and grain, piles of salt beef and pork, rows of fishing-nets, and stronger nets for hunting the stag and the wild boar; with herds of cattle, pigs, and sheep, in the pastures below, and nearly fifty chickens. In the halls and passages were trophies of arms, cuirasses, helmets, arbalètes, couleuvrines, bombardelles, lances, and swords; "the most of them rusty," for their day was over. The furniture was partly sold by order of the king, partly bequeathed to the Bishop of Tortosa, and partly sent over to the Château of Tarascon.

The Lady Alix was the last of many famous predecessors in that boudoir, which was scattered to the four winds at her death. Some of them went into the church, as Ermeline, Abbess of St. Sauveur at Marseilles, in 1203; Aybeline, a nun at Mollégès, in 1283; Barbe, Béatrix Florette, Constance, Catherine, and Nazarèthe, who were in turn in the Convent of Noble Nuns at Aix. But the daughters of so strong a house could not often choose so quiet lot. Both policy and blood called them imperiously to a larger life, and, if we may trust their traces, they lived it as heartily as their brothers in their own fashion. That Stéphanette, whose sister's dowry brought such trouble to Provence, was a distinguished leader of the poetically amorous society, which was chiefly cultivated at the court of her rival and brother-in-law of Barcelona. The songs and sighs of Troubadours did not invariably end in merely music. The first lady proclaimed by the unhappy Guilhem de Cabestan was Bérengère des Baux; but, for his sorrow, he then chose Tricline de Carbonelle, the wife of Raymond de Seillans, who slew him, and made a dish for the lady's table from his heart. Fouquet the poet, was so stricken with grief at the death of Adélasie des Baux that he became a monk, and eventually rose to be Abbé de Thoronet, Bishop of Marseilles, and Archbishop of Toulouse, leaving numerous compositions upon the virtue and beauty of his lady on his death.

Sometimes the woman refused the homage of the Troubadour, as did Baussette, who scornfully rejected the verses which Roger d'Arles brought to the castle of Les Baux; sometimes; again, the barons themselves did not disdain to turn a pretty rhyme or two in competition with the Troubadours, as did Raimband des Baux for Marie de Châteauvert in 1236, or that Guillaume d'Orange who derived from the same strong family. But the ladies of Les Baux were chiefly content to provide inspirations, as did that Passe-Rose of the lovely name whom I have mentioned earlier; or Clairette, the theme of Pierre d'Auvergne; or Alasie, the Queen of Beauty at the court of Signe, as Jeanne at that of Avignon; or Rambaude whose charms were sung by Sordel; and there

"Pavillon de la Reine Jeanne" at Les Baux

were doubtless many more to whom such lines were addressed as that ancient Provençal love-song of "Magali," which I have reproduced in my appendix from the version, and the pretty tune, saved from oblivion by Mistral. But I shall have more to say, perhaps, of Provençal poetry another time; and I must pass on from the ladies of the house of Les Baux to the next lady who lived in the halls they had deserted: an appropriate successor; for she was Jeanne de Laval, the second wife of the royal Troubadour, the good King René.

The lands and castle of Les Baux passed to René by virtue of his title of Count of Provence; and it is owing no doubt to the money he spent in embellishing the place for his wife that we have the lovely little "Pavillon" in the valley still left us to admire. There is now only a field of grain within the walls that once held Jeanne de Laval's garden, and all the pleasant walks and shrubberies in which her courtiers and her maids-of-honour strolled and flirted. At each angle was set a tiny summer-house, of which only this one is left; a little gem of rustic Renaissance architecture, with its round arches set between Ionic pillars, and the delicate frieze beneath its tiny dome. The place is called Baumanière in the Vallée de la Fontaine; and it is good to know that René's successor, Charles d'Anjou, approved and ratified the privileges he had granted, privileges which still kept for a little longer the peculiar flavour of independence and of aristocratic solitude around Les Baux. But in 1481 Les Baux passed, with all Provence, to the kingdom of France; and the king was Louis XI. Romance seems to shudder and fly hurriedly away at the very name of him; and but a little more need now be added to explain the desolation of Les Baux today, and to say something of the other ruins that remain in it apart from its old castle.

In 1528 the barony of Les Baux was given by François I to Anne de Montmorency, Grand Constable of France, and Master of the King's Galleys. The hideous results to Provence of the invasions of the Emperor Charles V, whose path was devastated before him to prevent his progress, must have fallen more lightly on Les Baux owing to the presence of the Constable himself. The king recognised his value; and François I came all the way to Les Baux to thank him, and it is at this visit that we first find the name of Claude de Manville, as captain of the town under Montmorency,[17] a name which is inseparably connected with the Huguenots at Les Baux. Of the Protestant party Baron des Adrets was the head, in the Rhone valley, and after the Massacre of Vassy, in 1562, he seized the town and château of Beaucaire. The year before, de

Montmorency had been taken prisoner in the battle of Dreux; and he was killed at St. Denis in 1567. Jehan de Manville, who had taken charge of Les Baux in 1561, was unable to prevent the Huguenots from getting in, and for three months they worked havoc on the emblems of Catholic religion in the castle and the town. In September they were turned out again, with considerable severity; but by 1563 the agreement between Condé and Catherine de Medicis gave them complete freedom for the practice of their religion and the enjoyment of their civic rights. In 1570 Jehan de Manville was back again.

His house is the fine Renaissance building which is almost the first ruin you see on the left hand, at an angle of the little street leading up into the town from the inn, the street called the "Grande Rue." Over the window of the oratory, which still shows indubitable traces of its former beauty, is carved the famous motto of the Reformation: POST TENEBRAS LUX, and the date 1571. In the church is the chapel of the Manville family, which was built by Claude in 1546, with their arms of a golden lion and a silver fortress, and a prettily vaulted roof. Several of their dead lie beneath it. This same Claude de Manville built the Hospital of St. André, in 1542, part of which was behind the Romanesque chapel of St. Blaise (in the Rue des Fours, continuing the Grande Rue) and part in the valley. The lands given him by François I extended outside the walls immediately beneath the rock on which the château was built. These are now the property of the Prince de Manville-Bianchi, by whose generosity the ministry of Beaux-Arts has been able to restore the church, and to preserve some of the ruins that were only classified as "Monuments Historiques" when it was too late to save them all.

In 1614, François de Lorraine, Duc de Guise, in the course of a formal progress through Provence, made his entry into Les Baux on a Saturday afternoon at the end of May. He and his suite seem to have spent a very pleasant Sunday in the château, and salvoes of artillery were fired as every toast was drunk. The duke desired to show his comrades that he was as expert in one form of entertainment as in the other, and loaded one of the cannon with ball, aiming at a broken wall among the ruins. The piece exploded; part of his right leg was blown away; and in a few days he was buried in the church of St. Trophime at Arles. By 1621 de Manville had to consent to give up the protection of the Protestants in Les Baux; and the Catholics have remained "in power" there ever since.

The last man who held the title of Seigneur and Baron of Les Baux was Antoine de Villeneuve, who was a partisan of the Duc d'Orléans against Louis XIII. The king sent Charles de Grille, Sieur d'Estoublon, to take possession of Les Baux by royal authority; but de Villeneuve's men resisted, "even to effusion of blood," and though many of de Grille's soldiers were introduced disguised as women, they could not hold the place. The king's lieutenant at once sent Captain de Saucourt and a company to summon the town to surrender; but the citizens held out "in the king's name"! They were straitly besieged, and sent despairing messages to the king, refusing to open their gates, until de Saucourt showed them a letter from Louis himself, dated the 18th of June 1631, from St. Germain-en-Laye. But this was not all. His Majesty's advisers apparently bethought them that this strong place had been somewhat too wilful. Orders for destruction arrived, and were slowly carried into effect. A mason of Tarascon, named Pol Reboul, struck the first blow on the château on the 11th of March 1633. The engineer, Bugon de Baril, completed the work of demolition with gunpowder on the 8th of April. In less than a month the walls that had stood for some seven centuries were ruined.

One more strange turn of fortune's wheel remained for Les Baux, even after Richelieu had wrecked it; and this was caused by the ambition of Spain to become possessed of Monaco. The young Honoré de Grimaldi, seeking the protection of Louis XIII, who had no desire to see the Spaniards conveniently planted between Genoa and Nice, so near to his own territories, arranged by the treaty of Peronne for the independence of Monaco, and the protection of a French garrison, in 1641, together with sufficient lands in France to compensate for the loss of any Italian revenues confiscated by Spain. Grimaldi got the Spaniards out of Monaco by a cleverly audacious ruse; and was rewarded by lands in France which were called his Duchy of Valentinois; and in 1643 Les Baux was created a marquisate in the possession of the Grimaldis, Princes of Monaco, and Dukes of Valentinois. The title that had been held by Diane de Poitiers, and by Caesar Borgia, added perhaps the last touch of sinister romance that was needed to complete the history of Les Baux. A little country pleasure-house, beneath the ruins of the fort, was enough for the Grimaldis; and even that was knocked to pieces by the Revolution, which also cut down every forest on the mountain-slopes.

The last Grimaldi who was Marquis of Les Baux was Honoré Camille Léonor; and in 1791 Les Baux became the property of the nation. It has become poorer and more desolate every year since then; and I must renounce the task of even trying to pick out some semblance of a story from the crumbling stones that still cumber its mean streets. There is a "Hôtel de Monte Carlo," in Les Baux,[18] no doubt in memory of past Grimaldis; and there is an admirable guide called M. Farnier, who "has constituted a little museum of the relics he has picked up," to use his own expression. To him I can cheerfully leave the explanation of the Maison du Notaire Royale, with its handsome chimney-piece; of the Hôtel des Porcellets, with the pietà above its door; of the Chapelle des Pénitents, with a sun-dial above its entrance; of the great Hall of Ceremonies, with its sixteen-rayed star, a floor that has been dug out four feet deep for limestone, and traces of round-headed Romanesque, pointed Gothic, and square Renaissance, all mingled together upon its outside walls; of the Tilting Yard, called "Les Arènes," built for mild bullfights, in 1840, out of the castle ruins; of the queer arrangements for catching rain-water on the sloping glacis behind it; and of the still imposing remnants of that marvellous castle in which so much of the history of Provence was made.

For myself, I like to leave Les Baux with the memory of Alexandre Dumas, who leaned over its escarpment and looked out along the plain for those pale hedgerows that the Provençal farmers made out of the bones of Marius' battles. He wondered at the little church, as you will wonder too, for it is the only building with any pretence to being weather-tight in the whole place. Its charming entrance, its altar for the sheep-shearers, its dark and massive arches, its little presentment of the Holy Maries in their boat—all are in sombre keeping with these silent ruins. Dumas, I regret to say, took away with him the little wooden figure of a saint; but it caused him such pangs of conscience that he said before it, when he got back to Arles, one of the heartiest prayers he had offered for many a long day, and maybe he has long ago atoned for a theft which was a loss to no one. For as he entered the little, cold, dark building (in the days before its restoration) he heard a sound of sorrow at the eastern end. Upon an open bier, before the high altar, lay the dead body of a little girl. Her two tiny sisters knelt on either side. Her mother sat crying in a corner, and continued sobbing after the good Alexandre had thrown her his whole purse. Her little brother tried to toll the bell for a service at which no priest was present. A dozen or so of beggars had looked in to see the sight. They comprised the whole population of Les Baux.

NOTES

1. "Princesses of Les Baux, Huguette, Sibylle, Blanchefleur, Baussette, who throned it on high upon your rocks of gold, lovely were ye in form, and joyful of spirit, gracious in love, and generous of delight...The wind still howls in all its mighty strength between your ruined doors and through your tottering turrets. The Rhonewind riots down your corridors...."

2. This tradition is preserved in the Convent of the Celestins at Casaluccio, near Aversa, upon the tomb of Raymond des Baux, Grand Chamberlain of Queen Jeanne of Naples: "*Illustrissimae Bauciorum familiae quae a priscis Armeniae regibus quibus stella duce mundi Salvator innotuit originem duxisse patet.*" (Of the most illustrious family Des Baux, who trace their origin from the ancient kings of Armenia to whom the Saviour of the world gave the sign by the guiding star)

3. Towards the end of 1904 the Nobel prize for imaginative literature was divided between Frédéric Mistral and Echegaray, the Spaniard; and I learn that Mistral, with his usual patriotic generosity, intends to devote the money to the improvement of his Provençal Museum, which will probably be removed to a house more worthy to contain its many treasures.

4. Mary Darmesteter, *Contemporary Review*, November, 1892.

5. See the end of chap. iii. vol. I.

6. The Latin name in the deed is "Balcius." I do not pretend to offer any etymological explanations of the word.

7. This deed of gift is preserved in the archives of the Bouches du Rhone (Reg. B. 1069. fo. 230. vo.), and begins as follows: *Notum sit omnibus quod Raimundus Berengarii, Barchinonensis comes, et Dulcia conjux ejus, fecerunt placitum cum Raimundo de Baucio. Illud vero placitum fuit tale: quod comes dedit Raimundo de Baucio omnem honorem illorum sceleratorum qui fuerunt de moete Gilberti comitis inculpati: quod est citra Duranciam, excepta villa Sancti Maximini. Et dedit ei dominium quod habebat in Berra, et justiciam et arbergia; et dedit illi in villa de Mejanis arbergia et bastimenta quae faciet ibi, et...Factum est hoc placitum in villa de Fos, in secundo anno postquam redierunt de Maiorgas...anno Domini incarnationis M.C.XVI.* (Let it be known to all that Raymond Bérenger, Count of Barcelona, and Dulcia his wife have made an agreement with Raymond des Baux. The agreement was on these terms: the Count gave to Raymond des Baux all honour belonging to those criminals who were convicted of the death of Count Gilbert: what is on this side of Durance, except the town of St. Maximinus. And he has given to him the lordship which he had in Berre and rights of justice and of settlement, including the right to build in the town of Mejani... This agreement was made in the town of Fos on the second year after they returned from Majorca... in the year of our Lord 1116)

8. He married Précieuse de Lacon, from whom his son Hugues de Baux (or "Bassis") inherited the chief office of Sardinia. The last important survivor of his line was Eléonore de Baux, wife of Brancaleone Doria, who was fined and exiled by John of Aragon in 1392.

9. Bertrand also had Meyrargues, Puyricard, Eguilles, and Marignane; and in 1213 he married the daughter of Mabile, Viscountess of Marseilles, whose dowry largely increased his wealth. William of Orange fought on the side of the Church in the Albigensian Crusade, and was taken by the "heretics" near Avignon, where he was flayed alive. He married twice, and left two sons.

10. The Count Raymond Bérenger (IV) of Provence had four daughters: Marguerite married St. Louis, King of France; another married King Henry III of England; a third married his brother, Richard, King of the Romans, and Duke of Cornwall; the fourth, Beatrix, was the wife of Charles d'Anjou, and thus Provence, as her dowry, became the county of the brother of St. Louis, and the uncle of three other kings of France. This was not enough for Beatrix, and she was not content until her husband was not merely Count of Provence, but King of Naples, Sicily, and Jerusalem; Senator of Rome; Vicar Imperial of Tuscany, and Seigneur of Placentia, Cremona, Parma, Modena, Ferrara, Reggio, and many towns in Piedmont and Romagna. The Sicilian Vespers were but a part of the price the French had to pay. Provence had lost her independence when France continued that debt of defeat and death which "the fatal gift of beauty" exacted of her to the full in those ill-starred Italian campaigns I sketched in *Old Touraine*.

11. Though Bertrand's son Raymond, Comte d'Avelin, succeeded him at Les Baux, his third son, Agout, is the only member of the family of Les Baux, whose name I can find in *Froissart*, and as might be imagined, it is honourably connected with a stubborn siege, during the English expedition in Languedoc, led by the Earl of Derby in 1344, in which took part the Earls of Pembroke, Oxford, and Stafford, Sir Walter Manny, and others, five hundred knights and squires with two thousand archers. The fighting is described in the first hook of *Froissart*, beginning at the hundred and second chapter. "Sir Agous de Baus" is mentioned as the captain of la Réole in chapter one hundred and nine, and when he "knewe that the people of the towne wolde yelde up, he went into the castell with his company of soudyers, and whyle they of the towne were entretyng, he conveyed out of the towne gret quantyte of wyne and other provisyon, and then closed the castell gates, and sayd, howe he wolde nat yelde up so sone." Then Lord Derby accepted the surrender of the town, hoping that thereby he would get the castle later, and in the town Sir Walter Manny found his father's body entombed, which he removed to Valenciennes. But Lord Derby, after eleven weeks, found he could not undermine the rock on which the castle stood; yet he got some way and the garrison grew alarmed; so "Sir Agous dyscendedde downe fro the hygh towre, and dyd put oot his heed at a lytell wyndo, and make a token to speke with some of the host"... and when Lord Derby had brought Sir Walter Manny and Lord Stafford to speak with him, he offered to yield the fortress if he and his men might depart, "our lyves and goodes saved." This the

Englishmen refused. Then Agout des Baux asked for the lives of his soldiers, saying: "Sir, knowe for trouthe, that yf the lest of us sholde nat come to mercy, as well as the best, we woll rather sell our lyves, in suche wyse that all the worlde shulde speke of us"...So Lord Derby granted honourable surrender, with their armour... "Than they dyd on their harnesse and toke their horses, wherof they hadde no mo but sixe; some bought horses of thenglyshmen, the whiche they payed for truely. Thus Sir Agous de Baus departed fro the Ryoll, and yelded up the castell to the Englysshemen, and Sir Agous and his company wente to Tholous." I confess that this honourable feat of arms, so handsomely recognised by the English, lends its best interest, in my eyes, to these barren Provençal ruins that are stained with so many less attractive memories.

12. "In the same season," writes Lord Berners, translating *Froissart*, vol.I. chap. clxxvi, "ther was a knyght called Sir Arnolde Cervoll, and most comonly named archpreest, he assembled togyder a great company of men of warr of dyvers contrees suche as lacked wages in other places: after the takyng of the Frenche kynge, they wyste nat where than to wynne any thyng in Fraunce: so first they went towardes Provence and toke by force many stronge townes and castelles, and robbed all the countrey to Avygnon, and they had none other capitayne but this knyght the Archpreest: the pope Innocent the Sixt, and the cardynalles beyng at Avygnon had of that company great dout, and kept there men day and nyght in harnesse, and made good watche. When this archpreest and his company had robbed all the countre, the pope and the clergy fell in treaty with them, and so on a sure apoyntment they came to Avygnon and they were as hononrably receyved as thoughe there had ben a kynges sonne; and often tymes this knyght had dyned with the pope and with the cardynals, and they had pardon of all their synnes, and at their departyng they had in rewarde xl thousande crownes for hym and his company; so some of his company departed, but styll the archpreest kept his company togyder."

13. Froissart adds that "Les gendarmes ne vivent pas de pardons ni n'en font point trop grand compte, fors au détroit de la mort."

14. Mistral's poem, *Nerto*, describes the flight of Benedict from Avignon to Chateaurenard, and the subsequent proceedings in Arles. It is one of the best "historical imaginations" of the Popes in Provence ever published, as is also the well-known tale in Daudet's *Lettres de mon Moulin*.

15. Turenne's portrait is worth preserving here in the language of a contemporary eyewitness: "Ce fléau de Provence ...estoit de taille pleine at quarrée, plus tost grand que petit, avoit les membres forts et robustes, la teste grosse et ronde, le visage plain et gras, le teint couleur de miel, les sourcils et les yeux de mesme, à l'entredeux des sourcils ayant la chair surenflée, ce qui causait deux plis qu'il faisoit en se renfroignant; avoit le nez tirant sur l'aquilin, les lèvres grosses et rouges, avec un peu de moustache noire...ressentant son homme de haute et bonne maison..."

16. The fortunes of the house of Orange, in which Las Baux had so large a share, have been sketched in the third chapter of the first volume, in its last pages. The branch of François des Baux, Duc d'Andrie and Seigneur of Berre, lost its estates in 1374, but was carried on by Raymond des Baux des Voisins, Prince of Tarentum, whose modern representatives are the family *Del Balzo* of Naples, who bear the arms of Les Baux and Orange.

17. The Manvilles seem to have originally come from Normandy, where Henri and Pierre de Manville served under Pierre de Brézé in the fifteenth century. Jean migrated to Toulouse in 1463 and held office in the town before his death in 1481. His son Claude, it was, who was captain of the galleys at Marseilles, and then captain, under Montmorency, of Les Baux, of which the king created him Seigneur in his own right in 1544. He married Philippine de Brion, but, being without issue, handed on Les Baux to his nephew, Jehan d'Aymar of Toulouse. A collateral branch was represented in Languedoc down to the Revolution by the Prince de Manville-Bianchi.

18. Where "lunch" is a perilous adventure, and any other form of hospitality impossible.

Part II: Carcassonne

"...The baseless fabric of this vision
The cloud-capped towers, the gorgeous palaces,
The solemn temples, the great globe itself,
Yea, all which it inherit, shall dissolve
And, like this insubstantial pageant faded,
Leave not a rack behind..."

—

"Il n'a jamais vu Carcassonne."

THERE was once a farmer in Languedoc who always promised himself the happiness of a journey to Carcassonne; but whether it was the market of the "Ville," or the battlements of the "Cité" which was the greater attraction I cannot tell. Seed-time and harvest, winter and spring, followed one another, and as he lay a-dying the gossips echoed Nadaud's sad line which I have placed at the head of this chapter, "He has never seen Carcassonne." It might no doubt be the epitaph of many an Englishman who has spared himself a week upon the Riviera, or even journeyed past Toulouse; and it applies to more than merely pilgrimages unfulfilled. It shall never be said of any traveller in Provence who reads this book if I can help it.

There are two places with the name of Carcassonne today, but there was only one before the middle of the thirteenth century; and the "new town," laid out in squares and parallels like any urban mushroom in the Western States, was founded at the will of St. Louis, and built under Philippe le Hardi, after the same squarely mathematical alignments which controlled the internal architecture of Aigues-Mortes. With this I shall have little to do; for, estimable as may be its present inhabitants, and untarnished its long record of development, it is but the stepping-stone, the very doormat (as Henry James once said) of its elder sister on the hill across the Aude.

To many of us a mediaeval fortress is a thing of stage-craft, a matter of nimble trickery behind the footlights; at most the rapid flash of such intuitively created mystery as stops our turning pages at one of Doré's best vignettes in the "Contes Drolatiques." But here, by the river Aude, within an easy morning journey from Toulouse, is the reality of six centuries ago, with no theatrical carpentry too visibly at work, with nothing between you and the Visigoths save the unrealised and priceless healing of a sympathetic architect. "Restorer" were a name soiled by too base uses for such work as Viollet-le-Duc has here achieved. He has evoked, with a sure hand, the lines and towers of the past; set them so firm upon the untorn bases of their first foundation, that even the encircling air about that immemorial place of arms seems dim with its full host of mail-clad warriors, still stirring with the pennons of their chivalry, and echoing to the shout of onset and defiance.

Look at it first from a distance, from that little stilted bridge across the river, to which you are led willingly down a long avenue of acacia-trees. Aloof, alone, high-set upon its solid hill, the ancient Cité stands within her double ring of frowning walls and lance-like pinnacles, each rounded roof a massy helmet, each buttress a colossal shield. By two gates only may you enter: by the Porte Narbonnaise, magnificently flanked by tall defences and bristling with solid outworks, cunningly interlaced and triply guarded; and by the Porte de l'Aude, which looks towards Toulouse and is approached by a steep paved way, now grassgrown. The green that typifies forgiveness now clasps the base of those enormous ramparts which once rose straight from the forgotten moat, as if in heavy folds of some stone curtain stretched from tower to tower between the fortress and the world.

Carcassonne

"Die Welt ist nichts als ein Orchester,
Wir sind die Instrumente drin..."

And as the overture is finished, it is time for that curtain to go up, and to let us look closer at the stage it shrouds, at the scenes where so many actors—heroes and villain both—played their last part in the tragedy of Carcassonne.

Though known to the Roman generals, Carcassonne showed nothing of her future fortunes until Rome had fallen. With Theodoric, King of the Visigoths, who held the entrenchments on the hill in 436, began the first fortifications that can still be traced, in an oval line which was only smaller than the existing interior line at the south-western angle. Its towers were cylindrical outside, square on the inside, and based upon huge uncemented blocks that may well have been of late Roman construction. They were joined by a tall rampart with the sentinels' walk along the top, defended by square battlements. On the outer face, at about the level of the internal ground, were round-headed windows, furnished with wooden shutters swung on horizontal bars, through which the archers shot. For a large part of their height these towers are solid, and were therefore a fine defence against the mines or battering-rams of the period.

The little plateau, thus so early and so strongly fortified, is set at an angle which commands the valley of the Aude, the natural pathway from Narbonne to Toulouse, between the foothills of the Pyrenees and the Black Mountain, and it is also the key to the roads from the Mediterranean to the ocean and from France to Spain. For this reason Clovis besieged it, ineffectually, in 508. For more than two hundred years afterwards the Visigoths stayed on, until the Moors and Saracens swept over the Pyrenees and held the southern towns of France. They left no traces in the masonry of the place except in the breaches they made in several parts of the walls; but one of their queens, Carcas, is said to have given her name to the fortress after her heroic defence of the town against the Franks whose archers had shot her husband on the walls. The legend probably arose from the inscription, "UNICA SUM CARCAS," once set up over the stone bust of a woman at the Porte Narbonnaise; a sentence which is more likely to have typified the pride of the inhabitants of the ancient city and their claim that alone it should be called Carcassonne, after the new town across the river had been founded.

Pepin took the fortress for the Franks in 759, and Oliban, who held it for Charlemagne, was the first count who declared his independence, and handed on his power. His descendant, Roger, thoroughly strengthened the Visigoth walls, founded the church of St. Nazaire, though nothing of his work is left, and began to collect around him some of the elements of a court, for which a flourishing industrial quarter soon grew up in the faubourgs round the walls, supplying leather and clothwork for the nobles and their ladies. After Roger's death his vassal knights revolted and besieged the fortress. But the Countess Hermengarde, wife of Raymond Trencavel, roused the Carcassonne militia, called out and armed the neighbouring workmen, under the leadership of her son Aton, and soon dispersed the rebel barons.

The Trencavel dynasty thus seemed firmly based upon popular affection, bound to them by the best ties of victorious comradeship in arms; but in 1096 Bernard Aton was in such trouble with his burgesses that Pope Urban II had to come in person to make peace between them, and to give his blessing to the nave of the present church of St. Nazaire, which was just being built. One result of the quarrel was that a certain number of the inhabitants were bound over for the future, as "châtelains," to keep the towers and walls in good repair, and to be responsible for the safety of the town. In about 1130, under Roger III, the château itself was built into the old Visigoth ramparts behind the Porte de l'Aude, and for the next fifty years the inner line of fortifications was constantly strengthened; but there was only the inner line when Carcassonne suffered the greatest siege of its history, and went through the tragedy which is the darkest association of its historic name.

To understand the position on that fatal first of August, when Simon de Montfort led a French army against a French fortress, I must go a little further afield to explain the horrible episode in Provençal annals which is known as the Albigensian Crusade.

What is now roughly known as the Albigensian "heresy" began in the mountains of Piedmont and Dauphiné, where men revolted against the symbolism, the mysteries, and the poetry, through the medium of which the Christian faith was universally offered for acceptance. Their opinions were fortified and spread by Pierre de Bruys and his disciple Henri de Lausanne. In Lyons one Pierre de Vaud was the head and front of their offence, as in Italy was Arnaldo da Brescia. They refused baptism, the Mass, the adoration of the Cross, the traffic in indulgences. What was originally a logical revolt of pure reason against dogmatic authority soon took unfortunately varying forms, and then reached unpardonable extremes. Their demand for separation from the Church—a thing unimaginable before, and never to be tolerated then—was the measure at once of their earnestness and their lack of worldly wisdom. The persecutions they endured, down to the Massacre of St. Bartholomew, and even later, are the proof of their sincerity. With the truth of their convictions, in the later and more adaptable doctrines of Luther and the Reformation, these pages have no concern; but it may at least be said that nothing based on lies could have endured so long or could have roused the heroism of nations in a cause that will never die while the religious formalities, which express individual belief in the Divine, exist. Religious persecutions form a subject that is most repugnant to every thoughtful mind; but unfortunately they bulk large in human history from the time of the first Pharaohs downwards, and they have left some of the deepest scars upon that small portion of the universe which it is my present business to describe. Something, therefore, must be said of them; but merely as an explanation of the facts before us.

A little consideration of the geographical conditions of Languedoc and Provence will at once show how favourable was their soil to any new and attractively imaginative propaganda. I use this last epithet because the revolt against the excessively mystic symbolism of the end of the thirteenth century was, in a sense, the last step possible in "imagination." The destruction of all symbols became inevitable because their work was over and they could mean no more; extremes, in fact, had met, as is so commonly the case after a course of over-nurtured decadence. The reaction, of course, did not take this form alone. Besides and beyond the passive resistance, the destructive criticism, the negation, that appealed to some minds, there was the brilliant vitality, leavened by common sense, illuminated by artistic feeling, which roused in other, subtler intellects, the magnificently exuberant fruition of the genius called "Gothic." As little with that side of "Gothic" as with its architecture are we here concerned. The "Albigensians" show the reverse of the picture; the foreign, exotic side, as opposed to the characteristically French.

Consider the colours on the palette. Languedoc had held the Saracen capital in Narbonne. Jews swarmed all over it; centred in Carcassonne, Montpellier, Nîmes. The Counts of Toulouse were Counts of Tripoli as well, and something more than the flavour of Oriental luxury had returned out of the East with the Crusaders. The literature of the Troubadours was the literature of love; and near the Rhone Valley love can never be Platonic; the "decisions" of their "Queens of Love" remain to prove it. "No true love can exist between wife and husband," said Eleanor of Guienne, and "a man may take a second lady-love to prove the temper of his first." Ermengarde, Countess of Narbonne, declared that a divorced man might well be the lover of his wife when once she had another husband. Such sayings should be taken, not as individual blots upon a fair reputation, but as symptoms of a temperament, indications of a frame of mind that was ready for every breath of novel doctrine. And there were many; though "Manicheism" has somewhat overpassed the rest, because of its great council held at the very centre of its heresy, Béziers, Carcassonne, Toulouse. Brought here from Bulgaria and Constantinople, it carried the old Persian theories of dualism into every phase of thought: the universe and the individual soul; the one race and the other; the God of Good, and the God of Evil; the spirit and the flesh. Thus taught the Manichean Pope, Nicetas of Constantinople, in his Rome which was Toulouse.

Inextricable confusions of interpretation were the natural result for every orthodox critic, and their self-contradictory accusations of doctrine need not concern us. But one clear cleavage leaps to light. The danger to the true Pope and to his Church, his World, was irrefutable. We need not refuse, either to him or to his workers, an equal ardour of sincerity, an equally unselfish flame of zeal. The foundation of the Dominican Inquisition, the abuse of the confessional, these were but the symptoms of that zeal, not here to be examined otherwise.

Politics, both external and internal, lent the shadow of a darker background to the whole. At the beginning of the thirteenth century, Germany's hostility to the Holy See was weakened by division. The crown of France was docile, even to taking back a hated queen. The Greeks had been subdued, for the empire of Constantinople had become (for sixty years) a French dependency. The Rhone and Languedoc alone seemed separate. Their lords were a King of Aragon and a King of England, both of uncertain faith, and drawn together by their common variance with Rome. That variance implied a difference from the rest of France, a difference which the movements of Crusading armies had already revealed to astonished northern captains marching southwards to the sea. After Toulouse or Avignon had been reached, the people seemed to change as greatly as the face of their country. Bargaining and marketing took the place of chivalrous ardour; disdainful opulence appeared instead of sturdy soldierhood, in this land of olive-oil, of garlic, and of figs.

In such a powder-magazine the spark was not long in blazing.

The Abbé of Citeaux strove to convert these heretics by the glamour of his ecclesiastical and luxurious pomp. He was soon taught stronger measures by a fanatic Castilian noble, who was Dominic, the founder of the Inquisition, that fatal weapon in the hands of Innocent III. Raymond VI, Count of Toulouse, roused the Pope to final conflict by reckless plundering of ecclesiastical property, by continuous defiance of the Papal will, by flaunting his immorality,[1] his agnosticism, his friendship with heretics and Jews. Pierre de Castelnau, the legate of the Pope, roused him to anger by his denunciations, and suffered the fate of Thomas Becket, at St. Gilles in 1208. The hour struck; and vengeance delayed not in her coming.

In titles, the Count of Toulouse was strong indeed. Marquis of Northern Provence; Master of Quercy, Rouergue, and Vivarais; of Agenois through the King of England; of Gevaudan through the King of Aragon; Duke of Narbonne; and suzerain of Nîmes, Béziers, Uzès, Foix, and Comminges; he was yet uncertain of receiving loyal help from all. The Vicomte de Béziers, for instance, with whom rumour unceasingly connected the assassination of de Castelnau, held by the Comte de Foix, and asserted independence; and he was not alone. The Count of Toulouse began, therefore, by the outward signals of submission, and was scourged in the church of St. Gilles, where Pierre de Castelnau lay buried. The Pope accepted his repentance, but exacted further punishment. To save himself, the wretched count had to see, even to appear to assist, the whole fury of the Pope's crusade concentrated upon his nephew, the young and heroic Vicomte de Béziers. The point of attack was well chosen. The vicomte's territories were the centre of the greatest number of the heretics, and he was not strong enough to make too widespread a resistance; whereas, had the Count of Toulouse been chosen as the scapegoat, a head and leader of a United South might necessarily, and involuntarily have been called into being. As a matter of fact, the Pope at first succeeded in uniting his friends against a divided foe.

The Papal Crusades of 1209 were led by the Archbishops of Rheims, Sens, and Rouen, the Bishops of Autun, Clermont, Nevers, Bayeux, Lisieux, and Chartres, the Duke of Burgundy, the Counts of Nevers, St. Pol, Auxerre, Bar-sur-Seine, and many more. With them was Archdeacon Theodosius from the Cathedral of Notre Dame in Paris, a master of siege-craft, and a mighty maker of engines for assault and battery. At their head was Simon de Montfort.

Béziers was the first town he besieged; and the names of the accused were read out for surrender. But the men of Béziers refused to give them up, and as soon as de Montfort's army began to entrench their camp, they burst out of the town and attacked it. The sally was repulsed easily by the

Entrance to Carcassonne (from a drawing by C.E. Mallows)

guards; and the officers, following the routed men of Béziers in their flight back through the gates, found themselves masters of the city. A temporary embarrassment arose as to which were infidel and which were orthodox. "Slay them all," said the Abbé of Citeaux; "God will know His own." Over forty thousand persons perished. The Abbé himself modestly restricted his own claims to twenty thousand in reporting matters to the Pope.

"Then," says the Chronicle of Languedoc, "those in the town who could, both men and women, withdrew into the great church of St. Nazaire, and the priests of the church tolled the bells until all within it were dead. Neither the sound of the bells, nor the priests' garments, nor the clerks, availed to save any from the edge of the sword. Not one escaped. This butchery and murder was the most pitiful thing ever seen or heard of. The whole town was pillaged, and fire was set to every house till all was devastated, as may still be seen, and not a living thing survived. This was a cruel vengeance, seeing that the vicomte himself was neither heretic nor sectarian…and people from all nations of the world assisted in it to the number of some three hundred thousand, who had come together, as was said, because of the promises of pardon and indulgence given them."

The horror of that holocaust spread far and wide. Every town opened its gates to de Montfort's army. Carcassonne alone stood firm, and in it was the hot heart of the Vicomte de Béziers, bleeding from the slaughter of his men. He was straightway besieged. His son, Raymond de Trencavel, was sent for safety to the Comte de Foix. His uncle, the King of Aragon, begged for terms. Safe-conduct was offered to the vicomte, with twelve others only. He refused at once, saying he would be flayed alive first. "Not one of my men shall the legate have, by my will; for it is for my sake that they have put themselves in peril." The siege began on August 1, 1209, and the defence was desperate. So hot was the fighting, aided by the skill of Archdeacon Theodosius, that in spite of constant sallies at night, in spite of unceasing heroism along the ramparts, de Montfort won the place after fourteen days of continual slaughter.

Want of water and famine had done what sword and mine had failed to accomplish. Every family from the countryside had fled for refuge within the vicomte's walls; when the wells were tainted there was no more hope. The vicomte held out until all the crusading forces were gathered round him then made a way of escape for his vassals by a subterranean passage which let them out into free country; and then fought until there were no more left to keep de Montfort out. Even so, four hundred and fifty wounded men were left. Four hundred of them were burnt; the others hanged. The vicomte himself, treacherously promised his life, was at first imprisoned in one of his towers during the rest of August. But his indomitable courage and his undying popularity throughout the country were too dangerous. By November he was dead.

This second massacre had turned the gorge of the best leaders of the Church's army. But some one had still to watch by the smoking cinders and the clotted blood. Some one had to be rewarded with these blackened ruins and maimed victims of St. Dominic and Innocent III, the guerdon for keeping watch that heresy did not once more raise her head from among the corpses and the ashes of her punishment. Simon de Montfort accepted both the task and its reward. The Crusading army fell away from him, glutted with butchery. The Comte de Foix at once appealed both to Philip Augustus and to the Pope, but was put off. The Count of Toulouse was offered such terms of reconciliation as even he could not accept. De Montfort's wife roused him a new army; and fresh soldiers hurried from the north on hearing that the harrying of the south was still in progress. The miserable Albigeois, burnt and hacked out of Carcassonne and Béziers, now fled to various isolated forts. A multitude took refuge in the Château de Minerve near Narbonne. They were besieged without a hope of succour, without a single prayer for mercy. The whole hundred and forty of the survivors threw themselves into the flames, men and women alike, when de Montfort's soldiers took the place. The same hideous scenes were renewed at the Château de Termes; and here, as before, Archdeacon Theodosius showed his holy skill in the machinery of assault. The cross was fixed above his engines, and for all who were unhappy enough to survive them his fires were lighted. At the taking of the Château de Lavaur the Seigneur of Montréal was led out with eighty other nobles to he hanged. He was a tall man, and his weight broke down the hastily-erected gallows, so the rest had their throats cut, and his wife was hurled down a well, which was then filled up with stones. The few of the garrison who remained were burnt alive.

It was now time to turn to the Count of Toulouse. His town was deliberately condemned to the same fate as Béziers by its bishop; and the clergy left it in procession, singing their litanies, and calling down death upon their people as they went. But even de Montfort seemed to have slaked his thirst for slaughter; or perhaps because there were so few heretics left to kill, he moved away from before the walls of Toulouse, where Count Raymond was helped by the Counts of Foix, of Béarn, and Comminges. At Castelnaudary, de Montfort was only saved from defeat and death by the discipline of his troops, who just managed to keep off the fiery onset of the house of Foix. Then Don Pedro, King of Aragon, challenged Simon de Montfort to bring his men to battle. The Crusader grimly accepted, gave his knights the Sacrament, and showed them Don Pedro's love letter to an inamorata in Toulouse. At Muret, near that town, the armies met, and Don Pedro did not survive the utter destruction of his forces. The Albigensian "Crusade" was over; the "heresy" had been stamped out in blood and fire. When the details were brought to Innocent III, his confidence in the justice of his cause, in the righteousness of his instruments, was rudely shaken. The blood of the slain seemed to cry out for vengeance; the love for Holy Church seemed hardly likely to increase. He was yet further troubled by the representations of the Comte de Foix. But all hope of reparation had long passed. Whole populations are not massacred with impunity for an idea. That idea was visibly shaken. The only certainty that remained was the immense loss of life, the widespread desolation.

In 1218 Simon de Montfort was slain beneath the walls of Toulouse; his strong heart had been broken long ago. His son, Amaury, gave up to Philip Augustus, King of France, all his blood-stained heritage of the south, save a few towns that still clung to independence.

Young Raymond de Trencavel, son of that Vicomte de Béziers so foully slain in Carcassonne, had married the sister of the King of Aragon, but when he claimed his heritage from Louis VIII, in 1226, it was denied him. Carcassonne had become a part of the royal domain under the king's seneschal. So he gathered troops in Aragon and Catalonia and took Montréal, Montolieu, Saissac, Limoux, Azillan, and Laurens, and then marched on Carcassonne. Two accounts of the siege have come down to us: the first from Guillaume de Puy-Laurens, Grand Inquisitor for the district of Toulouse; the second, the formal report addressed by the royal seneschal, Guillaume des Ormes, to Queen Blanche, the mother of Louis IX.[2]

The fortress still had only its single lines of defence, an oval of about four hundred metres long by half that width. The château was behind the triangular defences which joined the barbican of the Porte de l'Aude to the main circumvallations of the western face; and it will be easy to appreciate these dispositions on the spot if you remember that the Cité is to the east, and the Ville Basse to the west of the Aude, while the still-existing twelfth-century bridge over the river points in almost a straight line from west to east, slightly inclining towards the south, as you may verify from the lines of the Cathedral of St. Nazaire, which lies south of the château within the walls.

As the invading army of September 17, 1240, came from the south they had no need to cross the Aude in order to invest the place; but the only reinforcements possible to the besieged must come from the north-west, over the river, so the Vicomte Raymond de Trencavel held the bridge, and arranged his army so as to cut off the fortress from the stream. For the same reason he at once seized the faubourgs all round the Porte de l'Aude, and strengthened his position by the fortified mill on a bridge across a small arm of the Aude, two hundred and fifty metres to the south of the big bridge. Others of his forces encamped on the ground between these bridges, facing the steep hill of the fortress; and others again watched the northern extremity of the walls, and the Porte Narbonnaise. All were strongly entrenched. A sally of the defenders against the captured faubourgs was repulsed, but to prevent its recurrence furious attacks were simultaneously made on the great barbicans of the Porte de l'Aude, and of the Porte Narbonnaise, and on the projecting piece of plateau which then extended beyond the main defences of the southern angle. The arbalétriers kept up such a storm of missiles that no defender could show himself alive beyond the walls, and a huge mangonel was raised against the western barbican. The eastern gate was attacked by mines, the hollow ground being eventually filled with burning wood which gradually produced the sinking-in of the defences above it.

The first breach in the walls occurred on the southern plateau between the cathedral and the angle of the fortifications; but the besieged were ready with a palisade that stopped all further entry; and when the northern angle just seemed to be sufficiently undermined to be on the point of falling, the garrison stopped further progress by a countermine. The vicomte was pressed for time, owing to the probable arrival of the enemy's reinforcements, and he no doubt attacked before the defence was sufficiently weakened; for the general assault he ordered on the twentieth day was everywhere repulsed, and four days afterwards he was forced to retreat before the appearance of the royal army. He had not been successful but his attempt had taught the French a lesson. King Louis IX determined that this key-fortress of the south should be henceforth impregnable.

The first of the royal commands having this object showed a clear appreciation of events. The faubourgs were levelled, and their inhabitants bidden to find a home elsewhere. It was built for them, later on, in the Ville Basse.[3] The next step was even more important. The whole of the external line of walls and towers, as we now see them, was forthwith built, enclosing the weak point on the plateau to the south, and extending the defences of the Porte Narbonnaise at least thirty metres eastward. Philippe le Hardi carried the work to completion before his death in 1285, and Carcassonne was the base from which he attacked the King of Aragon, and the sure refuge to which he could always retreat in case of accidents. The date of the walls between the south-west angle and the Porte de l'Aude is fixed at 1280, owing to the order given by the king, in August of that year, in Paris, that four barred windows might be put in them for the convenience of the bishop, on the understanding that they should be walled up in case of siege; and they may still be seen. The outer walls were finished before any reparation was done to the inner line, in which the bossed stone-work is all later than the exterior buildings. But nothing was added after the thirteenth century was over; and the work was so well done that the fortress was never taken by storm again.[4] It never opened its gates after the rest of Languedoc had been taken by Edward the Black Prince in 1355, though he had stormed and burnt the lower town, and the whole countryside had just been desolated by the plague. The copies of the Archives, preserved in the Cité, made up for the losses incurred by the conflagration in the lower town. "La chevaucheé du Prince Noir" was the name given to this raid in Languedoc, from which the prince brought back a thousand waggons of plunder to Bordeaux.

The French king, though he had raised an expensive levy, did not think it worth while actively to oppose what does not seem to have been much more illustrious than a raid for the frank purposes of booty. The lower town suffered heavily, and the only bright spot in a somewhat sordid adventure is the heroic defence made by the consul Davilla, who died in the breach he could no longer defend, and whose funeral was honoured by his foes as well as by his countrymen. The town was rebuilt by Jean d'Armagnac, the king's lieutenant in Languedoc.[5]

Carcassonne (from a drawing by C.E. Mallows)

Both towns remained inviolate, thanks to the efforts of the seneschal, Pierre de Villan, from the ravages of the bandits called "Grand Companies," which du Guesclin was soon to lead over the Pyrenees. In the disorders that followed the death of Charles V in 1380, Languedoc, which had formerly been under the governorship of the Duc d'Anjou, was passed on by him to the Duc de Berry; but Gaston Phoebus (III), Comte de Foix, refused to acknowledge his demission from the post of lieutenant which was similarly handed on to the Comte d'Armagnac; and the Cité stayed by Gaston until the Council of Regency in Paris peremptorily ordered their obedience. The desolation caused by these quarrels was reflected in a general insurrection of the unemployed poor, which was only subdued by very drastic measures in 1383. Six years afterwards, the young King Charles VI, then in his twenty-first year, visited Carcassonne, and passed on to Foix, where I have seen that tall donjon-keep which looks out from a strong spur of the hills towards the Pyrenees on one side and the plains of Languedoc upon the other, a fitting memorial of its famous masters. Gaston Phoebus received the king with a picturesque loyalty all his own. A hundred gentlemen of Béarn and Ariège appeared before the king at Foix, each driving a pair of oxen, which they presented to his Majesty.

In 1412, Carcassonne once more held out defiantly against the attacks of John the Fearless, Duke of Burgundy; but by the middle of the century famine and misery once more oppressed the country, and the bands of brigands known as "écorcheurs" roamed up and down it. But a hundred years later it had recovered sufficiently to give a brilliant welcome to Francis I. It is to the credit of Guillaume de Joyeuse, governor of Languedoc, that though Charles IX personally visited the fortress in 1565, he absolutely refused to carry out the orders for a "Massacre of St. Bartholomew" here, or at Limoux, Castelnaudary, or Béziers. But toleration seems to have been impossible for long in a land so seared with the traces of religious struggle; and in 1584, the Calvinist Montmorency, head of the party called the "Politiques," held the fortress against the lower town, which was of "the old religion" as represented by Joyeuse, the champion of the "Ligue". But the accession of Henri IV led to the loyalty of the Cité, and the estates of Languedoc were held there soon afterwards.

The church of St. Nazaire within the double walls of the hill-fortress must not be forgotten by the most casual visitor. The beginning of its nave I have already mentioned, and the work in it cannot be later than the end of the eleventh century, or earlier than 1085. The transept, with the apse and the chapels, dates from the beginning of the fourteenth century; but the whole was reared upon the foundations of more ancient work which is still traceable in the crypt. On the south side of the transept is the tomb of Bishop Radulphus, dated 1266, and carved with statuettes of the canons of the cathedral in their surplices. The choir and transept, built by Bishop Pierre de Roquefort from 1300 to 1320, are exquisitely finished, and very rich in decoration. The stained glass is especially remarkable; and the tomb of the bishop himself is in quite the best style of the fourteenth century. The tomb and statue, often attributed to Simon Vigur, Archbishop of Narbonne, who died here in 1575, are in reality fourteenth-century work; nor is the slab, supposed to commemorate the famous Simon de Montfort, any more authentic; but the bas-relief, let into the wall of the right-hand chapel of the sanctuary may well represent the death of de Montfort in his attack on the walls of Toulouse. The whole church was carefully and beautifully restored between 1844 and 1860 while the fortress itself was being brought to life again, and it is a curious note of later northern "Gothic" amid the walls and ramparts of an earlier age, and of a more southern character.

NOTES

1. Even the broadest views of aristocratic licence revolted against four wives, three of whom were living at one time. They were Beatrix, sister of the ill-fated Comte de Béziers; the daughter of the Duke of Cyprus; his cousin, the sister of Richard Coeur-de-Lion and, after the death of this last, the sister of the King of Aragon. When he was ill, he insisted on being carried to Toulouse in order to be near his "bons hommes," the heretics. Little wonder that contemporary orthodoxy called him "limb of Satan, son of perdition, and firstborn of the devil, a fervid persecutor of Holy Church, a supporter of the infidels, a torturer of the faithful, a criminal apostate, the gutter of whose heart is open to every form of sin."

2. See *Bibl. de l'École des Chartes*, II. Série, t. ii. p.363.

3. The Act empowering the building of the Ville Basse was signed at Aigues-Mortes in 1248, in the form of a letter to Jean de Cravis, Seneschal of Carcassonne, bidding him give house-room, by arrangement with the bishop, who was indemnified for the site, to all the inhabitants of the old faubourgs, except those suspected of treachery with the vicomte during the recent siege.

4. Viollet-le-Duc has calculated the minimum of the defenders necessary for the double line of walls, as follows: —

Fourteen towers on the outer wall at twenty men each,	280
Twenty men in each barbican,	60
Reinforcements for attack at any other point of the walls undefended by towers,	100
Twenty-four towers on the inner wall at twenty men each,	480
At the Porte Narbonnaise,	50
Along the inner walls where unprotected by towers,	100
Garrison of the château,	200
One captain to each division,	53
	<u>1323</u>

With a further number of some two thousand workmen, servants, and common soldiers, a total of three thousand men would be enough, at need, to hold the fort.

5. It may be interesting here to preserve the offer of twenty-five thousand crowns of gold which the Black Prince refused before he sacked the town. It runs as follows:—

"Au très illustre prince et seigneur Edouard, prince de Galles, fils aîné du roi d'Angleterre: le prieur des Frères Prêcheurs, le gardien des Frères Mineurs, le prieur des Carmes, le prieur des Hermites de Saint Augustin, avec leurs religieux. Les prêtres de l'Eglise Saint Michel, les prêtres de l'Eglise Saint Vincent, le Commandeur de Sainte Eulalie de Palajauel, le commandeur de Saint Antoine, l'Abbesse des soeurs de Sainte Claire, la prieure des soeurs de Saint Augustin, la prieure des soeurs repenties, avec leurs religieuses, très humbles suppliants de votre Excellence, vous demandent, autant qu'ils peuvent, qu'il vous plaise par votre charité et douceur que le bourg de Carcassonne ne soit point brûlé et qu'un autre nouveau dommage ne soit point ajouté à celui qu'il a déjà souffert. Si votre Excellence nous refuse cette grâce, il sera nécessaire que leurs maisons soient brûlées et leurs Eglises abandonnées, et le service divin cesse…et afin que l'abondance de votre pitié paraisse plus, nous vous supplions qu'il vous plaise agréer l'offre que les habitants du bourg ont faite à votre Excellence, offre d'une rançon de vingt-cinq mille écus d'or…c'est la très humble grace que nous sollicitons.—4 Novembre 1355."

Part III: Aigues-Mortes

Aquae multae non potuerunt exstinguere charitatem nec flumina obruent illam.

(Many waters cannot quench love; neither can the floods drown it)

I HAVE twice visited Aigues-Mortes, from Nîmes, by railway; and after hearing the accounts of more adventurous travellers who have either tried the canal from Beaucaire, and seen nothing, or gone by road, and seen too much—for huge swamps varied by level plains are not inspiring—I have concluded that the railway is best. By whatever route he may select, the traveller who has seen Carcassonne must on no account forget that the only fortress which can be compared to that magnificent stronghold is the walled quadrangle of Aigues-Mortes, which is chiefly famous for two royal visitors, St. Louis and the Emperor Charles V; and the memory of the great Crusader has lasted the more strongly of the two.

This City of Dead Waters is thoroughly well named; and the process that has been going on along Provençal coasts could scarcely be better traced than in the four lines of "littoral" which are still visible between the old Abbey of Psalmodi and the sea: the four coastlines, that is to say, which have gradually been pushed further and further out to sea by the slow waters of the sand-filled Rhone, flowing into a tideless Mediterranean, past a triangle of soaked soil, in which there is scarcely as much land as water. The very gradual nature of the process here during the last seven hundred years may be judged from the fact that the Crusading fleet of St. Louis only touched the open waters of the Mediterranean at almost the exact spot where those waters are flowing now. The old canal he used is used no longer, and the "Grau St. Louis" at its mouth is almost entirely choked up; but the route he followed westwards, from beneath the spot where he had built the Tour de Constance, can still be imagined, along the north of the Étang de la Marette, and so through the Étang du Ponent to the Grau St. Louis. By the sixteenth century the port had been changed to the south-east of the town; and when the Emperor Charles V sailed up to the Grau de

The Walls of Aigues-Mortes

Croisette to meet the Pope and Francis I, in 1538, he struck due east across the Étang du Repausset, and so past what is now the Beaucaire Canal and into the north corner of the Étang de la Ville.[1]

The solitude and apparent abandonment of Aigues-Mortes are perhaps in keeping with the forgotten majesty of its unassailable and lonely strength. Surrounded by marshes that exhale perpetual ague; beside the sea, yet not a practicable harbour; it is guarded by huge walls of masonry that no man would ever desire to scale, and its sentinels are disease and desolation. Those mighty ramparts have been untouched since Boccanegra built them for the son of the Crusading king; and they are as strong today, as you may see by walking round them, as when they were set up. Those who have strolled round the walls of Chester or of York will remember a strange feeling that ordered life has lasted there, uninterrupted, from the days of the Romans until now; and modern buildings and the stir of modern occupations seem not inappropriate within the girdle of their ancient certainty and peace. But he who walks along the sentinel's pathway round the ramparts of Aigues-Mortes experiences a very different feeling. They guard nothing that we know as modern. The shadows and the ghosts of old Crusaders are the garrison they hold, and it is a shrunken population, in a withered chessboard of haggard-looking streets, which seems to struggle into the semblance of activity and life. I shall not easily forget the shock with which I came upon the flaring poster of some travelling dramatic troupe, stuck up against the pedestal of the statue of St. Louis: "Les Folies Aiguesmortaises": it would be difficult to conceive a more ghastly invitation to be gay.

Some travellers delight to be "modern" everywhere, as some artists (both with pen and pencil) rejoice in drawing the sharp contrast between ancient splendour and the frequent jarring notes of everyday necessities, of squalid commonplaces which may be seen from China to Peru, but may be surely now and then forgotten. To such as these I would recommend the visit to Aigues-Mortes of Alexandre Dumas, the elder. His travelling footsteps are a delight to follow everywhere, and he had the art, even when he emphasised the moment's slender circumstance, of expressing it in terms that have fitted the emotion of all centuries. Need I say that he discovered the bleached bones of an actual Crusading galley on the shore from which he first set eyes on the Mediterranean he was to make so much his own? And shall we criticise the obvious error that no such galley ever left material traces of its sojourn, at least if we may judge by his description of the interesting relic so appropriately displayed by his zealous host the very next morning after his arrival? He had driven from Nîmes along the Montpellier road to Lunel, and from there turned eastwards on a causeway through the marshes to the Tour Carbonnière. Not a sound or sight of life broke the stillness of the watery solitudes, save when sometimes a heron, screaming, flew slantwise from the sedge. The gateway of the tower was opened by a douanier, yellow with fever, trembling with a fit of ague, and dying slowly at the Government's expense.

The Tour Carbonnière was the advanced post of Aigues-Mortes, which can be seen in the distance when you have gone ten minutes further along the road. It was built at the same time as the greater fortress, and the suns of Provence have even here bestowed on it the fading gold of autumn leaves which is the distinctive beauty of Provençal monuments. It was strengthened and restored by the military authorities of Nîmes in 1858, and is destined to as long a life as the dead town it guards. Close by it the name of Sylve Godesque, on one side of the Canal de Beaucaire, preserves the memory of the ancient forests long since vanished; and on the other side, a little northwards, is the site of the old Abbey of Psalmodi, which was sacked by the Saracens in 720 A.D., but continued its existence for some time afterwards. An interesting detail about it is that a deed of gift of 788 preserves the fact that it was then called "Insula Psalmodia" (much like the "island of Moutmajour" already mentioned), which shows that the sea cannot then have been far from the "earliest coastline" marked on the little map here given of the marshes of Aigues-Mortes. This proves, again, that the second and third of these coastlines were formed much faster than the fourth, and that after the

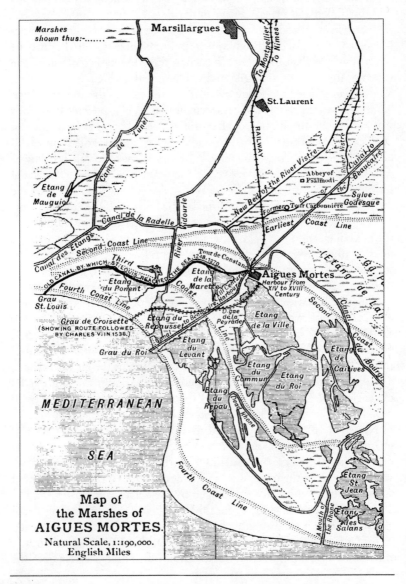

Map of
the Marshes of
AIGUES MORTES.

Natural Scale, 1:190,000.
English Miles

fourth had established itself very little change has been observable for several hundred years. The period of transition and change, in fact, may be said to have approached its end by about the year 1000 A.D., and any further alterations will take far longer to become visible. The best way to realise the lines of this very watery landscape is to look at it from the top of the Tour de Constance, at the north angle of the town.

It was from the Abbot of Psalmodi, in August 1248, that St. Louis bought the site of Aigues-Mortes, where there seems already to have been a tower called "Matafère"; and it is significant of the separation of Provence from France that the French king had to take this means of securing any Mediterranean harbour at all for his Crusading fleet. The site given by the abbot to him and to his heirs for ever contained, at that date, "the town of Aigues-Mortes with its fortifications," and certain territory round it, both to north and south; and the "consideration" for the bargain was certain royal property near Psalmodi, which was granted in exchange to the abbot, though the king's rights of high and low justice were reserved.[2] The "town" was no doubt rebuilt with the straight streets that can now be seen intersecting each other at right angles, and leaving an oblong "place" in the middle, much after the pattern of the lower town of Carcassonne, which was laid out in the same period. The "fortifications" were also probably limited to the Tour Matafère, or some primitive donjon-keep, which was expanded into the Tour de Constance, beside the magnificent walls of Boccanegra. But it is certainly true that a canon of Maguelonne records in 1160 that ships from Genoa, Constantinople, and Alexandria had brought merchandise here. This indicates that St. Louis chose wisely when he found another seaport necessary, which should be his own property, besides the Marseilles which his wife Margaret of Provence had prevailed upon her sister, the Countess Beatrix, to lend him for the occasion. The port of Narbonne was already silted up. Maguelonne was under its own bishop. Montpellier's harbour was under the King of Aragon. Agde and St. Gilles belonged to the Count of Toulouse. Provence itself was not to become French for another two centuries. St. Louis, in fact, had very little choice. As soon as he had secured Aigues-Mortes, he saw to its future prosperity, by granting the inhabitants many valuable privileges and exemptions, so that when the walls were finished later on they are said to have sheltered as many as ten thousand souls.

When Alexandre Dumas arrived, the population had shrunk to between two and three thousand, a quarter of the houses were empty, another quarter were ruined, and a third quarter were pulled down to make room for gardens. It is true that in visiting the place ten years after I had seen it first, there was a noticeable difference in the liveliness of the town, and especially in the excellence of the hotel in the central marketplace; but you must not expect any of the southern spirit that may be seen elsewhere, and I should still shrink from sleeping there at night. The good Alexandre was so fortunate as to be the guest of the mayor; and, after the heroic adventure of the royal galley already mentioned, he went a-fishing near the lighthouse; and he records with joy how he hooked a monstrous dogfish so heavy (it was at least eight pounds, it appears) that mortal man could not achieve its capture on a line; so "Jadin shot it through the body with my carbine," and it forthwith formed the foundation of an enormous Bouillabaisse. Soon afterwards he drove back to St. Gilles by way of the Canal de Beaucaire.

The famous iron rings, still to be seen at the corner of the walls near the Étang de la Ville, are no more the relics of the moorings of St. Louis' galleys than were those maritime wreckages which Dumas was shown the actual vestige of any crusading fleet. The walls themselves were built long after that fleet had sailed back for the last time without its master, and the rings can only have been used by casual fishing boats. The old canal by which St. Louis passed from the Tour de Constance to the Grau that bears his name can still be traced along the line marked in my map, but it is absolutely impracticable to-day; and we can only see with the eye of faith the fleet of a thousand vessels, probably very much like the two-masted, lateen-rigged barques scratched on a prison wall in the Castle of Tarascon, on which St. Louis embarked his six-and-thirty thousand soldiers for the Eastern voyage by way of Cyprus. His faithful Joinville sailed from Marseilles, and from there joined the main fleet. He gives a vivid description of the perils of the sea in those days.[3]

St. Louis had started on the Crusade from Aigues-Mortes with no idea of self-aggrandisement or territorial ambition. When he lay, some time before, in such grievous sickness that many thought him dying, he had commanded that the red cross should be placed upon his garments and his bed-gear. Terrible news out of the East had reached Paris, and the heroic king seemed only able to cling to life by the passionate faith which stirred him to obey the call of God as the avenger of the infidel. At first the Pope himself seemed to oppose it, for the policy of Innocent IV was to turn the arms of France against either England or the Emperor. But St. Louis took no care of politics, or cared for them only to redress past evils. He paid an indemnity for his losses to Trencavel of

Carcassonne and Béziers. He called to his banner all the soldiers who had fought on the Albigensian side in the horrible civil wars of Simon de Montfort. He seemed determined to expiate that bloodshed by the new Crusade, and to found in Egypt a colony where homeless Frenchmen might thrive and prosper, and in time become the outpost of Christianity against the Saracen in the Holy Land.

So in 1248 he reached Aigues-Mortes with all the flower of his chivalry, having left his kingdom to the care of his mother, Blanche de Castille, the widow of Louis VIII. With him went his young and beautiful wife, Marguerite de Provence, one of the four famous daughters of Raymond Bérenger and Beatrix of Savoy. With him were his brothers: Charles d'Anjou, for whom the kingdom of Sicily was waiting, and Robert d'Artois, who was to die in Egypt. Joinville gives a list of the Crusading knights as long as the catalogue of Homer's ships, and among them were the lords of Auvergue and Béarn, of Brittany, Burgundy, Montferrat, and Brabant; Chateaubriands, Talleyrands, and Montmorencys. For six weeks the camp was pitched near Aigues-Mortes; and the lion of Venice or the leopard of England floated high beside the fleur-de-lys of France. The pilots agreed to start upon a Friday, the 20th of August; and to the sound of "Veni Creator" the fleet put slowly out to sea.

For two years enormous stores of provisions had been collected in Cyprus, and there St. Louis was joined by the rest of his fleet, which now amounted to eighteen hundred vessels. They reached Damietta and took it, on June 7, 1249, and there they wasted precious days in rest, and pillage, and in vain discussions. His brother Alfonse, who was to have brought reinforcements to Cyprus, had not yet appeared. The luxury and idleness of that seductive island was continued in Egypt, where swift military operations were the only hope of the invader. After months of delay the enemy grew courageous. When the French took thirty days over the march from Damietta to Mansourah for which Bonaparte in 1798 allotted only four, the Saracens joyfully hurled Greek fire upon the invaders, who worked painfully for fifty days more at damming up the Nile near Mansourah, only to find that a ford had been ready for their passage all the time. Robert d'Artois and his Templars hurled themselves into the town of Mansourah, which the Mamelukes promptly closed upon them, and every Frenchman was cut to pieces. Behind, and knowing nothing of this tragedy, King Louis was fighting valiantly among his knights upon a raised causeway, and there held out until the evening, when the news was brought him of his brother's death. But he rescued Charles d'Anjou from a determined attack of the

Saracen cavalry and at last the persistent enemy drew back. St. Louis gave thanks to God in the midst of his sorely harassed soldiers.

Next morning his camp was full of wounded men, and hundreds of his knights had been severely burnt by the Greek fire. Even more were stricken with sickness from a strange plague that seemed to arise from eating too freely of the Nile fish. The priest who came to say the Mass at Joinville's sickbed had to be supported in a fainting-fit, and died soon afterwards. Even the king had to help to bury corpses which no one else would touch, and at last himself fell a victim to the malady. He might have escaped safely to Damietta, but he would not leave his men. His wounded and sick he sent back by water. Himself he started painfully by land. In a little house on the way he was so weak that he was obliged to take rest, and he laid his head on the knees of "*une bourgeoise de Paris*," who happened by some strange chance to be so far from home.

The whole time, the Saracen cavalry hung on the flanks of the retreating army and slew without mercy, having no room for prisoners. Some, in their despair, denied the Christ. All who did not were massacred. A few of the highest rank were taken prisoners and reserved for ransom, and among these was the king. They offered Damietta and 400,000 gold besants as ransom. The Sultan had already accepted these terms, when his own Mamelukes cut his throat beside the French galleys. One of the murderers, with his hand still bloodstained, rushed into the very presence of St. Louis, crying, "What will you give me now that I have slain the enemy who would have taken your own life?" But St. Louis answered nothing. Thirty Mamelukes, with naked swords and battle-axes in their hands, had come on board; and the French, thinking they would forthwith be beheaded, had begun to confess their sins to a priest in the company of the Count of Flanders. "For myself," writes Joinville, "I could at that moment bethink me of none of my sins, but considered that the more I defended myself and became wounded, the worse it would be for me. So I signed myself with the cross, and knelt at the feet of a Mameluke who held a huge carpenter's axe, saying, 'Thus died St. Agnes.' The Constable of Cyprus knelt beside me, and I said, 'I absolve you of your sins by whatsoever power God hath given me.' But when I rose to my feet I had forgotten his reply."

Within three days of learning of her husband's capture, Queen Margaret bore a son, John, whom she named Tristan; and her bedchamber was guarded throughout her trouble by an old French knight of eighty years, whose orders were to slay her if ever the Saracens got in.

Freed at a great price, the king passed on to Palestine, where he rebuilt the walls of Cesarea, Jaffa, Sidon, Acre, and other towns, until news reached him of his mother's death, and he began his journey home. Meanwhile the tidings of his capture and defeat had roused such passionate resentment in France that the poorer people, who were deeply attached to him, and were naturally quite ignorant of much that was going on, ascribed his continued absence to the machinations of the Church and the aristocracy; and great crowds of pilgrims, known as "Pastoureaux," assembled to march over seas and rescue their beloved king. Mingled with this devotion to his personality was a strain of religious mysticism, somewhat akin to the Albigensian heresies, which led these frenzied rustics to massacre the priests and to follow a Hungarian who proclaimed himself the bearer of a letter from the Virgin Mary. Only after much trouble and bloodshed were these disorders quieted, and St. Louis at last came back to France. Near Cyprus his galley suffered some mischance against a hidden rock, but he insisted on staying on board and having her repaired, for if he had continued the voyage in another ship, some hundreds of men, "whose bodies are as dear to them as mine to me," would have been left in Cyprus without hope of returning home. It is easy to imagine the hold upon the affections of his people which was enjoyed by a king who showed such unselfishness as this.

Before St. Louis started on his first voyage from Aigues-Mortes, Simon de Montfort, son of the terrible leader of the Albigensian Crusade, finding that the queen, Margaret of Provence, would never forgive the desolation inflicted by his father on her country, had passed over into England, where Henry III, who had married Margaret's sister, Eleanor, received him with the highest honours as Earl of Leicester,[4] and made him governor of Gascony in 1248. There de Montfort carried out his duties with such severity that he was recalled to England and quarrelled with the king. In 1258 the "Provisions of Oxford" were drawn up, and the dispute between the people and Henry III was referred to the arbitration of St. Louis, who decided in favour of his brother-in-law. De Montfort accepted this judgment, which annulled the "Provisions of Oxford," and was confirmed by the Pope, as the signal of revolt; and he roused the interest of every city in England by the famous scheme for introducing their representatives into the first English House of Commons. The victory of Lewes placed him for a time at the head of the state in 1264.

Henry III had inherited so much of the punishment of John Lackland that he had been obliged to take refuge in the power of the

Pope, and even to attempt the spoil of the unhappy house of Suabia by buying the title of emperor for his brother, Richard, Duke of Cornwall (husband of yet another sister of St. Louis' queen), and securing for that brother's son the equally empty name of King of Naples.

But if it is appropriate that, in a history of Provence, we should notice how much was done for the freedom of the English people by the son of him who sacked Béziers and Carcassonne, it is no less important that we should observe the strange quadruple cord which binds the politics of Europe at this time to the destinies of the house of Provence. For we have seen that the King of England and his brother had married two sisters of the Queen of France, and that all three wives were princesses of Provence. It is to yet a fourth sister of the same family that our thoughts are turned by the mention of the Pope's policy in Naples, and the downfall of the house of Suabia; for what King Louis refused for himself, he permitted his brother, Charles d'Anjou, to accept, and through "this dark man who slept so little," came the kingdom of Naples to Beatrix, the heiress of Provence. Tall, strong, and fierce-looking, with an olive-dark skin and a great nose, Charles d'Anjou, says Villani, was wise and prudent, firm and faithful, ever eager for new wealth to prosecute his ambitious enterprises. He conquered Manfred easily in the battle for the last shred of Barbarossa's ancient power, at which the brilliant natural son of Conrad, the true descendant of Frederick II, was slain. Later on, Corradino, the heir, was beheaded. Immediately Charles filled the country with his financial agents, and so harassed every one with taxes that the Pope soon regretted that this strong and avaricious Frenchman had been called in, even against the Saracens, who were the allies of the Suabian family.

Meanwhile St. Louis was once more stirred to take up the Cross against the infidel by the terrible news that seventeen thousand Christians had been massacred in Antioch, and many thousands more sold into slavery. In 1267 he came into the great hall of the Louvre carrying the Crown of Thorns, and his brothers, Alphonse de Poitiers and Charles d'Anjou, with many other princes and nobles, joined him in spite of the cynical discouragements of Pope Clement IV. Even his friend Joinville refused to go. But St. Louis was the very personification—and he was the last, the most splendid personality—of the Middle Ages; and in a short time he had assembled another great camp round Aigues-Mortes, where the soldiers waited some two months. At length, in Genoese galleys, he started his army on the voyage; and because the Sardinian ports were closed, he followed the advice of Charles d'Anjou and sailed to Tunis, and waited for his brother among the ruins of Carthage, which were filled with the corpses of the conquered Saracens. In a week the plague broke out, and death followed swiftly upon high and low. The king's youngest and best-beloved son died. Within a few hours St. Louis was dead himself, upon a bed of ashes, praying for the salvation of the people in whose country he was lying sick, and murmuring with his last breath the name of the Holy City. With him died the kingly chivalry of the Middle Ages, and in him expired the personal Christianity of the ancient world. His son, Philippe le Hardi, returned to France as the heir of nearly every member of his family; but the strongest of them all was Charles d'Anjou.

This Charles, whom the Pope began to fear more and more, for the kingdom of the Two Sicilies had already become the least of his ambitions, had married his daughter Beatrix to Philippe de Courtenay, titular Emperor of the East. It was against this figurehead that Pope Gregory X raised an equally impotent Emperor in the person of Rudolph of Hapsburg; and it is a strange coincidence that, through the good King René of Provence and his connection with Lorraine the house of Hapsburg was later on to provide the present Emperor of Austria, who thus has the blood of Provence in his veins through the marriage of Maria Theresa with Duke Francis Stephen in 1765. But Pope Gregory's plot with Rudolph of Hapsburg was only a part of the machinations that were soon astir against Charles d'Anjou. Sicily itself was roused to the sullen menace of revolt by Procida, a doctor from Calabria, who had been at the court of Frederick II, and the friend of the unhappy Manfred.

Procida first tried his hand at plotting in Spain; then left it, disguised as a Franciscan, for the court of Paleologus in Constantinople, and so passed on to the Pope. Finally he went to Sicily, which he found ripe for his teaching and full of discontent.

On Easter Monday, the 30th of March 1282, every man and woman in Palermo, Sicilians and French as well, were on their way to hear vespers at Monreale. It was the end of Lent, and the hot season had begun; and, as usual, the quarrel started over a woman. The French had strict orders to allow no one to carry arms at any assemblage of the people. One Drouet, a too zealous official, stopped a betrothal ceremony to search the bridegroom. He went too far; for he searched the bride as well; and the girl fainted. In a flash he was himself disarmed. In another moment he was slain. At nightfall not a Frenchman was left alive in Palermo, except the viceroy, who was packed off as fast as he could travel to Aigues-

Mortes. At Calatafimi the only man spared was Porcellet, who was eventually buried in the Alyscamps at Arles. Other towns followed suit, and Messina prepared to receive the attack of the avenging Charles d'Anjou. But Don Pedro of Aragon sent men to its help, keeping himself well out of danger, and Admiral Roger de Loria brought a fleet to check Charles's Provençal galleys. In 1283 Charles's son, Charles le Boiteux (he whose daughter Clémence was to marry Charles of Valois later on), was taken prisoner. In January 1285 Charles d'Anjou himself was dead.

But the Pope, with the national hatred of Aragon, adjudged Naples to his own countryman Charles of Valois, the son of Philippe le Hardi, whose cause was at once taken up by the fleets of Genoa, Marseilles, Aigues-Mortes, and Narbonne. Again Admiral Roger de Loria displayed his seamanship and skill successfully; and the French had to retreat to Perpignan, having lost every inch of ground in Spain.

It was during the fifteen years of his reign (from 1270 to 1285) that Philip III of France built the fortifications of Aigues-Mortes. They form an almost exact quadrangle of chiselled stone, covered with mason's marks; and at one point of the sentinel's walk along the ramparts is an undoubted chessboard, scratched with the point of dagger or halberd on the grey stone. There are fifteen towers at the angles, at each side of the gates, and along the curtain-walls. The chief entrance is that to which the traveller first comes from the railway station. It is called Porte Vieille, and originally led to the Tour Carbonnière outside, and was partly protected by the Tour de Constance on the right. Through it you pass into the market square with the statue of St. Louis. The chief gate on the other side is more to the east, and was called Porte de la Marine, because it gave entry to that part of the Étang de la Ville by which the galleys of the Emperor Charles V approached the town.

This type of fortress closely follows the models built by the Crusaders in Syria, Cyprus, and the East; and of them all it alone remains as the best example of the Genoese work of Boccanegra in the thirteenth century. It has been said that the plan was copied from Damietta; but if any of these Eastern cities is to be taken as its model, Lenthéric points out that Antioch is the most probable. Even then the Tour de Constance, the only part of Aigues-Mortes in which we can trace the hand of St. Louis himself, is distinctively different, and there is mention of this tower in writings of Pope Innocent IV dated 1246. The Gothic vaulting in the little chamber known as the oratory of St. Louis is particularly good; and the magnificent hooded fireplace in the lower story is especially to be noticed, with the sentinel's walk that goes all round the chamber, and the deep-set windows that show the enormous thickness of the walls. Higher up, these windows were put to strange and terrible uses; for each one of them became a dungeon. The most terrible associations of the Tour de Constance are not connected with the "Dark Ages," but with the enlightened administration of the "Roi Soleil" and his successors.

In August 1880 one of the windows was being cleaned out. Wrapped in the coarse cloth of a mattress were found two women's shoes, one of a young girl, three children's slippers, some playing-cards dropped by the soldiers of the guard, a pewter spoon, some pieces of earthenware, and a few fragments of old letters, the last of which were sent to the Consistory of the Reformed Church in Nîmes, of which Antoine Court was pastor in 1715. They tell the last chapters of a sad story of religious persecution, some of the first pages of which were written in blood upon the walls of Béziers and Carcassonne, as I have just described. Beginning among the poor and humble, the French Reformed Church spread and expanded until it seemed about to claim the throne itself. The "religious wars" showed that the Protestants were a real political power, but they fell with La Rochelle in 1629. From then until the Revocation of the Edict of Nantes, nearly sixty years afterwards, they were more and more bitterly persecuted, until the bare right of toleration was repealed, and the horrors of the Waldensian massacres of 1655 seemed likely to spread over the whole of France.

In 1686 a young man of twenty-four from Nîmes was hanged, after torture, at Beaucaire for daring to wish to be ordained. In 1698, Claude Brison, another native of Nîmes, who practised as a barrister at Toulouse, and then became a minister of the reformed faith, was executed at Montpellier. In 1715 Antoine Court, who had been called "Luther's eldest son" at school, was appointed to the Reformed Church of Nîmes, and in spite of mortal peril he and five other pastors carried on their worship. One was hanged in 1718, two more in 1728, a fourth in 1732. In 1720 a midnight meeting for prayer was held in a cavern called the "Grotte des Fades," or "Fairies' Cave," near Nîmes, under the presidency of Antoine Court. Two companies of soldiers surrounded them, and fifty men, women, and children were arrested. Nineteen were sentenced to transportation to America, and were marched through France, with incredibly brutal treatment, to La Rochelle. There the English chaplain prevailed on the authorities to let him bring the survivors in safety to England. Six, less fortunate, were condemned to the galleys. The women were sent to prison in the Tour de Constance at Aigues-Mortes, where there are records of Marguerite Forestier, widow of Pierre Prunet, and of Sarah Granier, wife of Jacques Chabanel, both of Nîmes.

Antoine Court himself escaped the soldiers in 1720, and, being generously assisted by King George I and the Archbishop of Canterbury, he was able to open a theological college at Lausanne in 1729, where he lived for thirty years, visiting his old congregations in France from time to time until his death.

In 1724 Louis XV issued an edict that all pastors were to be put to death; all who harboured them to be sent to penal servitude; and all who attended a Protestant service to be imprisoned for life; besides many other bitter and grievous civic disqualifications. In 1730 Pastor François Roux wrote to Antoine Court a letter still preserved at Geneva, describing the meeting he had called on March 27, 1730, at the "Mas des Crottes," some seven kilometres from Nîmes.[5] The soldiers suddenly rushed in and secured ten prisoners. The man was condemned to the galleys, and the nine women sent to the Tour de Constance, by the judgment of the Marquis de la Fare, Intendant of Languedoc, rendered on April 3, 1730. It is to two of them that the letters so strangely found in 1880 were addressed, and they have been deciphered by the care of M. Charles Sagnier.

The first was written by Catherine Gauteyret, her mother-in-law, to Suzanne Mauran, who was not yet twenty-six years old, and was the newly married wife of Barthélemy Mauran, a master baker of Nîmes. Her wedding had been first blessed (in October 1729) by a Catholic priest. But she was desirous of consecration by a pastor of her own reformed religion, and with this object she attended the meeting held at the Mas des Crottes by François Roux. Her state of health prevented any possibility of escaping the soldiers. Four months after her imprisonment in the Tour de Constance she gave birth to a son, who was baptized there on August 18, 1730. She was unable to read or write; and the terrible conditions under which she had to face her trouble may be judged from the fact that her husband's mother sends her some planks of wood (from St. Laurent d'Aigouze, near Aigues-Mortes) to make a bed, with two sheets, and some napkins.[6] She was still in prison when her husband died in 1739. Only after twelve and a half years of misery did she sign the "act of abjuration" which procured her release. In 1746 she showed how little value she attached to this, by marrying Antoine Brouzet, another Protestant. In that faith she died in 1777, and the son who had been born to her in the Tour de Constance had to make special request that her body might at last be laid in peace within the grave, for even burial was a privilege denied to Protestants.

Another woman seized at Crottes and sent to Aigues-Mortes was Elizabeth Michel; who, at twenty-two years of age, had married Antoine Jullian, a dyer of Nîmes, and who was cast into the Tour de Constance at the age of twenty-nine, with her hair cut off close to her head, as was done with all the women, and her property confiscated. In 1730, some eight months after her imprisonment, her husband writes to tell her that petitions have been laid before M. le Marquis de la Fare for her release. The letter is addressed to her under care of Madame Jeanne Lestrade, wife of M. Antoine de St. Aulas, major of the garrison of Aigues-Mortes, the same lady who stood godmother to the boy born in the Tour de Constance in August, and who therefore may be justifiably suspected of some little tenderness of heart to the unhappy prisoners. In May 1731, Elizabeth's husband wrote again, expressing his joy that her health remained unaffected, and giving her news of her four children, the youngest of whom she had left at only four months old. Within three days he wrote again. But in 1739—nine years after her first imprisonment—he is still unavailingly petitioning the Intendant of Languedoc for her release. The freedom granted seven years previously to Isabeau and Suzanne Amalric, who had been captured with her, lent an even greater excuse for leniency, had excuse been needed. At last, after twelve years and seven months, having just seen Suzanne Mauran go free twelve days before, she felt unable to bear more, and she went through the formula of recantation, which was so bitterly insisted upon by the authorities. On October 30, 1742, the king himself at Versailles gave orders for her release to the Duc de Fleury, governor of Aigues-Mortes; and she went back to Nîmes and to her husband, only to find that what little was left of their property was to be still further diminished by annual fines. She had been given liberty to die, apparently, but no more. From 1739 to 1755 twenty livres were taken from her property every year by the tax-collector. From 1755 onwards the impost was doubled. In 1779 her faithful husband was still bombarding the deaf authorities with petitions for her relief from these exactions, for she persisted in clinging to life, though eighty years of age; and she had round her twelve grandchildren by one son "who hopes for yet the thirteenth in good time, out of the twenty-two children he has had." Seven years later she was still alive, and still protesting; and her family at Nîmes still cherishes the receipt for the iniquitous tax of 1786. That is the last trace of her; but she had at least earned the privilege of seeing the Edict of Toleration signed only one year later, in 1787; and we may venture to hope that this sturdy Protestant lady even survived to hear about the Revolution.[7]

Before the Revolution, and long before the stout-hearted Elizabeth Jullian had finished her complaints to the authorities, the horrors of the Tour de Constance had stopped. I could have multiplied the instances of misery within it, and of massacres without, but I have said enough; and it is pleasant to leave Aigues-Mortes in the good company of the Prince de Beauvau, who closed these terrible prisons in 1767. The scene is described by his nephew, Stanislas-Jean de Boufflers, who accompanied him on the visit to Aigues-Mortes which he made at the instance of Paul Rabaut, the Protestant minister.

"We found at the entry of the tower," writes de Boufflers, "an eager guardian, who led us through a dark and twisting passage, and opened a great clanging door on which Dante's line might well have been inscribed: *Lasciate ogni speranza voi ch' entrate.* I have no colours in which to paint the terrors of the picture which gradually grew upon our unaccustomed eyes. The scene was hideous yet pathetic, and interest in its victims struggled with disgust at their condition. Almost without air and light, fourteen women languished in misery and tears within that stone-walled chamber. As the commandant, who was visibly touched, entered the apartment, they all fell down together at his feet. I can still see them, bathed in tears, struggling to speak, unable at first to do anything but sob. Encouraged by our evident sympathy they all began to tell us their sorrows at once. Alas! the crime for which they were thus suffering was the fact that they had been brought up in the same religion as Henri Quatre. The youngest of them was fifty, and she had been here since she was eight years old. In a loud voice that shook with emotion the marshal said 'You are free!' and I was proud to be his servant at that moment."

The Prince de Beauvau had only had leave to release three or four, but he wrote to say that "these unhappy women had all an equal claim on justice and humanity. I could make no choice between them. After they had gone I closed the Tour de Constance, in the hope that it will never again be used for such a purpose." The minister in Paris was furious at an interpretation of orders which he considered as an abuse of confidence. But the marshal answered that "while it is true his Majesty may deprive me of the command he has graciously bestowed, the king can never stop my doing my duty in accordance with the dictates of my conscience and of humanity."

It is a good word with which to leave the tower that was built by the most saintly King of France, and that was put to such base uses by his successors; and it is significant that the swamps and deadly marshes of

Aigues-Mortes should have been thus cleansed thirty years before the deluge of the Revolution changed the rest of France. Aquae multae non potuerunt exstinguere charitatem.

NOTES

1. See map on p. 288

2. The deed, as quoted by Lenthéric, runs as follows: "*De quitatione terrae de Aquis Mortuis Domino Regi facta ab Abbate et conventu Salmodii et permutatione ipsius: Omnibus praesentes litteras inspecturis, Remundus, permissione divina Abbas Salmodii et ejus loci conventus, salutem in Domino. Notum facimus quod nos, unanimi et deliberato consensu, territorium in quo situ est villa de Aquis Mortuis et fortalicia ejusdem loci...Domino Nostro Ludouico Deo Gratia illustri Regi Francorum quittavimus et concessimus ab ipso et heredibus ejus perpetuo possidendum...*" (Concerning the surrender of the land of Aigues-Mortes to the King made by the Abbot and community of Psalmodi and its exchange. To all who shall inspect these documents Raymond, by the granting of God Abbot of Psalmodi and of the monastery of this place, wishes salvation in the Lord. We make it known that we, unanimously and with considered agreement, have surrendered the territory in which is placed the town of Aigues-Mortes and the fortifications of that place... to our Lord Louis by the grace of God noble king of France and have granted possession of it to him and his heirs in perpetuity...)

3. "We entered in the August of 1248," he writes, "on board ship at the rock of Marseilles, and the door of the vessel was let down to receive the horses we were to take with us over sea. When all were entered, that door was shut and caulked like a ton of wine because it is below the waterline when the ship is out at sea. Soon afterwards the master cried to his sailors on the prow, 'Are we all ready?' and they answered, 'Yea, verily.' And when the priests and clerks were aboard he bade them all go up to the deckhouse and sing and pray to God for His safe conduct. So all therewith began to sing with a loud voice, from one end of the ship to the other, that splendid hymn 'Veni, Creator Spiritus,' and the sailors, under God, set sail. Straight-way the winds thundered in the canvas, and we soon lost sight of land, seeing nothing save sea and sky only, and day by day we drew further and further from our point of departure. And by all this I mean you to understand that very foolish were that man who should undergo such peril knowing that any mortal sin were on his soul; for such an one may go to sleep on an evening, and the next morning he knoweth not whether he will find himself at the bottom of the sea."

4. This earldom, Simon, though fourth son of the Albigensian Crusader, inherited through his mother; and a secret match with Eleanor, the sister of the English king, and widow of the second William Marshal, linked him to the royal house of his new country. At first the nobles opposed him, but Earl Richard of Cornwall gave up their cause; then the Church attacked his wife, but she made a pilgrimage to Rome. The greatness of his reputation on both sides of the Channel may be seen in the fact that he

was able to refuse the Regency of France, which was offered him by the nobles during the absence of St. Louis. He inherited the strict and severe piety of his father. Temperate and pure in life, he was yet singularly hot-headed and impatient; above all, he was resolute, unshakable, and steadfast in his ambitions. He "stood like a pillar" in the cause of the Commons and the people against the misgovernment of the king, even when the nobles left him for the royal party; and the "Provisions of Oxford," primarily introduced by a foreigner, were ordered to be observed in the first royal proclamation which has come down to us in the English tongue. The new force created by de Montfort in English politics, when he summoned two citizens from every borough to sit beside the two knights from every county in the Parliament assembled after his victory of Lewes, was perhaps the greatest contribution made to English constitutional government by any single subject. For his reward, he was slain, fighting desperately to the last, at the battle of Evesham in 1265. "From me he learnt it," he cried, as he recognised the military skill of Edward's onset on that fatal day. "From me he learnt it," his spirit might have exclaimed, when Edward I called the great Parliament of 1295, and modelled it on that of 1265. In all essentials, the character of Parliament has remained the same until this day.—See J. R. Green's *Short History of the English People.*

5. The summons to these meetings was generally in somewhat disguised language. Here is one of them: "Garrigues, 10 Avril 1770. Monsieur Fromental m'a chargé de vous écrire pour vous prier d'avertir les fidèles de votre église de se rendre vendredy prochain au porche de la Meterie de M. Bousquet de Nîme où il se propose de donner à déjeuné."

6. Here are the pathetic fragments of this letter: "28 Août 1730. A Mademoiselle Sussont Maurane à la tour de Constance. Mademoiselle et bele fille. Je vous felisite du fis que Dieu vous a donné Et moy qui vous enbrase de tout mon ceur vous soitant mille beneditions et que Dieu vous le veuil conserve par sa sainte grase. Je vous envoie…bant pour un lit et sing planche pour m…nogier de Saint-Lauran. Je vous envoie…et dux linseul et de serviete quan…en…lit en le vous soitant vous me…pour dauntan que j'ay…"

7. I need quote only one of the patient and persistent husband's letters. It runs as follows:—"Nîmes cest 16e X^{bre} 1730. Ma tres chere Epouse Je vous diray comme je n'auroit pas tant tardé à vous faire reponse sil nest fait…comme jay attendu dun jour a autre…celle fin de pouvoir vous envoyer quelque chose de positif; je vous diray comme jay receu une lettre de la part de la belle mere de mon frere laquelle nous tachons de faire tenir a M. le Marquis de Lafare a celle fin de le faire resouvenir de la promesse qu'il a faite a Monsig^r larchevesque de Romans pour quil vous donne votre elargissement. Je nay plus rien a vous dire si non que vous vous reposiés toujours sur la providance et datandre constenmant sans vous inqueté parce que dans le moment que nous y pensetont le moins cest sera alors que votre delivrance set terminera, est que Dieu vous faira eprouvé combien Ilest pitoyable envers ceux qui le reverent je vous diray comme je me porte bien…moy je prie le Seigneur pour…avec un attachemen…ma tres chere epouse affec…fide…Jullian."

CHAPTER XI

Avignon

Part I: Bricks and Mortar

"…C'estoit L'Isle Sonnante, et entendismes un bruit de loing venant
frequent et tumultueux, et nous sembloit à l'ouyr que ce feussent cloches
grosses, petites, et mediocres, ensemble sonnantes…nous doubtions que
feust Dodone avec sea chauderons, ou le Porticque dit Heptaphone en
Olympie, ou bien le bruit sempiternel du colosse érigé sus la sepulture
de Memnon en Thèbes d'Egypte."
—RABELAIS.[1]

THERE are some spots, in great and ancient cities of the world, which
seem to resume within themselves the history, not merely of the racial
centre which they represent, but of all those centuries which saw their
greatest splendour. Such are the Palatine of the Caesars, or the Vatican
of the Popes, or the Kremlin of the Tsars; and such is Avignon.

Within that mighty mass of architecture on the Rocher des Doms,
which was palace, fortress, shrine in one, seven Popes centralised the
attention of Christian and political Europe upon Avignon for almost a
century.[2] Behind its huge buttresses have been received the ambassadors
of Louis of Bavaria, of Charles le Bel and of Philippe VI of France, the
envoys of the Khan of Tartary and of the Emperor of Constantinople.
Here the Bishop of Cahors was condemned to suffer the most atrocious
penalties for his alleged plots against the Pope; here the great Tribune,
Rienzi, chafed in his prison; here Queen Jeanne of Naples faced her
accusers and bought her pardon at a price; here Urban V
excommunicated Bertrand du Guesclin, and patched up peace between
England and France; here Benedict XIII held out against all

Christendom, and refused to pass to other hands the dignity with which his cardinals had invested him. Something of the lives and personalities of these Popes must here be said; for though journalism has now vulgarised the secrets of the Vatican, the papal halls of Avignon had lost all their sacrosanct characteristics long before the Revolution desecrated the palace which Benedict XII, Clement VI, and Urban V had built, enlarged, and strengthened. The Republic has certainly done its best to deface and degrade the most historic building on the soil of France, by ruining its rooms, filling them with soldiers, and whitewashing its walls. But there is some hope that before the first decade of the twentieth century is over, the fortress of the Popes will receive at least the dignified neglect due to so stupendous a monument, and will be saved from the fate in which both the palace at Avignon and the château of King René at Tarascon are now (1905) so shamefully allowed to languish. Sheer ruin, as at Beaucaire, were infinitely preferable to the mean squalor and the revolting conditions of the barracks and the gaol, which now disgrace these two memorials of faded and despised magnificence.

This mass of architecture, which dominates not only the modern town of Avignon, but a great part of the history of Old Provence, is best seen at first from Villeneuve-lez-Avignon on the other side of the Rhone, or from that road which leads up to the Fort Saint-André, and shows upon its lower slopes the Tower of King Philippe le Bel, which once guarded the western end of the now ruined Pont St. Bénezet. It is worth considering the river and the bridge a little more closely before we examine the other buildings upon either bank. The Rhone's course from Lyons to the sea is 329 kilometres, of which 85 only are passed after Avignon. Between Lyons and Avignon it receives the waters of the Saône, the Isère, the Drôme, the Ardèche, and the Durance; and though the drop is over eighty centimetres in every kilometre between the Drôme and the Ardèche, it is only forty-nine centimetres between the Ardèche and the Durance, which means that the water is almost half as flat again as it was before, with a current which must normally be too slow to carry down the sand and mud suspended in the stream. This means that the slightest obstacle has produced a bar of sand, and modified the flow of the river and the formation of its bed. Old islands have disappeared; new ones have arisen. Conditions are never absolutely stable. In former centuries the maps show that the usual current was on the right or western bank, which therefore gave the best harbourage for boats, and there was navigable water beneath the Tower of Philippe le

Bel and the walls of Saint-André, whereas the bank beneath the Rocher des Doms was shallow, sandy, and deserted. Exactly the contrary is the case today, and there is deep water beneath the walls of Avignon, owing to the engineering works of the last forty years.

Though the water was shallow near the old Palace of the Popes, there was much more of it, and their Rock must often have stood out like an island from the plain submerged by inundations from the Durance, the Sorgues, and the undiked bed of the old Rhone. In those far-off days, the absence of a swift stream was one reason for the growth of the little fishing village and market which was the first Avignon. It was military and naval considerations which built Villeneuve, for the King of France, upon the opposite and deeper shore. Tossed from one hand to the other in the early centuries after Charlemagne, Avignon became in turn Italian, Provençal, Burgundian, the fief of Toulouse, the dependency of Forcalquier. At last she declared herself a Republic under a Podestat, with continual internal revolutions that never seem to have stifled her commercial prosperity. But her dalliance with the heresy of Toulouse brought all the terrors of the Albigensian Crusades upon her. King Louis VIII at once demanded safe passage across her famous bridge, and when that was stoutly denied him, he formally acquainted the Emperor, the nominal suzerain of Avignon,[3] with his royal determination to reduce the city.

This operation took longer than was expected. The bastion near the town which defended the bridge was practically impregnable, and the bridge itself was unfit for the transport of an army; so the baggage and the troops had wearily to cross over on pontoons to the northward of the town. A plague broke out while this was going on, and famine within her gates compelled Avignon to surrender, after three months of heroic resistance, on the 12th of September 1226. The king tore down part of the walls, executed the chief officers of the defence, and then walked through the main streets of the town bareheaded, in sackcloth, with a taper in his hand, as an expiation for the horrors of war. The *confrérie* of the Grey Penitents preserved the memory of his remorse for more than six centuries afterwards. Being excommunicated at the time, for heretical friendship with Toulouse, Avignon had no mercy to expect from the Pope, and she received none. With her citizens' money the Fort of Saint-André was built on the opposite bank as a perpetual menace of royal displeasure. Every fortified house and every remnant of Roman occupation was destroyed. The place was left, as the price of its "absolution," with nothing but the most necessary shelter for its humiliated and starving inhabitants. The Republic of Avignon could not survive the shock, and died ingloriously in 1251. The sole remnant of its existence and its power are the ruined arches of the Pont St. Bénezet.

In Roman times the only fixed bridges between Lyons and the sea had been at Vienne (which lasted, being of stone, until the seventeenth century) and at Arles. The construction at Vienne, probably the work of Trajan, was long considered one of the wonders of the Rhone, and was carefully kept in repair from year to year, with solid masonry. The only stonework in the wooden bridge at Arles was the huge buttress on each hank, one of which may still be traced at Trinquetaille. The historic passage between Tarascon and Beaucaire was nothing but a ferry, for Hannibal's bridge was only temporary. Even under Louis XIV five or six permanent bridges were considered sufficient for the distance which is now served by at least twenty viaducts, every one of which seems indispensable to modern traffic. The reason for the change is that until the eighteenth century, and even later, the natural road was the river itself, and bridges were only a hindrance to passing boats and vessels. It was no doubt some such consideration as this last which induced the magistrates to oppose the curious demand of a stranger named Benoît, or Bénezet, that a bridge should be built to join their town with the eastern shore in 1177. But he persisted with a strange fanaticism, and in 1188 was accomplished what was little short of a miracle in those days.

Pious historians were not long in affirming that it was a miracle indeed. Bénezet, say they, was a little shepherd of twelve years old, who kept his mother's flock near Viviers.

"The word of Christ came to him to build a bridge over the Rhone at Avignon. But he knew nothing of the Rhone; he feared to leave his own country and his flock of sheep; he had but three farthings in the world. 'Obey,' said the Voice, 'and an angel shall lead thee.' So an angel appeared in the form of a pilgrim, and they journeyed to the Rhone; and the child was frightened at the size of the river. 'Fear not,' said the angel, 'for in this boat thou shalt pass over, and in Avignon thou shalt go before the bishop and his people, for the Spirit of God is with thee.' Now the boatman was a Jew, and when he was besought by Bénezet in the name of God and of the Virgin, he refused, and taunted the child; but at length be was over-persuaded, and as there was nothing more to take, he took the child's three farthings and ferried him across. So Bénezet went straight to the church in which the bishop was preaching to his people, and stood in front of the

pulpit, and said in a clear voice, 'Listen to me, all of you! Christ hath sent me to you that I may build a bridge over the Rhone.' Then the bishop was angry at being interrupted by so worthless-looking a little boy, and ordered him to be taken off to the officer of the guard and dealt with according to his insolence and his untruth. This meant that he was in perilous likelihood of being flayed alive. But the child said to the officer, just as clearly as he had said to the bishop: 'Christ hath sent me to you that I may build a bridge over the Rhone.' 'What!' replied the officer, 'can a little beggar boy do what neither God nor St. Peter, neither St. Paul nor the Emperor Charlemagne, have been able to accomplish? If you can move this stone, as a beginning, and carry it to the river, I may, perhaps, believe that God hath sent you.' Now the stone was very thick, thirteen feet long by seven broad, and thirty men could hardly move it, for it was a fragment of a Roman building destroyed by the Saracens. So Bénezet knelt down and said his prayers, and seized that mighty block, and lifted it as easily as any pebble, and carried it across the town upon his shoulder, and placed it on the bank of the Rhone where the foundations of the first arch were to be laid. Then the officer of the guard and all the people fell down and worshipped him, and all the town were very glad for him. And in the first day five thousand pieces of gold were gathered, and every one brought money for the young stranger, who was visibly inspired by God. So the work began at once; but before it was all accomplished Bénezet died, in the eleven hundred and eighty-fourth year after the birth of Christ; and he was buried in the chapel on the bridge itself, and four years afterwards the bridge was finished by his comrades."

These "comrades" were no doubt members of that Brotherhood of Bridge-builders who were descended from the Collegium Pontificum of Rome, as the Comacine architects were from a similar fraternity; and it is possible that this particular "Collegium" was the origin of all the religious *confréries* of the Middle Ages, for there was much of the brotherliness of true religion about their proceedings. In Italy, in Spain, in Portugal, in the British Islands, traces of their early activity are to be found. They seem to have worked independently in each country, bound together only by their common origin in Rome, and by their common work for the public welfare, supported by the public alms. They wore a white dress, with two arches of a bridge in red upon their breast, and a cross above. The most important details concerning them are given in the bull of Nicholas V, dated 1448, concerning the beginning of another famous bridge across the Rhone at Pont St. Esprit in 1265, and the special privileges granted by the Holy See to all who helped in its construction. This was not finished until 1307, and it had its own hospital and chapel, which were centres of the pious zeal of those who collected funds for its building and its maintenance. Almost the whole of Christendom seems to have heard of the efforts being made. No fewer than eighteen Popes gave their blessing to the work. Charles VI of France took it under his special protection, and the royal favour lasted actively in its support until the reign of Louis XIV. Extraordinary precautions were taken to save its black, polished pavement from injury, and its arches from too great a weight. King Louis XI himself went over it on foot in 1474. Marshal Bassompierre, unable to transport his cannon in pontoons, as the king had done with his baggage-waggons, was obliged to carpet it thickly with straw in 1525. Only in 1774 were men careless enough to allow carts and carriages to cross it. The whole eight hundred metres of its length are still as strong as they were six centuries ago; the keen angle of its central point, to which the lines from each bank converge, still bravely spurs away the downflow of the stream and the mason's mark on every stone still gives an almost perfect history of its building and its frequent reconstructions. In the last half of the nineteenth century an iron span had to he substituted for two of the original twenty arches, to allow large vessels to pass under the right bank; and the whole roadway was broadened to a uniform width of seven metres, which alters the ancient aspect of the building, but does not alter the fact of the magnificent strength of the first bridge on which the later work is founded, and which has borne all the necessary enlargements that are the essential consequence of increase of traffic in the lapse of time.

It was as an energetic and talented member of the Brotherhood which built the Pont St. Esprit that Bénezet came to Avignon to build the bridge there a century earlier. His hospital, his oratory by the bank, were the centres of his successful propaganda. The quarry of Villeneuve furnished his stone. The bishop and the consuls of the Republic of Avignon gave him all the assistance in their power. The bridge, finished after his death in 1188 had three-and-twenty arches, one of which was over low-lying land on shore, and each was thirty-two metres fifty broad, resting on piles, which varied in thickness from seven metres fifty to eight metres ten. The line was by no means straight from one shore to the other, but on the whole it showed the same angular spur against the stream which was afterwards built in the Pont St. Esprit. The breadth of the carriage-way was three metres ninety; and on the third pile from the town rose the little chapel which for nearly five centuries held the body of the canonised architect. Only after the terrible winter floods of 1669 had seriously shaken the structure was his body moved to the chapel of the hospital at the bridgehead by the town, until the pile had been strengthened by great bands of iron. But Louis XIV desired the sovereignty of the bridge as against the Church's claims; and the saint's body was therefore moved to the royal Church of the Celestines, where it remained until the Revolution turned it out into the parish church of St. Didier; and there, not without further misadventures, it remains until this day.

The firm line taken by Louis XIV may well have been prompted by the recollection of the famous lawsuit over the same bridge, and the rights of the river, between the Pope and the French king in 1500. The king, whose garrison was in the Tower of Philippe le Bel, claimed that he held from there the bridge and both banks of the stream, including the bed of the river. The case was fully argued out to the joy of every lawyer in Provence; and after the story of the original St. Bénezet had carefully been investigated and proved, the verdict was given to the Pope.

In spite of the anxiety shown in this lawsuit, and in spite of the care taken to build openings in the piles for floodwater, the famous bridge has not lasted like that of the Pont St. Esprit; and this for the very obvious reason that the older construction was never kept in such constant repair, owing to unceasing wars and disturbances. The deathblow to its permanence was really dealt by Pope John XXII in 1331, who passed the care of the chapel to the chapter of St. Agricole, and commanded the consuls of Avignon to watch over the repairing of the bridge. As soon as the construction was left in secular hands it began to fall into ruin. The besieging army of the French king, in 1226, had already broken down several arches. More went in 1298, as is known by a legacy left for their special repair. In 1331 the Brotherhood of Builders placed on record the fact that they established a ferry whenever the bridge was broken, as it must have been about that time, for only eight years afterwards Benedict XII had to warn Peter IV of Aragon to cross the Rhone at Beaucaire. In 1352 there is record of Hugues de Sade having given two thousand golden florins to the restoration fund instituted by Clement VI for the restoration of the four arches near the town, and his arms may still be seen upon the first of them. The disorders of the reign of Benedict XIII were even more fatal to the long-suffering bridge, for the Pope was by no means anxious to keep open the communications between himself and the Dukes of Anjou and Bern, who were in Villeneuve in 1395. This lamentable series of disasters went on steadily, until in 1679 the task of repairing them was given up. There is no need to invoke the legend of a destructive devil who cast down every new arch that was added to the ancient work. The carelessness and impiety of man are more than enough to explain the wreckage that we see today. The primitive wooden structure by which the modern traveller crosses to Villeneuve is a sadly decadent successor to the stout masonry of St. Bénezet and his brave brotherhood.[4]

The chapel of St. Bénezet is different from its former self; but recognisable. The Romanesque floor is four and a half metres beneath the modern roadway, but the old staircase to its entry exists no longer, and was indeed altered after the repairs already mentioned in 1352, when the "Gothic" chapel was added to the Romanesque work beneath it. Like the bridge itself, this little shrine remains as the evidence of a twelfth-century skill and an enthusiasm for good work, which may serve as the model for all construction of the kind that has ever been attempted under similar conditions.

The bridge leads to Villeneuve; and it is with real regret that I must frankly confess to having no space here to deal with Villeneuve as it deserves. I can only say "Go Over and See What can be Seen." Very few travellers are wise enough to do so; but those few are well rewarded. The ruined monastery, broken and even degraded as it is, is well worth a visit; its front door, its central fountain, its cloisters alone deserve your admiration and respect, The magnificent fortress of Saint-André on the hill above is also a splendid specimen of military architecture, and a few months ago there was still the quiet grace of a nuns' garden within its huge walls; but France, which seems sometimes to care so little for its ancient monuments, has of late appeared to desire to destroy every modern possibility of religion and romance as well. So the monasteries and the convents of today are suffering the same fate as the crucifixes and the processions of an age when Liberty, Equality, and Fraternity had not yet become the motto of republican iconoclasm, and when monotonous democracy had not yet planed down every characteristic difference to the vulgar level of official ignorance. There is a church in Villeneuve, too, with a strange tower, that must be visited, and one or two extremely interesting pictures in the museum; and it is an education in mediaeval architecture to look up at the tower of Philippe le Bel from its foundations. Still, it is the view across the stream that is the inevitable focus of your interest; and from this eastern bank the little cathedral of Notre Dame des Doms is the first building that attracts and holds the eye. It must be more closely studied, though the frescoes with which Simone Memmi covered its porch have long since vanished, and we can see no more the Virgin in Glory, the Christ among the clouds, the St. George in armour and on horseback, slaying a dragon, while St. Margaret kneels by his side. Within its walls were enthroned Innocent VI, Urban V, and Gregory XI; Louis d'Anjou was crowned King of Naples; Charles IX, Henri III, and Louis XIII were humble pilgrims; John XXII and Benedict XII were commemorated by splendid monuments; and Domenico Grimaldi, the Christian admiral at Lepanto, was one of the one hundred and fifty-seven bishops and cardinals who were buried there.

As an example of that careful development of a Provençal style from Roman workmanship which I have already noticed in speaking of St. Trophime, the south entrance of the cathedral of Aix and the west porch of the cathedral of Avignon are among the most important examples. This latter, indeed, has often been mistaken for the actual remnant of a Roman building, but it is now known that it was built and dedicated in 1069, on a site first consecrated by the piety of St. Martha of Tarascon, ruined by the Saracens, and restored to all its ancient splendour (with several legendary additions) by the care of Charlemagne. Originally the church, which is changed almost out of all knowledge, from its primitive

The gate of Fort St. André, Villeneuve-lèz-Avignon

arrangement, was a simple nave of five bays with a pointed tunnel vault and double vault arches resting on plain piers. The outer pier of each group of piers is cut away towards the top, to permit of the insertion of a small column, channelled, fluted, or twisted. At the base of the vault was a small decorated cornice. Beyond the fifth bay was the dome, included in the choir. The apse was rebuilt in its present ungainly form in 1671, when the whole church was slightly lengthened.[5]

The west porch, so classic in its detail that it was long thought to be a Roman construction, is a small rectangle, rather broader than it is deep. An engaged and channelled column, with pseudo-Corinthian capital, on a low pedestal, fills each outer angle, and upon that rests a shortened entablature, richly carved. In the centre of the plain, pointed pediment is a small, round opening, the forerunner of the splendid western window of the northern churches. Below the entablature is a round arch, resting on plain pilasters with egg and dart moulding beneath its outer edge. Only the south arch remains of the two which once opened on each side. The round tunnel vault within has been partly restored, and the inner portal reproduces the design of the external architecture. The fading fresco of Simone Memmi is on the tympanum.

For more than seventy years this little shrine was the premier church of Christendom; yet very little was done to it by the Popes, who exhausted their treasure and their energies on the fortress-palace at its side. Their finest monuments are the tombs of John XXII, and of Benedict XII, which is now in the chapel of the Annunciation, between the second and third bays on the north side of the nave. The galleries that surround the cathedral from one side of the choir to the other were built by Archbishop Azo Ariosto in 1671, who changed or removed much of the older structure in the process; and scarcely any of the present chapels can be said to have formed part of the original plan. The huge western tower, quite out of proportion with the building, in a line with the façade, is the most interesting of the later additions; but even the dignity of this was utterly lost by the placing of a colossal gilded statue of the Virgin upon a pyramid at the top in 1859.

Yet nothing can destroy the natural magnificence of a site with which that of Durham Cathedral can alone compare. Approached by a splendid flight of steps and inclined planes; with the palace of the Popes on one side, the Rocher des Doms upon the other, and the Rhone beneath; this little cathedral forms part of an architectural group only surpassed by St. Peter's and the Vatican itself; and to the

Vatican of Provence we must now turn, to see what little is still visible of its ancient splendours.

Not much after all can be written by way of explanation of a mass of buildings which are difficult enough to understand, even when you walk over them.[6] But I must try to reconstruct the background of the strangely complicated picture in which the personages of this extraordinary French fourteenth century may be fitly placed. Clement V, who helped the King of France to destroy the Knights Templars, was himself content to live in a Dominican convent now vanished. His successor, John XXII, Bishop of Notre Dame des Doms,[7] stayed at first in his own old palace near the little cathedral in which he had customarily officiated. But he soon found that a bishop's palace was not large enough for a Pope; and after fitting up a private chapel for himself in the Church of St. Stephen, he bought up gardens and houses from the old quarter near the Rocher des Doms, and thus secured sufficient space for the great mass of buildings that was soon to rise. He began well; and by joining the art of Pierre Dupuy de Toulouse to the masonry of Cucurron he secured a luxury and magnificence in the arrangement and furniture of his rooms, which soon impressed upon Avignon the advantages of having a Papal Court in their city. At Bédarrides, and at Châteauneuf (where "the Pope's vineyard" is still famous), he had country-houses of almost equal splendour, and he was careful to build a new bishop's palace for his nephew, Arnaud de Via, which is now called the "Petit Séminaire." But the most important thing for his successors was the enormous treasure he left behind him in bullion, plate, and precious stones.[8] Benedict XII at once took advantage of so good an opportunity, and was indeed practically obliged to take precaution for the safety of the treasure his predecessor had amassed.

These precautions resulted in a complete reorganisation of the whole mass of buildings. The first palace was either destroyed, or hidden in new work, and a fortress of tremendous strength was built round the whole, with four towers, of which that known as Trouillas[9] is the highest, not far from the east end of the cathedral, and slightly to the south of it. In 1904 this part of the palace (which extends a hundred metres beyond the north-east corner of the entrance court) was occupied by the Archives, and not visited by travellers. Next to the Tour de Trouillas is the Tour de la Glacière, from which the long apartment, known as the Salle Brûlée, extends to the north-east corner of the entrance court. The northern line of Benedict XII's palace, extending parallel to the south wall of the cathedral, contains his private chapel on the east, and the Tour de la Campane at its western angle. Within these containing wings is a cloister; but none of the buildings set up by Pierre Poisson before 1334 were open to the public when I was last in Provence.[10]

The arms of Clement VI, beneath the vault of the entrance through which you may now penetrate the palace, are a sign that he built nearly the whole of the massive masonry round the great entrance court, with the help of Pierre Obreri, a French architect, between 1342 and 1352; but the courtyard itself was levelled and cut down out of the living rock by Urban V after 1362, and completed by the wing which forms the eastern façade. The area occupied by this court alone is no less than 1800 square metres and the whole palace occupies 6400 square metres. Scarcely anything except the impression of its enormous size and strength remains. Even the splendid pointed windows that looked out upon this court have been squared into common rectangular openings to suit the needs of the garrison. If regimental necessities had stopped at this, there might have been less need for objurgation and complaint. Unfortunately the housing of French soldiers, even of French officers, has implied irreparable damage elsewhere in the palace.

By what was once a splendid stairway of white marble you are led into the old chapel that was the hall of the consistory, with two naves divided by a row of massive pillars. The room in which Queen Jeanne pleaded before the Pope has now been split up into several superimposed dormitories for soldiers, and the whitewashing and carpentry necessitated by these lamentable changes have so ruined the original structure that it will be difficult ever to reproduce the dignity and splendour of the original construction. The beauty of its decorations has at any rate gone for ever; and the remnants of the prophets and sibyls painted by Italian artists are but a sad reminder of how much has been lost.

The intentions of Clement VI have fortunately been recorded. He wished the frescoes to represent Christ upon His throne, delivering judgment, between the Virgin and St. John the Baptist, with saints and bishops round them, and all the peoples of the world beneath. Besides cutting the whole scheme of the design in half by the dormitory floors, the officers and soldiers have amused themselves with slicing off various heads of the figures which pleased them; a practice which has deprived the rest of the world of the work of Simone Memmi, who came to Avignon in 1338 and died there in 1345, and of Matteo Giovanetti of

Viterbo. The oratory of Clement VI and the private chapel of Benedict XII have been similarly desecrated; and until the State takes up the definite responsibility of guarding what is left, the task of explaining the pitiful remnants of Italian and French art is not one which I can usefully continue. So I shall only mention the interior of the palace as it occurs in the story of its inhabitants. Nothing, however, can destroy the splendid effect created by the exterior, with those mighty engaged arches which form the largest machicolations in the world. Every gate is defended with a portcullis, every wall is crowned with machicolated parapets. If it was the home of the Vicar of Christ, it was very clearly also meant to be the fortress of the Church Militant here upon earth. On the north the cliff of the Rocher des Doms plunges straight into the river. On the south the buildings penetrate the town itself. The east walls are fifty metres higher than the neighbouring houses. To the west the advance works of the citadel linked it to the guardhouse of the bridge. Ten years of terrible siege, when Benedict XIII was holding out in it, left scarcely a trace upon its strength. The garrisons that wrecked its interior, though even they are powerless to destroy its outer walls, have been the regiments of modern France.

The main architectural importance of Avignon is that it contains, within itself and Villeneuve, a wonderful series of fourteenth-century buildings; civil, military, and ecclesiastic. Its main historical importance is as a link in that development of the Papacy of which I sketched the beginnings in the first chapter of this second volume. I have now briefly to explain how it was that the Popes came to Avignon, and what influence their presence there had upon the general politics of Europe.

NOTES

1. "...It was the Ringing Island; and we heard a kind of confused and often-repeated Noise, that seem'd to us at a great distance not unlike the Sound of great, middle-siz'd, and little Bells rung all at once...Some of us doubted that this was the Dodonoan Kettles, or the Portico call'd Heptaphone in Olympia, or the eternal Humming of the Colossus rais'd on Memnon's Tomb in Thebes of Egypt."— Motteux's Translation.

2. The list of Popes who lived outside Rome contains, of course, more than seven names, and the nine chiefly connected with Avignon may well be given here at once, with the dates added for the sake of clearness: Clement V (Bertrand de Got), elected

June 1305, died in April 1314; John XXII (Jacques Duèze, Bishop of Avignon), died in October 1334; Benedict XII (Jacques Fournier), died April 1342; Clement VI (Pierre Roger de Beaufort), died Decemher 1352; Innocent VI (Etienne Aubert), died September 1362; Urban V (Guillaume Grimoard), died December 1370; Gregory XI (Pierre Roger de Beaufort), who removed to Rome in 1376, but died in 1378; Clement VII (Robert of Geneva), died in 1394; Benedict XIII (Pierre de Luna), deposed in 1409 and 1417, and died in November 1424; after whom the Great Schism came to an end.

3. As I have mentioned in my preliminary pages, the western or right bank is still known as "Royaume," the left, or eastern bank, as "Empire." This is because the ancient kingdom of Arles (which extended along the eastern bank of the Rhone and the lower Saône) was ceded to the Emperor Conrad II in 1033, and the title was never forgotten. The western bank was equally firmly styled "the king's" ever since the cession of Languedoc to the crown in 1271. It should be remembered that in describing a river "east" and "west" are according to the compass; but "right" and "left" are always taken from the point of view of a man looking down stream.

4. More details of this historic bridge may he found in Lenthéric's magnificent volume *Le Rhône,* and it may be hoped that a similar book will be some day written about the Thames and London Bridge.

5. Fuller details of this most interesting building have been published by "Barr Ferrée" in *The Architectural Record* for March 31, 1896.

6. The architects were chiefly French. Under Pope John XXII (1314-1334) it was Guillaume de Cucurron; under Benedict XII (1334-1342), Pierre Poisson; under Clement VI (1342-1352), Pierre Obreri; under Urban V (1362-1370), Jean de Loupières, Raymond Guibaud, Guillaume Nogayroly, and others; who each contributed something to what Froissart was moved to call "la plus belle et la plus forte maison du monde."

7. *Doms*=Latin *domus*; Italian *duomo*; German *don*; the principal church; in Provence called often "La Major."

8. "*Dicitur Joannes XXII reliquisse in aerario tantam vim auri quantam nullus ante eum pontifex, scilicet viginti quinque millionum et amplius.*" (John XXII is said to have left a greater amount of gold in the treasury than any pope before him, certainly 25 million [probably gold florins] and more)

9. Trullatium.

10. Map of the Palace of the Popes

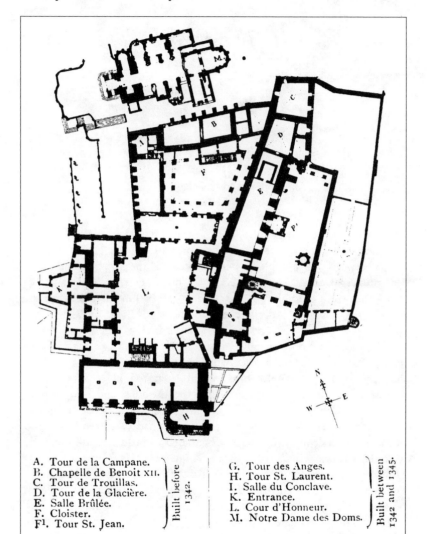

A. Tour de la Campane.
B. Chapelle de Benoit XII.
C. Tour de Trouillas.
D. Tour de la Glacière.
E. Salle Brûlée.
F. Cloister.
F¹. Tour St. Jean.

} Built before 1342.

G. Tour des Anges.
H. Tour St. Laurent.
I. Salle du Conclave.
K. Entrance.
L. Cour d'Honneur.
M. Notre Dame des Doms.

} Built between 1342 and 1345.

Part II: The French Popes

"Avignoun, la fiholo de Sant Pèire
Que dins soun port n'a vist la barco à l'ancro,
E n'a pourta li clai à sa centuro
De merlet, Avignoun, la gento vilo
Que lou mistrau estroupo emai descouifo
Eque de tant qu'a vist lusi la glòri,
N'a counserva que l'inchaiènço d'elo!"
—MISTRAL.[1]

THE fall of the Empire of the West, and the rise of Imperial power at Constantinople, only increased the dignity and power of the Pope in Rome between 476 and 590. When the power of the Emperor and of the old municipal aristocracy decayed, the Church grew stronger still, for people turned to their bishops and to the Pope. By Gregory the Great the Papacy was raised to a decisive eminence in 604, and by 731 it was definitely freed even from the Eastern Emperor. The crowning of Charlemagne in Rome in 800 was the first symptom of that alliance between the Papacy and France which was to receive its most striking illustration in the presence of Clement V at Avignon five centuries afterwards. When the Emperors began to misunderstand the position, they were humbled at Canossa by Gregory VII; and the lifelong labours of Hildebrand left the Papacy stronger than it had ever been at the end of the eleventh century. The Crusades exalted its influence still more. By Matilda, Countess of Tuscany, nearly a quarter of Italy was left to the Holy See; and Frederick Barbarossa himself had to kiss the feet of the Pope at Venice before the twelfth century was over. Innocent III made his power decidedly felt in every court in Europe before his death in 1216, and his friars became a vast army, devoted to his service, who overran all Christendom in his name. The inveterate hostility of Gregory IX and Innocent IV crushed, as we have seen, the house of Hohenstaufen, and once more France was called in by the Papacy, when Charles d'Anjou, in the Pope's name, took possession of the Sicilian kingdom. The presence of Anjou in Italy began a decadence of papal prestige which was directly caused by the active intervention of the Popes in European politics. Celestine V was the mere instrument of the King of Naples. His successor, Boniface VIII, discovered that, in ruining the Hohenstaufen, the Papacy had mortally weakened its own strength; and neither his bold policy nor his keen intelligence could avert the inevitable disaster. His quarrel with Philip IV of France was foredoomed to utter failure; and the violence of Sciarra Colonna, or the legal sophistries of the Toulouse advocate, Guillaume de Nogaret, were scarcely necessary to deal its deathblow to the mediaeval Papacy. At Anagni, Canossa was avenged. At Avignon, the price was paid. The victor had little difficulty in electing a nominee of his own to succeed the brokenhearted Boniface. Bertrand de Got, Archbishop of Bordeaux, was elected Pope, as Clement V, in June 1305; and as it was easy to represent that Italy was in too disturbed a state to receive him, he took up his abode in Avignon, which was held by Charles II of Anjou and Naples, as Count of Provence. The *camerlengo* had brought the tiara from Rome, and in November Clement V was crowned at Lyons in the presence of the King of France and his two brothers, Charles of Valois and Louis d'Evreux. An accident during the subsequent procession gave rise to ill-omened remarks; for a wall, crowded with spectators, suddenly fell down, the Pope was borne to the ground, and a ruby was lost from the tiara. Twelve of his suite died of their injuries, and among the victims was the Duke of Brittany. Even the King of France did not escape injury.

It might be imagined that the Papacy must inevitably and at once have suffered from the transference of its central seat. But this was not the case. Its powers were too deeply rooted in the imagination of mankind for any temporary change to stir the foundations of this vitality. The only question was which nation should secure those powers for its own advantage. France did not hesitate. Bertrand de Got ruined his old enemy the Archbishop of Bourges by the simple method of settling the papal court at Bourges for a long enough period to exhaust its resources, a process in which it is said that the Pope's mistress, a lady of an ancient and noble French family, was always willing to assist. But the validity of King Philip's acts was recognised, and the obnoxious bulls of Boniface VIII were revoked. Nothing more was needed to establish the sanctity of the Papacy; and when nine new French cardinals had been elected, and all the Italians called to Avignon except three who were made the Church's vicegerents in Italy, the process was complete. The Pope, indeed, found himself strong enough to oppose and successfully defeat

Philip's nomination of his brother Charles of Valois to the Empire; he even went further, and openly declared the papal suzerainty over the Empire. The lamentable tragedy which ended in the execution of Jacques de Molay and the destruction of the Order of Knights Templars[2] (an order which, it should be noted, was never attacked by those Troubadours who dilated very frankly on the vices of Papacy, clergy, princes, and even thrones), was but a symptom of the unscrupulous uses made of the papal tribunals by the recklessness of King Philip. The accusations began in April 1307. They proceeded after the Pope had reached Avignon, across the Bridge of St. Bénezet, on 28th March 1309; they only ended on the scaffolds and the faggots of the 14th of March 1314. A month afterwards the Pope who had legalised the murders and spoliations of the king was dead at Roquemaure; in November of the same year Philip himself had passed before that Higher Tribunal to which the dying Jacques de Molay had solemnly summoned his unjust accusers.

Riots against the Italians in Carpentras, and disorders generally among the papal court and its surroundings, delayed the next election for two years; and it was not till the 5th of September 1316 that the Bishop of Avignon was crowned as John XXII. In the meantime Italian influence had begun its work in Provence, and especially in Carpentras and the Comtat-Venaissin, where schools of rhetoric and literature were opened by refugees from Italy; and art followed them across the Alps. Even if no proofs were forthcoming of the visit of Dante Alighieri to the Rhone valley, his presence as a political exile from the strife of Guelph and Ghibelline would be quite natural. The arrival and the sojourn of Petrarch in Provence rests upon a more certain basis. His life at Avignon is known. His love-story has immortalised Vaucluse. The wealth of Avignon, as the centre of all this, became assured.

The quarrel for the Empire between Louis of Bavaria and Frederick of Austria only increased the prestige of the Pope, who boldly claimed his superiority to both. When the victory of Mühldorf seemed to serve the ambitions of Louis; when the Imperial crown was placed upon his head by that same Sciarra Colonna who had been the hero of Anagni, John XXII soon showed that the days of Boniface VIII were over. The Emperor's theatrical anti-Pope was crushed and driven into humiliating submission. The Ghibellines were everywhere put down. Louis was driven from Italy, and compelled to take refuge in theological disputes. John XXII maintained his position unimpaired against every attack, even of the doctrines of the Franciscans, the writings of William of

Occam, and the brilliant political pamphlet (the *Defensor Pacis)* of Marsiglio, a work which foreshadowed the sovranty of the people and the official position of the ruler in a way which the nineteenth century was alone to change from theory into accomplished fact.

But the Pope was not free from opposition even in Avignon itself. However many new French cardinals he might create, there still remained an Italian nucleus in the sacred Conclave, and the Italian party was continually hostile to the French. An echo of these dissensions is heard in the sordid and superstitious details of the trial of the Bishop of Cahors for sorcery. The miserable prelate was dragged through the streets of Avignon, flayed alive by the common hangman, and thrown to the flames on a scaffold in front of the papal palace. This building was already being begun with the help of the large sums that flowed into the Papal treasury as soon as it had become fixed and organised within a permanent abode. The cruelties perpetrated on the Jews by the brigands, to whom the name of "Pastoureaux" still clung, may have been the strongest incentive to build walls that were as much to shelter as to isolate the sanctity of the Pope. About a thousand of these unhappy outcasts took refuge with their treasure in the Tower of Verdun. The "Pastoureaux" surrounded them, and troops of robbers from all the countryside were continually reinforcing the besiegers, attracted by the rich booty that the Jews were guarding. At last only eighty fighting men, with some three hundred women and children and aged persons, survived within the fortress. Those of their comrades who had been captured in the sorties were hideously tortured before their eyes at the foot of the castle walls. In the final loss of ammunition that ensued, old men had hurled their coffers of money on the heads of the besiegers, women had thrown the dead bodies of their children against the attacking foe. At last a huge fire was built up in the courtyard, and all the possessions of the besieged were placed upon it. Then the Jews killed each other, until only one remained alive; and the brigands at last took the ruins of the castle. Fortunately the regular troops of the Governor of Languedoc were strong enough to scatter the bandits before they could advance on Avignon; but the papal court had learnt its lesson, and the palace was no longer left open to attack. John XXII had not done much more towards this necessary project than collect the money for his architects and workmen, when he died, on the 4th of December 1334. His body was laid in state in Notre Dame des Doms, where his magnificent tomb may still be seen. He was succeeded by Jacques Fournier, who was crowned the next January as Benedict XII, an upright but feeble-minded Cistercian, of poor parentage and rather weak will, as may be imagined from the message he sent to Philip VI of France, that "if he had possessed two souls, he would willingly sacrifice one to do him service, but as he had only one soul, he could not go beyond what he thought right."

Three years after Benedict's election, the Electoral princes declared at Rome that he who was elected by a majority became straightway King of the Romans, and could exercise his imperial rights without any papal confirmation. The tenuity of German kingship and the shadowy phantom of the Empire only made this assertion the more direct a proof of papal weakness. But extreme doctrines produced a natural reaction, and before Benedict was dead men's religious sympathies had once more begun to uphold his cause against the secular sceptre of the Emperors; and no doubt the new Pope's anxiety in matters of doctrine, and the public refusal of Italy to accept the presence of the Holy See, gave an added sanctity to the great palace at Avignon which Benedict reared to take the place of John's first buildings. By his care was raised the immense fortress on the northern side of the present mass, dominated by the Tour de Trouillas, and honeycombed with secret passages. Within it were received the ambassadors of the Khan of Tartary and Pedro IV of Aragon. The safe-conduct of men of all nations within the papal city— "the City of Christendom"—was warmly asserted by the Pope's rescue of Nicolini da Fieschi from the prison of Villeneuve, into which the King of France had thrown him, and the punishment of all directly concerned in that unlawful outrage. But Benedict did not live long to enjoy the powers his honesty and foresight had created. He died on St. Mark's Day, the 24th of April 1342; and it is characteristic of him that it was by his orders that a third crown was added to the papal tiara. The first, originally a present from the Emperor of Constantinople, had been sent by Clovis to the Church of St. John Lateran. The second was added by Boniface VIII. The "triregno" was completed by the miller's son.

Clement VI, the next Pope, was of a very different quality and character from his predecessor, for Pierre Roger de Beaufort was the scion of a noble house, and the Pope had no mind to give up the habits of the cardinal. So the companionship of the beautiful Cécile de Comminges did not cease when her lover assumed the tiara; and it was for her that Clement VI bought for his nephew, Guillaume de Beaufort, the viscounty of Turenne which became so famous in Provence during the life of that Princess Alix whose misfortunes I described at Les Baux.

The Tomb of Pope Benedict XII at Avignon

Though it was the diplomacy of Clement VI which finally vanquished Louis of Bavaria and apparently subdued the Empire, the Papacy by no means profited to the extent that might be imagined. Secure at Avignon, for the moment, the Pope paid for the comparative remoteness of his court, and the greater freedom offered there for his luxurious habits, by the loss of that free criticism which in Rome might have proved a valuable safety-valve for public opinion, and would have always acted as a salutary check on papal errors. The conflict with Louis of Bavaria really marked the end of the unquestioned, mediaeval sovranty of the Holy See. Questions as to the origin and limits of the papal power had been asked all over Europe. Many had never yet received an answer. Clement VI was crowned in May 1342, at Avignon, in the presence of John, heir to the French throne, and of the Dukes of Bourbon and of Burgundy; but in 1343 there came to Avignon, in the embassy of eighteen deputies sent from Rome, two Italians whose personality was even more powerful than that of the Princes of the Blood; for they were Petrarch and Rienzi; and their chief mission was to persuade the Pope to take a more direct interest in the affairs of Rome, if not to restore to the Eternal City the presence of the Pontiff of the world. The most significant answer of Clement VI was the strengthening and extension of that papal palace of Avignon, which he had determined should be the worthy shrine of his magnificent court. Rienzi was to know its dungeons later on. Petrarch was to castigate its vices. But all Europe revolted against the extortions to which its luxury gave rise.

One of the new cardinals was the Pope's young nephew, Pierre Roger, then only eighteen years of age, who was afterwards to become Gregory XI. The Pope's family and all his court were provided for at the expense of Christendom, and papal aggression, which had gradually grown through the unconsidered effect of various appeals and judgments, reached with the Popes of Avignon a height unknown before. In England, fighting desperately with France throughout the greater part of the fourteenth century, the antagonism to papal taxes was warmly abetted by national hatred of the Pope's surroundings; and every other country joined more or less fervently in the protest, for the only district which did not feel the presence of "the army of provisors" was the papal States, and they remained in dire confusion throughout the absence of their overlord. But Clement VI was content, provided the money came in from one source or from another; and he considered himself still further secure when the ownership of Avignon had been firmly handed over to him by Queen Jeanne of Naples.

Of this celebrated and unfortunate lady I have already had to speak in previous pages, and if it be possible, I must say more of her later on, for there is scarcely a more romantic or more ill-starred figure in the fourteenth century than this Mary Stuart of Provence. After the murder of Andrew of Hungary, her first husband, a crime of which Petrarch and Boccaccio alike acquitted her, the Pope promised to be godfather to her unborn child; and Philippe de Cabassole, that friend of Petrarch whose château still stands in ruins above the spring of Vaucluse, held the boy at the font, as the papal representative in Naples, on Christmas Eve, 1345. But peace was far from being assured to the unhappy mother, and the strong-handed intervention of Hugues-Raymond des Baux, Grand-Seneschal of Provence, in her affairs has been described already. In 1347, Queen Jeanne took as a second husband her father's cousin, Louis of Tarentum;[3] and soon afterwards she sailed for Provence, where she found herself promptly arrested by the barons of Les Baux and other Provençal towns, who were determined to prevent her handing over their beloved country to any northern potentate, or even to the King of France. Her handsome husband, the merest puppet of the alcove and the bedchamber, proved quite unable to ride the whirlwind which seemed the invariable companion of his unquiet consort; and after some delay in Genoa, he sailed secretly to Aigues-Mortes, travelled in haste to Beaucaire and there awaited events at Villeneuve-lez-Avignon. Not until all danger from the Duke of Normandy's demands had passed, not until Jeanne had sworn never to alienate any portion of Provence, was she allowed at liberty; and her husband accompanied her on the triumphant entry into Avignon on the 15th of March 1348.

Eight cardinals followed her canopy of cloth of gold; which was escorted by the Papal Guards; and Clement VI commenced proceedings by awarding the Golden Rose to the husband, who also received the retrospective sanction of the Holy See for his union to the queen. It only remained solemnly and formally to clear her of the imputation of murder.

The scene in the great "Salle du conclave," then brilliant with the frescoes of Simone Memmi and his pupils, must have been an impressive one during that terrible year when Avignon, outside the papal palace, was being devastated with the horrors of the plague. On one side sat the Pope surrounded by the high officers of his court; on the other were Queen Jeanne and her husband and her maids-of-honour. Between them stood the accusers, the Grand Justiciary, and the representatives of Hungary. Crowding at the end near the great staircase came the throng of papal dependants, the retainers of the Provençal nobles, and the citizens of Avignon. It was not before Christ's vicegerent on earth that this young queen, already twice a wife, who was to be four times a widow, now pleaded her cause; but before a crafty, courtly man of the world, who thoroughly understood and sympathised with every note of passion in her story, and who meant to get his full material advantage out of all. We may imagine the irresistible appeal of Beauty in distress, the eternal argument of victorious Phryne. Contemporary evidence is enthusiastic over the lady's eloquence as well, and she was well equipped with Latin and rhetoric, and literature, for any such attempt. But it is safer to put the result down to very mingled reasons. That result was her unequivocal acquittal, and the blessing of the Pope. She went back at once to Villeneuve with her husband, out of the countless dangers of the pestilence-stricken streets of Avignon. There she waited until the news came that her inveterate foe, Louis of Hungary, had himself been chased from Naples by the plague; and she saw a chance of returning to her kingdom and her faithful people; for Jeanne was as beloved in Naples as in Provence. The sole difficulty that arose was money for the journey and for the immediate necessities of her Italian administration. Her need was the Pope's opportunity.

In June of that same year, Queen Jeanne and Louis of Tarentum formally sold Avignon to the Pope for the sum of 80,000 gold florins of the coinage of Florence, which is some indication of the nature of the transaction. "To him that hath shall be given" was evidently a motto Clement VI appreciated, and the richest prince in Christendom was able to add one of the brightest jewels in the Provençal crown to his already overloaded tiara at a very reasonable cost.[4]

As might perhaps have been expected, Jeanne's fortunes did not prosper after these transactions. Provence, which could forgive her almost anything, was nearly angry over the loss of Avignon. Naples, with the fickle passion of the south, began to clamour for another trial, if only to get rid of the constant enmity of Louis of Hungary. The Pope was obliged to go through another farce of proclaiming the queen innocent, even if she had actually murdered her first husband, by the hypothesis of sorcery and witchcraft which had driven her to actions over which she had had no control. Only by this obvious concession to the credulity of the scum of Naples was any possibility of peace secured; and in January 1351 Jeanne and her husband were crowned within the city.

About four months before this John, Duke of Normandy, succeeded Philip VI upon the throne of France, and soon afterwards paid a visit to the Pope, in which piety and politics were about equally commingled, residing during his stay at the palace in Villeneuve, formerly inhabited by Queen Jeanne. A number of new cardinals were created, to strengthen the French faction in the Conclave, among them the ambitious Spaniard Gilles d'Albornoz, and Raymond des Ursins. While Naples was celebrating the coronation of its queen, Avignon beheld the splendid fêtes organised by the new King of France upon the island of Barthelasse, and a fashionable reputation was given to the water-festivals upon the Rhone, its islands, and its bridges, which has lasted until this day.[5]

In December 1352 Clement VI died suddenly. Petrarch has left a scathing account of the manners and customs of his court, comparing it to the two Babylons (of Assyria and Egypt), the four labyrinths of Avernus and of Tartarus, and bestowing on it almost all the horrors of Dante's *Inferno*. It is true that the Courts of Love, of which Avignon was a celebrated centre, were not exactly calculated to increase the papal prestige for chastity and continence; but without excusing individual errors one may at this distance of time justly consider the general value of the cultivated society which the papal court encouraged, the benefits conferred upon the South of France by the arts and sciences thereby fostered, and the material increase in prosperity and power of the town which was the focus of these various influences. I am as little concerned here to estimate the moral character of Clement VI as to weigh the Borgias in that balance which history is too often wont to fill as much with the eminent position of the culprit as with the sins of which he can be fairly proved guilty. It is enough, here and now, to remember that the whole position of the Papacy at Avignon was extraordinary and abnormal. It is unnecessary either to apologise for its chief actors or to exaggerate their faults.

It might certainly have been thought that any advantages derived from the comparative security of Avignon had come to an end with the reign of Innocent VI, who was Pope from 1352 to 1362. That meteor of unrest, Rienzi, was among the first of the notable visitors to Avignon during the new Pontificate. As we have seen, the dramatic tribune had been here already, before his vaulting ambition had o'erleaped itself. This second visit was very different. Then he had boldly proclaimed that passionate patriotism for the Eternal City which had been more delicately expressed by the poetic accents of the studious Petrarch. He had gone back to Italy and roused the very stones of Rome to mutiny against the patrician families. He had been raised to the full splendour of that tribunician power which had been evoked from the dead centuries of the past when Jacopo Arlotti crushed the Colonna and the Orsini, and the people invited the Emperor to enter Rome upon their own authority in 1312. That evocation was repeated with a tenfold splendour, and with the aid of every artifice, by Rienzi in 1347. He succeeded because, at bottom, his ideals were noble. He failed because his methods were unworthy. At first not only the common people of the capital, but the great men of the world, and nearly all the cities of Italy were captivated by what seemed to be the realisation of that golden dream which was common to Rienzi, to Petrarch, and to Dante, which was a conception of the true Roman citizenship that inevitably prepared the way for modern nationalities. This, without doubt, Rienzi foresaw; and this inspired him, with an almost mystical fanaticism, to continue at all hazards on his perilous path. He had, indeed, gone too far to return.

Having once got the patricians into his power he was not strong enough to use his opportunity. A passion for theatrical effect, a lack of reticence and real dignity, a disregard of perspective and proportion which was the heritage of sudden power—these things fatally weakened a career which in many ways must arouse our sympathy now, as it aroused a temporary enthusiasm then. But having freed the people, Rienzi was not able to convince them that freedom has its price, not in eternal vigilance only, but in taxation too. As soon as they discovered that the renaissance of old Rome meant more than shouting, they drew back. The Pope had no difficulty in pulling the strings of a high policy to which the tribune had no access. On the 15th of December 1347, Rienzi was barricaded in the Castle of St. Angelo. Soon afterwards he fled to Naples, and there spent some two years in mystic contemplation on Monte Maiella. In 1350 he went to plead the cause of Rome in person before the Emperor Charles IV. But the Emperor, who owed some useful warnings to the Holy See, sent him forthwith under guard to the Pope, by way of grateful recognition for past assistance.

Even this did not disabuse Rienzi of his confidence in his own star. The peoples of the countries through which he passed thronged to see "the deliverer of Italy." His entry in Avignon was almost a triumphal procession. But it ended in a prison in the Tour de Trouillas. Even when it suited the Pope to put an end to a situation which enabled the changeable Romans to cry out for the return of "the martyr in the cause of freedom," Rienzi did not realise that his release meant merely that he was to be a profitable pawn in further papal and Imperial games. Innocent VI chose the strong and subtle soldier-cardinal, Albornoz, as his chief instrument in the next Italian gambit; Rienzi, though he went as the chief actor, was in reality the piece that was to be sacrificed. It is easy now to criticise the sensuous passionate, ill-balanced dreamer, to point out his errors, to enlarge upon his weaknesses. But we must remember too that he had a faith which had once moved mountains, and that in the abstract his ideals were pure and right. It is a tragic figure that moves out of Avignon; driven by a relentless fate to irremediable doom; his mind and reasoning faculties unbalanced as the preliminary to the final ruin.

Three knights of Provence took a large share in the last scenes of Rienzi's life. They were the famous Montréal, known throughout Italy as Fra Monreale, the great condottiere, and his two brothers Bertonna and Arimbaldo. These latter the tribune, now raised at his own desire to the dignity of senator, placed in high command near his own person. From their more dangerous brother he was content to borrow fighting-men and money. When Fra Monreale claimed repayment he threw him into prison, and with a harshness as misplaced as had been his former leniency, he sent him forthwith to execution on the scaffold. The scarcely hidden sympathy for a successful brigand at once began to smoke and smoulder. Fra Monreale might have pillaged every wealthy town in Italy; but Rienzi had not disdained to profit by the exactions of the brave soldier he had now beheaded. Indeed his first action, after the fatal sentence had been carried out, was to equip fresh troops against the patricians with the condottiere's money. It was in vain that Arimbaldo and Bertonna were released. The further execution of Pandolfo, a rich citizen, fanned the popular excitement into a flame. The people he had freed stormed the Capitol. He strove to escape in disguise; was recognised by the gold bracelets he had forgotten to take off; and was instantly stabbed to death. For two days the corpse was exposed to the insults of the populace on the very spot where he had once swayed the heart of every Roman with the passion of his fiery eloquence.

Rienzi died as he was meant to die. It was Albornoz who succeeded. Proceeding warily yet without delay upon his path, the cardinal gradually attained his ends; and the Pope, having dismissed Rienzi from his mind, sought refuge in his country house at Villeneuve from the pomps and splendours of a pontifical court for which he felt a growing distaste as he drew nearer to his end. This house he had begun to plan when, as a simple cardinal, he bought a farm from the Abbé of St. André. Eventually (on

2nd January 1356) he dedicated it to St. John the Baptist as a Carthusian monastery, with the beautiful name of "Vallée de Bénédiction." The fine entrance from the main street is, of course, of later date, and only shows how long its dignity and influence lasted, a fact which may be also gathered from the foundation, by this same mother-house, of the Carthusian monastery of Marseilles, in 1633. To his beloved building in Villeneuve Innocent VI left his cross, his chalice, and his pontifical ornaments, and here he wished to be buried. His magnificent tomb has been removed, but may be seen in the church of the "Hospice-Hôpital," which stands among its gardens and cypress groves in Villeneuve. The Chartreuse, now little more than a degraded wilderness of still lovely ruins, was yet further beautified after this Pope's death by one nephew, the Bishop of Carcassonne, and then by another nephew, the Cardinal of Pampeluna, who left it a rich heritage in lands and gold, as did yet a third nephew, the Bishop of Paris, Auxerre, and Maguelonne.

The traces of these former splendours may be seen in the exquisitely designed fountain in the central court of the Chartreuse; in the beautiful groinwork of the cloisters near what are now almshouses; and in many details of carving and stonework that have survived the spoliation and neglect of centuries. It is no doubt due to the impulse thus first given by Innocent VI, and continued by his relations, that we owe the presence in the museum and the church of Villeneuve-lèz-Avignon of several paintings by the early French school which are of the highest interest and value, and were rightly appreciated for the first time when they were seen in the Louvre in the wonderful exhibition of the "Primitifs" for which they were lent to Paris in 1904. That known as the "Virgin of Pity" was particularly remarked by connoisseurs. It still shows the careful work upon a thick gold background, characteristic of the early fifteenth century. A strange, oriental-looking town lifts its domes and minarets on the horizon at the left above the head of the donor, an old surpliced priest, with small, keen eyes, prominent cheekbones, and sparse, grey hair. The Virgin, her face emaciated with sorrow, holds upon her knees the stiffened corpse of the Christ Crucified. On either side of her are the kneeling figures of St. John and of the Magdalen. It is a painting full of sincerity, and rendered with a skill as great as the pious enthusiasm which inspired it.

Far more important is the magnificent "Coronation of the Virgin," once attributed, as were so many things in loyal Provence, to the good King René, but now known to have been painted by Enguerrand Charenton (born in 1410), who lived at Avignon from 1447 onwards, and painted this as the reredos for the chapel of the Chartreuse in 1453. In spite of its too evident decay, this splendid painting still retains the harmony of its dignified colour-scheme, and the impressiveness of its largely-conceived design. On high, above the battlements of a city, the Virgin is being crowned by the Trinity, surrounded by a choir of angels and by the heavenly company of priests and martyrs. The colour as a whole is rather lighter than is usual in the Provençal school, and somewhat recalls the style of Fouquet, both in this and in certain details of the surrounding cherubim. The face and hands of the Virgin are characteristically French in treatment, differing both from Italian and from Flemish work; and though some critics detect the influence of the school of Fra Angelico in certain accessory details in the painting of the cardinals and bishops, the work as a whole is distinctly "northern" in feeling, as it is French in execution; and it is the more valuable inasmuch as no other work by Charenton is known in Provence.

The Porch of the Chartreuse, Villeneuve-lèz-Avignon

The affection of Innocent VI for Villeneuve may be easily understood if we remember that the papal palace was several times disturbed, and literally imperilled, by such attacks as that of the brigand "Arch-priest," de Servoles, whose depredations have been already described in my chapter on Les Baux. Public security, in fact, scarcely existed in France during the imprisonment of King John and the triumph of the English arms. Scarcely was de Servoles finally beaten back, by bribes as well as force, when other bands of brigands, known respectively as "Alpéruges" and "Tard-venus," came up against Avignon; and a great flood, produced by the overflowing of the Durance and the Rhone, added to the misery of the inhabitants. But the new walls proved too strong for the freebooters, and the Pope brought in corn by river for the inhabitants; and at length to some extent restored prosperity to the town, which had by now fully given him its allegiance. Wearied out by constant anxieties at home, by the expense of the campaigns of Albornoz in the papal states, and by the difficulties attendant on the death of Queen Jeanne's second husband, Louis of Tarentum, Pope Innocent VI died in September 1362. He had adhered loyally to his task of restoring order both in Italy and Provence; but it was too great for his strength, and his frail body refused to accomplish any longer the tasks his will imposed upon it

He was followed in the chair of St. Peter by Guillaume Grimoard, Abbot of St. Victor in Marseilles, who had been papal legate at the distracted Court of Naples, and was elected Pope as Urban V after the violent intrigues of the Conclave of Cardinals had resulted in their inability to choose any member of their own body present. So grave was the peril considered, that the legate was hurriedly summoned from Italy to Marseilles before the result of the election was made known to him or to any one else; and he entered Avignon almost by stealth on the 31st of October 1362; but John of Navarre, Peter of Cyprus, and Waldemar of Denmark provided the unusual spectacle of the presence of three kings at his coronation in November in the Cathedral of Notre Dame des Doms.

A man of great learning, of widely established reputation, and of sincere piety, Urban V must have felt completely out of touch with the intrigues of the papal palace; and the measure of his zeal may be appreciated by the fact that after the papal states had been partially brought into obedience and passivity by the stern measures of Albornoz, he openly announced his determination to return to Rome. The outcry of the luxurious cardinals and courtiers of Avignon may be imagined. They were perfectly willing to buy off the continuous stream of robbers and brigands by continual ransoms from the papal funds; and even the unusual policy of awarding places to merit, and of insisting on decorous behaviour, did not reconcile them to the abandonment by the Pope of the country in which nearly all of them were his compatriots. This is the real reason why Urban's well-meant efforts to live in Rome finally failed. He was, after the first enthusiasm was over, a stranger in a foreign land, and the difficulty was felt on both sides. Other considerations also incline me to believe that the voyage to Rome was, in the Pope's own mind, merely a temporary expedient, with the double object of performing a conscientious duty in restoring some measure of repose to that distracted city, and of escaping for a while from the twofold inconvenience of brigandage without and tortuous intrigues within the palace at Avignon. It is, for instance, difficult to imagine that a Pope who was about to sever all personal connection with the Rocher des Doms would build the Tour des Anges, would add still more to the mass of buildings on the east of the palace, and would plant fresh gardens and shrubberies in its immediate neighbourhood. Nor can I think that wholly disinterested zeal would go so far as to raise the height of the ramparts Innocent VI had built round the town, and to increase their extent and strength to a very remarkable degree.

Less than five months after Urban's succession, he found himself faced by very considerable domestic difficulties owing to the severe frost, which stopped the flow of the Rhone and killed the fruit-trees. The necessities of the papal commissariat, in the way of good burgundy, were indeed provided for by the monks of Cluny, who managed to keep the Holy Father well supplied with excellent Beaune in spite of every difficulty. But the common people were not so privileged; and the constant distress occasioned by the "Grand Companies," a highsounding name for large congregations of bandits, added to the misery of the whole district. Avignon's old enemy the "Archiprêtre" had indeed been compelled to fly before the Emperor Charles, and was promptly assassinated by his own men near Mâcon. The Emperor took advantage of the opportunity, not only to visit Avignon, but to get himself crowned King of Arles in St. Trophime, in 1365, in the presence of Amadeus of Savoy, the seneschal of Provence, and eleven bishops, much to the alarm of Queen Jeanne, who was only reassured by the immediate announcement that her rights had been in no way diminished by what was, after all, a mere theatrical revival of long-vanished dignities. But the ceremony, and its immediate occasion, were by no means sufficient to crush the evil of unlicensed brigandage. The turbulent princes of Les Baux overran Provence with fire and sword, only in the next year; and soon afterwards a more serious danger arose than any which had yet menaced the peace of the country.

Henry of Trastamare, resolved to depose the blood-thirsty maniac, who, as Pedro the Cruel, reigned over Castile, bethought him of using the "Grand Companies" as a convenient instrument. France was but too glad to get them out of the country on any pretext. Bertrand du Guesclin, taken prisoner by Chandos, was ransomed from the English in order to provide a leader strong enough for so undisciplined a rabble; and by gathering his old comrades round him he soon got together so formidable an army that he was able to approach Avignon, to obtain the blessing of the Pope, at the head of thirty thousand men. There are at least two meanings to the word "blessing"; and du Guesclin soon made it clear to Urban V that his army understood it in the sense of two hundred thousand livres. A cardinal hastened to suggest that plenary absolution might be a worthy substitute. "Sire," replied Bertrand, "icy y en a moult qui d'absolution ne parlent point et trop mieux aiment l'argent"; and his men began to pillage the countryside as a slight indication that they were quite in earnest. The Pope hastened to raise one hundred thousand francs in taxes from the citizens of Avignon, and to send the money to du Guesclin. But as soon as he was informed how it had been procured, he returned it to Urban, saying it was only from the Pope himself that he could accept that sum. So from the papal exchequer it was unwillingly withdrawn, and du Guesclin forthwith led his army towards the Pyrenees.

No one can be surprised that Urban should desire a change of air after these unfortunate experiences, and should listen with indulgent sympathy to the patriotic outbursts with which Petrarch called upon him to go forth to Italy and Rome. He therefore gave the Comtat-Venaissin in charge to the poet's friend, Philippe de Cabassole, and left Avignon on the 30th of April 1367. On his arrival in Viterbo, on the 9th of June, he was greeted by a crowd of people who were only too glad of a chance to complain of the severities of his legate, the Cardinal d'Albornoz. Urban was unfortunately weak enough to yield to their clamours, and begged the cardinal to leave his presence and prepare to answer his accusers as soon as called upon. This strong-willed soldier-priest had been recalled in disgrace to Avignon some time before, owing to disturbances in Rome which had practically compelled the Pope to give his sanction to the reform party in that city. But he had been sent back as papal legate to Naples, and had given Urban sound advice as to dealing with the internal politics of Rome when the Pope should have arrived there. All was forgotten when the mob of Viterbo shouted for his disgrace. "I have served you too well," said the proud prelate the next morning, "and I am sorry that I did so." Already stricken with a mortal disease, Albornoz never recovered from the public indignity of papal ingratitude, and in two months he was dead.

With Urban's sojourn in Rome I must not here concern myself. One of its most brilliant episodes was the visit of Queen Jeanne, already a widow for the third time; for her third husband, James of Majorca, had died after two ineffectual efforts to conquer Aragon and make a name for himself in Spain. She was received with the honour of the Golden Rose; for the Pope thoroughly understood the political value of her apparently inexhaustible potentialities as a bride. One of the strongest claimants for her kingdom of Provence was Louis d'Anjou, son of King John, and brother of Charles V of France. Louis obtained from the Emperor the titular rights of the royalty of Arles, secured the help of those fighting brigands whom du Guesclin was quite ready to put at his service after their Spanish campaign was over, and promptly crossed the Rhone to lay siege to Tarascon and Arles. One of the few historical occurrences of which the town of Tarascon was the actual scene was the repulse of du Guesclin at this time (1368) by Bérenger, a gentleman of Avignon, who died in its defence. Du Guesclin passed on to Arles, which offered the most obstinate resistance. Rallying to the standard of Queen Jeanne, Aix, Marseilles, and the towns of Provence rose against the invader:—

> *"Tarascoun, e Bèu-Caire, e Toulouso, e Beziés*
> *Fasent bàrri de car..."* [6]

In a short time Louis d'Anjou returned to Languedoc, having done nothing, and when he heard that Queen Jeanne was quite prepared to make him her heir (and in fact he became so, after her death) he must have been relieved to think that he had done no more harm to his inheritance.

The King of France, delighted at the turn affairs had taken, and recognising the diplomatic value of conversations between Queen Jeanne and the Pope near Rome, to which the enemies of both persisted in giving a very different meaning, acknowledged Urban's share in these transactions by formally ceding to him that portion of the famous

Bridge of Avignon which extended as far as the Chapel of St. Bénezet, a cession which the Pope received more as an indication of good-will than as any addition to prerogatives he considered long ago his own.

But when the King of France sent Louis d'Anjou to Aquitaine as the champion of that district against English injustice and exactions, the Pope saw that if further war between the two countries was to be prevented he must be on the spot. So, in spite of every protest, even of the frenzied letters of Petrarch, he announced his return to Avignon in September 1370, taking advantage of the temporary tranquillity of Italy. Two months after his return to the Rocher des Doms he was dead. It appeared as if a judgment had fallen upon him for deserting the Eternal City to which he had once made up his mind to return. The appearance of yet another of "the Provençal Popes" in Rome led to even greater disasters both to Avignon and to the Papacy itself; for with the death of Urban's successor, Gregory XI, began the Great Schism which disturbed the whole of Christendom.

The new Pope, another Pierre Roger de Beaufort, and nephew of Clement VI, was only thirty-nine at his election, and had been a cardinal since the age of eighteen. Sickly and frail in body, kindly and agreeable in manner, he was perhaps the only man in the papal court who was not prepared to welcome his accession as Gregory XI; for he knew his own weakness where others could only admire his industry and intellect. The fatal step of returning to Italy he postponed, it is true, for six years; but he finally took it through dread of losing all hold upon his Italian estates, a dread which was quite intelligible from the general antipathy created, not only among the small princely dynasties, but also among the free democratic governments, by the determination of a foreigner to bring the States of the Church immediately under his power. This was mainly owing to the establishment of French governors, a mistake which Albornoz had been far too wise to commit; and if Florence had only been able to rally the rest of Italy around her she might have regained all that Albornoz had conquered. But the Italian republics, if they had some of the brilliancy, reproduced all of the jealousy of the Hellenic communities; union seemed as impossible to the one as to the other; and Rome was quite ready to welcome the Holy Father when at last he made up his mind to go to her.

These were the general reasons for Gregory's return. But particular occurrences also exercised a very strong influence upon his decision, and the chain of causes that ended in his ill-omened departure from Avignon begins (once more) with Queen Jeanne.

It will be remembered that this unhappy lady's first husband, Andrew of Hungary, had been murdered at Aversa, in September 1345. Upon the same balcony, whence his mutilated corpse was cast into the garden, Charles, Duke of Durazzo, husband of Queen Jeanne's sister, was also murdered, in 1348, by the implacable Lewis of Hungary. His brother Louis had, as son, another Charles of Durazzo (or Duras, as he is sometimes called in the French fashion); and this Charles Queen Jeanne contrived to marry to his cousin Margaret, declaring both of them (with a strange duplicity which will be easily recognised after what has gone before) to be her heirs, and thus contrived to patch up for a time the quarrels with which her house was constantly beset. But the King of Hungary remained an enemy whom nothing could appease; and his annoyance at the cession of Sicily from the kingdom of Naples was trebled by this declaration of a new inheritance. So Queen Jeanne determined to make one more throw for fortune, and chose a fourth husband in Otho, Duke of Brunswick, a Guelph, with the blood of Este and of Brandenburg in his veins. Charles of Durazzo, who, above all men, owed her gratitude, was the first to revolt against her new step, pretending that there was still a possibility that she might have children. While he was rousing armed resistance on the one side, Barnabo Visconti appeared on the other, eager to take advantage of the general disturbance by continuing his incessant quarrel with the Pope.

Amadeus of Savoy was sent from Avignon by Gregory XI, at the head of all the forces that could be got together in Provence and the Venaissin, to oppose Visconti, who was soon obliged to send Andrea Doria to the Rocher des Doms to beg for terms of peace. But these were refused as soon as it was seen that Visconti was playing a double game and only trying to gain time; and the Emperor Charles IV joined the Pope's side by hurling edicts, as terrible as any papal bulls, against the towns of Italy.

Famine and pestilence desolated Avignon in 1374; but the pause that followed them saw the origin of what was to be a greater scourge to Mother Church than either; for at this time Pierre de Luna was created cardinal, who was afterwards to become the famous Benedict XIII. Almost the first news of Italy that reached Avignon after this ominous election was the revolt of the men of Florence, which was immediately caused by the treacherous attack made on them by the English condottiere, Sir John Hawkwood, at the instance of the Pope, their actual ally; but was really based upon far deeper and more fundamental differences. Gregory XI answered with the thunders of his excommunication; and it was only the extraordinary ambassadress chosen by the city who saved it from complete impoverishment through loss of trade and commerce. The Pope and the Emperor combined were too strong enemies,

Of all the strange, historic figures who have passed through the streets of Avignon, that of Catharine of Siena is perhaps the least intelligible to us today. There is something of that innocent mystery about her which shines through the marvellous tale of Joan of Arc; and of all that her presence meant in the papal palace on that 18th of June 1376 I cannot begin here to suggest the significance. Like the Maid of Orleans, and like the greater Child before them, "sitting in the midst of the doctors both hearing them, and asking them questions," Catharine astonished the cardinals with her understanding and her answers. There were the same rumours of hysteria, of unnatural trances, of visions in this case as in others. But she accomplished the hard facts of her mission. The Pope withdrew his interdict. It also turned out afterwards that she had not exaggerated the effect of her energetic appeal to the Holy Father to return to Rome. The embassy from the Eternal City, headed by Luca di Savelli, strengthened his resolution to take this important step. He was finally determined by the report of possible schisms, sent him by his legate from Italy.

By a Bull of the 23rd of August 1376, he made what arrangements were possible for the safety of his faithful people of Avignon, and for the government of the Comtat Venaissin, and in September, accompanied by thirteen cardinals, he left Avignon. His horse refused to carry him from the palace, and he had to change his mount before he could proceed. On the 27th of March 1378, he died in Rome, his last hours harassed by a sound prevision of the disorder that should inevitably follow.

Of the twenty-three cardinals who at that time existed, sixteen were in Rome, one was absent as legate in Tuscany, and six had remained in Avignon. Of the sixteen, one was a Spaniard, four were Italians, and eleven were French. The position was full of the most tremendous possibilities for the future of the Church. All Christendom had remonstrated, at one time or another, against "the apostasy of Avignon." Rome herself, remembering the aspirations of Rienzi, and with the utterances of Catharine of Siena still ringing in her ears, now saw her opportunity at last. A Roman Pope must be elected to restore some order into the States of the Church. The gates were guarded, and the cardinals were strictly watched. They sent their own valuables and the papal treasure to the Castle of St. Angelo, where the papal chamberlain, the Archbishop of Arles, secured the governor and the garrison. The sacred Conclave in the Vatican was disturbed by the inrush of an excited mob shouting for the election of a Roman. Bartolommeo Prignano, Archbishop of Bari, was chosen, and took the title of Urban VI. As is usual in times of stress, a compromise had been arrived at, and the new Pope was selected as nothing more than a respectable figure-head, against whom no party could have any violent objections, and who had never even been a cardinal. He sadly disappointed every one by proving resolute, self-willed, determined to enact reforms, full of enthusiastic piety, and absolutely bereft of all political experience, of all tact, of any shred of dignity. A greater misfortune could scarcely be conceived.

The French were quick to recognise their mistake. The governor refused to hand over the Castle of St. Angelo to Urban VI. His insolence towards Otho of Brunswick turned even him and his wife, Queen Jeanne, against the unworthy occupant of the Holy See. The dissentient cardinals withdrew to Anagni; and wrote to the four Italians who remained with the Pope that the late election had been forced upon them by the Roman mob. They laid the same arguments before the University of Paris, and before Louis d'Anjou, and the King of France, who at once declared their sympathy. On the 9th of August 1378, they issued an encyclical letter to the whole of Christendom; and then began a bitter war of pamphlets. The creation of twenty-eight new cardinals by Urban hastened the crisis; and on September 20th, the rebel cardinals elected Robert of Geneva as Pope, who took the name of Clement VII. It was but natural that he should emphasise the divisions by leaving Italy, and it was but obvious to go to Avignon. To Avignon, therefore, Clement VIII betook himself on the 10th of June 1379, and this is why there was once a Pope on the Rocher de Doms at the same time as there was a Pope in Rome.

With the Great Schism this book has little to do. It is but another manifestation of those phases of religious dispute of which we have already heard too much; and from its crowded and inglorious scenes I can but choose those which are closely connected with Avignon itself; or which are necessary to the comprehension of what passed in the Valley of the Rhone.

As far as personality went, the suffrages of aristocratic Europe must have naturally gone to the well-born prince at Avignon, who in stature, in bearing, and in character gave evidence of his high descent. For Robert of Geneva, the condottiere, was changed as greatly, though in a very different way, as was Bartolommeo Prignano, by the sudden rise to the dignity and greatness of the tiara. Yet even among the compatriots of Urban VI there was the undoubted strength of that sudden, strangely passionate outcry for national individuality which had been roused in Italy around Urban, in spite of the defection of his native country, Naples, with Queen Jeanne. But through all the turmoil of Italian intrigues, the one clear light is that which shone from Catharine of Siena, who alone cried aloud, from devoted and self-sacrificing motives, for national unity and ecclesiastical purity; and she died at the end of April 1380.

Clement VII was not slow to show his contempt for Italy and all things Italian; and his coronation of Louis d'Anjou as King of Naples, at Avignon, in May 1382, was but the most brilliant episode in his constant support of French influence against Urban VI. To us it means something more, for it implies the death of poor Queen Jeanne.

Declared a heretic, schismatic, and traitor, by Urban VI, attacked by that Charles of Durazzo whom she had so often befriended in his youth, Jeanne had been compelled to proclaim the brother of the French king as her heir. While she was besieged in Castel Nuovo, watching in vain for Provençal galleys that never came to help, her husband was surrounded and taken prisoner in a sortie, and she had to surrender to Durazzo. Finding that nothing could bend her indomitable spirit, he strangled her in prison, on the 12th of May 1382; and before the end of the month Louis d'Anjou was crowned king of her kingdom. The Provençal galleys came at last, but came too late. The ill-fated queen had found her only rest within the grave. By September 1384, Louis d'Anjou himself was dead. The fatal heritage of Naples had begun to exact its toll upon the best blood in France; a second Louis d'Anjou appeared to take up the burden of his father, and was in turn crowned King of Naples by Clement VII in Avignon. In October 1389 the most disastrous Pontificate in the history of the Church ended with the death of Urban VI.

Provence suffered, as we have seen in my chapter on Les Baux, from the disorders occasioned by the murder of Queen Jeanne, because Turenne, guardian of Alix des Baux, and owner of vast property in the district, espoused the cause of Charles of Durazzo against the house of Anjou; and Marie de Blois, though her son Louis (II) of Anjou and Provence had been crowned by the Pope, in the presence of King Charles VI of France, was unable to secure the recognition of his rights by Marseilles until a Papal Bull had confirmed them, and until she had sworn never to have any dealings with the murderer of their beloved queen. At Arles the same promises had to be repeated, so great was the affection still felt for the memory of Queen Jeanne throughout Provence.

The death of Urban VI must have led Avignon to hope that the embarrassment of a dual Papacy had at last been ended. But this was far from being the case. The King of France was, of course, Clement's strongest ally, though Burgundy remained neutral, waiting for what the cardinals in Rome might do. Castile, at the instance of John I, son of Henry of Trastamare, the enemy of the English, had formally recognised Clement in March 1381. By 1390 Navarre and Aragon had joined the same obedience, by the diplomacy of the indefatigable Cardinal Pierre de Luna. The University of Paris, which might have been neglected in Rome, was near enough to Avignon to render its open hesitation sufficiently embarrassing; yet even this was for a time partly overcome. Every preparation was made for possible difficulties when news of the election of the Neapolitan cardinal, Piero Tomacelli, by the fourteen cardinals in Rome, reached Avignon. The newly crowned Boniface IX was a worthy antagonist indeed. Vigorous, prudent, chaste, heedless of mere formalities, determined to assure his position in Italy by wise politics, and above all by the power of wealth, he slowly strengthened himself by every means he recognised as possible. England alone, where the inevitable loss of prestige entailed by the Schism had produced, in Wyclif, a formidable opponent to the Papacy, escaped the rapacity of Boniface, which was necessitated as much by his championship of the cause of Ladislas (son of Charles of Durazzo) in Naples, against Louis (II) of Anjou and Provence, as by any other single reason. The debt was repaid by timely help when the Pope was in danger from the rebellious Roman people. His position seemed safer still when, in 1394, Clement VII died at Avignon.

In 1390 Provence had suffered almost as much as Naples from the strife between the houses of Durazzo and Anjou; and when plague broke out as well, the Pope withdrew to the château of Beaucaire, where he first heard the news of the opposition of the University of Paris; and though this was visibly weakened, it no doubt embittered Clement's last years, and he died of sudden apoplexy on the 10th of September 1394. Both the King of France (who had begun to realise that the inconveniences of a schism were not counterbalanced by the presence of an "Antipope" at Avignon) and the University of Paris at once exhorted the cardinals at Avignon to suspend any further election until a formal embassy could be sent to them. But the letters containing these urgent messages of delay were judiciously left unopened by the Conclave,[7] which at once bound over all its members by oath to work actively towards the extinction of the Schism. Of the whole College of twenty-four, three were absent, three refused to sign the oath, and eighteen proceeded to deliberate. Perhaps the loudest in his protestations that, if elected, he would resign if it were necessary for the good of the Church was Pierre de Luna. He succeeded as well as any impregnable widow, and conducted his little campaign with so much skill that he was elected Pope on the 28th itself, and took the title of Benedict XIII. The name is a worthy one with which to connect the last of the Popes in Avignon with their rocky fastness on the Rocher des Doms. No beleaguered captain ever held out more fiercely than did Pierre de Luna. Against France, against Christendom, against the protests of the civilised world, he remained unmoved. Death alone put an end to his indomitable obstinacy in retaining the tiara; and the first to make trial of that iron will were the Dukes of Berri, Burgundy, and Orleans, who headed the promised embassy to Avignon from the King of France and the University of Paris, on the 22nd of May, and took up their abode in Villeneuve. Their mission proved absolutely fruitless, and when they became too insistent, the wooden arches of the mended Bridge of Bénezet "caught fire," and traversing the Rhone in an open boat was not to their liking.

Soon the University of Toulouse was brought to the side of Benedict, who considerably weakened even the University of Paris by giving rich posts about his own person to its most brilliant scholars, In June 1397, Avignon, which was beginning to get used to greeting famous guests, saw the ambassadors of England, France, and Castile, who bore messages, similar to those sent to Rome, that the Schism "must end by the 2nd of February 1398." The mention of a date only pledged Charles VI to violent measures; so the madman of France proceeded to arrange with Wenzel, the drunken King of the Romans, what measures should be taken for the betterment of Christendom. In July 1398 a royal order was signed withdrawing the French allegiance, which cut off from Benedict all power over the ecclesiastical revenues of France. Trusting that this would terrify Benedict into submission, Charles VI sent D'Ailly, Bishop of Cambrai, as an ambassador to Avignon, while Marshal Boucicaut waited at Lyons to enforce the royal wishes by strength of arms if need were.

Froissart (in chapter CCXXIX of the sixth volume of Lord Berners's translation) has much to say of the result, as follows:—

Whan the bysshop of Cambraye had refresshed hym at his lodgynge, and had chaunged his apparell, than he wente to the Popes palayes. And whan he came in the Popes presence he made his reverence, but nat in such wyse

as he ought to have doone...and whan the bysshoppe came to the utter-
aunce of the mater, howe the Pope shulde resygne and depose hymselfe fro
the papall dygnyte, and that he that was at Rome shulde do likewyse,
with those wordes the Pope beganne to chaunge colour, and lyfte up his
voyce and sayd: I have endured great payne and traveyle for the churche,
and by good election I was created Pope, and nowe to depose myselfe, that
shall I never do during my lyfe; and I wyll that the Frenche kynge knowe
that for all his ordynaunce I wyll do nothynge therafter, but I wyll kepe
my name and papalyte tyll I dye... Than dyvers other of the cardynalles
sayd: Syr, shewe us what ye wyll do. Than Benedyc aunswered and
said...As longe as I lyve I wyll be Pope, and I wyll nat depose myselfe
nouther for kyng, duke, erle, nor other treatie, nor by no processe nor
meanes, but that I wyll abyde Pope...Saye to our sonne of Fraunce, that
hyther unto I have taken him as a good catholyke prince, but nowe by
synister meanes if he wyll entre into great errour, he wyll repente it. I
praye you to say to hym fro me, that he be well advysed howe he enclyneth
to any thynge that shulde trouble his conscyence... (Whan Syr
Boucyquaut, marshall of Fraunce understode, he sayd to the bysshop of
Cambray): Syr, ye are best to retourne into Fraunce, ye have no more to
do here, and I shall execute that I am commaunded to do by the kynge and
his uncles. The next daye the marshll set clerkes awarke to write...and sent
to the senesehall of Beaucayre, that he shulde close all the passages as well
by the ryver of Rone as by lande, to the entent that nothynge shulde entre
into Avignon. He wente hymselfe to the Pownte Saynt Esperyte, and closed
there the passage over the ryver of Rone, that nothynge shulde entre that
way into Avygnon. Thus the marshall dayly gathered men of warre, and
many came to serve hym, some for obeysaunce, and some to pyll and robbe
theym of Avygnon...Benedic had of longe tyme purveyed his palays with
wyne, corne, larde, oyle, and of all other thinges parteynynge to a fortresse
and also he was of his person hygh and cruell, and wolde nat be abasshed
for a lytell thynge...At the towne of Villeneuve, without Avygnon, whiche
partayned to the realme of Fraunce, was the seneschall of Beaucayre, with
fyve hundred men, and kepte the entre on that syde, and the marshall of
Fraunce, with two thousande men was on the other syde of Avignon, and
he sent to theym of the cytie that without they wolde obey and open their
cytie, that he wolde burne all their vynes and houses abrode in the coun-
trey aboute to the ryver of Durense...So they entred into treatie with the
marshall of Fraunce, the whiche toke such effecte, that all the men of
warre entred into the cytie of Avignon, and it was apoynted to besiege the

palays...Howebeit (Penedyc) sayd that he wolde nat submytte hymselfe,
to dye in the payne, and so he kepte hymselfe close in his palais, which was
as stronge a place as any in the worlde, and most easyest to be kepte, so that
it be well vytayled...and the palays was so kept that none coulde issue out
nor entre in. They lyved with that store they had, for of vytayles they had
suffycient for two or thre yere, but they lacked woode to make fyre with-
all, and to sethe their meate, whiche made theym abasshed.

Though eighteen of his twenty-three cardinals went over to Villeneuve
and joined the French king in renouncing the stubborn Pope, though the
two cardinals who had stayed with him were taken prisoner in their effort
to escape, Benedict still held out. His brother Rodrigo de Luna was a
powerful military assistance to him. An attempt of the besiegers to enter
by way of the sewers was foiled, and every man was captured as he entered
the kitchen from the subterranean passage. An exchange of prisoners
followed; and still the siege dragged on. At last terms were offered to
Benedict that he should not leave Avignon without permission, and that
he should abdicate in case Boniface abdicated, died, or was ejected. He at
once grasped the opportunity of delay, accepted the terms, and grimly
waited four years more for what the chance of circumstance might bring.
I can conceive few more humiliating incidents in Boucicaut's brilliant
career than the withdrawal of his army, after Benedict's stubbornness had
worn out the patience of the king, and after Rodrigo de Luna had had an
undoubted advantage over the besiegers by the strength of the artillery he
used so well from behind his lofty walls, even after an outbreak of the
plague had desolated both palace and city. Nor were even the barren
results of diplomacy to last long; for as soon as the Marshal's army had
been withdrawn, Benedict brought in his own Catalan mercenaries,
terrorised the town, and announced that he should disregard all promises
made to the King of France under pressure of military necessity. Boucicaut
had turned angrily to the suppression of Turenne; and no doubt the
drowning of that notorious brigand in the Rhone, in 1400, gave the
Marshal some little satisfaction for his inglorious campaign. At least he
had restored some measure of tranquillity to the rest of Provence, as was
described in the first part of my eleventh chapter.

The end of the fourteenth century witnessed, as may easily be
understood, a profound outburst of shame and sorrow at the unhappy
condition of the Church. This took the form, as again was natural in
those strange days, of passionate belief and mystic exaltation, of a weird

crusade, from Provence throughout the South of Europe, of bands of penitents clad in white accompanied by flagellant friars, and heralded by the usual miracles of a contagious fanaticism. Boniface IX found himself too much of an Italian prince to make much headway against Benedict XIII as the true Vicar of Christ. France, on the other hand, found that in exchanging papal dues for royal exactions, she had but chosen scorpions instead of whips; and the terrible unrest occasioned by the madness of King Charles VI added to the alarm of all good Christians. Among the contending factions that quarrelled round the royal lunatic, it was natural that the Duke of Orleans should find his chief support in the South. Louis d'Anjou, too, worsted in his fight for Naples by Ladislas and Boniface, turned naturally to Pope Benedict, who had crowned him king, and visited the proud captive of the Rocher des Doms at the end of August 1402, in order to restore him that obedience of Provence which no French king could then either take away or give. The chief result of these differing courses was a gradual reaction in favour of Benedict, and its practical issue was his escape from the palace of the Popes, by the combined agency of Orleans and Anjou, and the assistance of Robert de Braquemond, to Châteaurenard.

In one of the most fascinating scenes of that delightful poem, *Nerto,* Mistral has described how the beautiful young daughter of Baron Pons de Châteaurenard suddenly appeared in the Tour de Trouillas from the subterranean passage that led from her father's donjon-keep to the Rocher des Doms; how she was led by Rodrigo de Luna through the Daedal passages and past the Babylonian pylons of that sinister fortress, till they passed together up the great marble staircase and found, in the vast Hall of Conclave, Pope Benedict XIII sitting alone beneath the frescoes of Simone Memmi; and how the withered but indomitable Pontiff arose to follow her, standing for the last time above his battlements to bless his people, and then entering, with her, the subterranean passage that led him to Châteaurenard.

Whatever were the real details of the escape, its effect was immediate and striking, when, on a March morning in 1403, Avignon awoke to her helplessness without her Pope, and France suddenly realised that Benedict was no longer prisoner. He had taken nothing with him save the Pyx with the Holy Elements, and that autograph letter in which the unhappy Charles VI had once promised him obedience; but he had the powerful houses of Anjou and Orleans behind him, and he was wise enough to ask his recreant cardinals to dinner with his bodyguard in attendance. The Universities of Orleans, Angers, Montpellier, and Toulouse supported the Duke of Orleans in his demand for recognition. All the steeples in Paris rocked with joybells, when the poor king, in a piteous interval of repentant lucidity, acknowledged Benedict to be "the true Vicar of Jesus Christ on earth."

But they little knew with whom they had to deal. Benedict forthwith proclaimed that all acts performed during the period of disobedience were null and void, and refused to recognise any ecclesiastical appointments made by the king. A hailstorm of letters, interviews, and protestations followed. Each side gave way a little. Benedict was polite, but firm. He even took the first steps towards a conference with the rival Pope. In the midst of them Boniface IX died in Rome, on the 1st of October 1404. Sixteen days later the nine Roman cardinals elected the Neapolitan, Cosimo dei Migliorati, who took the title of Innocent VII, and lived scarcely two years in the turmoil of contending factions by which he was surrounded. Benedict meanwhile, visiting Marseilles, Tarascon, Pont de Sorgues, Nice, or Savona; trailing his pontifical dignity through the dust of the Provençal highroads; going even as far as Genoa in a pretended desire to meet his rival half way, which deceived nobody, was confronted at last by the reiterated withdrawal of the obedience of France, hastened by the violent opposition of the University of Paris. Again he was given breathing space by the death of Innocent VII, in November 1406. Every one, except Benedict himself, seemed worn out by the struggle. The fourteen cardinals in Rome took refuge in the old, threadbare expedient of electing "some one who was solemnly bound to make the restoration of unity his chief duty," and they chose the Venetian, Angelo Correr, a man of eighty years, who took the title of Gregory XII, and at once seemed to give practical proof of his sincerity in the cause of unity.

Benedict was in Marseilles in the autumn of 1406, and there he received the embassy from France, and from Gregory, with the greatest suavity. Savona was suggested as their meeting-place. Europe at once betrayed a state of almost comical excitement over its eagerness to keep the Popes up to their engagements. But each of the Holy Fathers pursued his own devious course in utter disregard both of Europe and of his own promises. Benedict proved just as stubborn as ever. The fine enthusiasms of the aged Gregory melted like wax before the covetous importunities of his own family; and he began to make difficulties about Savona. Meanwhile Benedict had retired to the monastery of St. Honorat in the Îles de Lérins, which I described in the first part of my ninth chapter, and was as polite as ever, emphasising his own willingness all the more when he realised the difficulties of his rival. When Gregory only got as far as Siena, Benedict triumphantly awaited him at Savona, on the 1st of November 1407, strictly according to contract. More negotiations followed, until the historian is driven to remark that "one Pope, like a land animal, refused to approach the shore; the other, like a water beast, refused to leave the sea." Benedict was probably the only man in Europe who was still thoroughly amused and interested. He had actually procured help from his old enemy Marshal Boucicaut, now French governor of Genoa, and was only just forestalled by Ladislas in making a dash on Rome itself. Gregory, who was then at Lucca, at once took up the role of an Italian patriot ready to defend the Eternal City at all hazards against Benedict and France; and proceeded forthwith to create new cardinals. The assassination of the Duke of Orleans on November 23, 1407, further weakened Benedict's side; but, in reply to the French King's threat of neutrality, he issued a menace of excommunication and interdict in a bull from Marseilles next May. The University of Paris tore the bull into shreds, and on June 15th Benedict sailed from Porto Venere to take refuge in Perpignan, where he summoned a General Council for November. Gregory replied with an invitation to another Council elsewhere. Then the cardinals of both Popes wrote to announce their defection and to summon a third Council at Pisa, in May 1409. Benedict's Council reported in favour of his abdication, and Pierre de Luna was, as usual, politeness itself; but when the envoys sent to Pisa with the news were imprisoned at Nîmes, he replied by excommunicating the "rebel cardinals" of Pisa. The sessions of the Council of Pisa proceeded, however, just the same; and at the meeting of May 25th both Popes were declared contumacious and guilty of the charges brought against them; and both were "deposed" on June 5th. On June 26th, the cardinals elected Peter Philargi as the new and true Pope, and he took the name of Alexander V. Christendom now beheld the astonishing spectacles of three Popes at once, and a new meaning seemed given to the triple tiara; for neither Gregory nor Benedict admitted the validity of what had passed at Pisa. Gregory declared his opposition at his own special council at Cividale. Benedict withdrew to the rocky fortresses of Peniscola on the coast, created more cardinals of his own, and gave orders to his nephew, Rodrigo de Luna, to keep firm hold of Avignon, in case "the true Pope" should return.

But the Rocher des Doms had seen a Pope within its palace for the last time. Even Rodrigo was driven out of it by the citizens of Avignon and the envoys of Alexander V, who was himself a corpse on the 3rd of May 1410 at Bologna. The eighteen cardinals present in that town promptly elected Baldassare Cossa as John XXIII, a man who might have made a fine general, but who was nothing short of a grotesque incongruity as the Vicar of Christ. In his turn he made preparations to lay hold of Avignon; and it was while his legate was in the palace that the fire broke out in the buildings, north-east of the entrance-court, now known as the "Salle Brûlée." But the fate of John XXIII was sealed at that most extraordinary politico-religious drama known as the Council of Constance, by which he was solemnly deposed on May 29, 1415; and this time the deposition proved effectual. By the 4th of July in that same year Gregory XII had abdicated. But Benedict XIII absolutely refused to recognise either the Council of Constance or the representations made to him at Perpignan by the most powerful princes in Europe. Finally he withdrew again to his own fortress of Peniscola. On April 1, 1417, he was declared guilty of contumacy by the Council of Constance. He signified his contemptuous indifference by continued silence. They formally deposed him next July; but he remained a Pope whatever they might do. By November the cardinals assembled in conclave at Constance elected Oddo Colonna, who was called Pope under the title of Martin V.

In September 1420 Martin was being hailed with boisterous enthusiasm in the streets of Rome; and it is his greatest credit that he not only restored order and a measure of prosperity to that unhappy city, but also brought temporary peace to distracted Naples by arranging that Queen Jeanne (II) should adopt Louis (III) d'Anjou as her heir; and it was through that adoption that the titles of Naples, Sicily, Jerusalem, Anjou, and Provence were united in the good King René, Louis' brother, who became Jeanne's heir when Louis died.

While Benedict lived the Great Schism could not be terminated. But even the strenuous vitality and the dignified obstinacy of Pierre de Luna at last came to an end. Worn out in his ninetieth year by extreme old age, he died at Peniscola in November 1424. Baldassare Cossa had died some time before. Gregory XII had gone too. Benedict had outlived them all, and he was never beaten, to the very end. His victory lasted even beyond the tomb; for in his last illness he had created several cardinals, and these in turn elected a canon of Barcelona, who claimed the Papacy as Clement VIII. The only importance of that claim lies in the fact that the negotiations which extinguished it were successfully carried through by one Alfonso Borgia, who was the first of that fatal family to be introduced into the Papal Court. The Great Schism was over at last; and the tale of the Popes in Avignon is ended.

NOTES

1. "Avignon! St. Peter's foster-daughter, who saw his boat at anchor in her port and bore his keys upon her belt of battlements; Avignon! That beauteous city with her unbound tresses tossed by the Mistral's blast, who has seen the splendour of so glorious a Past, yet has kept nothing of it but a forgetful carelessness…"—*Lou Pouèmo dóu Rose*, cant. viii.

2. See *Old Touraine*, vol. i. p.45, where these iniquitous proceedings are shortly described, and references are given to further authorities on the subject.

3. For the intervention of the Grand-Seneschal, refer back to the first part of chap. xi.; see also Mistral's *La Reine Jeanne*.

4. The Comtat-Venaissin had been ceded to the Holy See, in the person of the papal legate, by Raymond VII, Count of Toulouse, in 1228 but the citizens of Avignon refused to recognise the transfer of their city to the Pope until Innocent VI confirmed their privileges and franchises, and the bargain was only fully sealed in 1358. Even then the town insisted that its falcons should appear upon the civic arms beside the papal keys. That the sum agreed upon was actually paid to Queen Jeanne in cash is proved by accounts in the Vatican, and in the Neapolitan Archives. Further, though Louis XI (in 1476), Louis XIV (in 1663 and 1688), and Louis XV (in 1768) claimed the ownership of the city, the rights of the Holy See never lapsed until the National Assembly destroyed all evidence of the papal purchase in 1791.

5. Even the old nursery rhyme may have its origin in this early festival and its numerous successors:—

"Sur le Pont d'Avignon
L'on y danse tout en rond.
Les beaux Messieurs font comme-ça
Et puis encore comme-ça…" etc.

6. "Tarascon, Beaucaire, Toulouse and Béziers were at bay behind the ramparts of their flesh and blood."—MISTRAL.

7. Some authorities say that the messengers heard of Pierre de Luna's election before they had reached Avignon.

CHAPTER XII

The Good King René

Part I: The Troubadours

"Ah! mounte soun li bèu Troubaire
Mèstre d'amour! Fiéu acabaire,
Fiéu relenqui d'ilustri paire,
Dóu grand fougau d'amour noun vous soubro un coupèu." —
CALENDAL.[1]

THE reign of King René in Provence is not merely the arbitrary date of
the termination of this little history, it is a true dividing line between
ancient and modern literature in the Valley of the Rhone. After him we
come to stern matter-of-fact. In his reign there were still audible the
echoes of the Troubadours, of those Provençal singers of whom he is
perhaps a dilettante example, but at any rate the last, until the revival of
the modern Félibres, and the poems of Roumanille, Aubanel, Mistral,
and the rest. There is, therefore, a certain fitness in the choice of him as
the subject of my final chapter, and that chapter I have divided into four
parts. The old troubadours of Languedoc serve as my fitting
introduction to Petrarch and Vaucluse; at Beaucaire we shall hear the
strains that northern minstrels brought into the southland; at Tarascon
and Aix we meet René himself; first in his great castle by the Rhone, and
then in his court at the capital, where little now remains of the beauty
and the culture with which he was surrounded except the glowing
colours upon some few canvases, and the wonders of the cathedral
architecture. Through all this runs a bright thread of romance; for every

lesser Dante dreamed of his Beatrice, every small Petrarch worshipped the Laura of his ideals. All over Provence lived ladies as famous for the "Gai savoir," for scientific lovemaking, as for their own attractions; alternately the theme of poems and the patronesses of the poetaster. Their names alone make a charming sound, like silver bells set all aswing upon a mellow summer evening.

Stéphanette, Adalazie, Mabille, and Jusserande, who from Les Baux and Avignon, from Hyères and from Claustral came to the merry-makings of Pierrefeu and of Signe; Clarette des Baux, Cécille de Caromb, Hugonne de Sabran, daughter of Forcalquier's Count, Isabelle des Berrilhans, Alaette of Aix, Elys of Meyrargues, these would meet at Romanin; at Avignon forgathered Béatrix d'Agoult, Jehanne des Baux, Doulce de Moustiers, Antonette de Cadenet, Rixende de Puyvert, and Blanche de Flassans, whom her friends called Blancaflour.

Perhaps I cannot begin better than by telling you the tale of one of them, and I will not spoil it yet by saying who she really was, or whom she really married, or what was the precise date of the occurrence; for you shall take her as typical of her fair predecessors, though happier than many of them, and her name shall be called Clémence. So now to the poet's words:—

In the old days there was a Count of Provence who was lame upon one leg and limped as he walked, because God made him so. But the beauty of his daughter Clémence was as the splendour and immensity of ocean. For though our rulers of Provence were sometimes poor, and sometimes lame, they had most marvellously lovely daughters who turned the hearts of more men than the very fairies; so this Lady Clémence was as a perfect ray of fine, light gold; and would that God would shed such rays on me Now the heir of the kingdom of the Franks had heard tidings of this lovely lady, and, being suddenly smitten with desire for her, had neither rest nor ease. But mark how often base suspicion lurks in the heart even of the highest. Listen while I tell the tale. The heir of the Franks had speedily sent down an embassy into Provence. So there was a feast, and the important question was asked and answered to the great joy of both sides; and then the ambassadors begged for private speech with the lady herself. So the oldest of them all took up his tale as follows:—

"Sweet Lady Clémence, clear star of the South, remember that every rose doth hide a thorn; and now we must not forget our behest to tell you something that will surely bring the blush to your cheek. Pray be not angry

with us that we do so. Well must you know that your good father, if we may venture with respect to say so, is a little lame. Ah! there is our difficulty; for you remember the old proverbs that by shoulder or by shoe a child takes after its parents; and that a badly grown boy can never be an emperor. Imagine, sweet lady, what the English would say—a malison upon them—if the children of the Queen of France were hump-backed or lame! So our lord, the prince, by way of guarantee that you are without bodily defect and may well hope for a healthy man child, desires that you should show yourself to us just as you were born."

Then that Provençal lady cried aloud: "Such insolence from a Franchimaud was only to be expected! Still, it shall never be said that any lady of Provence blushed to hear that she was badly made and yet refused to prove the contrary. Wait here till I return. Now chastity and modesty be my apparel!"

So, on that word, she moved like summer lightning from the hall. She cut her laces and untied her threads, and swiftly at her feet fell down her gown of royal brocade and velvet, until she wore nothing but the simple shift a bride wears on her wedding night. And so the girl in gentle dignity walked back to them, the heavenly graces of her lovely form all showing through the thin, transparent tissues as she passed in front of the ambassadors. Then the oldest of them all spoke out again.

"Fit for a king indeed, O lovely maid, a treasure for the throne and for all France! But deign to remember my lord's whole command. Let the star shine out without a cloud between, without a veil before! And think that my lord offers you his crown in guerdon." So, with a winning grace, with never an instant's more delay, the Lady Clémence unbound her long hair that drooped in heavy curls behind her, crying, "Never shall it be said that for a shift I lost the crown of France!" So in an instant fell that filmy veil from off her; and as the daystar shines upon the mountain top, the Venus of Arles shone suddenly upon them all. And each one wished he were the heir of the kingdom of the Franks. But there must be ever some who gain and some who lose, in the great game of Love, and beauty is like dew upon the rose. So every man and woman in Provence clapped their hands for joy of their sweet Lady Clémence, when they heard of her courage and her pride; for she that does no evil thinks none; and from Clémence, that star of loveliness, descended the long line of Valois kings.[2]

I fear that the ladies who inspired the majority of the Troubadours were not always as chaste or modest as Clémence, even if they were as fair. Whether the famous "Courts of Love" actually existed is not for me to determine. The name certainly corresponds to a tendency in society which is not inaccurately described by some such title. The influence on manners and morals thus exerted has been already touched upon occasionally, as lightly as such themes need ever be mentioned in these pages. But it is necessary now to realise something a little more accurate about a form of poetry which begins to be prominent at the end of the eleventh century and begins to die out at the end of the thirteenth. It can be traced back to earlier days, as it can be followed into later generations; but that is not my province. I have only to make clear that the chief inspirations of its sonnets and lyrics were drawn from what we should now call the illegitimate love of married women.[3] So bare and bold a statement needs explanation, even if it does not demand excuse. Both are comparatively simple.

The high-born lady of the late eleventh century lived a rather dull life, and conditions did not improve for her until the Renaissance. Her marriage usually represented nothing better than the union of two fiefs, or the amalgamation of two fortunes. Love entered into it so rarely, the woman was so frequently considered as nothing but the mother of the heir, that any chance case of real affection was seized upon at once by every bard as marvellous. By these outbursts, and by the affections of the commoner people who were able to give way to the dictates of their heart, the truth of love, as the highest mortal passion, was kept alive; and it was recognised that every woman, whatever her birth, might feel that passion. The conditions of noble wedlock gradually elevated the ideal of love above every circumstance of marriages that only emphasised the material benefits of conjugal union; and the irresistible fatality of the natural passion was sung in every phase of its manifestation, until it became the source of all perfection, mental, moral, or physical, in the lady and her knightly adorer. That she incurred grave risks in gratifying her affection was a leading principle in her lover's life. He tried to compensate her by his patience, by his discretion, his unbounded courtesy, his unstained valour, his ready self-sacrifice. Hope must be ever nearer to him than fulfilment; but his reward will ever be far greater than his deserts when it does come. His ideal was thus gradually and delicately drawn out into an infinity where time and space were of but little account, where an innumerable code of gallant precepts filled his life, and the thought alone of his beloved became more precious than the close comradeship of more material swains. His quest was certain of victory in the end, for love was irresistible. "Ask and it shall be given unto you." The woman; on the other hand; if she had read that "God is love," was also ready to believe that "Love is God." Married, she was the mere chattel of her husband; but she was her lover's queen. She could send him forth upon high enterprises, or she could listen to the outpouring of his art. She was sometimes too frail to resist the consequences of that perilous situation. But shall we cast a stone at her? Shall we not remember rather that, through the hazardous conventions of the extraordinary cult she wove around her shrine, the brutality of man was raised to a higher level than Provence had known since the Roman Empire. In arts, in language, in civilisation, France was bettered as a whole by the Troubadours. The cataclysm of blood that swept them from the valley of the Rhone, and plunged Provence into another night of barbarism, was the Albigensian Crusade, from which the Italians of Avignon were her chief deliverers.

The language of the Troubadours needs explanation as much as their point of view. Romance poetry, like the Romance languages, descends from the Latin; and the oldest poetry in Provence was no doubt directly taken, not from such models as Virgil, Catulius, Horace, and those who inherited the Hellenic metres, but from the popular Latin of the people which survived after the Goths had overwhelmed the "classic" authors in the ruins of the Roman Empire. This common speech lasted through various channels; its vocabulary was dignified by the liturgy of the Church, and amplified by the popular festivals. A better cradle for the youth of minstrelsy than the Valley of the Rhone and the Côte d'Azur could hardly be imagined. Its dazzling sun and glowing climate appealed as much to Byzantine governors of Marseilles as to Saracen conquerors of Narbonne or Arles or Carcassonne. The serenade of modern Spain is of extremely ancient ancestry; and when Raymond Bérenger (III) of Barcelona married Douce, the heiress of Provence at the beginning of the twelfth century, he must have found that many Moorish influences to which he was accustomed on one side of the Pyrenees had already made themselves felt upon the other. The value of Arabic literature must not therefore be forgotten. But it was not paramount. After the Romans came the Visigoths, who must have imported a genius instinctively Teutonic. Before the Romans, even before the Greeks and Phoenicians, there were Celts. The Celtic peoples are essentially poetic; and the interwoven patterns of the Book of Kells may perhaps be the reflection, in a different medium, of that complicated prosody and rhyme which tinged the compositions of the Celtic Troubadours. From these most ancient sources, then, Provençal poetry arose, influenced first by Celtic, then by Greek, then by Latin, then by Teutonic, and then by Arabic inspirations. As we have already seen, Provence was the most adaptable country in the world, and ever ready for some new thing. The sterner, slower men of the North were amazed at the versatility, the laxity, the broad-mindedness of the South. At last the various influences at work produced a definite result. The mingled notes of many nations, slowly harmonised throughout the ages, gathered to a resonant chord of melody; and, as was only natural, it was in connection with the most ancient rites of autochthonous religion that this melody was heard; it was at the festival of the spring in Aquitaine that the May songs and dances of the Troubadours first sounded.

Such solemn festivals as that of Christmas had been celebrated by the people, since before the Merovingian era, not with Latin hymns only, but with songs of a simple character, with carols in the vulgar tongue, with more daring efforts at satire or gross jesting, and, in the spring, with songs of love. The chorus, or refrain, was an essential sign of these popular songs. Those which were peculiarly adapted to May contained a conventional description of the spring; they were chiefly concerned with the young women, to whom the boys' thoughts lightly turned at such a season; there was a disregard of serious respectability, even of morals, which was excused as being a necessary part of the joyous abandonment to happiness and love appropriate to the month. The essential structure of the Troubadours' lyrics needs here no more definite delimitation.[4] The very prominence given to women, not only as subjects of songs, but as dancers in the festivals, is a dominant note in one as in the other. It was a prominence handed down to these May festivals from the pagan feasts of Venus, just as the Bacchanalia of Roman vineyards has lasted down to this day in the villages of Provence; and that prominence involved inevitably the supremacy of love, which was the keynote of the Troubadours' lyrics. It was at first a delighted expression of that imaginary emancipation from law and rule which was all the keener because it was recognised as only temporary. The Troubadours exalted it to the height of their undying fervour, to the summit of their infinite ideal; and Guilhem, ninth Duke of Aquitaine, was the first Troubadour; his granddaughter Eleanor was the first Troubadour-Queen of chivalry, of romance, of sentiment.

Eleanor had held her first court in Bordeaux. She then became a Queen of France, and after her divorce she became the queen of Henry II of England in 1152, and ruled domains that extended from the Tyne across the Channel to Normandy, Anjou, Maine, Brittany, and Touraine, and further south to Poitou, the Limousin, Gascony, Auvergne, Guienne. Before this second marriage she had gone to the Crusades with her first husband; and the mixture of romance and warfare thus acquired was never lost throughout her life. Among those who sang her praises in the Limousin was the lowly-born Bernard de Ventadour, whose verses even Petrarch deigned to praise; and her son was Richard Coeur de Lion, born in Beaumont Palace, Oxford, the English Troubadour-King, who once held, not inappropriately, the fief of Arles. I must follow out this pleasant byway of my subject no further, except to emphasise a fact, too often forgotten, that French was the spoken language of the cultivated Englishman until the middle of the fourteenth century, and therefore the development of Provençal poetry up to that date is of the deepest interest to us. But I must pass on to some of the poets of Provence. One that has never been forgotten was one of the earliest, who took part in the Crusades of 1147.

Geoffroy Rudel, Prince of Blaye, heard tidings, through the pilgrims of Antioch, of a beautiful Lady Mélissent of Tripoli. He crossed the sea, and after a long and stormy voyage he died in her arms, thanking Heaven that he had been allowed only to look upon her face. This pathetic story attracted the garrulous Nostradamus, from whom Uhland, in 1814, took many singular details for his ballad. Heine's imagination played round it with the subtly complex emotion of his own grim genius, and called the ghosts of the dead lovers from the tapestry of Blaye.

> *"Melisanda! teure Närrin,*
> *Du bist selber Licht und Sonne;*
> *Wo du wandelst, blüht der Frühling,*
> *Sprossen Lieb' und Maienwonne."*

It has appealed to Browning, to Swinburne, to Madame James Darmesteter,[5] to Carducci; and each has interpreted its sorrow and its self-sacrifice as seemed good to them. It inspired "La Princesse Lointaine" of Rostand in a different vein:—"Ma bonté n'est pas grande," he makes her say. "Non, mais tout simplement *je soigne ma légende.*"

The tale of Peire Vidal brings us nearer to the places we know in these chapters. His first love was Alazais, Viscountess of Marseilles, from whom he stole a kiss as she lay asleep in the hall, and when she woke and called for help he was soundly drubbed out of the castle. Then her good-natured husband met him at Les Baux and brought him back again to receive a formal present of the stolen kiss, and to amuse the careless viscount with his rhymes and antics. But Peire grew tired of waiting for a reward that never came, and Madame Alazais grew bored by repeated protestations in every kind of metre; so Vidal went westwards across the Rhone, and there his second flame was Louve de Peinaultier, who dwelt with her husband at Cabaret, near Carcassonne, about the year 1190. Desirous of proving the extent of his devotion to the "She-wolf," he dressed himself in a wolf's skin, and on the Black Mountains he was hunted in earnest by the shepherds and their dogs, and brought back half-dead and mangled to his lady-love. He died indeed in 1209, and though his unbalanced mind was full of eccentricities, he had the certain spark of genius. In spite of every frailty he achieved success; and his vigorous poems upon political subjects have lasted down to our own day, with his love-sonnets and his fantastic lyrics.

Raimbaut de Vacqueiras was another who sang at the feasts and tourneys of Les Baux and of Orange, for he was the favourite of Prince Guillaume des Baux, son of him who married Tiburge, heiress of Orange. This Guillaume came into his own in 1181, and Raimbaut de Vacqueiras was the Tyrtaeus of his constant quarrels with Raymond (V) of Toulouse. A poem on a tournament of the time at Les Baux has come down to us, describing the downfall of the Count of Beaucaire and of Barral of Marseilles. He wrote five idioms fluently in a single poem, to show that as many languages were necessary to do fit honour to his lady; but perhaps he is most famous in literature as having written the poem on a Genoese lady, in which Italian is first used as a literary language by a writer of distinction, about seventy-five years before Dante.[6] His famous "Carros," dedicated to the beautiful Beatritz de Monferrat, is said to have been imitated by Boccaccio, and to have suggested the "Trionfo d'Amore" to Petrarch. Certain it is that Raimbaut must himself have known Vaucluse, and we may well take Petrarch, the originator of modern literature, as the last of the Troubadours. Their influence was with him all his life, in a more human, more sympathetic sense than it is seen in Dante's mystic vision of his Beatrice. From the first moment when Petrarch met his Laura, her beloved image filled his heart and roused his highest gifts. He idealised and perfected that lyric poetry which was the natural form of those Troubadours' songs in which Dante recognised the spark of an immortal fire that should never be put out.

Raimbaut de Vacqueiras lived in the brief noon and perfect

blossoming of the old Provençal poetry which began with Duke William of Aquitaine, with Marcabru, with Bernart de Ventadorn, with Bertram de Bon, and went on through the years of Peire Vidal to Sordello, and so to the decadence of Guiraut Riquier at the end of the thirteenth century, of whom some ninety lyrics and sixteen epistles have been preserved. Through Dante and Petrarch it may be said that all modern lyric poetry descends from this Provençal stock, which had such vigorous offshoots in Spain, in Portugal, in Italy, in France, even in Germany. It was mainly due to two reasons that Provençal poetry died: to the Albigensian Crusade and to the absorption of Provence by France. It lasted in other countries long after Provence herself had ceased to be a separate nationality; and as the classic language of a certain style it inspired the poets of many nations to form a national language of their own. For its merits were largely those which have made Horace and the Hellenic writers the perfect and imperishable moulds of form; the "Émaux et Camées," as Théophile Gautier puts it, of the thought and expression of the world. Through this the rough life of the twelfth century was raised to something higher; and in Dante's "Paradiso" is the idealised culmination of the Troubadours' dream, the spiritualisation of the lady-mistress whose apotheosis is celebrated in such homage as no poet ever paid before.

Enough has been said in my chapter about Carcassonne to suggest the connection between the Albigensian "heresy" and what has been here explained of the Troubadours' theory of life and love. A certain laxity in morals was undoubtedly encouraged in the upper classes by the doctrines sung by their especial poets. It was also supposed to be fostered in the lower classes by those teachings of Manichaeism and the duality of principles, which were connected with the Albigensians. But the aristocracy of every age has assumed that all deviations from the path of virtue should be restricted to their own society; vice was not to be popularised by any coarse degeneracy in the unfashionable poor. Whatever the "seigneur" might do, the "villein" must at any rate obey his priest. So any freedom of thought in the vulgar, such as was encouraged by Albigensian preachers, would be strongly attacked both by the aristocracy and the Church. But the Church went further still, for the Albigensians were in favour of the text of the Bible; and since the only language in which that text could be translated from the original into Provençal was the language of the Troubadours,[7] all such translations were obviously encouraged by the special interest both of the poets and of the ladies to whom they chiefly sang. In time the poets gave more practical expression to their sympathies. The reading of the original text produced the invariable revulsion against priestly dogmas and interpretations which is visible (under similar conditions) in many other times and places. "God confound thee, Rome!" sang the Troubadour, Guilhem de Figueira, "thou draggest all who trust in thee into the bottomless pit. Thou forgivest sins for money..." Or again, "Ah! false and wicked clergy," cries another, "traitors, liars, thieves, and miscreants, your balance is gold and your pardons must be sought by silver..."

Obviously Rome could not allow this to go on unchecked; and her crusade against the Albigensian heretics was therefore inextricably involved with the repression of the dangerously eloquent singers who recklessly criticised the clergy and the Church in verses as glowing as those with which they sang the duties and the pains of love. The Pope might be indulgent to the exaggerations of a few poetasters or to the mistaken creed of some score love-lorn ladies; but this was going too far. Several nobles too were actually on the side of the Albigensian rabble: the ill-fated Vicomte de Béziers, the Counts of Toulouse, Foix, Béarn and Comminges, Guy de Cavaillon, and others, as we have seen. So the Church began to take a legitimate revenge by claiming such singers as Izarn, or Bishop Fulk of Marseilles, as her own champions. "In eight points," thunders the orthodox Izarn, recreant to his craft, but faithful to his creed, "have I convicted thee, obstinate heretic, and ere thou art delivered to the flames, take this to comfort thee at thy burning." The main authority for the horrible campaigns that devastated the south is an epic poem by an anonymous Troubadour, entitled "Aisos es la Cansos de la Crozada contr els Ereges d'Albeges." With the annihilation of the society which had furnished its chief patrons, the minstrelsy of the Troubadours vanished; and with it went the literature and the culture which it represented. The wintry centuries that followed do not seem to have made up, either by morality or prosperity, for their orthodox enthusiasm; and the feudal castles of the south remained till the Renaissance "bare ruin'd choirs, where late the sweet birds sang." The nightingales of Provence migrated to Italy and Spain.

Charles d'Anjou, who inherited Provence from the last Troubadour-Count Raymond Bérenger (IV), knew nothing of that Romance dialect which we now call Provençal, which expressed the nationality of the land up to 1245, and which lingered on until 1481. The name "Provençal" had at first been given, somewhat inaccurately, by Frenchmen from the north to the whole southern *Langue d'Oc*. It became attached to it for ever through its associations with the good King René, whose sympathies were more with Provence than with Anjou. After his death, after "the Rhone had fallen into the sea," and Provence had been incorporated into France, the language suffered many changes, and people, from the highest to the lowest, spoke strange mixtures of many tongues.[8] Important documents had to be registered in Provençal for the local courts and sent up to Paris translated into French. In 1790 it was decreed that the new code should be translated into Provençal, as was the case with other local idioms. The preservation of the Provençal dialect thus officially assisted was still further assured by the work of the historian and philologist, Raynouard of Brignoles, in the department of the Var. That work was given wider recognition by his admission to the Academy as perpetual secretary in 1808; and when M. Villemain made his speech on the award of the Prix Montyon by the Academy to Jasmin, in 1852, the salvation of the old Provençal by Raynouard was very properly remembered. Through him, and through many of his successors, besides Jasmin, the language was preserved. But it remained for others to give it that vital touch which was inevitable as soon as its possibilities as a spoken, written vehicle of modern thought were fully realised.

To Roumanille and the Félibres that realisation is chiefly due. In 1855 appeared their first organ, *L'Armana prouvençau*. In 1859 was published Mistral's *Mirèio*. In 1876 the laws and statutes of the society called the "Félibrige" were put in writing. The *Revue Félibréenne* was soon as popular in Paris as in Provence; and *La Romania*, published by Paul Meyer and Gaston Paris, gave at once the stamp of the highest scholarship to the new movement. Fortunately the Renaissance of Provence was not allowed to degenerate into a fashionable Parisian fad. The poems I have quoted here and there throughout these pages are sufficient to prove that the local pride in local characteristics—which is the firmest buttress of a great nation's strength—has been worked out among the appropriate surroundings of local enthusiasm and love. The magnificent Provençal dictionary, in which Mistral enshrined the language he has done so much to make immortal, is the best proof that his poems are a true and sincere reflection of his people and his own country. The centre of the movement of which he is still the head was Avignon. One of its loveliest and most ancient shrines has ever been Vaucluse.

NOTES

1. "Ah! where are those good comrades now, those Troubadours who were the pastmasters of Love! To you, spendthrifts that you are, and sons degenerate of an illustrious stock, scarcely one spark remains of that great furnace of the Love of ancient days."—MISTRAL.

2. See "La Princesso Clemènço" in Mistral's *Isclo d'Or*, of which I do not like to call this a translation; it is rather a version of the tale in the form given it by the poet of Maillane. Students who insist on knowing accurately who people are may like to see, in "La Princesso Clemènço," that Margaret who was daughter to "Charles le Boiteux," Charles II of Anjou, Naples, and Provence, who was the son of Beatrix, Countess of Provence, and of Charles d'Anjou, the brother of St. Louis. Charles II married Mary, daughter of Stephen of Hungary, and had children: Philip of Tarentum; Charles Martel of Hungary; John, Duke of Durazo; Robert of Anjou, Naples, and Provence; Blanche, who married James II of Aragon; Eleanor, who married Frederick of Sicily; and Margaret, whom I take to be this Clémence, who married Charles of Valois, son of Philip III of France, brother of Philip IV, uncle of Philip V, and father of Philip VI. The father of Clémence died in 1309. Her husband died in 1325, and his son, Philip VI, succeeded to the throne of France in 1328; his daughter Mary married her cousin Charles, the son of Robert of Anjou, Naples, and Provence, and their daughter was the famous Queen Jeanne with the four husbands.

3. See Gaston Paris, in *Romania*, xii. p. 518, and elsewhere.

4. See Gaston Paris, *Origines*, p. 46, etc.

5. Now Madame Duclaux.

6. I believe the first appearance is recognised in the four rhymed lines in the Cathedral of Ferrara in 1133; and there is also a rude song by a Tuscan joglar before Raimbaut de Vacqueiras. Soon after him are found the Cantilena Bellunese, four lines composed in 1195; and between that and the famous hymn of St. Francis of Assisi there is only the fragmentary poem from Monte Cassino. See Justin H. Smith, *The Troubadours at Home*, i. 414.

7. The earliest translation known of five chapters of St. John's Gospel (probably for liturgical use) is one made in Provençal in the middle of the twelfth century. See J. H. Smith; also the last chapter in J. F. Rowbotham's *The Troubadours and Courts of Love*.

8. Philologists who like to trace such matters may sift the Latin, Romance, French, and Provençal out of the following letter, written by King René, in July 1468, to Jean Allardeau, Bishop of Marseilles: "*De par le Roi*. Moss. de Marsella e mon compère. Da parte d'alcuni poveri homini a moi e stato humilmente supplicato comep la supplicatione loquale qui interclusa ve mandamo chiaramente intenderete

di alcuno loro errore e fallimento. Et considerato sono homi maritimi et che hanno de gli altri carrighi assai, ove cognoscerete sia coso di pieta per quanto tocha a moi volemo loro sia in vostra Guardia. Dots al ponte sey lo vi giorno de jullet de l'anno MCCCCLXVIII."

Here is an extract from the Registers of the Estates of Provence under King René, on October 9, 1473: "Le nom de nostre Senhor Dieu J. C. et de la siena gloriosa mayre e de tota la santa cort celestial envocant loqual en tota bona et perfecta obra si deu envocar, car del procesit tot bon et paciffié estament del tres que hault et tres que excellent prince et senhor nostre lo rey Regnier per la gracia de Dieu rey de Jérusalem, de Aragon, de ambos la Sicilias, de Valencia, de Sardenha et de Corsega,duc d'Anjo et de Bar, Comte de Barcelona et de Provensa, de Forcalquier et de Piémont. Thuision deffension de aguest sieu pays de Provensa ev de Forcalquier; et confusion et destruction de ses ennemis..."

Finally I may quote (from Henri Oddo, who preserves these typical extracts) the letter of a rich farmer's son at the end of the fifteenth century: "Senhe payre à vous de bon car mi recoumandi, la present es per vous avisar como yeu ay resaput vostra letro en laqual mi mandas del cap de Besonhos, yeu ay resaput ma raubo ambe mas canupas, calcuno libres...Et tot vostre emble fils Peyron Bonpar."

Part II: Vaucluse

"Non era l'andar suo cosa mortale,
Ma d'angelica forma, e le parole
Sonavan altro che pur voce umana."
— PETRARCH, sonn. 69.

ON a fine spring morning there are few more lovely expeditions in Provence than the drive to Vaucluse from Avignon. Leaving the Hotel de l'Europe, you pass the old ramparts of the city and its newer walls, until a turning to the right, near some tram lines beneath a railway bridge, brings you to the long Marseilles Road, all fringed with trees. Large milestones, with the magic name of "Vaucluse" inscribed upon them, soon begin to point the right way forward to the east along a level country that lies between Rhone, Durance, Ouvèze, and the many branches of the Sorgues; a well-watered land, fertilised by constant streams and warmed by the Provençal sun; where the prosperous country houses have each their little avenue of shade that leads from the front door to the fine main road along which your carriage rolls so easily.

For some ten kilometres the direction has been rather south of west, to avoid the hills around which are built Caumont, Châteauneuf, St. Saturnin, and Morières. But at the bridge on your right, called Pont de Bonpas, which carries the main road from Paris over the Durance to Marseilles, the route goes slightly northwards along the right bank of the river, upstream; and on your left are the ruins of an old castle, with machicolated towers and huge buttresses that rise from the last rocky ramparts of the hill that slopes down from the north. A little further on is a row of queer little dwellings hollowed out of the rock itself, with doors and windows carved in the living stone; and so you reach the village of Caumont, where a telegraph-post, marked with a plate of blue metal, shows the turning to the north and east that leads on towards Thor. Upon the slopes above the road is what looks like a deserted hamlet, with empty cottages that cluster round a deserted steeple. Near them are some brickworks and a number of tiny manufactories of tiles. On the other side of the road, to the right, is Pieverde, the spot where Laura was born.[1]

By degrees, in the distance to the north, appear the villages of Gadagne and Châteauneuf, with their church and castle perched on the very verge of the hill, and standing out against the sky. This is well seen from the stone that marks the third kilometre on the road from Caumont, and on the next hill in the northern distance, but more eastward, are the ruins called "Thouzon," where are grottoes in the rock. Two kilometres further on, the road, which has already crossed the railway, turns somewhat sharply to the right and develops into the long, straight avenue of trees that leads to Thor. On your left appears the fine old wall and gate of the town, with its clock and bell-tower, and the motto "Taurum Stella Ducit" beneath a bust of Pierre Goujon d'Alcantara, the founder of free public schools in France, who died in 1840. Still taking turns to the right, whenever there is a choice, you find yourself at last on a long level stretch of highway pointing a little south of east, and the mountain slopes of Mont Ventoux begin to show clearly on the horizon straight ahead, slopes that gradually show up as a huge white cliff, with a vast cauldron-shaped cleft in its centre.

The next village is L'Isle, "the island," on the Sorgue, to which another ingratiating avenue of trees welcomes the dusty traveller, with the railway on his right hand. This is twenty-one kilometres from Avignon, and the waters of the river Sorgue begin to be the dominant feature in the picture, for "L'Isle" is like a little Venice full of water-wheels, which drip and murmur softly in the pleasant air as you pass the Hotel St. Martin, and the gendarmerie, towards the statue of the Virgin, where yet another avenue of trees begins that leads to smiling country set with green meadows and watered with whispering streams. Past a stone obelisk and another bridge, the highway turns to the right, and you face eastwards again for that mysterious cauldron that has grown clearer in the cliff. About four kilometres from L'Isle, the road seems to dip downwards, and there is a perceptible rise in the general temperature of the air, as you pass beneath a huge stone aqueduct with a foaming stream beneath it. Now the carriage follows the banks of a little river, of singularly clear water, bluish-green; and the rocks, of a strange striated limestone, close in on either hand. A little further down—or rather up the stream—between these narrowing cliffs that will be green with vines and olive-trees, the "Vallis Clausa" ends in a high grey cliff; and before you reach the cliff itself, the level ground on each side of the highway opens out for the buildings of the hamlet of Vaucluse. The water-wheels are turning everywhere. On one side is a tiny church. On the other is a delightful little inn (named from the twin divinities), where trout and asparagus rejoiced our hearts after a long drive, and where we rested before wandering into fairyland beyond.

And fairyland it is. Vaucluse, with all its memories, can never be desecrated or vulgarised. There are the usual attempts to do so. But they fail. Nature herself is here on too grand a scale. Man has left here too poignant traces of immortal passion and undying love. The syllables of Petrarch and the sighs of Laura are on every breeze. Theirs are the images reflected in the crystal surface of that mysterious pool which wells from the deep heart of the mountain and pours forth its everlasting streams through the cascades of the young river towards the village of Vaucluse. It is a symbol of love and life; of love deep-seated in the elements that make the world, rising with strength irresistible towards the sunlight; foaming through the first years of youth and ardour, flowing at last with ordered stillness, turning the water-wheels of traffic and of commerce, but never losing the heaven-blue of its source, the undying, fundamental power that shapes and sways the universe.[2]

It is but a few minutes' walk from the church of Vaucluse to the fountain which wells out of the heart of the limestone cliff to make the river Sorgue. On the way you must turn aside for a moment to the right, where, near the traces of an old Roman aqueduct, tunnelled through the heart of the rock, is a garden that may have been Petrarch's garden, and a laurel that may have sprung from one he planted. A little further on, after you return to the path that follows up the course of the swift stream, you see the ruins of a castle, perched high on the ragged shoulder of a cliff. It was the home of Petrarch's friend, Philippe de Cabassole, who was born in this district in 1305.

The young Philippe, educated by the clergy of Cavaillon, was made archdeacon and provost of that town in 1333, and created a bishop the next year by Pope John XXII. By Robert of Anjou he was made chancellor to the duchess, and at the duke's death he became guardian of his granddaughter, the famous Queen Jeanne, to whose court at Naples he was eventually obliged to go; and there he stood sponsor, for the Pope, to the son of Jeanne and of Andrew of Hungary. His integrity, sound learning, and talent for diplomacy were good reasons for the many delicate missions with which he was entrusted by the Pope, and in 1359 he was made Patriarch of Jerusalem. He was Vicar of Avignon and the Venaissin in the absence of Urban V at Rome, and in 1368 was raised to the dignity of cardinal. By Gregory XI he was sent as legate into

Italy, and died in Perugia in 1372, but was brought back to be buried at the Chartreuse of Bonpas, whence his body was solemnly transferred to the church of Caumont in 1833.

The friendship of such a man with Petrarch, who appreciated his modesty as much as his real talents, is easily intelligible. Cabassole's château above the fountain of Vaucluse was his by right of the seigneur, as Bishop of Cavaillon, and here Petrarch first met him, about the year 1338, in the beginning of a friendship which death alone was to sever. Their correspondence shows a long-continued intimacy equally appreciated by both; and while the poet sometimes ascended to the château to talk over those political affairs with which both friends were so well acquainted, the diplomatist often came down to the garden beside the waters of the Sorgue where Petrarch told and retold that story of his love which no man could hear unmoved. It is a pleasant thought, in that beautiful spot, to remember this pair of cultivated men, the dreamer and the worker, talking over their hopes, or reading verses to each other. As Petrarch once wrote to Cabassole :—

> *"Valle locus clausa toto mihi nullus in orbe*
> *Gratior, et studiis aptior ora meis."*

> (No place is dearer to me and better
> for my studies than Vaucluse)

Petrarch was just one year older than his friend, and was born in Arezzo, in August 1304. Expelled, as Dante was, by the political troubles of his country, he took refuge in the Venaissin, and first studied at Carpentras. After spending so much of his life in the Vaucluse country, he died, like Cabassole, in Italy.

> *"There is a tomb in Arqua—reared in air,*
> *Pillared in their sarcophagus, repose*
> *The bones of Laura's lover: here repair*
> *Many familiar with his well-sung woes*
> *The pilgrims of his genius. He arose*
> *To raise a language, and his land reclaim*
> *From the dull yoke of her barbaric foes:*
> *Watering the tree which bears his lady's name*
> *With his melodious tears, he gave himself to fame."*

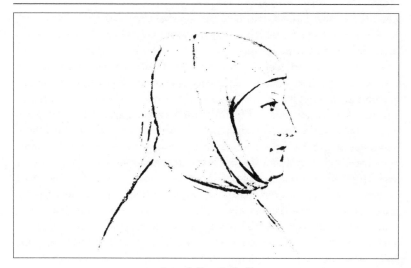

Petrarch (Jane E. Cook)

Of all the life that lay between these two events, it is the burning episode of Laura's love that haunts the memory longest. The patron of the word's literature before he reached middle age, beloved by his contemporaries, and having nothing left to ask from material ambitions, Petrarch poured out his whole genius upon his one affection; and we actually know very little of the details of his personal life, and so little of the truth about his Laura that the most incredible legends have for long passed current about them both. Without going outside the actual words he left behind him, chiefly in his own hand-writing, it will be possible to draw some slight sketch of the man, and of his love, which may be incomplete but will at all events be based upon no fanciful hypotheses. He was a man as other men, in spite of being a clerk in holy orders. Marriage might be forbidden him by public opinion, yet in the Avignon whose vices he was swift to censure, he had himself left two illegitimate children. But the highest and the best of him was Laura's; and that tie was the only one that ever bound her heart or body. Her continued chastity, which lasted till her early death, was but a reflection of that eminently religious caste of mind which he so often describes in her; it was probably her strongest attraction to him; and it has given her immortality.

"My body," writes Petrarch, "in my younger years was remarkable not so much for strength as for dexterity in many ways. I do not boast of any excellence of figure, beyond what might be pleasing to those of greener years. I was of vivid complexion, between fair and dusky, with lively eyes, and sight which remained extremely keen for many years, and unexpectedly failed me after my sixtieth year, so that I had reluctantly to have recourse to spectacles. Old age came upon a body always healthy, and surrounded it with the usual array of ailments."[3]

Laura must have had a surname in her life, but she attained immortality without one. The only thing I feel sure about it is that it was never changed. From a certain punning habit of her lover's, it has been suggested that it was de Sole. No one can contradict that. From Petrarch's own writings we find that she was born "at the foot of some hills," on the way from Avignon to Vaucluse, in a countryside, in a tiny spot that scarcely seemed to deserve so great a glory. Professor Flamini, from a study of Francesco Galeota's sonnet, fixes this spot near Caumont, at the place called Pieverde, "between two rivers," the Sorgue and the Durance. Here, too, she lived all her life; and the greenness of the grass surrounding her "Pieverde" is very frequently mentioned by her poet, who evidently noticed its contrast to the arid plains of Avignon. Innumerable references to the country occur in almost every description of their meeting. She is "seated on the grass," for instance; she is followed through a meadow and a wood; she sometimes sat on a large stone, or beneath a tree, and in that calm atmosphere there were many violets in their season. She often took off her shoes, which left her feet bare. On one occasion Petrarch saw her bathing; on another she was sitting "like a flower in the grass." From high ground near Vaucluse her residence was visible, "near yet far-off." The poet can see, from his mountain-spur, "the sweet plain where she was born," and longs once more (after her death) to see "her tresses loosened to the breeze." Her house was near grass and water and young trees, in a shady place—but it is needless to emphasise the fact that Petrarch never thinks of her or speaks of her as either having been born or having lived in Avignon, or any other town. The very different terms in which he sometimes speaks of her abode do not imply anything except a reference to her circumstances and surroundings. The "dark and vile prison," the "mean drudgery" of her life, the "rose born in harsh briars," the "unworthy environment," the coarse place of her residence compared to the humility of her lover's heart, the "treasure in the mud"—all these things refer to the somewhat squalid farmhouse of her birth and upbringing. She was not rich, and she came of no rich or famous family.

Petrarch first met her at six in the morning on a Good Friday, when he was twenty-three. His heart took fire like tinder as her golden hair was twisted by the breezes into a thousand pretty knots, while she walked about in the grass and talked, wearing a green dress with violets at her bosom. Caring little for mere conventionalities ("fera"), she sometimes scattered her hair, and then most winsomely gathered it up. But she was careful of the proprieties too ("onesta"), though only sixteen at that first meeting in the April of the year, and the April of their lives. Purer than a white dove, she bound her lover fast "with words and nods," and their courtship lasted, untainted, for one and twenty years. This surely means that the legend of the meeting in the Church of Ste. Claire at Avignon must be abandoned. That legend depends chiefly upon a note found soon after Petrarch's death in the copy of Virgil he usually carried with him. But Mr. E. J. Mills has pointed out that not only is the handwriting of this note not Petrarch's, but it contains statements which he has himself contradicted, apart from the main incongruity of the description of the first meeting I have just given, out of his own writings, with the surroundings of a church interior in Avignon on a Good Friday morning. The time and place of her burial, for instance, and her lover's knowledge of her death, are not given in this note as they are described in writings we know to be Petrarch's; nor is the "Ludovicus" mentioned in it (who is Lombardo de Serico, nicknamed "Socrates," his confidential secretary) likely to have brought a mere "rumour" of a death which he saw "with his own eyes" (Petr., Ecl., X.) and of which he gave the minute particulars recorded in the "Triumph of Death." The note was probably added, soon after Petrarch's death, by this secretary. It would be considered a pious duty. It would also add to the value of the Virgil, and, as Mr. Mills has mercilessly observed, "Petrarch died in Lombardo's debt."

Laura herself, says her lover, had exquisitely white skin, and on her cheeks the tender red "of roses plucked by virgin hands." Her large and brilliantly black eyes were of a singular purity beneath black lashes, often downcast, and golden hair. Though living in poor conditions, she was of an old family, precocious in wisdom and intelligence, apt in conversation, a sweet singer, serene and fearless in temperament, and of a religious disposition which increased as she grew more delicate when years went on. Averse from the idea of marriage, she cared little for "society," and was happy in her solitude, or with the friends around her. That she must have been unknown in Avignon is clear from Cardinal Colonna's letter (which cannot have been "merely malicious") inquiring whether the Laura of the poet's verses really existed, or was but an imagination of the writer. "You say," replies Petrarch, "that I have forged some fantastic name of Laura, so that there may be a woman for me to talk about, and for whose sake many will speak of me, while as a matter of fact the only 'Laura' is the Laurel of Poetry...my verses are a sham, my sighs, pretence...yet you know my pallor, and my pain. Your letter is an insult to my sorrow." No stronger terms are needed to show how real Laura was, and how far she lived from Avignon. It is worth considering, too, whether Petrarch spoke enough French to make himself understood, as intimately as he must have done, to any but an Italian exile like himself. The colour of her hair and eyes suggests that Laura was Italian. Of her face we can now get no clearer vision than of Beatrice's, of many another woman who swayed the hearts of men, so unintelligibly yet so certainly. The two portraits, said to be of Laura, in the Avignon Museum are utterly apocryphal. We know that Simone Memmi painted her; on the porch of Notre Dame des Doms, on the façade of Santa Maria Novella at Florence, in the church of the Angels at Siena, in the palace of Benedict XII at Avignon, in the miniature he exchanged with his friend Petrarch for two sonnets. The drawing here reproduced is based on the portrait in the Laurentian Library, the most

*Laura (From a drawing by Jane E. Cook after the original
in the Laurentian Library, Florence)*

authentic now discoverable, and the most accordant with what Petrarch describes of her life and characteristics.

It was natural that some great family in Avignon should at some time or other, have claimed her as of their stock. There may well have been a Laura de Noves, who married a de Sade, but she was not Petrarch's love. No phrase or word that Petrarch ever used of her is used exclusively of married women. But in his repetition of such words as "casta," "pudica," "onesta," especially of "santa," I can only see the ecclesiastic's description of virginity, not the mere acknowledgement that a wedded wife was never unfaithful to her vows, a wife, too, who (if de Sade be correct) had sealed her union with the pledges of eleven children. Are we to believe that any wealthy husband, even in papal Avignon, would have permitted a courtship of twenty-one years with a poet who was known to have had two illegitimate children in that city, and whose only "return" (to use the fashion of that day) could have been the poetry which reached its highest value after all concerned were dead? Is it not easier to understand that a woman of Laura's religious temperament, valuing, as she would, the religious profession of Petrarch, must have invariably refused him either marriage or illicit love?[4]

Laura died in 1348, and was buried beneath "a few stones," in "a petty grave" ("poca fossa") probably beside that road still called the "Chemin des Morts" at Caumont, near the little chapel of St. Sebastien, and opposite to the farmhouse where she had lived.[5] She died victorious, to the last, over the promptings of his passion and her own. "I' non son forse chi tu credi," she had said once, and, after the first few years of struggle, Petrarch believed and honoured her. "The little that I am," he writes, "she made me. Whatever reputation or glory be mine would never have come to me if the weak seedling of virtue placed by nature in my heart had not grown up and blossomed in that noble love of hers...She drew me from the society of the base; she guided me in all my ways; she spurred my tiring Muse, and roused my fainting spirit."

> *"Basso desir non è ch' ivi si senta,*
> *Ma d'onor di virtute. Or, quando mai*
> *Fu per summa belta vil voglia spenta?"*

In a time when the morals of Italians may be judged from the tales of Petrarch's friend, Boccaccio, when Avignon itself was filled with the debauchery of which a corrupt and luxurious papal court was the centre,

Petrarch was himself not altogether unspotted from the world. But Laura kept him from falling any further; and at what a cost can be imagined[6] only by those who heard that passionate voice reading, from his very soul, the eloquent lines that have expressed the pain of lovers from his time for ever, in the innumerable turns of phrase, in the exquisitely modelled cadences of the language he was the first to forge into so subtle and so beautiful an instrument of thought. Her gentle spirit lingers still where it was wont to inspire the poet of Vaucluse, though, as he wrote after her death, "a dark night is now falling on those hills from which her flight to heaven was taken, upon those meadows where her eyes did make the day."

NOTES

1. Most probably. As will be seen, I reject the theory that she was the wife of a De Sade, and the mother of eleven children, or that Petrarch first met her in a church at Avignon. A study of the text, in which Petrarch gives all the details we shall ever know, inclines me to believe that the interpretation of E. J. Mills *(The Secret of Petrarch,* 1904) is in the main the most probable yet published. Though there is much in the book with which I cannot agree, the main conclusions are fortified by the latest researches of M. de Nolhac of Versailles and others mentioned in my preface.

2. Nothing better has been written about the physical characteristics of the Pool of Vaucluse than the seventh chapter of Charles Lenthéric's splendid second volume of *Le Rhône,* pp.174-265.

3. For this and other extracts see Edmund James Mills, and Lenthéric's *Le Rhône,* vol. ii. p. 258, etc.

4. As a matter of fact there is every indication that she may have considered herself physically unfit to marry any one, apart from any other considerations. For there are many allusions to some internal trouble that the medicine of those days would not have been able to diagnose. She evidently died of the effect of a chill on a constitution already thus enfeebled. The story of the plague is as unfounded a legend as the marriage and the rest. The very full description of her last illness and death, as given by Petrarch himself, makes it utterly impossible either that the plague caused her death or that she was buried in Avignon. She was buried where she was born, at Pieverde, and the touching coincidence may well be true, that she died at six on the Good Friday of 1348, exactly on the twenty-first anniversary of her first meeting with Petrarch.

5. *"Carpe iter hac qua nodosis impexa capistris*

Colla boum, crebrasque canum sub limine parvo
Videris excubias, gilvosque ad claustra molossos.
Ille locus tua damna tegit; jamque aspice contra,
Hic Galatea sita est, qua nil Natura creavit
Pulchrius in terris..."

(Journey this way, where the necks of oxen
Are tied with knotted halters and you may see any watching dogs
At a small doorway and brown molossian dogs at the enclosure.
This place covers what you have lost; behold, here Galatea
Is buried, than whom Nature created nothing
Lovelier on earth)

A passage which may be taken in its literal meaning of Laura's grave, from Petrarch's Eleventh Eclogue. [Laura was buried at the church of the Franciscans. The knotted halters of the oxen symbolise their rope belts with three knots for poverty, chastity and obedience; the watching dogs their vigilance and the molossian dogs their brown habits].

6. *"Nullis mota precibus,"* he writes, *" nullis victa blanditiis, muliebrem tenuit decorem, et adversus suam simul et meam aetatem, adversus multa et varia quae flectere adamantinum licet spiritum debuissent, inexpugrabilis et firma permansit."* (Moved by no prayers, overcome by no flattery, she retained her womanly propriety and despite her and my own youth, despite many different factors which ought to have swayed her adamantine spirit, she remained unconquerable and resolute)

Part III: Beaucaire

"Dox est li cans, biax est li dis,
Et cortois et bien asis,
Nos hom n'est si esbahis,
Tant dolans ni entrepris,
De grant mal amaladis,
Se il l'oit, ne soit garis,
Et de joie resbaudis,
Tant par est douce."[1]
AUCASSIN AND NICOLETE.

THE traveller in Provence will probably first see Beaucaire from the eastern (or left) bank of the Rhone as he looks across the river from Tarascon. If he is wise he will cross the bridge without delay, and almost the first thing he will notice is the opening of the great canal that leads from the Rhone to Aigues-Mortes. Then he will see, further upstream on the western shore, the famous fields in which is still held the phantom of what was once the greatest fair in all the south of France; and above all are the towers and battlements of the château; the walls where Aucassin was shut fast in prison because of his love for Nicolete. That love-story I shall tell here, for it has been told as well as the story of Vaucluse, though in far smaller space, and to me it has always been the central and abiding interest of Beaucaire. But there are other things that may be quickly mentioned first, for Beaucaire has a history of its own that goes back to Rome, and forward to the present day; and in its beautiful Hôtel de Ville you may see the best monument of its more modern chronicles.

This Hôtel de Ville should be the first aim and object of your little pilgrimage, for it is a pleasant walk there, and any one will tell you how to reach it. But I must not linger over the beauties of its Renaissance architecture, its charming courtyard, its dignified staircase, its exquisitely decorated windows that look out upon a busy little market square where they sold us asparagus and fresh peas on the twelfth of April, onions, leeks, and garlic, cheese, and cakes. From here we passed along the Rue du Château towards the hill on which the castle stands. That hill has been pierced by the new street out of the town, so that it is now difficult to realise the wide extent of the original castle walls; but from the top of the high donjon you may understand it, and as you pass up the stone steps into the beautiful garden that the township of Beaucaire has made within those ancient battlements, the fleurs-de-lys of France are growing in a wild profusion on every slip of terrace, guarded by formal trees of yew and box, clipped into round or oval shapes. They stand side by side with taller pines that clothe the sloping hill, and the eye is carried downwards to the strong curves of the Rhone flowing in the distant haze, where a great barge swings in the mighty current of the river and gropes to her anchorage along the quays below the bridge.

The red roofs of the town seem to cluster close beneath the castle-walls as you look down on them; and in the castle-courtyard, with its ancient well of water set fairly in the midst, the roses—tiny yellow roses in a shower of blossom—cover every space of grey stone with a spray of gold. On this side of the river is a small church spire, copied from the larger spire of St. Martha on the eastern shore. Close beside you is that little gem, the chapel of Beaucaire, to which a stairway leads from the lower outworks, crowned by a "Gate of Honour," the last remnant that is left of the castle that Aucassin knew.

The ancient site of Beaucaire was the Ugernum of the Romans, where Avitus was proclaimed Emperor in 455, where St. Césaire, Bishop of Arles, was imprisoned in 528. The fortress that stood where the ruined castle still remains was given by Theodobert, grandson of Clovis, to Gontran, King of Burgundy and Arles, in 503. It was pillaged by the Goths in 585, and disappears from history till the beginning of the eleventh century. By that time "Ugernum" had become "Bellicadrum," the "lovely place," Beaucaire; and the first mention of Beaucaire in documentary evidence is the division recorded of the possessions of Bérenger, Count of Narbonne, who died in the year after William the Conqueror had won at Hastings. To his son, Raymond, Beaucaire was ceded in 1067, and the castle was fairly begun on the ruins of the old Roman fort. After the quarrel between the two sisters, Stephanette and Douce, Countess of Provence, Beaucaire was allotted to the Count of Toulouse; and in 1168, during his seigneury, occurs the first mention of the famous fair which was held for so many centuries afterwards, from the 22nd to the 28th of July, and flourished on the privileges granted by nearly every seigneur or French king who succeeded. In 1174 Beaucaire was the scene of an ostentatious display of pageantry, very much like the

Field of the Cloth of Gold later on, to celebrate the truce made between Raymond (V) of Toulouse and his enemy the King of Aragon, at the instance and mediation of Henry II of England. Money was literally "thrown about," for one Bertrand Raimbaud had the fields near the Castle ploughed, and then sown with crown-pieces. Guillaume Gros de Martel cooked all the meat on his estate at once by the light of wax candles in his kitchen. Raymond de Venous was cruel enough to burn thirty of his horses to show how many more he had left in his stables. This Count of Toulouse died in 1194 at Nîmes. His son and heir, the sixth Raymond, married the English Princess Jeanne, and we have heard of him already in speaking of the Albigensian Crusades at Carcassonne. At the partition of the plunder, Beaucaire, which had been previously granted in fief to Simon de Montfort by the Archbishop of Arles, and was no doubt thereafter considered as his property, was reserved by papal decree as part of the inheritance of young Raymond (VII) of Toulouse; and when the heir came back to Provence from an interview with the Pope, he forthwith set about claiming Beaucaire by force of arms in 1216, and was hailed as their rightful sovereign by all the people of the district.

The siege that followed is the first serious military operation with which Beaucaire was connected. Raymond, a boy of about nineteen, whose address in arms was only equalled by his personal courage and brilliant popularity, first threw himself into the town, which was entirely on his side, and then attacked the castle which was garrisoned by Lambert de Limoux for Simon de Montfort. Refusing all terms of surrender, Lambert held out manfully against every assault until he seemed likely to be reduced by sheer famine, both of food and water. Then Guy and Amaury de Montfort moved to his help, and the mighty Simon himself brought up reinforcements to the help of the fortress-key of Languedoc. Then began a siege within a siege; for while Raymond furiously attacked the castle, his own lines in the town were straitly harassed by de Montfort's men outside. The usual barbarities of that time were perpetrated on both sides; but young Raymond continued to hold the advantage of better lines of communication and an inexhaustible commissariat. The black flag, raised as a signal of despair upon the castle keep, urged de Montfort to extraordinary efforts; but his mines were destroyed by the men of Beaucaire, who were inspired to continuous gallantry by the zeal and courage of their young leader. A sortie from the town ended in a regular pitched battle, after which both sides retired to their own lines in good order. The black flag rose once more, and de Montfort made another attempt. Drawing out young Raymond's forces by a feint attack he strove to envelop him on both flanks; but the Count of Toulouse, helped by Dragonet, his governor, and by Raimond de Rabastens, his bravest knight, still held his own, and neither side could claim a victory. De Montfort then sent a "forlorn hope" of a hundred picked warriors to attack one gate of the town while

The Chapel of the Castle of Beaucaire

he made a demonstration himself at the other side of the walls, opposite Tarascon. But neither succeeded. Then a message came that the heroic garrison of the castle had killed their last horse, and had eaten nothing for thirty-six hours. Simon was compelled to capitulate, and withdraw to Nîmes; and the honour of having beaten that experienced and sturdy general on almost the only occasion of his defeat rested with young Raymond at Beaucaire. The renown of that exploit no doubt spread to the north of France, and may well have inspired the chivalrous figure of Aucassin in the famous poem I shall shortly describe.

Young Raymond married Sancia, daughter of the King of Aragon, and by her visit to Nîmes in 1218 that town was also rescued from de Montfort's power; and four years afterwards the fortunes of that strange family began to fall, in Provence at any rate. Their possessions were ceded, as far as Amaury de Montfort could cede anything, to Louis VIII, King of France, to whom the citizens of Beaucaire did homage during his siege of Avignon. St. Louis, the next king, confirmed the royal tenure, which was never again to lapse while royalty endured; and by him the castle and its fortifications were put in the state which can still be traced in the ruins now visible. He built the famous triangular keep which may be visited today, and he dedicated the lovely little chapel to the Virgin Mary for the worship of the royal garrison. These matters were probably arranged during the king's visit in 1248, when he stopped at Beaucaire on his way to embark at Aigues-Mortes for the Crusades. In the next year "Young Raymond" died. Beaucaire, in future, was to be in much the same position towards Tarascon, as was Villeneuve to Avignon: the king's town as against the independent city—the city of the Pope in one case, and of René of Provence in the other. Before we leave Beaucaire the independent, before it is merged into the Kingdom of France, we must look a little more closely at the castle and the life within it, as we may imagine it towards the close of the twelfth century and the beginning of the thirteenth.

At that time the average population was very much what it is today. But the life was simpler, and the simple needs of the majority were provided for by a far smaller cultivation of the soil than is now visible. The forests were therefore far larger, and much more land was lying waste, nor was a man very safe as he fared across the countryside, for the protections and privileges of the towns extended but a little space beyond their walls, and scattered castles were as often nests of robbers as harbours of refuge. The barons, too, were frequently at war with one another; and when they were at peace their mercenaries kept the road on their own account, and became bands of "routiers," or freebooters, whose highest development we have seen when du Guesclin held the Pope himself to ransom. Trade, however, was better managed than might sometimes be imagined, and shared with religion a regularity of control and a strictness of observance that are not often realised in histories of that time, though they are evident from countless little hints in the original documents of the period. The fair of Beaucaire is a good example of this. Like the small city that it really was, it had its own count and its own justices. It was attended by the merchant-princes of the world, men who thought nothing of a journey to Alexandria twice a year, and by the great dealers of all the cities of France, Nîmes, Avignon, Marseilles, Paris, Rouen, Chartres, Bourges, Tours, and the rest. Communications were easier than we can realise now, and none the worse for being slower, because the commodities for sale were seldom perishable. A man might go up the Seine, or the Loire, and he would have but little land travelling (comparatively) in his journey before he could trust himself and his merchandise to the Rhone, and float down the current to Beaucaire. The place was equally easily reached by the light trading brigs which plied round the Mediterranean coasts and scarcely ever sailed out of sight of land. From Genoa and Pisa, from Venice and from Egypt, from all the ports of Spain, from the north coast of Africa, from Greece and the Levant, the treasures of the south and east were brought overseas and up the Rhone to the great meeting-place of north and west. As was natural where so much business was a-doing, the money-changers drove a merry trade as well,[2] a trade of far more importance than its descendant of to-day. The jewellers and artificers in precious metals, whose craft was so gorgeously encouraged by the Church, were also there; and each trade was bound up in its own Confrérie, quartered in its own part of the great fair, and guarded by its special patron saint. No doubt a vast deal of exchange and barter went on. Even down to the beginning of the nineteenth century you might have seen oranges from Spain, leather from Morocco, tobacco and dates from Africa, perfumes, dyes, and carpets from Egypt and Turkey, oil from Provence and Genoa, cloth from France and England, furs from Norway and Russia, wines from Bordeaux and Burgundy, sardines and anchovies from Perpignan, scents and soaps from Grasse, drugs and medicaments from Montpellier, knives from Châtellerault, velvets from Vienne and Amiens, horses from as far as Prussia. The first boat that anchored within the prescribed time at the quay of Beaucaire was rewarded by the municipality with a sheep or a barrel of wine. The river was wellnigh choked with continuous arrivals. It is nothing wonderful that the writer of "Aucassin and Nicolete" should have described a shipwreck beneath the castle walls. There must have been many in the twelfth and thirteenth centuries, and there have been many since.

At the present day the power of purchase has grown to such a large extent that what were the luxuries of our grandparents are the necessities of our children. But the taste for what is absolutely the best thing to be found remains as restricted as it ever was, because it has nothing to do with money. In what we are pleased to call "the barbarous ages" of seven centuries ago, taste was as rare a thing, but just as real. The lady in the castle on the hill had little else to think about in the long periods of waiting between one fair and another, between the scanty opportunities of spending money and the still more infrequent occasions when it might well be spent. At the end of the twelfth century she wore an over-dress of lightest écru-silk from the Damascus looms, diaphanous and exquisite, cut in three pieces that fitted perfectly over her figure. Both skirt and corsage could open down the front, and were united by a bodice which could be unfastened from behind. The sleeves, that fitted closely to the elbows, spread out into long trumpet-shaped petals at the wrist. The belt, a thing of dainty jewellery, served only to conceal the line of union between skirt and bodice. Through this transparent silk glowed the purple robe beneath, trimmed with ermine. At her neck showed white linen, embroidered in gold threads. Her hair was thickly braided with soft strings of pearls, and kept in place with a gold circlet. Her fan was of fine ostrich-feathers, set in a golden handle, finished with a ruby at its point. And all the details of this dress might have been bought at the great fair of Beaucaire. All of them, or many like them, were worn by that Châtelaine to whom "the old prisoner," who wrote the "Chantefable," recited the first version of "Aucassin and Nicolete."[3]

There was war between Count Bougars of Valence and Count Garin of Beaucaire, so that the land of Beaucaire was harassed every day; and Count Garin was old and frail, and his heir was Aucassin. "Fair was he, and slim and tall, and featly fashioned of his body and limbs. His hair was yellow, in little curls; and his eyes were grey and laughing;[4] his face was clear and shapely; his nose high and well-set, and so richly seen was he in all things good, that in him was none evil at all." But when his father bade him get to horse, and help his men in battle, he replied:

"Father, I marvel that you will be speaking. Never may God give me ought of my desire if I be made knight or mount my horse, or face stour and battle wherein knights smite and are smitten, unless thou give me Nicolete, my true love that I love so well." But his father would not; for Nicolete had been bought of the Saracens by the captain of the town, who brought her up and christened her, and she was not for such as Aucassin to wed. Yet the boy answered: "If she were Empress of Constantinople or of Germany, or Queen of France or England, it were little enough for her; so gentle is she, and courteous and debonaire, and compact of all good qualities." Then the count bade the captain of the town put the girl in ward, at peril of his life, saying that if he had her at his will he would burn her, so angered was he at the stubbornness of Aucassin. So the captain placed Nicolete in the upper chamber of his palace, which stood in a garden, with bread and meat and wine, and one old woman to keep her company, and sealed the door.

> *Nicolete is put in ward*
> *In a vaulted chamber barred*
> *That is painted wondrously*
> *With right cunning artistry.*
> *At the marble window-sill*
> *There was leaned the damozel.*
> *She had hair of yellow gold*
> *And an eyebrow of rare mould,*
> *Clear face, delicately fine,*
> *Never saw ye more divine!*
> *On the wood she gazed below*
> *And she saw the roses blow,*
> *Heard the birds sing, loud and low,*
> *And she wept, "Woe's me forlorn!"*

Then Aucassin, hearing the rumour that she was lost, or that Count Garin had bid slay her, went to the captain and asked news of her. But the captain said that she was not for him, neither as wife, for he must take the daughter of a king or count, nor as leman, for then his soul would lie in Hell and never enter Paradise. And Aucassin answered:—

"In Paradise what have I to win? Therein I seek not to enter, but only to have Nicolete, my sweet lady that I love so well. For into Paradise go none

but such folk as I shall tell thee now: Thither go the old priests, and halt old men and maimed, who all day and night cower before the altars and in the ancient crypts; and such as go in old threadbare cloaks and in old clouted frocks, naked folk and barefoot, covered with sores, perishing of hunger and thirst, and of cold and misery. These be they that go into Paradise, with them have I naught to make. But into Hell would I fain go; for into Hell fare the goodly clerks and goodly knights that fall in tourneys and great wars, and stout men-at-arms, and all men noble. With these will I go. And thither pass the sweet and gracious ladies that have two lovers or three, and their lords also thereto, and there go the gold and silver and the cloth of vair and grey, and the harpers and the minstrels, and the Prince of this World. With these I would gladly go, let me but have with me Nicolete, my most sweet friend."

So Aucassin went away sorrowing, and while he mourned his lady in his chamber, the din of battle rose about the castle because the Count Bougars of Valence was attacking it. Then, while the assault was at its height, entered Count Garin and besought his son to go out and encourage his own folk, and called him coward and caitiff that he would not defend his lands. But Aucassin would not, unless he might have Nicolete. Yet at the last his father granted him to have two words or three with her, and one kiss. So Aucassin armed himself and mounted, but he so dreamed of Nicolete that when he had spurred forth from the gate he dropped his reins and his foes began to lead him off a prisoner; and when he was aware of them, "Ha! God," said he, "sweet Saviour. Be these my deadly enemies that have taken me, and will soon cut off my head? And once my head is off, no more shall I speak with Nicolete, my sweet lady that I love so well." So he put his hand to his sword, and he was tall and strong, and his horse was eager, and he suddenly fell a-smiting right and left, and hurled out of the press, and lashed at the helm of the Count Bougars de Valence with so shrewd a stroke that he was stunned and fell; and he led him away prisoner by the noseguard of his helmet and brought him to his father. But when Aucassin reminded the Count Garin of the covenant between them, his father would have none of it. So the youth turned to Count Bougars and took his hand in his, and said: "Now givest thou me thy word that never while thou art living man wilt thou avail to do my father dishonour, or harm in body, or in goods." So the Count Bougars was sore astonied, and gave him the pledge, and was escorted back to safety. Then did Count Garin cast

Aucassin into a deep dungeon, because of his love for Nicolete, and while he was in prison Nicolete was fast shut in the upper chamber of the captain's palace.

Now it was summer time, the month of May, when days are warm and long and bright, and the night is still and clear. Nicolete lay one night on her bed, and saw the moon shine bright through a window, and heard the nightingale sing in the garden; so she minded her of Aucassin, her friend whom she loved so well. Then fell she to thoughts of Count Garin of Beaucaire, who hated her to the death; and she thought to herself that she would remain no longer there, for that if she were betrayed to the Count Garin he would make her die an evil death. Now she perceived that the old woman who kept her company was asleep. Then she arose and put on a gown of cloth of silk she had by her that was very good, and took towels and sheets off the bed, and knotted one to the other, and therewith made a cord as long as she might, and tied it to the pillar of the window and let herself slip down into the garden; then caught she up her raiment in both hands behind and before, and kilted up her kirtle, because of the dew she saw lying deep on the grass, and so went her way down through the garden. Her locks were yellow and curled, her eyes grey and laughing, her face featly fashioned, her nose high and well set, her lips more red than cherry or than rose in summertime, her teeth white and small; her breasts were firm and bore up her bodice as they had been two apples, her waist so slim that your two hands might have clipped her, and the daisy flowers that brake beneath her as she went tiptoe, and that bent above her instep, seemed black against her feet and ankles, so very fair was the maid. So she came to the postern and unfastened it, and went out through the streets of Beaucaire, keeping always in the shadow, for the moon shone very bright, and went on till she came to the tower where her friend lay. Now the tower was cracked here and there, and she crouched down beside one of the buttresses, wrapped in her mantle, and thrust her head through a crevice in the tower that was old and worn, and so she heard Aucassin wailing within, and making dole and lament for the sweet lady he loved so well.

Then she cut her curls of gold,
Cast them in the dungeon hold.
Knightly did Aucassin take,[5]

And of them much worship make,
And he kissed them and caressed,
And bestowed them in his breast.

While the lovers were thus talking to one another and speaking of their love, the town guards were heard at the other end of the street, as they made their rounds. So the watchman on the tower, who was kindhearted and had no wish that harm should come to Nicolete, warned her with a little song from the battlements. So she looked up and thanked him for his courtesy, and shrank back behind the buttress till the watch were passed, and then let herself down with great pain and difficulty into the fosse of the castle; and though the blood streamed from her wounded feet she went forward and found an old pike that had been thrown there in battle from the walls, and with the help of it she climbed up the steep wall on the further side and walked out a distance of two crossbow shots towards the great forest that stretched beyond the castle for thirty leagues this way and that, and laid her down to sleep in a little thicket. At prime, the next day, the shepherds came out from the town to a place where there was a spring on the fringe of the forest, and Nicolete was wakened by the sound of singing birds and of the shepherds, who were eating bread.

"Fair children," said she, "may the Lord keep you!" "May God bless you!" quoth he that had more words to his tongue than the rest. "Fair children," said she, "know ye Aucassin, the son of Count Garin of Beaucaire?" "Yes, we know him well." "So may God help you, fair children," said she, "tell him there is a beast in this forest, and that he come and hunt it, and if he can take it, he would not give one limb thereof for a hundred marks of gold, nay, not for five hundred, nor for any ransom." Then they looked on her and saw her so fair that they were all astonied. "Will I tell him thereof?" quoth he that had more words to his tongue than the rest; "foul fall him who speaks of it or tells him the tidings. This is but a fantasy you tell of, for there is no beast so great in this forest, stag nor lion nor boar, that one of his limbs is worth more than two deniers or three at the most, and you speak of so great a ransom. Sorrow be his who believes you, or who tells Aucassin. You are a fairy, and we have no care for your company, so hold on your road."

But at last she gave them five sols from her purse and they promised to tell him if he came that way, but not to seek him out.

Now Aucassin's father had taken him out of the dungeon and was making a feast to comfort him, but he was all woebegone because men said that Nicolete was lost. Then a good knight came up to him and advised him to take a ride in the forest to cheer him with the sight of the flowers and the sound of the birds. So he took horse and rode into the forest, and at about the hour of noon he found the shepherds at their fountain, Esmé and Martin, Fruelin and Jack, Robin and Aubrey, who were talking of the girl with the bright face and eyes of vair who had given them money.

"Fair boys," said Aucassin, "do you not know me?" "Yea, we know well that you are Aucassin, our damoiseau; natheless we are not your men but the count's." "Fair boys, sing me the song that anon ye sang." "Hearken by the Holy Heart," quoth he that had more words to his tongue than the rest, "wherefore should I sing for you if it likes me not? Lo, there is no such rich man in the country, saving the body of Garin the Count, that dare drive forth my oxen, or my cows, or my sheep, if he finds them in his fields or his corn, lest he lose his eyes for it; so wherefore should I sing for you if it likes me not?"

But at last he gave them ten sols from his purse, and they told him how "a maid came past, the fairest thing in the world, whereby we deemed she was a fay, and all the wood shone round about her." So they gave him the message, and he knew that it was Nicolete, and his heart was stirred within him so that he hurled through the forest till the briers tore his raiment, yet at vespers he had not found her; but he met some one down an old and grass-grown road.

Tall was he and great of growth, laidly and marvellous to look upon; his head huge and black as charcoal, and more than the breadth of a hand between his eyes, and great cheeks, and a big nose and broad big nostrils and ugly, and thick lips redder than a collop, and great teeth yellow and ugly, and he was shod with hosen and shoon of bullshide, bound with cords of bark over the knee, and all about him a great cloak doubled, and he leaned on a grievous cudgel.

So when he asked Aucassin why he wept, the young lord told him it was for the loss of a white hound. Then the man burst out with revilings, saying that his own cause for grief was greater.

"Wherefore so, brother?" said Aucassin. "Sir, I will tell thee. I was hired to a rich villein, and drove his plough; four oxen there were. But three days since came on me great misadventure, whereby I lost the best of mine oxen, Roget, the best of my team. Him go I seeking, and have neither eaten nor drunk these three days, nor may I go to the town lest they cast me into prison, seeing that I have not wherewithal to pay. Out of all the wealth of the world have I no more than ye see on my body. A poor mother bare me, that had no more but one wretched bed; this have they taken from under her, and she lies in the very straw. This ails me more than my own case, for wealth comes and goes; if now I have lost, another tide will I gain, and will pay for mine ox whenas I may; never for that will I weep. But you weep for a hound of the dunghill. Foul fall whoso thinks well of thee."

So Aucassin gave him twenty sols from his purse to pay for the ox, and rode on through the stillness of the night until he came to the place where Nicolete had made her a lodge of flowers, at a place where seven roads met. So for the sweetness of it, and for love of her, he put his foot out of the stirrup to alight from his horse that was big and tall; and he thought so much of her that he slipped on a stone so hard that his shoulder flew out of its place. But he managed to tie up his horse with one hand and crept into the lodge, and there lay looking up at the stars; and as he sang a little song to one of them, which reminded him of his lady, because it was the fairest, Nicolete heard him, being near at hand,

and came to him and threw her arms about his neck and kissed him, and finding his shoulder wounded she plied it so with her white hands (as God willed who loveth lovers) that it came again into place, and she bound flowers and grass and leaves upon it with the lappet of her smock, and he was quite healed.

> *Aucassin the boon, the blond,*
> *High-born youth and lover fond,*
> *Rode out from the deep forest*
> *In his arms his love he pressed,*
> *'Fore him on the saddle-bow:*
> *Kisses her on eyes and brow,*

On her mouth and on her chin.
Then to him did she begin:
"Aucassin, fair lover sweet,
To what land are we to fleet?"
"Sweet my sweetheart, what know I?
Nought to me 'tis where we fly,
In greenwood or utter way
So I am with you always!"[6]

Here the reader would perhaps gladly leave them, for the crisis of their trials seems reached; but the old singer has to make a longer song of it, and he tells how they were taken on board ship and driven by a mighty wind towards the fairyland of Torelore, where the king lay sick in childbed, and his queen was at the wars, where men fought with roasted crab-apples, and with eggs, and with fresh cheeses, and with mushrooms. So Aucassin very speedily scattered the king's foes for him. But a fleet of Saracens came by sea and stormed the king's castle, and Aucassin they put into one ship and Nicolete into another. Now Aucassin's ship drifted away in a storm and was wrecked in the Rhone, and the people of the country, who had run to the wrecking, recognised Aucassin and took him to Beaucaire, where his father and mother had died during his three years' absence in Torelore, so he was Count of Beaucaire, and held his land in peace and sorrowed for his lady. But Nicolete was taken in the Paynim ship to Carthage, and when she saw the walls of Carthage she knew well that it was the city in which she had been brought up, and indeed she was the daughter of the King of Carthage. Now Nicolete would marry none of the suitors whom the king offered her; so she ran away from Carthage, because all her desire was to Aucassin.

Then took she a certain herb and therewith smeared her head and face,
till she was all brown stained. And she let make coat, and mantle, and
smock, and hose, and attired herself as if she had been a minstrel; and she
took her viol and went to a mariner, and so dealt with him that he took
her in his ship. Then hoisted they sail, and fared on the high seas even till
they came to the land of Provence...

At Beaucaire, below the tower
Fared Aucassin, on an hour;

> *Round him his proud barons were,*
> *While he sat him on the stair,*
> *Saw the herbs and flowers spring,*
> *Heard the tune the song-birds sing;*
> *Of his love he thinks anew,*
> *Nicolete, the maiden true,*
> *Whom he loved so many years*
> *Then was he in dule and tears.*
> *Even then came Nicolete.*
> *On the stair a foot she set,*
> *And she drew the viol bow*
> *Through the strings and chanted so.[7]*

And when Aucassin heard news of his dear Nicolete from the harper, he wept for joy that there were tidings of her, and the harper promised that she should be with him in a little while. So Nicolete went away to the house of the captain's wife, for the captain, her father in God, was dead; and there she bathed herself and rested for a full eight days; and then she took a herb called *Eyebright,* and anointed herself, and clothed herself in rich robes of silk, and bade the captain's wife bring Aucassin to her.

> *Then Aucassin wedded her,*
> *Made her lady of Beaucaire;*
> *Many years abode they there,*
> *Many years in shade or sun,*
> *In great gladness and delight.*
> *Ne'er hath Aucassin regret,*
> *Nor his lady Nicolete.*
> *Now my song-and-tale is done.[8]*
> *I know no further.*

So sweet and simple a tale needs little commentary; but I must point out just two or three things in it that should be noted by any reader in Provence. The peculiar form of prose alternating with verse, the prose giving the episodic facts and the verse being usually an amplifying commentary, is very rare in any writer, and almost unknown after the thirteenth century.[9] From the numerous interpolations of verse in such tales as the *Arabian Nights*, it has been thought that Arabian forms may have entered into the poet's education as much as Hellenic; for if "Nicolete" sounds of Greek origin, there was a Moorish king in Cordova called "Alcazin" in 1019; but I do not think too much stress should be laid on Arabic origins, as I have noticed in speaking of the Troubadours, and the dialect of this poem is distinctly northern. The manuscript used by Mr. Bourdillon, from which I have quoted, is in the Bibliothèque Nationale (No. 2168 f. fr.) in Paris, and this copy on vellum is the only one known.[10] It is the work of a true poet, of an old and weary man, a "prisoner" he calls himself; and he may well have been the pilgrim from the Limousin whose sickness was cured by the sight and by the charity of some fair châtelaine, as Aucassin sings of Nicolete. He was old, but (as Mr. Lang has characteristically noted) he had the kindly sympathy of Thackeray at his best, and the thing that has most interested him is the love of these young lovers, and the character of his various personages. What better touches of artistry could we wish than the stubborn pride of the old Count Garin when he thinks his boy may make a mésalliance; the weak effeminacy of the King of Torelore; the good nature of the captain's wife; the sturdy independence of that Caliban-gargoyle, the ploughboy, whose hideous features have been preserved in many a thirteenth-century carving? The study of the shepherd-boys alone throws a flood of light upon feudal society in a free spirit of criticism that is very different from most of the accepted versions. The splendid reply of Aucassin to the captain of the town, preferring hell and its "brave company" to heaven without his Nicolete, would seem equally anachronistic to those who did not take into account the strange connection I have already emphasised between the Troubadours and the Albigensian tenets. The question of the date must necessarily remain so uncertain (pending fresh discoveries) that I am inclined again to hint at the appropriateness of taking the young Raymond (VII), who held Beaucaire for the Albigensians against Simon de Montfort, as a very possible type of Aucassin, the ideal knight, whose presence is invoked by his father to stir up the people of the town to fresh endeavour at the very sight of him. The change from the weeping, lovelorn swain to the hero who hurls into the fray among his foes, inspired by the one thought, that by the strength of his hands he may free his father and win Nicolete, is significant enough; and his popularity is frequently insisted on.

But it is on Nicolete herself that the memory dwells most fondly. Slowly yet surely the slight pure outline of her, at the beginning, is filled out with colours more and more enchanting. Each incident lends her form a greater beauty, her character a sweeter grace. High-souled, as ready for the self-sacrifice as for the joys of love; modest, yet never ashamed of the full passion that she knows is shared; strong and determined in her escapes from durance, yet tender and compassionate when there is need for it; firm in her refusals to the great ones of her world, yet winning and politic in her dealings with the shepherd boys, Nicolete is not merely a type of the perfect damozel of chivalry, she is an immortal character in the poetry of the world.[11]

NOTES

1. Good is the lay, sweet is the note,
Dainty too, and deftly wrought,
There is no man so distraught,
None so wretched, so fordone,
Sick with so great sickness none,
If he hear, shall not he cured,
And of gladness reassured, So sweet it is!
—F. W. Bourdillon's Translation.

2. Mr. J. H. Smith (vol. ii. p. 401 note) mentions that a mark weighed 226.28 grammes at Limoges, but 239.11 grammes at Montpellier. Two marks, or twenty sous, went to the pound, and one sou was twelve deniers, a denier being twenty-four oboles. Under Philip Augustus the pound had twenty-four sous, each weighing 13.356 grammes. Gold varied in proportion to silver from ten to twelve.

3. The translations I shall give from this poem, which is partly in prose and partly in rhyme, will usually be taken from Mr. Andrew Lang's elegant and dainty version. Those chosen from Mr. Bourdillon's scholarly edition will be specially mentioned; and from this latter are drawn any quotations from the original, or observations on the actual text. But I have sometimes taken a line from one of these authors and followed it by a line from the other, as each seemed to me to give better meaning, or a prettier English sound, to the text of the old French; so that neither Mr. Lang nor Mr. Bourdillon can be wholly held responsible for the extracts from the poem and the short sketch of the story that alone are possible in this place. To each I acknowledge my profound indebtedness, and that each may find more readers of their charming versions is my chiefest hope. The original is far too little known, even in its own country.

4. The original is "Il avoit les caviax blons et menus recercelés, et les ex *vairs* et rians,

et le face clere et traitice…" All beautiful eyes were called *vairs* in the songs of the Troubadours and the old romances; *e.g.* "Les ex *vairs* et rians plus d'un faucon mué" (Fierabras), or "Les iex ot *vairs* come cristal" (Barbazon), to which Bourdillon compares Chaucer's "Hir yen grey as is a faucon," or "eyen grey as crystalle stone," in "Sir Eglamour." There was evidently some confusion between the brightness and the colour of eyes called *vair*; *e.g.* "Si noir oel me sambloient *vair*" (Li Jus Adam). I have taken Bourdillon's interpretation, "bright grey," as being the most probable, in spite of the close juxtaposition of "vair" and "gris" in the list of colours in A. and N. § 6:—"Es s'i va li ors et li argens, et li vairs et li gris."

5. The original of this line is "Aucassins les prist, li ber," and Bourdillon rightly emphasises the beauty of the last two words, and the importance of their position in the phrase, comparing it to Virgil's "Constituit signum nautis *pater.*" Though the poet takes many words and phrases, which might be thought to be merely otiose epithets from the stock endings of the late "Chansons de Geste," he usually employs them with the fullest effect, as in this case; or again when the lover rides away with his lady on his saddlebow:—

> "Aucassin li biax, li blons,
> Li gentix, li amorous."

Every word tells in the pretty picture; or lastly in the description of Nicolete faring forth alone "right amid the bosky wood down an ancient path foregone," the words are the well-known phrases of many a "chanson," but they are singularly appropriate to their new setting.

6. Bourdillon.

7. Bourdillon rightly points out the beautiful word "dansellon" which occurs in her song.

> "Car ele aime un dansellon
> Qui Aucassins avoit non."

8. "No cantefable prent fin."

9. Changes of metre occur in the iambics and choruses of Greek tragedy, or in such modern examples as Tennyson's "Maud"; prose alternates with blank verse in Shakespeare; but this "Cantefable" is differently planned. When it was first recited, such rhymed parts as the warder's song of warning, a charming adaptation of the *Aubade*, or the song of the herdboys, Fruelin, Aubrey, and the rest, or the song of the disguised Nicolete… "*Escoutês moi franc baron…*" were made much more

realistic by being actually sung to music. Of the twenty-one rhymed sections, at least eighteen are obviously better framed in metre than in prose, and some of them, such as the tale of Torelore... "*En le canbre entre Aucassins*"...were equally obviously meant to be comic interludes, set to a comic tone. Aucassin himself (in section 22, the scene with the shepherds) says, "Encor aim je mix coster que nient," "I would rather have it told (in prose) than not hear it all," a sentiment which would no doubt reflect the preference of most of his artistic audience for verse, which they would regard as the illuminated miniatures round a manuscript, or as the freely ornamented border of a Bayeux tapestry.

10. Gaston Paris thinks the date is about the middle of the twelfth century, owing to various details in language and phraseology. He considers that one man wrote the whole as it stands, both prose and verse, for neither would be perfect without the other, and the word "cantefable" in the last lines seems to clinch the matter finally. Whatever difference there may be in the language is owing to the fact that the verse parts had to be written down, and were therefore more accurately preserved, whereas the prose parts might be handed on orally for some time, with the result that more modern phrases might occur in it when it achieved the final honour of being committed to manuscript. The language of Villehardouin, or of Joinville, in the form it has reached us, would be sufficient to show that the prose parts of this ballad would very probably wear a more modern look than the verse, even if they had originated together.

11. While that literature which saw her birth was in its prime, it was as well known in England as across the Channel. Yet neither in England nor in France was "Aucassin and Nicolete" again remembered until the lost manuscript was found about the middle of the eighteenth century. In a mutilated form the tale first appeared in the English tongue in 1786. In 1873 Walter Pater first drew general attention to it by his fascinating chapter in *Studies in the History of the Renaissance*. To Mr. Bourdillon and Mr. Andrew Lang English readers owe the best editions of the poem that have yet seen the light.

Part IV: Tarascon

"Celui qui a escript ce livre
Ne vous requiert chasteau ne place,
Mais que pour vous il puisse vivre,
Et soit toujours en vostre grace."

THE castle of Beaucaire now smiles across the Rhone where once it frowned defiance at the towers of Tarascon. No one can help smiling who first hears of Tarascon. "Ah!" they will say, "you mean the town of Tartarin!" But the Tarasconnais do not appreciate the joke. I do not care for it myself so much now as when I was first in Tarascon. I had come determined to see King René's castle, and after many hours of waiting I was provided with the following document:—"Nous, Maire de la ville de Tarascon, autorisons MM. Eliot et Cook à visiter le château du Roi René sous la conduite d'un gardien. Tarascon, le 12 Avril 1892. Le Maire. J. Roff." After taking oath that we carried no weapons concealed about our persons, we were admitted, and it proved almost as disappointing as the Palace of the Popes in Avignon. Thirteen years afterwards even this document was powerless. Ashamed, perhaps, at the base uses to which the château has been turned—for, like Fontevrault, it is the gaol of mean criminals—the local authorities are adamant, and the guardian is worse than Cerberus. We tried blandishments, "spargens humida mella soporiferumque papaver." He remained unmoved. We produced a letter in which the Minister of Fine Arts in Paris requested the assistance of every French official for the work on which the bearer was engaged, and added special permission for photographing the Historic Monuments. The guardian impassively waved it aside, even as the concierge at Avignon had done. Governments may totter; Ministers may rise and fall; Presidents may pass away or be elected; but the Concierges of France remain, the everlasting repositories of stolid power. "It is possible," said this one, "that Monsieur has permission to see the Historic Monument; but I will pray Monsieur to observe that he has no permission to see the gaol."[1]

It is probable that in a few years the castle of Tarascon will be taken under the direct protection of the Government, as is promised at

The Castle of King René at Tarascon

Avignon also, and then my readers will be able to see King René's house for themselves. For the present they must accept my slight description of the fortress that rose on the ruins of an old Roman citadel, consecrated to Jupiter, and built after both Hannibal and Marius had immortalised the memories of the famous ford across the river from Beaucaire. Provence contributed to the constructions here in 1283 and 1387, but the fortress was only changed into a habitable château after the first visit of King René on the 2nd of December 1437.[2] He made up his mind, apparently, that Tarascon was a good place in the spring and early summer, and here he chiefly took his royal relaxation after the cares of government at Aix. His chapel was built by Jean Robert, who was paid seven hundred and forty-six florins for wages between 1447 and 1449, and the construction was carried on under the care of Jean de Séraucourt, René's faithful servant and captain, at seven hundred florins yearly. This chapel is finely vaulted, and on its carved capitals may still be seen a sculptured priest who preaches to at least one attentive listener. It is near a flamboyant archway, and a recess with the date 1518, that shows the place was used for at least eight and thirty years after King René's death had passed it on to the Kings of France. The chapel is reached through a small private quadrangle, with a carved archway, and a "left-handed" spiral staircase on the right, one of four similar stairways which serve the whole building.

On the lowest floor of the living rooms is a dark apartment, which may well have been a prison, for on its walls is the sad inscription, "I called unto God in my torment and He heard me, and said I will save him." But I like to think that it was not so used under the good René, and that the curious "sgraffiti" on the walls were the work of his idle pages and men-at-arms while they waited their turn for attendance. Among these strange pictures, scratched on the plaster, as by a dagger's point, are a large number of vessels, with lateen sails; some with small cannon mounted on the poop; all of them most interesting records of the kind of trading-ships that plied up and down the Rhone from the Mediterranean in the early sixteenth century, and brought goods from every port in Europe to the great fair of Beaucaire. There are houses and castles roughly drawn as well; a great coat-of-arms above the door; and a board marked out for a game of chess, which is interesting, because among the books known to have formed part of King René's library at his death in 1480 is a treatise on the Game of Chess, dedicated to Bertrand Aubant, Captain of Tarascon, by the translator, John Ferron, a preaching friar.[3]

On the next floor is an eight-sided boudoir with a ceiling beautifully carved in wood, opening into a delightfully proportioned dining-room, with a hooded chimney-piece, and a window looking out upon the courtyard. Above this again is another octagon room; and if the "study," which René decorated with glass-painting with his own hands, may have been below, this upper room may have been Jeanne de Laval's bedroom, for the colours on the carved ceiling are still clear, and there are deep window seats where her ladies of honour could wait and watch what was going on outside. The roof of this wing of the building is a magnificent piece of architecture, and in far finer repair than the interior.

René did not limit his restorations to the château. He was equally interested in the famous Church of St Martha, and this must be visited by any one who goes to Tarascon. For though I have twice proved that sleep is impossible, with any comfort, in its hotels, and that the best way to see it is to arrive early in the morning and go on to St. Remy for dinner in the evening, yet there are several things worth noticing in its streets. The Hôtel de Ville, for instance, must on no account be missed, and there is a dark and odorous stable in which the image of the celebrated Tarasque itself reposes, which was once the central figure in the fêtes that modern republican governments have condemned. The streets, too, that lead to the town hall are arcaded picturesquely, as was the custom in all fifteenth-century towns, much after the fashion of our own Chester. But on the whole the town of Tarascon is disappointing; and after you have seen the curious mixture of the southern square tower with the northern round form in its castle, after you have admired the details of the entrance gateway, with the moat and separate drawbridges for horse and foot, after you have seen the round Norman towers that flank the town gate, there is no better thing to do than straightway to pay a visit to the church, dedicated to that St. Martha whom I spoke of in describing the campaigns of Marius, and whose victory over the Tarasque has been preserved in the name and armorial bearings of the town.

Originally constructed in the twelfth century on the ruins of a Roman temple, this church was reconstructed in the fourteenth, and contains many "Gothic" details in its southern plan. But the south porch is a very beautiful example of what the original workmanship was like, as will be seen from Mr. Mallow's drawing of it. The mouldings of the arch combine the classic egg and dart with "Gothic" dogtooth enrichments. The sculptured ivy wreath is unique in work of the time. The small arcade above shows fluted pilasters and round shafts alternately, resting on a Romanesque cornice of carved heads. The central pillar in the entrance reminds the visitor of the more magnificent portals of St. Gilles and Arles. Within are a number of pictures in which the handiwork does not seem to me to correspond to the great names to which they have been attributed; but the light is too bad to permit of close examination. Several are said to be by Parrocel, others by Vien, and many deal with episodes in the life of St Martha. There is a most interesting crypt, containing her tomb, and the sepulchral effigy of Jean Cossa, the faithful seneschal of King René, who composed the epitaph now over the statue a few years before his own death.[4] The two men had held a great place in the politics, the art, the civilisation of their time. Jean Cossa was five years older than his master, and died nearly four years before him. We shall hear more of him in the short description I must now give of King René himself, the last Count of Provence.

On the 1st of December 1400 Louis (II) of Anjou and Provence was married to Yolande of Aragon, in the cathedral of St. Trophime at Arles. Her picture is preserved on a stained-glass window in the Cathedral of Le Mans; and it is said that her husband, who got sight of her secretly in Montpellier before their wedding, fell at once desperately in love with the lady whom Juvenal des Ursins describes as "the loveliest creature one could wish to see." Events proved that she was one of the best and wisest of women too. So for once, in the tale of great alliances, political necessity was blessed by natural inclination, and on January 16, 1409, at three o'clock in the morning, was born to them, in the castle of Angers, a son called René after a famous and saintly bishop of that city.

Church of Ste. Martha, Tarascon

Before him had been born Louis (III), who died in 1434, after having inherited Anjou and Provence for seventeen years, and Marie d'Anjou, who became the queen of Charles VII of France. After him came Charles Count of Maine (whose son held Provence for scarcely a year after King René's death), and Yolande, who married first Jean d'Alençon, and secondly François, Comte de Montfort, son of the Duke of Brittany. But of all five children it was René who was to hold the greatest place in history, and the joy of Angers when he was born seemed a significant prophecy of his career. The tomb of his nurse, Tiphaine de Magine, was set up by himself in the church of Notre Dame de Nantilly, in Saumur, her birthplace. At the early age of twelve he was married to his ten-year-old bride, Isabelle de Lorraine, on the 24th of October 1420. Their eldest son, Jean de Calabre, was born in August 1427, and according to some authorities a year earlier.

No better influence could have guided the youth of René, and indeed of France, than that of his mother, Yolande, the mother also of the future queen of France. Charles, when dauphin, was well aware how much he owed her. It is significant of the thoroughly patriotic line she took in all her political dealings, that she was one of the first of the great ladies of France to shelter and encourage Joan of Arc. She was one of the three matrons who testified to the Maid's chastity. She was the first to proclaim the divine mission of the shepherd girl, and to renounce all her own dignity in its favour. She sent from Blois the convoy that was to help her in the siege of Orleans, and pawned the jewels of Anjou to pay for it. When the Maid was first summoned before the Duke of Lorraine, in March 1429, it was the aid of René, son of the Duchess of Anjou, that she asked, "to guide me into France." Robert de Baudricourt, who had been Joan of Arc's first helper, was René's lifelong friend; and when the time came René himself was not backward; for at the siege of Paris in the September of that year he was at her side; and when she was wounded by an arrow in the thigh, she was rescued from the moat and carried to safety by René, with the Count of Clermont and others. After that, René had to go fighting elsewhere, with his faithful Barbazan, who fell on the fatal day of Bulgnéville, in 1431,when René himself was sorely wounded and finally thrown into prison.

The death of his elder brother, Louis (III) d'Anjou, in Italy, in 1434, and of Queen Jeanne (II) of Naples soon afterwards, entirely changed the destinies of René, who thus came into a double inheritance. Duke of Bar and of Lorraine already, he now became Duke of Anjou, Count of Provence, and King of the two Sicilies. His wife Isabelle—for he was still in prison—went forthwith to take up his new kingdoms. His liberty was only bought in 1437 by the cession of Cassel and some lands in Flanders to the Duke of Burgundy. In November he was on his way across the borders of Provence, where he was received with joyful enthusiasm on every side, and by the 2nd of December he was in the castle of Tarascon. In the autumn of 1442 he had lost all real hold on Naples, and though he clung to the recognition of his rights by the constant use of the title "King of Sicily," it was a title and no more. But the influence of the great house of Anjou in Italy was by no means over. As one of the essential bases of Charlemagne's power, and of the policy both of St. Louis and of Charles V, that influence could never be forgotten when France inherited what Anjou had left. It cost France uncounted blood and treasure; but its effects are visible unto this day.

In 1443 King Charles VII was reorganising Languedoc after the succession of triumphs over the English which had begun with Joan of Arc. At Toulouse King René met him, and in the train of his wife Isabel de Lorraine was Agnes Sorel, lately arrived from the court of his mother, Yolande, Duchess of Anjou, who had died the year before. The fair Agnes may well have added to the gaiety with which the king welcomed his old playmate, and it is worth noticing that when she was ill at Jumièges, during the Normandy campaign of 1450, René was with Charles VII at her sudden death on the 9th of February. Her tomb at Loches is a sufficient explanation of her influence over both of them. In the autumn of 1443 died René's second son, Louis, at the early age of sixteen. The following spring saw the brilliant prospect of a throne across the Channel open before his daughter Margaret, who was then just reaching the beauty of her fifteenth year. Henry VI of England had sent the Earl of Suffolk and other ambassadors to France, in search of peace, and they were received by René in the town of Tours. On April 3, 1444, Margaret of Anjou was solemnly betrothed to Henry VI (represented by Suffolk) in the cathedral of Tours. In the next year she was married, Suffolk again being proxy for the English king, at Nancy, bringing the isles of Majorca and Minorca as her dowry, with which England might begin her ambitions of Mediterranean control. At the same time Yolande, René's elder daughter, was married to Ferry de Lorraine, son of Antoine de Vaudemont, and through her the blood of the last Count of Provence was to be transmitted to the Hapsburgs. Margaret, who made what was reputed to be by far the more brilliant match, was to see her only son,

Edward, slain after Tewkesbury, in 1471, and to break her heart in vain regrets in her old father's fading kingdom. But she had shown great qualities of ambition and endurance before the end, and it is not often remembered that the unquiet heroine of the Wars of the Roses was a princess of Provence.

Though René was often at Angers during the first half of his life, it was to the Provence he loved, the Provence where he was to die, that he seems ever to have turned with greater affection. His voyage there in 1447 has been fortunately described in detail. On board the galleys he kept always ready near Angers, he sailed up the Loire to Roanne, carrying with him his plate, his tapestry, his furniture, all covered in beneath the cloth of grey, white, and black that was his livery, below the banners embroidered with his shield that flew from every mast. The flotilla moved slowly from one town to another through the pleasant landscapes of Touraine. Sometimes a bridge (as at Saumur) had to be pulled down to let them pass, and built up again after they had gone. From Roanne great wagons took them gently across country to the Rhone at Lyons, where they embarked, after due rest and refreshment, and floated down the stream to Tarascon, taking from a fortnight to three weeks over the whole journey. On this particular occasion his visit was marked by his meeting with the Dauphin, who was

The Good King René (From the triptych called "Le Buisson Ardent" by Nicolas Froment in the Cathedral of Aix-en-Provence)

afterwards to be Louis XI. Two men more different, in heart, in mind, in character, the castle of Tarascon has never sheltered since, than the uncle and this nephew, whose piety had already begun to be obtrusive. For Louis spent his time apparently in visiting St. Martha's tomb, or the Grotto of the Magdalen at Ste. Baume, or that ancient church of the Holy Marys by the Sea, where René established the worship of the holy relics in the next year. The lower chapel there was begun by his orders in January 1449, by an architect named Robert, who was helped by Frozino d'Andréa, a Florentine, and Gaillard Nicon of Avignon. The relics of the saints had been discovered by René's workmen in 1448, and a Bull from the Pope proclaimed their authenticity.

During the same visit René founded the famous Order of the Crescent, which therefore takes precedence of the Order of St. Michael, founded by his nephew as the first order of chivalry created by the Kings of France, though it is later than the Golden Fleece already established by the Duke of Burgundy, the third of the great outstanding figures in contemporary history. This Order of the Crescent, then, was founded in Provence, to consist of fifty knights at most, who should hear Mass every day on penalty of fasting, and keep peace and charity between themselves and towards their sovereign. They wore a golden crescent every Sunday, on their right arms, enamelled with letters of blue, "Los en croissant," and scarlet cloaks. They must never be unfaithful to the Catholic religion, never use sorceries, never desert their flag in battle, and always meet once a year upon the feast-day of St. Maurice. They were also to succour the distressed, and particularly the widows or orphans of their comrades, to have compassion on the poor, and to speak no scandal of women. Among the first members with René were Ferry de Lorraine, Louis de Beauvau, Jean Cossa, Tanneguy du Châtel, Guy de Laval, Thierry de Lénoncourt, Francesco Sforza of Milan, Jean du Bellay, and Jacques de Brézé, who was admitted later. Guy de Laval was its first head, and René succeeded him, followed by Jean Cossa. The Bishop of Orange was chaplain, and Charles de Castillon the chancellor. But the institution, with all its noble ideals, did not outlast its founder.

It was very possibly owing to the chivalrous enthusiasm aroused by the foundation of this Order that Tarascon saw the most celebrated festival ever held there, which has gone down to history as the "Tournoi de Tarascon," or the "Pas de la Bergère," arranged while René was in his castle by the Rhone from May 17 to July 2, 1449. A full relation of all that happened was written down by Louis de Beauvau, Grand Seneschal of Provence, whose details are closely corroborated by the statements in the royal budget. The fête, which was partly a tournament and partly a shepherd's masque, lasted five days, presided over by Isabeau de Lénoncourt, who was dressed in grey damask with a scarlet cap. People streamed into Tarascon from Avignon, Marseilles, Aix, Salon, Nîmes, Montpellier, and Arles, and on the 3rd of June the fun began with a tilt between Pierre Carrion and Philippe de Lénoncourt, who came from Lorraine, and the encounter went on every afternoon from twelve to six. Tanneguy du Châtel, nephew of the famous provost of Paris, and seneschal of Beaucaire, went into the lists with the lovely Honorade de Pontevez-Cabannes behind him on his charger, but only just saved her from disaster after the furious onslaught of Ferry de Lorraine, who eventually obtained the prize. René himself brought fresh lances into the arena when Gaspard Cossa (brother of Marguerite de Lascaris) broke his weapon. The jousting ended with a round between Jean Bezelin and Lénoncourt, after which every one sat down to a feast provided by Louis de Beauvau, and the gay company only parted with the greatest regret for their own homes.

In 1453, René, who had already lost his mother and his second son, Louis, was still further afflicted by the death of his beloved wife on the 28th of February, in his arms, at Angers. Lorraine passed immediately to his eldest son, Jean de Calabre; and René once more went to Italy to forget his grief in another effort to win Sicily. He came back to Provence in exactly a year, and his return was signalised by the characteristically generous protection he at once accorded to the famous merchant-prince, Jacques Coeur, whom he had met, and no doubt admired, during the royal negotiations concerning the Papacy some five years before. For no crime but his prosperity Jacques Coeur had been imprisoned by Charles VII, and the royal procureur was now attacking his nephew, Jean de Village, Coeur's representative in Marseilles, and the admiral of René, for whom the sailor had often brought back strange animals out of the East, Saracenic weapons, Moorish vestures, and other curiosities. René refused to give up his admiral; and Jacques Coeur himself, whose house in Bourges still testifies alike to his good taste and his prosperity, fled through Provence, was rescued by the men of Arles from the king's agents at Beaucaire, and finally passed on to Italy and exile.

For some time after this René did not visit Provence, but the interval was filled by his marriage to his second wife, Jeanne de Laval, daughter of Guy de Laval and Isabelle of Brittany. One of her garden-pavilions we have seen already at Les Baux, and her portrait was painted, opposite his own, on the great triptych in the Cathedral of Aix called the "Le Buisson Ardent." The king and queen are kneeling, surrounded by their patron saints, one on each side of the magnificent picture by Nicolas Froment (of Uzès), representing the angel appearing to the Shepherds, and the Virgin and Child surrounded by a wreath of verdure on the hill above them. This large and splendidly-preserved painting was for some time attributed by Provençal loyalty to the brush of their beloved king himself. Recent researches have proved the attribution here given under which it appeared at the great exhibition of the "Primitifs" at the Louvre in 1904. It is not only a masterpiece of design, but it is exquisitely finished in the smallest details, even to the ornaments of the gold border round the central group, and of the splendid canopy above it. The figures of Moses (who is taking off his shoe), of the Angel, and especially of the Virgin, recall the treatment in the painting of the Annunciation, which is also at Aix; but the landscape background may be recognised as taken from the sunny shores of the Rhone between Tarascon and Beaucaire. This Annunciation (which also appeared in Paris in 1904) is now in the Church of the Madeleine at Aix, and has been successively attributed to Jan Van Eyck and Albrecht Dürer, but these names are but the panegyric of admiring

Jeanne de Laval (From the triptych called "Le Buisson Ardent" by Nicolas Froment in the Cathedral of Aix-en-Provence)

critics. The splendour of the conception, the perspective of the long quiet aisles, the detail of the carving, and the drawing of the figures, combine to suggest that school of art which was under the particular protection of the Duc de Berry, and the Burgundian style of much of the architecture may be explained by the known presence in Provence during the fifteenth century of many sculptors who were compatriots of Claus Sluter of Dijon. This is no doubt one of the most interesting pictures in the Provence which welcomed Jeanne de Laval so warmly as soon as she was married, for her subjects quickly recognised that this was such a love-match as is rare indeed among the great, and that with her, the choice of his maturer years, their beloved René was to enjoy the tender and poetic relaxations which lightened the last days of his life, and gave him happiness at home in spite of every external difficulty.

The somewhat empty title of the King of Aragon was added to René's many other dignities in 1466. But his son, the Duke of Calabria, was not long to enjoy an inheritance which he was in the act of enforcing by the strength of arms when he died in 1470 at Barcelona, in the vigour of his years, not without some suspicion of poisoning. It was a bitter blow to the old king, and Ferry de Lorraine, who might have carried on the work, was dead as well. René decided to leave France and Anjou, and to live his last years in Provence. This determination must have been still further strengthened by the sudden death of Nicolas de Lorraine, in July 1473, only two years after that of Edward, son of his daughter Queen Margaret. His only male descendant now was another René, son of his widowed daughter Yolande of Lorraine; and he foresaw but too well the miseries of the constant quarrels over his inheritance which Louis XI was not likely to appease. His nephew Charles d'Anjou was, he felt, not likely long to survive him, and the cession of Provence to France must have been authorised, as inevitable, before either of them died; that of Anjou was made by mutual arrangement with the heir in 1480. The interviews at Lyons, in which Louis XI began cruelly to assert his open covetousness of King René's lands—a covetousness which history cannot but condone in view of the unity and aggrandisement of France thereby achieved—were chiefly conducted by that same Jean Cossa who had helped the Duke of Calabria in his Italian campaigns, and who lies buried in St. Martha's crypt at Tarascon. Commines describes the meeting he saw between René and the King of France, and gives the speech of "John Cosse, seneschal of Provence, a woorthie gentleman and of a good house in the realm of Naples," adding that "the King being a wise Prince tooke this practice in good part, which the said John Cosse uttered indeed simply as it was meant, for himselfe was the onely contriver thereof. In short space all controversies between them were ended…"

The man was worthy of so good a master, and he died six months after his last diplomatic service for the house of Anjou he had so faithfully served. The founder of his line was that Fiacre de Cossa who was Master of the Household to Philip Augustus in 1180, and was said to have come originally from Maine, though his family settled in Naples under the protection of the house of Anjou. Of the same stock came Balthazar Cossa, who declared himself Pope John XXIII, and abdicated before his death in 1419 at Florence. Though Guardian of Woods and Forests, and Chamberlain to King René, Jean Cossa was more particularly attached to the service of the young Duke of Calabria; but apart from the full powers thus given him he enjoyed the intimate friendship and confidence of René himself, as is testified by the tomb and epitaph to his memory in Tarascon, raised after his death in 1476. The title "Count of Troy" came to him by his marriage with Giovanna d'Andria, by whom his surviving son, René, became Grand Falconer of France, and founded the famous house of Cossé-Brissac.

The meeting at Lyons, in May 1476, may well have been much assisted by those negotiations for the release of René's daughter, which had terminated when Sir Thomas Montgomerie handed her over to the French commissioners at Rouen on the twenty-ninth of the previous January. Louis XI had, of course, not paid fifty thousand gold crowns for the ransom of Margaret of Anjou without shrewdly calculating on a large return. She renounced all rights to the English crown and any claims that might exist by reason of her marriage. She handed over, further, to her deliverer all rights, whether present or future, which she might possess in the property of her father or her mother, more especially in Bar, Lorraine, Anjou, and Provence. But Louis did not gain all he hoped so quickly as he had expected; and the unhappy princess, deprived of almost all means of subsistence after her father's death, lived in a legendary sorrow in the manor of Reculée, near Saumur, to which she withdrew on her return from England, consoled only by the tales which Chastelain composed for her, "of the ruin of certain unfortunate great ones," and of their patience in adversity.

By 1476, René himself was back in Provence, determined to end his days amid the scenes and the populations he had loved all his life. Of the palace that he built in Aix, not a stone remains. It was wantonly destroyed in 1786. Ruskin's outburst has rarely been so vividly justified. "You talk of the scythe of Time, and the tooth of Time: I tell you Time is scytheless and toothless; it is we who gnaw like the worm—we who smite like the scythe." Of no place is this fierce invective against human spoliation so true as in Provence; but no place has so full a consolation in the beauty of those living monuments of an imperishable past, the women of St. Remy or of Arles. In the loveliness of their quiet faces, in the dignity of their dress and walk, in the ancient charm that seems impalpably to cling round their eternal youth, we may still find something of the Provence King René loved. In Aix, a town of fountains and front doors, which show that to the very end of the eighteenth century the capital still held its own as a centre of administrative and commercial life, nothing is left of the period of which these pages treat save its cathedral, its pictures, and its books. They shall be the last things we will look at together.

The cathedral of St. Sauveur at Aix-en-Provence presents a mixture of styles and epochs which are clearly distinguishable one from another, and offer a not unpleasing harmony as a whole. Taken as a group, with the church, the baptistery, the cloister, and the archbishop's palace, the buildings form one of the most interesting architectural subjects in the south, and it must be remembered that the south aisle, the baptistery, and the cloister are the oldest portions of all, and no doubt at one time formed a single church by themselves. The character of this aisle (dedicated in 1103) is almost identical with the original work in Notre Dame des Doms at Avignon, showing the same pointed tunnel vaults, the rectangular piers, the modified Corinthian capitals, the carved band carried at the base of the vault, and a dome treated just like that which is beneath the western tower on the Rocher des Doms. The position of this dome in the whole building, in the fourth bay of one aisle, with a somewhat unusual "presbytery" in the bay behind it, would prove that it must have formed part of an independent structure, even if there were no other evidence. The entrance portal of this same south aisle (built in 1080) is an exquisite example of that Provençal use of Roman details which we have observed before. The channelled columns, variously fluted, the modified Corinthian capitals, the block above the abacus, corresponding to an entablature—all are features of a transition-process emphasised by the larger columns on each side, which are manifestly taken from an actual Roman structure. On the right is a heavy wall of large blocks of finely cut stones, which was once part of the Roman temple of Apollo; and from this temple came the eight superb monolithic columns of granite and green marble, with Corinthian capitals, which carry the small round arches of the baptistery. These are no doubt the earliest relics in the whole cathedral; and though the baptistery was very much modified (and its lantern added) by Canon Jean de Léone

Part of the Cathedral Door, Aix-en-Provence

in 1577, it is still possible to realise something of its ancient style and proportions. The cloister is equally celebrated. The oldest parts were built by Prévôt Benoît in 1080; and, though ugly and unimportant buildings now weigh down three sides, the north colonnade stands free, and was probably roofed much in the same way as that of St. Trophime at Arles. Eight arches go to each side, resting on coupled columns with delicate shafts of every possible design, sometimes even bent and twisted together, and all with sculptured capitals. The corner piers are different, and squarer, with pannelled sides. In the eastern arcade the arches have a rich zigzag ornament, with grotesques set in the spandrils.

The "Gothic" portion of the cathedral was begun in 1285, and dragged on until 1534. The choir in the central nave (which shows a slightly inclined axis) is different from that usual in France, but, like Westminster Abbey, follows the usual Spanish model also seen in such Italian churches as that of the Frari in Venice. Within it, immediately above the stalls, is a gorgeous series of tapestries, which are attributed with great probability to Quentin Matsys, and once formed part of the decoration of old St. Paul's in London, as did the candelabra which are now in St. Bavon's Church at Ghent. The chief peculiarity of this central nave is that it is almost entirely enclosed in solid walls, with only a few small openings cut into the adjoining aisles. Its façade is a fine piece of fifteenth-century work, begun by Archbishop Olivier de Pennart,[5] and completed by Pierre Soqueti, who started his work about 1500, and carved his beautiful statue of the Virgin and Child on the central pier soon afterwards. The chief glory of the portal, and the gem so fitly framed in this fine architectural setting, is the splendid pair of doors most exquisitely carved in walnut-wood in 1504, and representing Isaiah, Jeremiah, Ezekiel, and Daniel, with the figures of the twelve Sibyls in two rows above them. They are finer work than Volard's doors, which were carved forty-seven years afterwards for the Church of St. Peter in Avignon, and they are very properly kept encased in wooden covers, but can easily be shown, and a portion of them was photographed for these pages.

Within the cathedral is a charming statue of St. Martha and the Tarasque, in the Chapelle de l'Université, which must on no account be missed, and several fine pictures, including "Le Buisson Ardent," already mentioned. The painting which represents the legend of St. Mitre shows the martyr walking about with his head in his hands between the kneeling figures of the donor and his wife and children. Behind them stretches the fanciful architecture of a fifteenth-century street. This reposed in a completely dark chapel of the cathedral till it was brought to the Louvre for the Exhibition of 1904, when it was seen that the rather awkwardly-placed figures of the donors had been added later, and that certain details, badly drawn and imagined, appeared side by side with the knowledge and the taste of the very different hand responsible for the executioner and the ladies watching from the windows. The bright light in which the whole picture is bathed is toned down, near the horizon, to that golden tint which is peculiar to the atmosphere of Provence, and shows that this is the work of a Provençal master with very different aims to those, for example, of Fouquet in the north.

We need not accept the enthusiastic attributions to King René of so many paintings in Provence, to acknowledge that he not only encouraged the art in others, but was himself an artist. During his long captivity in Burgundy, from 1431 to 1437, he may well have met Jan Van Eyck at Dijon; and his frequent and lengthy visits to the kingdom of Naples no doubt made him familiar with artists working before Perugino or Botticelli. But it was Flemish rather than Italian art which inspired his taste and led him above all to encourage the use of oil-painting among his favourite artists. Perhaps the most authentic of his own works are to be found among the manuscripts he so delighted to

Porch of a House in Aix-en-Provence

illuminate. The Bibliothèque Méjanes of the town of Aix, a collection most unworthily housed, and in constant danger from fire, contains a great number of very valuable books and manuscripts which would well repay extended study, and are guarded, near the beautiful sixteenth-century Belfry of the Hôtel de Ville, by the sympathetic and intelligent M. E. Aude, who was good enough to give me a list of his chief treasures. Among them is a clean and perfect example of *Hypnerotomachia Poliphili,* containing those unsurpassable woodcuts which have been variously attributed to Bellini, Mantegna, Carpaccio, or even Raphael, and were printed in Venice by Aldus in 1499. There is also a unique copy of the *Life of Antichrist,* published in Lyons, in 1480, and some splendid examples of sixteenth-century binding.

But the most interesting books for us are the two illuminated manuscripts known as the "Missel du Roi René," and the missal called the "Heures de la Reine Yolande." The chief beauty of King René's missal is in its capital letters, which may well have been his own work. Throughout the book numerous notes in his own handwriting occur on the margin, beginning with the date of his birth in January, and then recording the various family occurrences which I have sketched in this chapter: in February the death of his wife "Ysabel"; in March the birth of his daughter Margaret, Queen of England; in July his capture in battle; in August the birth of his first-born; in September his marriage to Jeanne de Laval.

His character comes more clearly before us as we read these notes he wrote; and we see a man who, in the best sense of the word, was versatile; who was ignorant of nothing great, or useful, or beautiful in his time; a prince whose honourable loyalty led him in his early years to stand in arms by the side of Joan of Arc; who, in maturer life, fought the battle of France in stubbornly struggling to preserve his own inheritance; who gave a queen to England, and to Lorraine a princess, whose blood still lives upon the throne of Austria. Through all the mischances of his life he never lost the privilege of creating his own happiness in his own way. Full of charity and loving kindness, not only to his own subjects, but to all the poor and the oppressed, he carried out strictly in his own life the principles on which he founded his chivalrous Order of the Crescent. Nor were the claims of a larger humanity forgotten. His love for women sometimes led him into paths where kings are best unseen. But his tenderness and affection to both his wives was unassailable and unchallenged. He built wisely and well; he encouraged the arts of painting and of manufacture; he instituted many religious ceremonies and many festivals which lasted in their full force into the nineteenth century, and will never be forgotten in Provence. He was full of interest in history, in geography, in the natural sciences; the friend of Charles d'Orléans, the protector of François Villon, he knew what good literature was; he gave us of his best; and some of his writing still remains to testify to his enduring charm of thought and manner. He held a great place in the world of his own day, as great, at one time, as either the Duke of Burgundy or the King of France. He escaped the terrible fate of the first; he never deserved a hint of the ignominy which some writers have too plentifully bestowed upon the second. Above all, he stands out, in an age which was rather too prone to that Machiavellian intrigue so praised by its historian Commines, as an honest politician. That is one reason why his material successes were not so great as those obtained by more unscrupulous players in the game of kings. His claim upon posterity lies rather upon artistic and intellectual grounds; upon the serenity he showed

A Woman of Arles (From a drawing by Jane E. Cook made in 1892)

in evil fortune; the dignity with which he faced defeat; the constancy with which he died, at Aix, on July 10, 1480, still in possession of his titles of inheritance and knowing that he possessed them for the good of France.

With him the tale of independent Provence is over; and with a phrase from the poem that described his last tourney of Tarascon, a poem addressed by his friend Jean de Beauvau to Louis of Luxembourg, I will leave you to wander through the valley of the Rhone that still remembers the good King René:—

> *"Pardonnez-moi s'il y a que redire*
> *En ce livret lequel je vous envoie;*
> *Meilleur l'auriez, si meilleur je l'avoye."*

NOTES

1. The dialogue continued:—

The Traveller. "Then, no doubt, you will have the goodness to show me the one while I close my eyes, very willingly, to the other."

The Concierge. "But I have the honour to point out that the gaol and the Historic Monument are the same building, and Monsieur is, to my regret, unable to give himself the pleasure of visiting the gaol."

The T. "Yet since the Minister permits the Monument, perhaps he includes the gaol, which is the same building, in that permission?"

The C. "I may suggest that Monsieur has laid no evidence before me of this inclusion."

T. "Well, may I photograph the Monument, according to this special letter which is now on your table, without visiting either the Castle or the gaol?"

C. "Monsieur is no doubt pleased to jest."

T. (getting a little warm). "Not at all. I am surprised to notice the very slight attention paid by a French official to a communication from a Minister."

C. "I take my orders from the Prefect of the Department and from no one else."

T. (unwisely sarcastic). "Is it yourself, then, or the Prefect, who is superior to the Minister of Fine Arts?"

C. "I will ask Monsieur to observe that the high level of this conversation should be carefully maintained, and that it is not I who forget to maintain it."

T. (completely cowed). "What, then, do you advise me to do?"

C. (coldly). "The Prefect resides in Marseilles."

T. Exit.

Four hours later.

T. enters waving a telegram. "The excellent Prefect accords his gracious permission on condition that you find the documents I have mentioned to be correct."

C. (blandly). "I will now take official cognisance of the documents referred to, and will copy them into my register."

Two hours later.

C. "The English visitors may now pass through the rooms of King René; but the Prefect says nothing either of the gaol or of the photographs."

T. (despairingly). "The rooms, then, and nothing else."

C. (with effusive politeness). "This way, monsieur; and no doubt madame will do us the honour of accompanying us..."

2. My authority for the king's itinerary is the splendid biography written by Lecoy de la Marche in 1875, which entirely supersedes De Villeneuve Bargemont (1825) and all other writers. René was at Tarascon on January 12, 1443 and during that February; on March 23, 1447, until April 11; on May 16, June 11 and 18, and October 10; in 1448 on February 4, May 11, June 19, July 13, November 26, and from December 7 to January 16, 1449. He returned there next April 1, and stayed there again from May 17 to July 2. He did not visit it again till May 12, 1457. A still longer absence lasted till November 5, 1469. Another visit began on November 20, 1471; but in 1474 he was here from March 28 till May 19. In 1476 he was at Tarascon on July 10, September 13 and 15; on August 21 of the next year and on September 28; on July 2, and from August 25 to December 31 in 1478; and in 1479, the year before he died, he came on January 4, and from the 9th to the 15th of the same month; from 1st February to the 30th of April, and for two days on the 3rd of May. He was here more often, in fact, than in any other place in Provence except Aix, his official residence.

3. This volume bears the arms of King René and is now in the Bibliothèque Nationale MS. fr. 2000.

4. "*Hic situs est Troiae Cossa de Scarpe Joannes*
   Qui comes et civis Parthenopaeus erat.
   Hic patriam liquit, tractus fulgore Renati
   Regis quem coluit, semper ubique fidus..."

   (Here lies Jean Cossa, who was count and
   citizen of Naples. He left his fatherland,
   drawn by the glory of King René, whom he
   served, faithful always and everywhere)

The date is given as October 1476. When Madame James Darmesteter was here (before November 1892) she seems to have thought this was the monument of Jean de Calabre, the son and heir of René, who fought through many a Neapolitan campaign. But that "brilliant young pretender" died in December 1470 at Barcelona; nor is it likely that a prince of the house of Anjou would be buried at Tarascon. René himself was buried at Angers, though he died at Aix in 1480.

5. See "Barr Ferrée" in the *Architectural Record*, 1896.

Appendix I

A LIST OF THOSE ROMAN INSCRIPTIONS TO WHICH REFERENCE HAS BEEN MADE IN CHAPTER VIII, PART II.

N.B. All are from Nîmes, unless otherwise stated.

(1) T. CORNELIO TITI FILIO [SA]TURIONI. [Beneath symbols which appear to be a dibble and a bill-hook.] (To T.Cornelius [Sa]turio, son of Titus)

(2) NÚNDINO PATRI ET MÁTERNAE MATRI PATERNUS FILIUS POSUIT. [Beneath a water-wheel and a dibble. Accents on the second letters of the first and fourth words.] (Their son Paternus set this up for his father Nundinus and his mother Materna)

(3) DIIS MANIBUS VALLONI QUARTINA FRATRI OPTIMO. [Above a pruning-knife of a peculiar form still found in southern vineyards.] (Quartina to the soul of Vallo, best of brothers)

(4) D. M. L. TREBONIO NICEPHORO PATILLO COPONI MAXIMUS EPAPHRODITUS AMICO OPTIMO. (Maximus Epaphroditus to the soul of L. Trebonius Nicephorous Patillus Copon, best of friends)

(5) PUBLIO BRITTIO SATURNINO. [Between a pair of square-tipped shears and a rough comb.] (To Publius Brittius Saturninus)

(6) SEX. SPURIUS PIPEROLUS AERARIUS SIBI ET SUIS VIVOS ET SECUNDAE UXSORI. (Sextus Spurius Piperolus Aerarius in his lifetime for himself and his family and his second wife)

(7) L. AVIDIO SECUNDO MUSICARIO FESTA UXOR. (Festa his wife to L.Avidius Secundus, maker of musical instruments)

(8) JULIAE LUC. FILIAE TYRANNIAE VIXIT ANN. XX. M. VIII. QUAE MORIBUS PARITER ET DISCIPLINA CETERIS FEMINIS EXRMPLO FUIT AUTARCIUS NURUI LAURENTIUS UCXORI. [From a tomb at Arles, carved with musical instruments.] (Autarcius to his daughter-in-law Laurentius, to his wife Julia Lucia, daughter of Tyrannia, who lived 20 years 8 months and was an example to other women both in her culture and character)

(9) D. M. C. ANTISTII ANT...MEDICI ET ANTISTAE IP...SYNEROS LIBERTUS. (To the shades of Caius Antistitius ... doctor

and Antistia … from their freedman Syneros)

(10) D. M. C. JULIO ALBO SESSORARIO SPURIA EUPLIA UXOR. (Spuria Euplia his wife to the shade of Caius Julius Albo, chairmaker)

(11) NON VENDO NISI AMANTIBUS CORONAS. [Above a woman seated behind a counter and holding a crown.] (I do not sell crowns except to those who love me)

(12) D. M. MARCUS MAGIUS SOTERICUS SIGNO HILARI AMICORUM AMATOR VIVUS SIBI FECIT UT ESSET MEMORIAE BONUM ITER VOCIBUS: FELICITER. [At Vienne.] (To the shade of Marcus Magius Sotericus, a good friend, who joyfully made this for himself in his lifetime so that his journey should be well remembered and reported)

(13) AETHERIUS MORIENS DIXIT HIC CONDITE CORPUS TERRA MATER RERUM QUOD DEDIT IPSA TEGAT. [At St. Colombe.] (When he was dying Aetherius said, Bury my body here. Let the earth, the mother of all, cover what she gave)

(14) HIC REQUIESUIT IN PACE MERCASTO QUI FLORENTEM AEVUM LX EGIT PER ANNOS JUCUNDAM VITAM HAEC PER TEMPORA DUXIT. [At Vienne.] (Here rests in peace Mercasto who led a vigorous and happy life for 60 years)

(15) D. M. MARIAE NEMAUSINAE MARIA MARITUMA LIBERTA. (Maria Marituma her freedwoman to the soul of Maria of Nîmes)

(16) D. M. LUCILIAE LUCII FILIAE SECUNDILLAE P. ATETTIUS SATURNINUS UXORI RARISSIMAE QUAE SEUUM VIXIT ANN: XX…LUCILLA LUCET. SECUNDILLA SALVE. (P.Aetettius Saturninus to the soul of his most excellent wife Lucilia Secundilla daughter of Lucius who lived with him 20 years… Lucilla shine forth. Secundilla hail)

(17) ATTIOLAE DUILCISSIMAE. (To sweetest Attiola)

(18) D. M. T. CALVII POMPEÍANI T. CALVIUS SECUNDUS ET POMPEIA QUINTI FILIA SEVERILLA FILIO PIENTISSIMO ET DÉSIDERATISSIMO QUI INDIGNE EREPTUS EST JUVENIS EXEMPLI RARISSIMÍ ANNORUM XVII MENSIUM V DIERUM VI. [Note the accents on the first e in Desideratissimo, the last i in Rarissimi, and the a in Pompeiani.] (T.Calvius Secundus son of T.Calvius Pompeianus and Pompeia Severilla daughter of Quintus to a most loving and loved son who was undeservedly taken from them. He was a most exemplary young man and lived 17 years 5 months 6 days)

(19) D. M. O DOLOR QUANTAE LACHRIMAE FECERE SEPULCHRUM JULIAE LUCINAE QUAE VIXIT KARISSIMA MATRI FLOS AETATIS HIC JACET INTUS CONDITA SACXO O UTINAM POSSIT REPARARI SPIRITUS ILLE UT SCIRET QUANTUS DOLOR EST QUAE VIXIT ANN: XXVII. M. X. DIE. XIII. JULIA PARTHENOPE POSUIT INFELIX MATER. [Tomb at Arles.] (O

grief, how many tears have made this tomb for Julia Lucina who was the dearest flower of her age to her mother. Here she lies buried within. O if only her spirit could be restored so that she might know how much grief there is for her. She lived 27 years 10 months 13 days. Julia Parthenope, her unhappy mother, set up this tomb)

(20) PERPETUAE QUIETI DOMITIO TATIANO INFANTI DULCISSIMO QUEM PRIMA AETATE FLORENTEM MORS DIRA SUBRIPUIT. VIXIT ANN: III.. MENS: VI. DIE: XIX. AGRIPINENSIS DONATUS PATER ET JOVINA MATER FILIO CARISSIMO POSUERUNT. (Perpetual rest to the sweetest child Domitius Tatianus whom grim death snatched in the flower of his first infancy. He lived 3 months 19 days. His father Agripinensis Donatus and his mother Jovina set up this tomb for their dearest son)

(21) [Brought from Marseilles to Aix in 1613.]

στῆθι παρερχόμενος τόνδ᾽ ΙΧΝΕΣΙ τύμβΟΝ ΟΔΕΙΤΑ
ΚΟΥΡΟΣ ΕΓΩ ΚΑΛΕΩ ΣΕ ΘΕΩ ΦΙΛΟΣ ΟΥΚΕΤΙ ΘΝΗΤΟΣ
ΗΙΘΕΟΣ ΚΟΥΡΟΙΣΙΝ ΟΜΗΛΙΚΙΗ ΠΑΝΟΜΟΙΟΣ
ΠΛΩΤΗΡΩΝ ΣΩΤΗΡΣΙΝ ΑΜΥΚΛΑΙΟΙΣΙ ΘΕΟΙΣΙΝ
ΠΛΩΤΗΡ ΚΑΥΤΟΣ ΕΩΝ ΠΟΝΤΟΥ Γ ΕΝ ΚΥΜΑΣΙΝ ΗΣΘΗΝ
ΕΥΣΕΒΙΑ ΤΡΟΦΕΩΝ ΔΕ ΛΑΧΩΝ ΤΟΔΕ ΣΗΜΑ ΠΕΠΑΥΜΑΙ
ΝΟΥΣΩΝ ΚΑΙ ΚΑΜΑΤΟΙΟ ΚΑΙ ΑΧΘΕΟΣ ΗΔΕ ΠΟΝΟΙΟ
ΤΑΥΤΑ ΓΑΡ ΕΝ ΖΩΟΙΣΙΝ ΑΜΕΙΛΙΧΑ ΣΑΡΚΕΣ ΕΧΟΥΣΙΝ
ΕΝ ΔΗ ΤΕΘΝΕΙΩΣΙΝ ΟΜΗΓΥΡΙΕΣ ΓΕ ΠΕΛΟΥΣΙΝ
ΔΟΙΑΙ ΤΩΝ ΕΤΕΡΗ ΜΕΝ ΕΠΙΧΘΟΝΙΗ ΠΕΦΟΡΗΤΑΙ
Η Δ ΕΤΕΡΗ ΤΕΙΡΕΣΣΙ ΣΥΝ ΑΙΘΕΡΙΟΙΣΙ ΧΟΡΕΥΕΙ
ΗΣ ΣΤΡΑΤΙΗΣ ΕΙΣ ΕΙΜΙ ΛΑΧΩΝ ΘΕΟΝ ΗΓΕΜΟΝΗΑ.

L. P. S.

(Stop, passing traveller, in your tracks.
I call to you, a boy dear to the God and no longer living,
An unmarried youth alike in age
To the saviours of seamen, the Spartan gods [Castor and Pollux, the Dioscuri].
Being a sailor I delighted in the waves of the sea
But, granted this tomb by the piety of my parents, I am finished with
Diseases and toil and pain and trouble.
For these are the harsh lot of the living
But among the dead there are two components
One of which is wafted about on the earth
While the other dances with the heavenly bodies.
I am one of this host, with the guidance of the gods)

(22) [Found at Marseilles, 1709. Re-produced in facsimile at Aix]

ΓΛΑΥΚΙΑ ΕΣΤΙ ΤΑΦΟΣ ΠΑΙΣ Δ ΑΝΕΘΗΚΕ ΝΕΟΣ
ΔΕΙΞΑΣ ΕΚ ΜΕΙΚΡΟΥ ΠΡΟΣ ΠΑΤΕΡ ΕΥΣΕΒΙΑΝ
ΟΥΚ ΕΦΘΗΣ Ω ΤΛΗΜΟΝ ΙΔΕΙΝ ΓΟΝΟΝ ΟΙΟΣ ΑΝ ΗΝ ΣΟΙ
ΓΗΡΑΙΩ ΤΕΥΧΕΙΝ ΟΥ ΤΑΦΟΝ ΑΛΛΑ ΒΙΟΝ
Η ΦΘΟΝΕΡΑ Δ ΥΜΑΣ ΠΑΝΤ ΑΔΙΚΟΥΣΑ ΤΥΧΗ
ΜΗΤΡΙ ΜΕΝ ΕΝ ΓΗΡΑ ΔΑΚΡΥ ΘΗΚΑΤΟ ΤΗ ΔΕ ΓΥΝΑΙΚΙ
ΧΗΡΙΑΝ ΔΥΣΤΗΝΟΥ ΠΑΙΔΟΣ ΑΜ ΟΡΦΑΝΙΗ.

(This is the tomb of Glaukias. His young son, who had shown reverence to his father since he was small, set it up. Poor wretch, you did not have time to see what a son he would have been in your old age, giving you livelihood and not a tomb. Envious Fortune, unjust to you in every way, has caused a mother to weep in her old age as well as making your unhappy son an orphan)
[See *Corpus Inscript. Græc. Siciliæ*, etc. (ed. Kaibel, Berlin), 2437.]

(23) [Found at Aix, 1839.]
Paulo sisle gradum juvenis pie quaeso viator
Ut mea per titulum noris sic invida fata
Uno minus quam bis denos ego vixi per annos
Integer innocuus semper pia mente probatus
Qui docili lusu juvenum bene doctus arenis
Pulcher et ille fui variis circumdatus armis
Saepe feras lusi medicus tamen is quoque vixi
Et comes ursaris comes his qui victima sacris
Caedere saepe solent et qui novo tempore veris
Floribus intextis refovent simulacra decorum
Nomen si quaeris titulus tibi vera fatetur
SEXTUS JULIUS FELICISSIMUS
SEXTUS JULIUS FELIX
ALUMNO INCOMPARABILI (ET)
FELICITAS F(RATRI).
[See *Corp. Inscr. Lat.*, xii. 533.]

(Please stop for a little, good young traveller, to learn from this inscription what the envious fates did to me. I lived one year less than twenty, virtuous, innocent, always approved for my sense of duty. I was handsome, skilled in the sports which young men play in the arena and in the use of various weapons. I often made sport of wild animals but I was also their healer and a friend of bear-baiters and a companion to those who kill the sacrificial victims and in Spring cherish the images of the gods anew with woven flowers. If you ask my name this inscription will tell you truly: Sextus Julius Felicissimus. Sextus Julius Felix to his unmatched foster-son and Felicitas to her brother)

Appendix II

MAGALI
Melodie Provençale Populaire
Transcrite par Fr. Seguin

Index of Places

Interlink's Bestselling Travel Publications

The Traveller's History Series

The Traveller's History series is designed for travellers who want more historical background on the country they are visiting than can be found in a tour guide. Each volume offers a complete and authoritative history of the country from the earliest times up to the present day. A Gazetteer cross-referenced to the main text pinpoints the historical importance of sights and towns. Illustrated with maps and line drawings, this literate and lively series makes ideal before-you-go reading, and is just as handy tucked into suitcase or backpack.

A Traveller's History of Australia	$14.95 pb
A Traveller's History of the Caribbean	$14.95 pb
A Traveller's History of Canada	$14.95 pb
A Traveller's History of China	$14.95 pb
A Traveller's History of England	$14.95 pb
A Traveller's History of France	$14.95 pb
A Traveller's History of Greece	$14.95 pb
A Traveller's History of India	$14.95 pb
A Traveller's History of Ireland	$14.95 pb
A Traveller's History of Italy	$14.95 pb
A Traveller's History of Japan	$14.95 pb
A Traveller's History of London	$14.95 pb
A Traveller's History of Mexico	$14.95 pb
A Traveller's History of North Africa	$15.95 pb
A Traveller's History of Paris	$14.95 pb
A Traveller's History of Russia	$14.95 pb
A Traveller's History of Scotland	$14.95 pb
A Traveller's History of Spain	$14.95 pb
A Traveller's History of Turkey	$14.95 pb
A Traveller's History of the U.S.A.	$15.95 pb

To order or request our complete catalog,
please call us at **1-800-238-LINK** or write to:
Interlink Publishing, 46 Crosby Street, Northampton, MA 01060
www.interlinkbooks.com